Dancing Backwards

A Social History of Canadian Women in Politics

Credits

Editor
Barbara Huck

Index
Adrian Mather

Associate editors
Peter St. John
Doug Whiteway
Deborah Riley

Prepress and Printing
Avenue 4 Communications

Design and layout
Dawn Huck

Library and Archives Canada Cataloguing in Publication

Carstairs, Sharon
Dancing backwards : a social history of Canadian women in politics / by Sharon Carstairs and Tim Higgins.

Includes bibliographical references and index.
ISBN 1-896150-30-6 (bound).--ISBN 1-896150-07-1 (pbk.)

1. Women in politics--Canada--History--20th century.
2. Women politicians--Canada. I. Higgins, Tim II. Title.

HQ1391.C3C38 2004   320'.082'0971   C2004-905511-9

Dancing Backwards

◆

A Social History of Canadian Women in Politics

By Sharon Carstairs and Tim Higgins

Foreword by Susan Thompson

With illustrations by Joshua Stanton

Heartland Associates Inc.
Winnipeg, Canada

Acknowledgements

For the first twenty years of my working life, before politics took hold of me, I was a high school teacher. The course I taught was called "social studies", but in reality I taught history, and with a very political bent. I have never found Canadian history to be dull and boring and I hope my enthusiasm was felt by my students. At least some of them have told me that they enjoyed my courses and that they would never forget to vote. I made all Grade 11 students work in political campaigns — municipal, provincial or federal, whichever was being held during that academic year — for the candidates of their choice.

Those years taught me that there was clearly a lack of resources concerning those who had made a success of politics, but it was not until I began teaching a course on The Emerging Role of Women in Politics at the University of Manitoba in 1993 that I realized how little I knew about the women who had been successful. I knew of Charlotte Whitton and Ellen Fairclough, but what of the first women in provincial legislatures, on city councils and on the judiciary? It was this that prompted my work on this book. Sitting in my home on Lake Winnipeg, I started to tell the stories of these women.

As with all books, there was help provided along the way. Michelle MacDonald, who began as a researcher in the Liberal Caucus Room at the Manitoba Legislature and rose to be my chief of staff when I became Government Leader in the Senate, has always been my greatest asset and my greatest critic when I start to put words on paper. Quite frankly, her assets are outstanding but it is her criticism that makes me do my very best work. One summer Christine Rowe, a co-op student who wanted to become a journalist, worked in my office. Though only in Grade 13, she had wonderful written skills and was put to work on editing. She was also a terrific sounding board, and would say at least once a day: "I didn't know that!"

However, the book truly jelled when Tim Higgins, who had a different story to tell, joined with me to make what we both hope will be a challenge to the women of Canada. We hope it will inspire them to do even more to make this country reflective of the needs and aspirations of fifty-two per cent of its citizenry.

My thanks also to Shelly Cory, who along with Ted Aubut searched the National Archives for the special photographs contained herein.

I would be remiss in not thanking my husband, John, who put off swimming and canoeing, the true purpose of being at the Lake, so that I could put a few more words on paper. And of course, the publisher, Barbara Huck, has truly turned this into reality. Without her, this book would not be. Enjoy, everyone.

Sharon Carstairs
August 2004

My part of this volume actually began life in 1997 as an outline for a three-part television documentary tentatively entitled "Leading Ladies". The programs, to be produced by Visual Productions of Winnipeg, would have examined the twentieth century through the eyes and voices of Canadian political women. Financial support for research came in part from Mayor Susan Thompson, who saw the proposal as a fitting millennium project for the capital of the province in which women first attained the vote, and from the Women's Directorate of the Province of Manitoba, which provided funding to hire a student, Karen Paquin, to assist with the research.

Though we made considerable progress, eventually the project languished for the usual reason that original Canadian television programming rarely gets made, i.e. filling out endless applications doesn't pay the mortgage. I moved on to other things, which included writing a couple of historical plays for Heartland Associates, the publisher of the present volume. Barbara Huck of Heartland had been involved with Leading Ladies from the outset, and I also knew her from my involvement with Winnipeg's successful bid for the 1999 Pan Am Games, which she co-chaired.

So when Senator Carstairs brought Heartland her fully researched idea for a series of biographies on women who had achieved political firsts in Canada, it was only a matter of time before *Dancing Backwards* was born.

Obviously, a project like this generates a long list of people to thank. I'd like to start with all the political professionals who generously took the time to speak with me. I include the Rt. Honourable Ellen Fairclough, the Rt. Honourable Kim Campbell, the Rt. Honourable Beverley McLachlin, the Honourable Iona Campagnolo, Her Worship Susan Thompson, Senator Michael Kirby, Senator Julie Pépin and the Honourable Marc Lalonde.

My colleagues at Visual Productions have been putting up with my historical non-sequiturs for going on a decade now. I thank them all for their forbearance and Darlene Mulligan, my producer, in particular, for suggesting *Dancing Backwards* as a title.

Dancing Backwards would not have become the book it is without the assistance of my wife, Liz. With a gentle smile, appropriate nod and occasional penetrating question, she helped me focus my thoughts and temper my enthusiasms during all those evenings in front of the fireplace. Enthusiasms that managed to escape Liz's attention were either tamed or excised by the experienced hand of my editor, Barbara Huck. Thank you, Barbara.

And finally, my gratitude to my co-author, the Rt. Honourable Sharon Carstairs, for assembling such a fascinating cast of characters. I can't think of a better way to have spent the last couple of years.

Tim Higgins
September 2004

Table of Contents

❖ Illustrations

❖ In Focus

Foreword

"Being a woman in politics is like being Ginger Rogers. You
have to do all the same dance steps as Fred Astaire, but you have to do
them backwards and in high heels."

Ann Richards
Former Governor of Texas

What a perfect quote! When Barbara Huck first shared it with me, my
involuntary reaction was a chuckle, followed immediately by: "My, oh my, how
true it is."

As the first woman to be mayor of Winnipeg, I would have to say that
each and every day of my 2,190 days in public office (but who's counting?) truly
did make me realize the truth of that quote. It took 118 years for a woman to be
elected Winnipeg's mayor and all of the challenges, barriers and "cultures" certainly were present in being the first woman to hold this office.

It started immediately, during my first campaign. Here I was … the
FEMALE candidate! I was a small business owner … I had no political experience
… (which meant that I had never held a political office or been in a political
campaign), no political party and no personal money.

The previous mayor, Bill Norrie, was retiring and the field of leading
candidates included the Deputy Mayor, (a Progressive Conservative) the chair of
the Finance Committee (a member of the NDP) and the chair of Planning and
Community Services (a Liberal). I make the political party distinctions because
not only were these men seasoned city hallers, but they also had the support of
their provincial party machines. By June 1992 (the election was slated for October),
a "back room boy" for one of those "leading candidates" had approached the members of my campaign team to advise them that I was a "nuisance" candidate; if I
continued to proceed with my campaign, I would be "frozen out of the big money".

The next missive was that I was too inexperienced. It was suggested
that I run as a city councilor in order to gain the appropriate political experience;
if I agreed, I would be guaranteed to be named Deputy Mayor when the "leading
candidate" won. I guess it goes without saying that the leading candidate lost. (I
have wondered whether Winnipeg's current mayor, who also came from the outside, was told that HE needed previous political experience in order to run for
office.)

Another memorable moment occurred just before the election. I was
required to participate in a "bear pit" session with three members of the city's
leading open line radio show. I'd had a tough run from the media and the radio

station's general manager had told me early in to the campaign that not only was the station going to endorse one of the city hall candidates, but also indicated that I was not a welcome candidate. I was floored by his position and went in to the bear pit session with a great deal of trepidation.

I had of course anticipated all kinds of difficult questions about my platform and policies, so I was completely taken aback when one of the first questions was "Candidate Thompson … you are a single woman … who will your escort be if you become Mayor?

Whaaaattttttttt? Clearly this was crucial information. Needless to say, I answered that Tom Selleck would be my escort, and we moved on to more substantive issues. And several days later, I won the election!

Like all the "first" women in this book, the results of my two terms in office were that a barrier came down, a door was opened and yet another crack appeared in the proverbial glass ceiling.

When Barbara Huck came to the Mayor's Office to discuss this project, I was absolutely delighted. Not only would it cover an important part of Canadian history, but it was yet another opportunity to celebrate Winnipeg's motto: "One with the strength of many". *Dancing Backwards* would profile the many women who had come before us and had helped to build a strong nation. By supporting it, I would be supporting an important part of our nation's story.

I come from a long line of female activists. On my mother's side, my great-grandmother, Lorinda Jane Davis Bellamy, of Edmonton, was a "suffragette", as they were called at the time, a friend of Nellie McClung's, a charter member of the Women's Christian Temperance Union (WCTU) and its president for seven years. She was also a founding member of the Edmonton YMCA and its president for the first four years. This activism has continued through generations of women in our family.

This book will inform and educate. But more importantly, it will entertain and inspire. *Dancing Backwards* will bring to life the women who challenged the status quo, who overcame enormous obstacles and who accomplished things many thought impossible.

As you read these stories and the history of these "first" women, I hope that you, like me, will be thankful, appreciative and indeed in awe of their courage, perseverance and determination and take their experiences and accomplishments as inspiration for your life and your dreams and your goals. Enjoy!

Susan Thompson
September 2004

Nellie's World

Aliens. In many ways, that might be the best description of some of the people you'll meet in this book, particularly in the first half. First-wave feminists — women like Nellie McClung, Emily Murphy and Agnes Macphail — were born and lived in a world that would be almost entirely unrecognizable today — the one that existed before the First World War. As it fades from living memory, connecting with this world becomes more and more difficult with each passing year. But let's try. Let's suppose, just for a moment, that it's 1902.

Politically, this is a world with about forty countries, of which only six really matter internationally. More than half the world's population is controlled by England, France and Holland. Countries that don't exist in 1902 include Finland, Norway, Hungary, Ireland, Pakistan, South Africa, Saudi Arabia and Israel. Italy has existed for only forty-one years, Germany, for just thirty-one.

Canada, comprised of seven provinces, is a semi-independent part of the British Empire and still largely rural. Our population is close to five and a half million, but only two million of us, or thirty-seven per cent, live in towns and cities. Our biggest city, Montréal, at 265,000, is smaller than Saskatoon today. We're very young (almost forty-five per cent of us are under twenty and we only live to fifty-seven, on average), very white and very Christian. The life span for men and women is roughly the same this year, largely because, in the absence of antibiotics or even, in many cases, antisepsics, complications from childbirth is the leading cause of death among women.

We, along with the entire Empire, are still mourning the death of Queen Victoria, who expired last year after a reign of sixty-four years (Queen Elizabeth won't reach that mark until 2016). Our new king, Edward VII, after six decades as Crown Prince, has just eight years left to enjoy the throne. With the exception of France, the rest of Europe is ruled by a glittering array of kaisers, kings, emperors and tsars, most of whom still wield real power.

Teddy Roosevelt is President of the United States, following the assassination of William McKinley by an anarchist last year. In Canada, Liberal Sir Wilfred Laurier has been Prime Minister since 1896, the first Québecois to hold the job.

In 1902, Beatrix Potter and Joseph Conrad are writing, Gaugin, Monet and Sargent are painting and Rodin is sculpting. Sir Arthur Conan Doyle will publish *Hound of the Baskervilles* this year, and Enrico Caruso will make his first recording. Emile Zola will die this year, John Steinbeck will be born and "our boys" are returning from Canada's first overseas military commitment, the Boer War. There is no Panama Canal (1914), no Grey Cup (1909), no United Church (1925) and no income tax (1917).

Walk into a general store or *dépanneur*, (there are no supermarkets, no malls, no suburbs) and you'll see many names you'll recognize — Coke, Pepsi, Campbell Soup, Shredded Wheat, Grape-Nut Flakes, Tootsie Rolls, Fig Newtons and, new this year, Triscuits. But you won't find any Corn Flakes (1907), frozen food (1924) or anything in spray cans (1926). There is only one national retailer in Canada — the Hudson's Bay Company. Timothy Eaton won't open his first western store, in Winnipeg, until 1905.

At your newsstand, you have the choice of at least two local quality newspapers (there are 112 dailies publishing across Canada. Winnipeg, for example, has three — the *Free Press*, *The Tribune* and the *Telegram*), plus any number of sensational tabloids. Magazines available include *Saturday Night*, the *Canadian* and something called *The Busyman's Magazine,* which will become *Maclean's* in 1911. *Time* won't start publication until 1923.

You can't buy a radio because wireless transmission is less than a year old and there are no stations, let alone receivers. There are no televisions, no movie theatres, no computers, no internet. Entertainment is live in 1902 — baseball, boxing, concerts, vaudeville and singalongs at the parlour piano.

Though records are available, home players are very rare. However, the public is spending many hours in phonograph parlours, where, for a nominal fee, listeners have the choice of as many as 150 titles. Records may have been only two or three minutes long, but people are still finding the idea of recording sound as amazing as they did upon its invention twenty-five years before.

> It has been said that Science is never sensational; that it is
> intellectual, not emotional; but certainly nothing that can be conceived

would be more likely to create the profoundest of sensations, to arouse
the liveliest of human emotions, than once more to hear the familiar
voices of the dead. Yet Science now announces that this is possible, and
can be done … Speech has become, as it were, immortal.

Scientific American, 1877

Powered appliances are just becoming available, but there's an excellent
chance that, even if you live in a city, your house hasn't been wired for the new
electricity yet. And, in the event that you are one of the lucky electrical pioneers,
you probably still can't use that new-fangled electric iron, because many utilities
are only running at night. The major use of electricity in 1902 is for street lighting,
and who needs Mr. Edison's light bulb during the day?

That being the case, you, your mother or your servant (since thirty-eight
per cent of working women are domestics) are keeping a wood or coal stove burning
all day. You're lugging 130 kilograms of coal a week to do this, and, of course, this
stove is either on or off — no individual elements means no hot midnight snacks.

One of you spends an enormous amount of time and energy on laundry.
In 1902, washing and ironing, done by hand, typically takes from Sunday night till
Tuesday evening. And though you're probably not still making your own soap,
there's a good chance you're still carrying water from outside — the 190 litres for a
typical wash weighs 190 kilograms. Of course, all that wash water, and the cooking
water, has to be carried out again, because you're likely not hooked up to the sewer
yet, either. And, you can add to that load the contents of the chamber pots, because
using an outhouse during a Canadian winter really doesn't bear thinking about.

Only the well-to-do travel for business or pleasure in 1902. For the vast
majority of new Canadians, the only trip they've ever taken is the one that brought
them here in the first place. And, if you were born in Canada, chances are good
that you've never been more than a few miles from home. But, regardless of the
purpose of the trip, it's done by land or sea. Even the rich can't buy an airline
ticket because there are no airplanes — the Wright Brothers haven't flown yet.

Worldwide, there are vast shipping fleets and over a million kilometres of
railway track, but no paved highways. Stand on a downtown street in any Canadian
city, and you begin to understand why. There are no cars. Although Carl Benz
invented the automobile in Germany in 1885, there are only 200 registered in all
of Canada; every one of them in Ontario. The people you see are getting around
by electric streetcar, by horse-drawn carriage, or on a relatively new invention
that's been all the rage for more than half a decade now — the safety bicycle.

These bicycles, which we call coaster bikes today, are especially popular
with women, largely because of the independence they confer. This is causing

consternation among husbands and fathers, not least because the costume required to ride them safely, named after feminist Amelia Bloomer, has revealed to the world that women have legs — an evidently shocking discovery. Female riders are regularly harassed because prevailing opinion has it that possessing legs is clearly a male trait, and impersonating a male is still a criminal offence in some parts of North America and Europe.

Add to this the dark suggestions from the medical community about the connection between bicycle seats and lustful behaviour in unmarried women, and we have the makings of real controversy. After all, it's generally accepted in 1902 that women don't have sex — they have babies.

Women's education is a hot topic, even though it's been almost thirty years since the first woman graduated from a Canadian university, Mount Allison, in 1875. Canada's and the Empire's first female lawyer was finally admitted to the Ontario bar in 1897. The first female doctor produced by a Canadian university graduated in 1883. There are no female architects, engineers or veterinarians.

But, in addition to questions about what women should be allowed to study, there's an ongoing debate as to whether it's safe to educate them at all. Women of the classes that produce suffragists are generally considered to be frail, helpless creatures — inherently ill, given to fainting spells and bouts of hysteria (from the same Greek root as hysterectomy — a medical comment if ever there was one). Long confinement is still common for pregnancy, and doctors tend to treat menstruation like a disease. All in all, women may simply be too delicate for the rigours of a university education. Consider this passage from Harvard medical professor Dr. Edward Clarke's best seller, *Sex in Education – A Fair Chance for Girls:*

> Miss D went to college in good physical condition. During the four years of her college life, her parents and the college faculty required her to get what is popularly called an education. Nature required her, during the same period, to build and put in working-order a large and complicated reproductive mechanism, a matter that is popularly ignored — shoved out of sight like a disgrace. She naturally obeyed the requirements of the faculty, which she could see, rather than the requirements of the mechanism within her, that she could not see. Subjected to the college regimen, she worked four years in getting a liberal education. Her way of work was sustained and continuous, and out of harmony with the rhythmical periodicity of the female organization. The stream of vital and constructive force evolved within her was turned steadily to the brain, and away from the ovaries and their accessories. The result of this sort of education was that these last-mentioned

organs, deprived of sufficient opportunity and nutriment, first began to perform their functions with pain, a warning of error that was unheeded; then, to cease to grow; next, to set up once a month a grumbling torture that made life miserable; and, lastly, the brain and the whole nervous system, disturbed in obedience to the law that if one member suffers, all the members suffer, became neuralgic and hysterical. And so Miss D spent the few years succeeding her graduation in conflict with dysmenorrhoea, headache, neuralgia, and hysteria. Her parents marveled at her ill-health; and she furnished another text for the often-repeated sermon on the delicacy of American girls.

Of course, even if a woman survives the ordeal of education, she's still not really fit for a role outside the home. According to Darwin — actually, loose interpretations of Darwin — millions of years of evolution have seen to that.

The first set of differences [between the sexes] is that which results from a somewhat earlier arrest of individual evolution in women than in men, necessitated by the reservation of vital power to meet the cost of reproduction … this creates a perceptible falling short in those two faculties, intellectual and emotional, which are the latest products of human evolution — the power of abstract reasoning and that most abstract of emotions, the sentiment of justice.

Herbert Spencer
The Study of Sociology

Given this obvious inferiority, it's clear to modern thinkers that anything women are doing can be improved upon. So, if there is one thing women are getting plenty of in 1902, it's advice. Even child rearing isn't exempt because, in this scientific age, Mother no longer knows best about much of anything.

The Dr. Spock of the day is Luther Emmett Holt, a New York paediatrician. His 1894 book, *The Care and Feeding of Children* will eventually go through seventy-five printings, and includes such advice as never playing with a baby under six months; splinting a baby's elbows to prevent thumb sucking and starting toilet training as early as two or three months. Suppositories could be used, if necessary, to help Baby understand what's required. Mrs. Max West, writing in the U.S. government publication, *Infant Care*, is concerned that bad habits such as masturbation be squelched as early as possible. And, should you find that her suggestion of tying the infant's limbs to the crib doesn't work, aluminum mittens and leg spreaders are commercially available.

Despite all these failings, under the law in 1902, an unmarried woman over the age of twenty-one has virtually all the same rights as an adult male, as long as she's white. The only exceptions — theoretically, at least — are that she can't vote provincially or federally, hold elected office, or serve a religious congregation as a minister.

For her married sister, life is rather more circumscribed. In 1902, a married woman has little, if any, existence independent of her husband. For example, she has no right to her own children. As sole guardian, the father may apprentice his children, give them up for adoption, educate them in whatever fashion pleases him and raise them in the religion of his choice. He has the right to all their wages until they reach twenty-one, as well as custody of their persons, which means if he wants to lock a daughter in her room for a year or two, he has a perfectly legal right to do so.

This state of affairs continues even after his death. The father can appoint a guardian who is well within his rights to bar a mother from any contact with her own children. Even if a mother is awarded custody of her children, the court can, and does, remove them if she tries to change their religion or do anything else Dad might disapprove of from the grave.

In most of the country, a wife has recently regained ownership of property she brings to the marriage, or has been bequeathed directly to her; but she has no right to any part of the estate — if her husband cuts her out of the will, there's no recourse. And, while she can make money by working for herself, say, as a writer or running a business, her husband can prevent her from working for anyone else by suing the employer for what amounts to homewrecking.

And speaking of homewrecking, the divorce rate is rising — there were eighteen of them in Canada last year; by comparison, there were 71,144 in 2000. Eighteen divorces, however, is actually a remarkable number when you consider that the country's only divorce court is the Senate and that a divorce actually requires an Act of Parliament. Adultery is the only grounds for divorce, but unsurprisingly, the definition of adultery is different for men and women. For a wife to prove adultery, the husband has literally to have moved his mistress into the family house. Even after that, a wife still needs further grounds before she can petition Parliament. Bestiality and sodomy (homosexuality — which is illegal, of course) are popular choices.

If the physical world of 1902 is strange, the mental landscape is even more so. The overriding world view, or *weltanschauung*, as the Germans have it, is the inevitable March of Progress. The educated classes look back on the triumphs of the past century, and see no indication that the expansion of wealth and liberal democracy will, or can, end. The evidence is everywhere, and obvious. Hasn't Mr.

Darwin shown that even life itself evolves inexorably toward higher and higher forms? (Actually, that's not what he said at all, but that's another story.)

It follows then, that not only will society continue to advance, but that it's perfectible. This understanding is what drives the social reform movements of this period — the firm belief that, in a world of Progress, a good cause and the Protestant work ethic are all that are needed to effect real improvement. Demon rum can be banished. The foreigner and the savage can be civilized. The perfect society is within our grasp, if only … well, if only the lower classes will play their part. That part, of course, mostly involves doing as they're told.

For upper middle-class reformers — a group that includes practically all suffragists — it's not unfair to suggest that the poor aren't so much people to be helped as a series of problems to be solved. There's a consensus that these problems won't be addressed by lessening the distance between the classes, the growth of socialism not withstanding. Far more constructive would be efforts to increase working class amenability to — or at least acceptance of — their place in society and their role in the economy.

Whether it's the role of women, working conditions in factories or the plight of the heathen overseas, the intent is not revolutionary — it's to foster increased productivity and social stability. Most suffragists want the vote so that the moral superiority inherent in women can be applied to the political system, which will, in turn, help the mothers of the race better shoulder their domestic responsibilities. Missionaries, for all their good works, are focused on converting natives into God-fearing third-class subjects of the Empire, not producing Gandhis.

After all, no less an authority than Jesus had said the poor will always be with us, and Darwin, as interpreted by sociologists like Herbert Spencer, has proved it with his doctrine of survival of the fittest. And in 1902, it's blindingly obvious who the fittest are, at least to the people in charge.

It is fearless energy, sturdy determination, versatile ability, peculiar aptitude for self government and unresting spirit of enterprise that characterizes the great Anglo-Saxon people … it is these characteristics that have brought [them] to their present dominant position in the world.

Lord Charles Beresford
The North American Review
December 1900

But being on the top of the heap doesn't just bring the Anglo-Saxon race privilege. The pervasive sense of responsibility that goes along with this perceived superiority is something that's almost incomprehensible today. In the world before the war, the cult of individualism that is so much a part of modern Western identity is largely confined to the frontier romances of Zane Grey. In 1902, reformers and missionaries are working for the less fortunate because they firmly believe that failing to do so would be shirking their duty to their class, their God and society in general. When Rudyard Kipling wrote in *The White Man's Burden*, "Go, bind your sons to exile /To serve your captives' needs," he meant exactly what he said.

Of course, this sense of responsibility extends beyond the downtrodden. There's also a duty to race and to civilization itself, which requires dealing with the potential threat represented by the same groups that duty bids us help. So Dr. Margaret Sanger promotes birth control among the poor, at least in part to balance the falling birthrates that threaten the future of the ruling class — her class. Nellie McClung supports the work of J.S. Woodsworth's All People's Mission in North End Winnipeg, as well as forced sterilization of the mentally defective (among whom, for instance, some "experts" include fifty per cent of prostitutes). And Judge Emily Murphy takes destitute young offenders into her own home, while writing diatribes on the "Yellow Peril" represented by Chinese immigration.

The juxtaposition of these two themes had been beautifully demonstrated at the 1900 Paris World's Fair. One of the exhibits featured a Colonial Village where modern people could examine how the objects of the White Man's burden lived in their native environment, thus clearly demonstrating why they needed our guidance. At the same time, the paying public was protected from any displays of primitive savagery by a suitably stout fence of the sort used at the Paris Zoo.

Nellie McClung

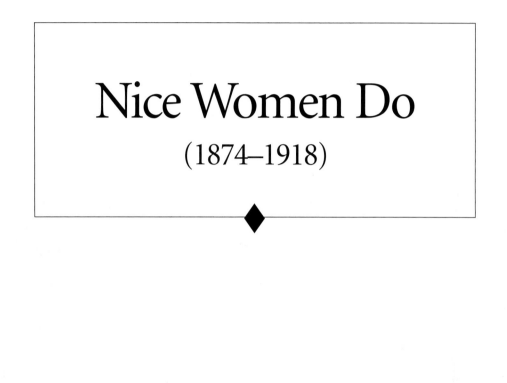

Nice Women Do

(1874–1918)

Scene: 1902

SOCIAL NARRATOR: She's in full Gibson Girl dress — floor-length skirt and high-necked, long-sleeved blouse with cameo broach at the throat. She's sitting on a stool holding a mirror as her maid puts up her hair.

(*To audience*) Oh, do sit down. I'll only be a moment. (*She goes on as she examines the maid's work in the mirror.*)

A few more pins on the other side, I should think.

(*As the maid complies*) Remarkably competent for an Irish girl. I'm very lucky to have her. (*The maid, who's finished, blushes and curtsies. The narrator waves her away and continues immediately, as though she's not present.*)

Help is so difficult to find these days, especially ones who know their place. So refreshing compared with all these girls going to shops and even offices. What future they see in taking jobs from men I'll never understand, although Charles does remind me that they're far cheaper to employ and much more easily managed. That may be true of a shop girl, but you can be sure he knows better than to try to "manage" me.

(*Crosses to rack and begins to put on jacket.*) Oh, I've finally had a letter from James in the morning post. He's leaving South Africa on the 15th, and expects to land in Montreal before Thanksgiving. His duty to go, one supposes, but I do think this war has been a sad commentary on British manhood. (*Putting on her hat*) Three years to put some Dutch bumpkins in their place? Really.

A propos of that, before we go, I've written a new ending to my presentation. Do tell me what you think:

Ladies, if the Anglo-Saxon race is to be saved, it seems clear that we are the ones who shall have to do it. If we are not to be supplanted by the offspring of immigrants and defectives, we must convince our young women that motherhood is both their joy and their duty. To see that our daughters assume their proper roles as guardians of the race, they must have more places at university. And above all — above all — the suffrage. There is only one way to bring true Christian virtue back into this sordid, this rum-soaked business of governance. We must have the vote!

Ladies, we face a daunting, some would say, an overwhelming challenge. But, of the outcome, let there be no doubt. We shall prevail, because we do His work. And, if the Lord be for us, who may stand against us? Thank you for your kind attention, and good night ... Well?

Oh good. Well, come then. There's work to do and great things to be won.

POLITICAL	SOCIAL / TECHNOLOGY

	POLITICAL	SOCIAL / TECHNOLOGY
1874	• Benjamin Disraeli becomes British Prime Minister • **Temperance Union established by Letitia Yeomans in Ontario**	• Civil marriage made compulsory in Germany • Tennis introduced in America • First Impressionist exhibition, Paris • **First Cdn nursing school in St. Catharine's, ON**
1875	• Rebellion in Cuba • Kwang Hsu becomes Emperor of China • Bosnia, Herzegovina rebel against Turkish rule	• Mark Twain writes *Adventures of Tom Sawyer* • Tchaikovsky creates Piano Concerto No. 1 • **London Medical School for Women founded** • First swim across the English Channel • **Mount Allison U: Canada's first female grad**
1876	• Korea gains independence • Serbia, Montenegro declare war on Turkey • Colorado becomes U.S. state • **BNA Act says women are not "persons"**	• Brahms writes Symphony No. 1 • Richard Wagner creates *Siegfried* opera • Alexander Graham Bell invents the telephone
1877	• Rutherford B. Hayes becomes U.S. President • Russia declares war on Turkey; invades Romania • First Kaffir War (South Africa)	• Patent Protection Law enacted in Germany • Complete works of Mozart published • Thomas Edison invents the phonograph • Famine in Bengal
1878	• Turkey and Russia sign armistice • Greece declares war on Turkey • Anti-socialist law enacted in Germany • John A. Macdonald returns to power in Canada	• Pope Pius IX dies • Gilbert & Sullivan produce *H.M.S Pinafore* • First bicycles developed in U.S. • Paris World Exhibition
1879	• British-Zulu War	• First electric tram exhibited • First telephone exchange established in London
1880	• Pacific War: Chile vs. Bolivia & Peru • J.A. Garfield becomes twentieth U.S. President	• Dostoevsky writes *The Brothers Karamazov* • NY City streets lit by electricity • Electrostatic generator
1881	• James.A. Garfield assassinated,Chester Arthur new U.S President • Political parties founded in Japan • Austro-Serbian treaty of alliance	• Savoy Theatre built in London • Canadian Pacific Railway founded • France establishes freedom of the press • Toronto weekly, *The Canada Citizen*, published
1882	• U.S. bans Chinese immigrants for ten years • Triple Alliance formed: Italy, Austria,Germany • John A. Macdonald re-elected	• Robert Louis Stevenson writes *Treasure Island* • World Exhibition in Moscow • Recoil-operated machine gun patented • Beginnings of psychoanalysis • **Single women, widow property owners allowed to vote on municipal bylaws in Canada**

POLITICAL	SOCIAL / TECHNOLOGY	
T I M E L I N E		
• French gain control of Tunis • First Canadian suffrage bill defeated in Parliament.	• Nietzsche writes *Thus Spake Zarathustra* • Robert Koch develops inoculation against anthrax • *Orient Express* makes first run	**1883**
• German occupation of Southwest Africa (Namibia)	• Statue of Liberty dedicated • **University of Toronto admits women**	**1884**
• Mahdi take Khartoum; General Gordon killed; British evacuate Sudan • Great Britain occupies Port Hamilton, Korea • Northwest Rebellion • Louis Riel hanged	• Sir Francis Galton develops fingerprinting • Benz invents single-cylinder car engine • H. Rider Haggard writes *King Solomon's Mines* • **Trinity College (U of T) awards degrees for women**	**1885**
• British PM introduces Home Rule in Ireland	• Surgical equipment first sterilized • Karl Marx's *Das Capital* published in English	**1886**
• Queen Victoria celebrates Golden Jubilee • Prince Ferdinand elected King of Bulgaria • John A. Macdonald re-elected	• Celluloid film invented • Phonograph sound quality improved	**1887**
• Cecil Rhodes granted mining rights • Suez Canal convention	• **Jack the Ripper murders six women in London** • **First beauty contest held in Belgium** • Pasteur Institute inaugurated	**1888**
• U.S. adds the Dakotas, Montana, Washington • London Dock Strike	• Eiffel Tower designed for Paris World Exhibition • Joseph Von Mehring & Oskar Minkowski discover the pancreas controls blood sugar • First May Day Celebration, Paris	**1889**
• First general election in Japan	• Discovery of antitoxins • Global influenza outbreak	**1890**
• Triple Alliance renewed for twelve years • Young Turk Movement formed in Geneva • Sir John A. Macdonald dies • Sir John Abbot becomes Canadian PM	• Beginnings of wireless telegraphy • Widespread famine in Russia • Thomas Hardy writes *Tess of the D'Urbervilles* • Oscar Wilde writes *The Picture of Dorian Gray* • Zipper invented	**1891**
• Gladstone becomes PM of Britain • Grover Cleveland elected U.S. President • Sir John Thompson becomes Canadian PM	• Tchaikovsky writes *The Nutcracker* • Internal combustion engine patented • Automatic telephone switchboard introduced	**1892**

	POLITICAL	SOCIAL / TECHNOLOGY
	T I M E L I N E	
1893	• Franco-Russian alliance signed • Trial over Panama Canal corruption in Paris • Laos becomes French protectorate	• Art nouveau appears in Europe • Henry Ford builds first car • World Exhibition in Chicago
1894	• Uganda becomes a British protectorate • Korea & Japan declare war on China • Czar Alexander III dies, succeeded by son Nicholas II • Sir Mackenzie Bowell becomes Canadian PM • Dreyfus treason trial (France)	• Rudyard Kipling writes *The Jungle Book* • Cinematograph invented • Flat phonograph record introduced • Argon discovered by William Ramsay
1895	• End of Chinese-Japanese war • Queen of Korea assassinated • Cuba fights Spain for independence	• Guglielmo Marconi invents radio telegraphy • X-rays discovered • First U.S. Open golf championship held • H.G Wells writes *The Time Machine* • Principle of modern rocket propulsion discovered
1896	• Utah becomes U.S. state • France annexes Madagascar • Russia & China sign Manchuria Convention • Sir Charles Tupper becomes Canadian PM • Sir Wilfred Laurier elected Canadian PM	• Nobel Prizes established • First modern Olympics held in Athens • Klondike gold rush • Helium, radioactivity discovered
1897	• Crete proclaims union with Greece • Turkey declares war on Greece • Germany occupies Kiao-chow, North China • Russia occupies Port Arthur	• Ronald Ross discovers malaria parasite • J.J. Thomson studies cathode rays, discovers electron • Bram Stoker writes *Dracula* • The Sultan of Zanzibar abolishes slavery
1898	• U.S. declares war on Spain over Cuba • Empress Elizabeth of Austria murdered	• H.G. Wells writes *The War of the Worlds* • Ramsay discovers xenon, krypton, neon • Pierre & Marie Curie discover radium, polonium • **Kit Coleman becomes first female war correspondent, covers Spanish-American war**
1899	• Philippines demands independence from U.S. • Boer War between Britain and Boers in South Africa	• Ernest Rutherford discovers alpha and beta rays • First magnetic recording of sound • Wilde writes *The Importance of Being Earnest*
1900	• King Umberto I of Italy murdered • Commonwealth of Australia created	• Freud publishes *The Interpretation of Dreams* • First trial flight of Zeppelin • **Canada passes Married Woman's Property Act** • Olympics held in Paris

POLITICAL	SOCIAL / TECHNOLOGY	
TIMELINE		
• Edmund Barton first PM of Australia • Queen Victoria succeeded by son Edward VII • U.S. President McKinley assassinated; VP Theodore Roosevelt becomes President • Social Revolutionary Party founded in Russia	• Pablo Picasso's begins his "Blue Period" • Ragtime jazz develops in U.S. • Adrenaline isolated as a hormone • Telegraphic radio messages sent across Atlantic • J.P. Morgan organizes U.S. Steel Corporation • Oil drilling begins in Persia	**1901**
• Independence of China and Korea recognized • U.S. acquires control over Panama Canal • Leon Trotsky escapes from prison in Siberia • **Women gain the vote in Australia**	• Hormone secretin discovered • Panchromatic plate invented • Coal strike in U.S.	**1902**
• Alaskan frontier settled • Russian Social Democratic Party splits: becomes Mensheviks and Bolsheviks	• First recording of an opera: Verdi's *Ernani* • First motor taxis appear in London • Henry Ford founds Ford Motor Company • First Tour de France • Wright Brothers achieve first flight	**1903**
• Russo-Japanese War begins • Treaty between Bolivia and Chile • Sir Wilfrid Laurier re-elected Canadian PM • Theodore Roosevelt elected U.S. President	• London Symphony Orchestra's first performance • **Helen Keller graduates from Radcliffe College** • Max Weber writes *The Protestant Ethic and the Birth of Capitalism* • Olympics held in St. Louis, Missouri	**1904**
• Demonstration in St. Petersburg crushed by police • Alberta & Saskatchewan become provinces • Japan defeats Russia	• First regular cinema established • Einstein develops Special Theory of Relativity • Rayon yarn manufactured • First neon lights appear	**1905**
• U.S. occupies Cuba • Roosevelt makes first foreign trip to Panama Canal • Armand Fallières elected President of France	• J.J. Thomson awarded Nobel Prize for Physics • Canada's Reginald Fessenden: first radio program • "Typhoid Mary" carrier found and incarcerated • "Interim" Olympics held in Athens	**1906**
• **Universal direct suffrage instituted in Austria** • Roosevelt bars Japanese from immigrating to U.S. • Oklahoma becomes forty-sixth U.S. state	• **Mother's Day established** • Immigration to U.S. restricted by law • First Cubist Exhibition in Paris	**1907**
• Union of South Africa created • Dutch establish rule in Bali • Laurier re-elected PM	• **Lucy M. Montgomery writes *Anne of Green Gables*** • First steel and glass building constructed in Berlin • Four-dimensional geometry formulated • Olympics held in London	**1908**

	POLITICAL	SOCIAL / TECHNOLOGY
	T I M E L I N E	
1909	• Civil War in Honduras • Anglo-German talks on control of Baghdad railroad • **International Congress of Women held in Toronto**	• Sigmund Freud lectures in U.S. on psychoanalysis • Admiral Robert E. Peary reaches North Pole • **Women admitted to German universities**
1910	• China abolishes slavery • Japan annexes Korea	• Halley's comet observed • Week-end becomes popular in U.S. • **Marie Curie publishes _Treatise on Radiography_**
1911	• Mexican Civil War ends • Revolution in Central China • Sir Robert Borden elected Canadian PM	• Roald Amundsen reaches South Pole • First flight from Munich to Berlin
1912	• Treaty of Lausanne between Italy and France • Woodrow Wilson wins U.S. election • Lenin connects with Stalin, takes over _Pravda_	• _Titanic_ sinks: 1,513 lost • Carl Jung publishes _The Theory of Psychoanalysis_ • First successful parachute jump • Olympics held in Stockholm
1913	• **Suffragist demonstrations in London** • Federal income tax introduced in U.S. • Balkan War	• Grand Central Station opens in New York City • Coal dust converted into oil • Basic ideas of jet propulsion established • Niels Bohr introduces theory of atomic structure
1914	• Peace Treaty between Serbia and Turkey • World War I begins with the assassination of Archduke Francis Ferdinand and wife in Sarajevo • Panama Canal opened	• Charlie Chaplin stars in _Making a Living_ • James Joyce writes _Dubliners_ • Patent suit in favour of Wright Brothers determined
1915	• WW I: Battle of Ypres 6,035 Canadian dead • WW I: Germans use chlorine gas	• Henry Ford develops the farm tractor • **Margaret Sanger publishes info on birth control** • Einstein postulates General Theory of Relativity
1916	• Italy declares war; Allies attack Zeebrugge • U.S. troops in Santo Domingo: internal conflict • Woodrow Wilson re-elected U.S. President • **Manitoba women get the vote**	• Olympics, scheduled for Berlin, cancelled • Jazz sweeps U.S. • **Margaret Sanger opens first birth control clinic in Brooklyn and is imprisoned**
1917	• WWI: Battle of Vimy Ridge • Russian revolution overthows Czar • **Louise McKinney first Canadian woman elected to a provincial legislature**	• Literacy requirements for U.S. citizenship • Trans-Siberian railroad completed
1918	• WWI: German offensive; Paris bombed • Nov. 11th: Armistice signed btwn Allies & Germany • **Canadian women get vote**	• H.L. Mencken writes _In Defense of Women_ • World's oldest radio station: CFCF Montreal • Eight-hour workday established in Germany

Nice Women Do

(1874–1918)

The women who led the fight for the vote are known today as first-wave feminists, to distinguish them from the activists of the sixties and seventies. Not that it's easy to confuse them. In attitude and beliefs, these Victorian women bore about as much resemblance to their "bra-burning",[1] consciousness-raising descendants, as their world does to the twenty-first century.

So who, exactly, would qualify as a feminist in 1902? Women who wanted to be man's equal in every way? Or women who just wanted a job? Activists intent on enhancing the roles of home and Mother? Or temperance workers trying to steer society down the path of moral living by banning vice? At the beginning of the twentieth century, the answer was, any woman who tried to challenge the status quo: i.e., all of the above.

Each of these various groups eventually supported women's suffrage. But with the exception of the equality feminists, who were actually a very small minority within the Canadian movement, the idea of equal rights or voting for its own sake was never really an issue in the period before World War I. For most activists, the vote was simply another means of advancing their particular agenda, whatever it happened to be — in other words, a lobbying tool. They would force politicians to listen by threatening them where they were most vulnerable — at the ballot box.

It's telling that the first women's suffrage organization in Canada was the Toronto Women's Literary Society, founded in 1876 by Dr. Emily Stowe. The idea of women sullying themselves in the dirty world of politics was entirely at odds with the idealized image of delicate, pure wife and mother that was then current.

---

[1] This much-publicized myth apparently began with the imaginative report of a *New York Post* reporter in 1968. Though a number of women had thrown bras and other undergarments into a trash can, none was ever burned.

The power of that image didn't faze the early proponents, such as Dr. Stowe and Flora Denison, who made no bones about the fact that, for them, obtaining the vote was just the beginning. They wanted a society where men and women were equals — in other words, they wanted social revolution. It was a bold vision, to be sure, but one that made female suffrage profoundly unpopular with large swathes of society, both male and female. As a result, strict suffrage organizations tended to be transitory and ineffective, or co-opted into more mainstream organizations like the Women's Christian Temperance Union or WCTU.

At the same time, urbanization, the rise of the middle class and greater access to a university education were producing a much larger group of women with both the time and the inclination to look beyond the home. What they were seeing in Canada's cities was not only disagreeable — it was a threat to those homes, to their way of life — to Progress itself. To these women, it was clear that what was needed was reform, not revolution.

In 1912, infant mortality in Canada was 118/1,000 live births (compare that with 4.95/1,000 today). Industrial slums were expanding in every city as immigration swelled the ranks of the working class. The population of non-Anglo Saxons continued to rise despite often horrific living conditions and soaring infant mortality. In 1912, for example, the infant mortality rate in Winnipeg's North End among people from central and southern Europe was an astonishing 372/1,000, while birthrates in wealthy neighbourhoods were steadily dropping. Sexually transmitted disease rates were climbing, threatening the health of future generations.

Much of the reform effort before the Great War was dictated by the mindset of the time — *noblesse oblige,* or the moral responsibility that came with privilege. Reformers were driven to help alleviate the suffering they saw around them, but there was also a large element of self-interest. Immigration and comparative birth rates seemed to cast doubt on the long-term future of the Anglo-Saxon race. Since, in the minds of English Canada's middle class, Progress was directly linked to their own wellbeing, something had to be done.

First, a little background. At the turn of the last century, Darwin, evolution and the survival of the fittest were all the rage among the secular elite. Darwin's idea — evolution through natural selection — went something like this:

Groups of living things have variations within their populations that give some individuals an advantage in a particular environment. These individuals are more successful and survive to produce more offspring, many of whom inherit the same variation. Over a number of generations, the variation that confers the advantage becomes more and more common, until finally it becomes the norm. Thus the population changes, or evolves. This process goes on constantly, whether the population in question is fruit flies, Galapagos finches, or us.

The problem, however, was that although Darwin's observations were painstakingly accurate, and his theory seemed a reasonable explanation for what he'd observed, neither he nor anyone else had figured out the exact mechanism. What produced the variation on which the environment acted? Remember, Gregor Mendel's 1860s hybridization studies had only been rediscovered in 1900, and Avery, Watson and Crick[2] were still half a century in the future.

In the absence of any definitive evidence, there were two competing explanations, both of which are still with us today. One, called environmentalism, or euthenics (this was nurture, from the Greek "to prosper") was based on the ideas of French naturalist Jean-Baptiste Lamarck (1744–1829). This school believed it was the environment that produced physical or behavioural variations between individuals and that these acquired characteristics could then be passed on to children. One frequently cited example from the period was the dockworker whose children were supposedly born with callused hands. If this were so, then changing the environment of people by improving factory conditions, for example, would not only help the workers, but automatically produce healthier children.

The opposing view, championed by Sir Francis Galton (1822–1911), was eugenics (this was nature, from the Greek for "wellborn"). Here, the variation was presumed to arise strictly internally, produced by what would eventually be called an individual's genes, though the term "gene" wasn't coined until 1911. This theory held that a criminal, or other defective, was born a criminal, and there was nothing an improvement in environment could do to change it. Under a strict interpretation of this idea, factory reform, rather than helping, could actually harm the race, subverting the laws of nature and the survival of the fittest by letting defectives live to reproduce. The only way to actively produce healthier children, this theory went, would be through selective breeding — superior people should be encouraged to have more children, while the inferior should be persuaded, or prevented, from doing the same.

> [In] Eugenics ... the first object is to check the birth-rate of the Unfit, instead of allowing them to come into being, though doomed in large numbers to perish prematurely. The second object is the improvement of the race by furthering the productivity of the Fit by early marriages and healthful rearing of their children. Natural Selection rests upon excessive production and wholesale destruction;

---

2   Oswald Avery, a Canadian, aided by Colin McLeod and Maclyn McCarty proved in 1944 that genes are made of DNA. In 1953, James Watson and Francis Crick, along with Maurice Wilkins and Rosalind Franklin, demonstrated how DNA works. Watson, Crick and Wilkins received the Nobel Prize for Medicine in 1962.

Eugenics on bringing no more individuals into the world than can be properly cared for, and those only of the best stock.

Sir Francis Galton
Memories of My Life, 1908

Although almost everyone agreed that the daughters of the superior classes should be having more babies — everyone but the daughters themselves, perhaps — for the Victorian/Edwardian reformer, euthenics had a much greater appeal. In addition to suggesting goals that might actually be achieved, reform based on euthenic principles had the happy consequence of producing results during the lifetime of the advocate — not an unimportant consideration during recruitment drives.

Reform work gave women's groups the opportunity to develop formidable organizational skills, and they were able to use those skills to exploit what even they considered to be woman's primary strengths in the public arena — her untainted moral authority and her biologically ordained talent for nurturing.

So, whether the cause of a particular group was more parks or better inspection of factories, compulsory education, mother's pensions or the promotion of home economics, the long-term goal rarely had anything to do with changing woman's traditional role in society.

The sensible dress movement was as much about healthier babies as freeing women from the tyranny of the corset. Groups that argued for expanded education for women were often looking to produce better mothers, not more doctors and lawyers. While home economics was giving more women a chance at a professional career, its real goal was helping women use science to create an improved environment for the development of the next generation.

Compulsory education was often about getting young people out of the debilitating environment of the factories before they and their potential offspring were permanently damaged. For the same reason, there was pressure for special legislation to protect female workers, even though such legislation made women less employable. In fact, many women's groups agreed with trade unions that unmarried women were selfishly taking work from men with families to feed.

All these organizations were considered feminist at the time — radical, even. But no matter how much they wanted to change society — and how much they were willing to move away from traditional liberal democratic values by supporting the expansion of government power in order to impose their views — at its most basic, their feminism was what has been called maternal feminism. And maternal feminism was actually about increasing the palatability of the status quo, not moving women toward equality with men. If women of good breeding and high intelligence could be inspired to turn their considerable energies to home and family, that was how the race would be saved and the future assured.

All this made support for suffrage problematic for many women. Here was an area, politics, which was about as far from home and family as it was possible to get, and an idea that reeked of social revolution. And yet, it was clear to many women's groups that their male legislators had no interest in passing their reforms, either because, as in divorce law, they were a threat to patriarchal power, or, as in the case of industrial reform, to their pocket books.

The answer, slowly, and in many cases, reluctantly arrived at, was to take up the cause of the small but vocal groups of suffragettes that had been constantly disappearing and reappearing since the 1870s. For example, despite the presence of Emily Stowe's daughter, Dr. Augusta Stowe-Gullen, among its founders, it took the National Council of Women until 1910 to formally support suffrage. The fact that this very moderate organization finally added votes for women to its platform shows how far the stigma of revolution had by then receded. This rehabilitation, if you will, had a lot to do with another reform effort underway during this period — the fight for the souls of Canada's drinkers.

> *Praise God from whom all blessings flow,*
> *Praise Him who saves from deepest woe,*
> *Praise Him who leads the Temperance host,*
> *Praise Father, Son and Holy Ghost.*
>
> *Temperance Doxology*, 1912

> The Women's Christian Temperance Union is no accident,
> but one of God's special creations. Throughout the ages since the fall
> of man, Divine Love has been raising up instrumentalities for the
> restoration of our race to its original standard of moral rectitude.
>
> Annual Report,
> WCTU BC, 1893

The period before the First World War was a time of tremendous expansion for Protestant churches in Canada, especially in the West. The Anglicans may have been there first, coming as they had with the Hudson's Bay Company, but, as the West was opened to settlement, Methodists and Presbyterians were in a very un-Christian competition to catch up. Virtually every new hamlet quickly had a Methodist and a Presbyterian church, often right across the street from each other. (Methodists, most Presbyterians and Congregationalists joined to form the United

Church of Canada in 1925, which explains why there are so many United Churches so close together in the downtowns of prairie cities.)

The evangelical fervour of this period, in its own, quiet English way, rivalled anything you might see in a fundamentalist prayer meeting today. Even though they couldn't be ministers, sit on the official board or have any formal role in church services, women were crucial to the running of the church. As Nellie McClung, who taught Sunday School at Young Memorial Methodist in Winnipeg, put it:

> Women may lift mortgages, or build churches or any other light work, but the real, heavy work of the church, such as moving resolutions in the general conference or assemblies must be done by strong, hardy men.

It was in church organizations like the Ladies' Aid and the Women's Missionary Society, to take the Methodist example, that many women learned the skills that would serve them so well in the fight for suffrage. These were not small organizations. By 1925, the women of the WMS controlled and administered a budget of over a million dollars — money that was completely separate from that of the Methodist Church itself.

While much of this missionary zeal was directed overseas where, for example, the WMS supported 275 missionaries around the globe, there was clearly work to be done at home as well. God's work. And that was the impulse behind the creation of the Women's Christian Temperance Union.

Founded in Canada in 1874 by Letitia Youmans, WCTU membership grew rapidly, peaking at over 10,000 nationwide by 1915. Like the members of most women's groups of the time, temperance women looked at the world and, in the spirit of Progress, saw problems that had to be solved; moral decay, poverty and, good church women that they were, the dilution of Anglo-Saxon, Protestant values. Unlike most of the other groups, however, they had identified the cause — demon rum.

If Canadians (by which, in most cases, they meant male Canadians) could be made to see the evils that flowed directly from drinking liquor — the abuse of women and children, crime, impure living, just to name a few — then surely they would see the light and abstain. By and large, Canadians weren't listening. Per capita consumption of alcohol was on the rise at century's end, as were society's problems.

When it became clear that moral arguments weren't working, the WCTU began to move away from temperance and toward prohibition. The issue was important enough, in their view, that if persuasion didn't work, they too would have to find a way to impose their beliefs on society at large. This didn't automatically mean support for suffrage, however. The idea of women voting was unpopular across the country; so unpopular, in fact, that even as committed a reformer as Letitia Youmans worried that association with it might damage the Cause.

In the absence of the vote, temperance workers' most potent tool was the petition. WCTU locals became experts at collecting impressive lists of signatures and delivering them to various levels of government. As a publicity generating device, the petition was very effective. But governments, and the liquor lobby, had an answer to this tactic — the local referendum. This was an ideal solution for governments — a chance to demonstrate their commitment to democracy, without the political risk of actually having to pass potentially unpopular legislation. Since the women who collected the names couldn't vote, while the majority of the drinkers, who were male, could, most of these referenda had predictable outcomes.

However, God's work wasn't about to be derailed by a few political tricks. The WCTU kept chipping away, and as urbanization and industrialization tended to exacerbate the drinking problem, it made perceptible, if slow, progress.

Finally, in 1898, its supporters convinced Prime Minister Wilfrid Laurier to hold a national referendum. It took place on September 26th, and, to many people's surprise, the prohibition side won by more than 13,000 votes. There was one, small problem, however. The only province where the proposition was defeated was Québec, where it never had a chance. No self-respecting Catholic priest was going to pollute the Communion chalice with grape juice, a fact that can't have been lost on Laurier. Given the rise of Québec nationalism after Riel's execution and the Manitoba Schools controversy, and the fact that the Liberals were in power because of the forty-nine seats they'd managed to win in Québec two years earlier, there didn't seem much upside to imposing prohibition. The referendum results were declared insufficient.

Clearly, if prohibition was going to become a reality, the movement required more political clout; the kind that would produce legislation. This led the WTCU into alliances with more secular women's groups like the National Council of Women, and eventually to support for women's suffrage. Though they needed each other, it was often an uncomfortable relationship. There were many areas where positions of the more rural, evangelical and conservative temperance union didn't mesh with those of the urban, upper middle class and more moderate social reform movement. Yet, they found ways to work together. And if it found its more radical stances being shifted farther toward the mainstream by the increasing presence of WCTU workers on executive committees, the social reform movement gained the energy and outstanding organizational skills of women like Louise McKinney, the Empire's first female legislator.

Louise McKinney was born in Frankville, Ontario, on October 22, 1868. Her parents were Richard Crummy, a first-generation Canadian from County Caven, Ireland and Ester Empey, a Canadian born of Irish parentage. Louise was their second daughter and fifth child and there were to be five more children in the family. She attended Athens High School and Smith's Falls Model School.

Louise has been described as a bright, fun-loving, popular girl with a great sense of humour and an enormous talent for debate. Though her later opponents probably had trouble believing the fun-loving part, these characteristics stood her in good stead in her life-long battle against the demon rum. Following graduation from high school in 1884, she accepted her first teaching position, though as yet she had no formal training. Teaching was not her first career choice — she had wanted to study medicine and deeply resented the fact that because she was a woman she was denied that opportunity.

After two years of on-the-job training, she attended the Ottawa Normal School and obtained her teaching certificate. Then, in the summer of 1893, she visited an older married sister in Drayton, North Dakota, and decided to stay.

For the next three years, she taught school, but it was in 1894, at the age of twenty-six, that she began what she considered to be her real life's work when she obtained a position as a paid organizer for the Women's Christian Temperance Union.

It was while engaged in work for the WCTU that she met James McKinney, also a fierce prohibitionist of Irish extraction. His father, John McKinney, farmed near Stittsville, Ontario, and had been born in County Derry, while his mother, Jane Lindsay, was Canadian born but again, of Irish parents. Louise and James were married at her family home in Frankville on March 10, 1896, then returned to the Dakotas. They had one son, Willard, whom they named after Frances Willard, the founder of the WCTU in the United States. Willard became a doctor, which must have delighted his mother. But one wonders whether, at the same time, she was somewhat resentful, because simply on the basis of his maleness, he was able to accomplish the goal she had so long desired.

In 1903, the family moved to Claresholm, Alberta, about ninety-five kilometres south of Calgary. As pioneers in what was then still the Northwest Territories, it's likely that they participated in discussions among their neighbours concerning when provincehood would be attained. As it turned out, they only had to wait two years.

Louise almost immediately established a local chapter of the WCTU in Claresholm and was installed as its first president. In 1904, when women from

LOUISE McKINNEY

Calgary, Regina, Saskatoon and Medicine Hat met in Calgary for their first convention, she was named the corresponding secretary of the WCTU for the Northwest Territories. Four years later, she became Alberta's provincial president.

She attended every national convention and many world gatherings, including those in Boston in 1906, Brooklyn in 1916, London in 1920, Lausanne in 1928 and Toronto in 1931. During this last convention she was acting president for the Dominion of Canada and was elected first vice-president of the World Union.

As were many temperance workers, she was very active in the Methodist Church. She and her husband helped to build the church in Claresholm and she taught in the Sunday School. In 1922, she was the only female delegate at the General Conference of Methodists in Toronto and three years later, she was one of only four women to sign the Basis of Union of the United Church of Canada.

It was typical of the times that all this was undertaken on a full-time volunteer basis. She'd had to resign as a paid organizer for the WCTU at the time of her marriage — even in a women's organization, respectable married women didn't work for money.

Those involved in the suffrage movement might have argued that the best case for giving women the vote was the ineffectiveness of the few elected men who agreed with them at getting legislation passed, or even persuading their colleagues that there was any merit to the idea whatsoever. The vast majority of male politicians remained in adamant opposition right to the bitter end, and indeed beyond. Many were, in the modern idiom, sexist, and proud of it. Some of these were true conservatives who were intrinsically suspicious of anything new. Others were political pragmatists, who saw no reason to expand the franchise until they saw a political advantage in doing so.

The federal battle can be said to have begun in April 1885, when Prime Minister Sir John A. Macdonald tabled his Electoral Franchise Bill. This bill, which had the goal of wresting control of the voter's list from the provinces, also included a provision for extending the franchise to property-owning spinsters and widows — Sir John evidently believing that most women would vote Conservative.

The bill, which set income, property and age requirements for male voters, did eventually pass. But Macdonald had to withdraw the suffrage section to placate a large segment of his own party, after listening to a series of speeches like the following:

Woman has been created for another kingdom. Her kingdom is powerful enough. They are supreme in almost everything. If you admit them to the political arena, we shall have to concede our places to them. It is all very well where a lady of property and rank may object that her butler has a vote while she has not. But that is due to the fact that the lady is a woman and the butler is a man. That is all. The reason is very plain. It may be said that there have been very illustrious women who have made their mark in history. But I should like to see any honourable member stand up and say that he would wish to be the husband of one of those illustrious women. If he were, he would be known as the husband of that illustrious woman and nothing else. He would be called the husband of Mrs. So-and-so. I hope that this Canadian Parliament will never sanction the theory of woman suffrage, a theory which I regard as most radical and which I dare to affirm it will be the duty of every well meaning Conservative to vote down.

> Joseph Royal, MP
> Debate on Electoral Franchise Act
> April 27, 1885

One of the great philosophical differences between Macdonald's Conservatives and the Liberal opposition was their attitude toward the centralization of power. The Electoral Franchise Act gave the federal government the final word on who voted. The Liberals felt that drawing up voters' lists should be a provincial responsibility, and swore to change the act when they came to power.

Macdonald won the election of 1891, but died three months later. Over the next four years, there were four different Conservative Prime Ministers: Sir John Abbot, who resigned due to ill health; Sir John Thompson, who was actually in favour of women's suffrage, but who died of a heart attack; Sir Mackenzie Bowell, who was forced by his own party to resign; and Sir Charles Tupper, who had been Prime Minister for fifty-four days when he lost the 1896 election to Wilfrid Laurier and the Liberals.

There was actually a second attempt to introduce women's suffrage during this period. It was in 1895, during Mackenzie Bowell's brief tenure as Prime Minister. Introduced as a private member's bill during the Manitoba Schools crisis, it had no chance of passing. But it did stimulate some memorable rhetoric in opposition:

> It will take away from the real charm and womanliness of women if they were given the franchise and allowed to mix in politics.

I can imagine that I might go home some evening and find, instead of my being expected, with tea on the table, nothing was done, because the absorbing question of the hour was politics. I might find a very nice-looking politician sitting in the parlour soliciting a vote. I am afraid that a good many married men might get tired of the situation.

But seriously, I believe it would take away a great deal of the charm of woman. I believe that woman's proper sphere is the home. I believe that there she has enough room to exercise all her powers and faculties, and there she has an influence that cannot be overestimated, over her husband and her children. This influence, I believe, would be lessened if women mixed up in political contests.

> James McMullen, MP
> Parliamentary Debate
> May 8, 1895

Mr. Speaker, to allow women to vote is, without any necessity, to impose on them a new obligation, a new duty, in addition to those which they have already as daughters, wives and mothers, in addition, as I have stated, to the numerous obligations they have as women. I have too much regard for women — and this is my way to show them my respect — to impose on them a new function, to overburden their weak shoulders, which could not bear such a heavy burden. The greatest regard one can have for women is to leave them where they now are, to the part they play as women and mothers.

> Sévérin Lachapelle, MP
> Parliamentary Debate
> May 8, 1895

Politics are not suited to the physical limitations which surround her sex; and although there have been women who were powerful in literature and politics, yet we find that these same women have also been obstructionists in politics and literature. Her Majesty Queen Victoria is held up to us as a great queen and one of the leading politicians of Europe, but there are many who think that even her position would have been better filled by a man.

> William F. MacLean, MP
> Parliamentary Debate
> May 8, 1895

Once in power, Laurier and the Liberals kept their promise, decentralizing the franchise by returning control over the right to vote in federal elections to the provinces. In that environment, it was only natural that the growing suffrage movement would shift its focus from Ottawa to the provincial capitals.

Meanwhile, over the years the energy and organizational skills of women's groups had become an asset for political parties, especially during election campaigns. In return, prohibition and suffrage slowly worked their way onto the platforms of opposition parties during the early years of the twentieth century, particularly on the prairies. By the summer of 1914, it seemed to be only a matter of time or, more specifically, the next election call before the goals were finally achieved.

The beginning of the end of their world occurred on June 28, 1914, in the Bosnian town of Sarajevo. Archduke Franz-Ferdinand, heir apparent to the Emperor of Austria-Hungary, was touring the provincial capital with his wife when their driver took a highly unfortunate wrong turn. Waiting along the alternate route was a young Serb terrorist, Gavrilo Princip, who succeeded in assassinating the royal couple.

Though there is little evidence that the Serbian government of the time actually planned the attack, the date alone was enough to give European governments pause. June 28th, or June 15th in the Orthodox calendar, was the anniversary of the seminal disaster of Serb history — their defeat by the Turks at the Battle of Kosovo in 1389.

Even if Belgrade didn't take a direct hand in the assassination, the government was certainly not unhappy that it had occurred — the dream of a Greater Serbia didn't begin with Slobodan Milosevic. With Austria-Hungary to the north in clear decline, and the Ottoman Empire to the south at least a couple of centuries past its best-before date, the Serbs calculated that they had everything to gain from the general war that the entire continent had been expecting for almost a decade. Unfortunately, the Serbs, along with everyone else, completely underestimated the effect the first truly industrialized war would have on their world.

The sequence of events that began when Princip pulled the trigger has gained a certain air of historical inevitability in the decades since — the war plans, the mutual defence treaties, the railway timetables. Everyone had their threat assessments, their historical rivalries and their war aims, and everyone believed that war was a completely legitimate instrument of foreign policy. But none of the above explains why. Why take the risk?

The French wanted revenge for their defeat in the Franco-Prussian War of 1870. The loss of Alsace Lorraine was bad enough, but worse, *les maudites Boches* had had the gall to crown their so-called Emperor at Versailles. They also, it seems, wanted an end to the self-doubt and ennui that seemed to flow from the same catastrophe.

Russia was already in trouble following its defeat by Japan in 1905 and the subsequent mini-revolution, even if the Tsar and his boyar advisors were too mentally arthritic to know it. Their support of Serbia against Austria in the cause of Slav brotherhood was ultimately a demand for Great Power reaffirmation in a world that had largely passed them by.

For the German General Staff, the Russian/French Entente was clear evidence that the Vaterland would be attacked sometime in the near future. The general staff's solution was preemption. In a classic case of failure of civilian control, the Kaiser and his government abrogated their responsibility to make foreign policy for the nation and listened to the generals. Hence the Schlieffen Plan and the sacrifice of Belgium's neutrality. Constant propaganda produced during the naval arms race with England over the previous two decades had prepared the public to go where the generals and their Kaiser led.

In Austria-Hungary, Emperor Franz-Josef had been on the throne since 1848. He and his ministers were not going to put up with the loss of yet another crown prince (the first having committed suicide with his lover in 1889), especially if the Serbs were behind it. Besides, Serb nationalism was a growing problem throughout the southern provinces, and since building schools and roads wasn't winning Austria any friends in the region, something more muscular would have to be considered.

Then there was England, financial colossus, and ruler of the largest empire the world has ever seen. England had little to gain and everything to lose by getting involved in a war on the continent, unless its government believed that a victorious Germany would pose a real threat in years to come and that it was better to fight now, with allies, than later, alone.

As part of England's global empire, Canadians had little choice in 1914. If London declared war, then we were at war. Despite that, war was not an unpopular decision, at least in English Canada. Rather like a teenager set to leave home and strike out on his own, Sir Robert Borden and his government were determined to use the war to prove that Canada's colonial days were over; we could be players on the world stage.

None of this, however, accounts for the excitement, the jubilation, and in some cases, the millennial rapture heard in the streets of every capital as war was declared, particularly among the middle classes. It took Europe and the Empire only thirty-eight short days, from June 29th to August 4th to turn their backs on a century of Progress and give themselves over to the serious business of slaughtering both each other and their world.

There may never be a completely satisfactory explanation for the Great War, but one thing seems certain. It was unlikely to have begun, and couldn't have been prosecuted to its disastrous conclusion, without the support of the middle classes.

> The Great War was the last to be conceived as taking place within a seamless, purposeful 'history' involving a coherent stream of time running from past through present to future. The shrewd recruiting poster, 'Daddy, what did You do in the Great War?' assumes a future whose moral and social pressures are identical with those of the past … Everyone knew what Glory was, and what Honour meant. It wasn't until eleven years after the war that Hemingway could declare in *A Farewell to Arms* that 'abstract words such as glory, honour, courage, or hallow were obscene beside the concrete names of villages, the numbers of roads, the names of rivers, the numbers of regiments and the dates.' In the summer of 1914, no one would have known what he was talking about.
>
> Paul Fussell
> *The Great War and Modern Memory*

One of the most far-reaching developments of the nineteenth century was, without a doubt, the appearance of the middle class or, as the Marxists like to call us, the bourgeoisie. Produced by the Industrial Revolution and liberal capitalism, by 1914, this group of increasingly educated, well-off men was administering nation-states and their empires, electing their governments, sitting in their parliaments and influencing their world views.

These are the people who embraced the idea of Progress most enthusiastically and who had the most to gain from the status quo. Yet, it was largely the young men of this class who were lining up at recruiting stations in that summer of 1914. Why?

At least part of the answer is to be found in the quote above. While this generation was not unaware of irony, it didn't — it couldn't — view the world with the ironic detachment that forms such a significant part of the environment of our time. That, as Fussell points out, was a product of the Great War.

This generation used terms like honour and glory completely unselfconsciously because these ideas were part of the fabric of their lives. War monuments from before WWI show it — no grim black monoliths with the names of the dead or great statues of the broken bodies of the fallen. In the nineteenth century, monumental architecture tended more toward depictions of triumphant generals on horseback. Glory was something to be pursued, honourably of course.

These ideals were taught in school. The popular fiction of the time —
novels by Rudyard Kipling, G. A. Henty, John Buchan and H. Rider Haggard —
was steeped in it. It was preached from the pulpit. There are many old churches
in England and Canada where you can still see battle flags and memorials to the
hallowed dead, modern United Church pacifism not withstanding.

On the other hand, the world was clearly changing. Anyone could see that.
Progress was inexorably civilizing the worlds described in those novels. David
Livingstone and Richard Burton had been replaced by bureaucrats in Africa
and India. In North America it seemed that was left of the Wild West could be
seen three times daily, as staged by Buffalo Bill and the Calgary Stampede. Both
Poles had been reached and the Panama Canal had made the Northwest Passage
irrelevant. Would there ever be another cavalry charge? Another International
Peace Conference might outlaw war entirely.

So in 1914, middle-class men went to war because they wanted to. For
many, it appeared a last chance for adventure in a world that had begun to seem a
little tame, an opportunity to test themselves before it was too late. If Brave Little
Belgium is having a spot of bother with Fritz, I suppose we'd better pop over and
lend a hand, what? In England, 300,000 men enlisted in the first month. The
Canadian Expeditionary Force had over 56,000 new soldiers by the end of 1914,
every one a volunteer.

It wasn't mass psychosis. In the world before the war, it made perfect
sense. And besides, they knew they'd be home by Christmas. So, they went. And
they went with the blessing, if not urging, of their mothers and sisters.

> *Oh, we don't want to lose you,*
> *But we think you ought to go.*
> *For your King and your Country*
> *Both need you so.*
> *We shall want you and miss you,*
> *But with all our might and main*
> *We shall cheer you, thank you, kiss you*
> *When you come back again.*
>
> Paul Alfred Rubens
> "Your King and Country Want You", 1914

War fever acted on most middle-class women just as effectively as on the
men. For the most part, suffragists on both sides of the Atlantic quickly moved
from relentless criticism of their governments to active support, at least on the
subject of the war effort. The most remarkable turnaround came in England in

the person of Emmeline Pankhurst, her daughters Christabel and Sylvia and her Women's Social and Political Union, or WSPU.

When ignored by the British government over the question of votes for women, Mrs. Pankhurst and her followers had, unlike her sisters in Canada, turned to civil disobedience and in some cases, terrorism, to make their case:

> Our task was to show the Government that it was expedient to yield to women's just demands. In order to do that, we had to make England and every department of English life insecure and unsafe. We had to make English law a failure and the courts farce comedy theatres; we had to discredit the Government and Parliament in the eyes of the world; we had to spoil English sports, hurt business, destroy valuable property, demoralise the world of society, shame the churches, upset the whole orderly conduct of life — That is, we had to do as much of this guerrilla warfare as the people of England would tolerate. When they came to the point of saying to the Government: "Stop this, in the only way it can be stopped, by giving the women of England representation", then we should extinguish our torch.
>
> Emmeline Pankhurst
> *My Own Story*, 1914

By August 1914, Mrs. Pankhurst and some thousand of her followers were in jail, ill from repeated hunger strikes, or in exile. Yet, within a week of the declaration of war, she had suspended her campaign, though in return for the release of her jailed colleagues, and dedicated her organization to the war effort and recruitment, remarking that "votes are irrelevant without a country to vote in".

By 1915, her newspaper, *The Suffragette*, had been renamed *Britannia* and was accusing government ministers of treason for not being sufficiently pro-war. The women were also active in the white feather campaign, in which they bestowed the white feather of cowardice on able-bodied men who weren't in uniform.

There was a white feather campaign in Canada as well, though the suffrage movement here never quite embraced the war with the zeal of Mrs. Pankhurst. In fact, the campaign for prohibition and the vote became even more intense once war was declared and this had much to do with the role of the WCTU.

Emmeline Pankhurst and the WSPU were, for the most part, equality feminists of the type that was quite rare in Canada. There was little sense of "doing God's work" in the English movement — Trust in God, She will provide, was a purposeful blasphemy; it still makes even liberal church people queasy — and temperance there was pretty much a spent force by the 1890s.

For the WCTU, however, though none of its members would ever have put it quite this way, the war was a godsend. Not only were the very people who were most likely to vote down prohibition referenda being shipped to France in ever increasing numbers, but the war itself was providing the best propaganda imaginable — the patriotic argument. How could anyone justify the use of scarce resources to make and distribute liquor when our boys at the front needed everything we could send them?

> Are we to "Be British" indeed, and remove a
> "greater enemy than the Hun" from our midst?
> Is the sacrifice made by our soldiers for us
> On the battlefield to be the only sacrifice?
> The Bar or the War. That is the Question of the Hour.
> *BC World*
> August 19, 1916

Saskatchewan went dry in 1915, followed rapidly by every province except Québec. More than forty years of effort by the WCTU had finally been rewarded.

The fight for the vote, meanwhile, was advancing all across the prairies as the war began, but nowhere was the campaign more high profile than in Manitoba. This was largely because of the public sparring between two very strong personalities — Canada's best-known suffragist, Nellie McClung and Manitoba's extremely Conservative Premier, Sir Rodmond Roblin.

By 1914, Roblin had been Premier for thirteen years, largely because the Roblin machine, as it was known, was unparalleled at dispensing favours at election time. One of the defining characteristics of government before the Great War was the lack of a professional civil service, which meant that government jobs and contracts were the foundation of political discourse. It was a language that Roblin and his Conservatives spoke exceedingly well.

The disagreements between Roblin and Nellie McClung had started as far back as 1901, when Roblin had repealed Manitoba's first prohibition act, passed the year before. His opposition to temperance made him a constant target of the WCTU, and his position on suffrage, which he was resolutely against, only guaranteed more friction.

Matters came to a head in January 1914. McClung was now a leader in the Manitoba Political Equity League, and on the 27th, she made a presentation before the Legislature on its behalf. Given Roblin's oft-stated position that, "nice women don't want the vote", his reply was predictable. He rejected her arguments out of hand, claiming that the culture and intelligence displayed by the delegation had nothing whatever to do with suffrage, but rather "the sacrifices men have made to the ideal of their heart".

The League members were hardly surprised by this rejection; in fact, they'd already prepared their response. The Walker Theatre had been hired for the following night, and the packed house saw one of the most famous pieces of political theatre in Canadian history.

The mock parliament idea was not new, the Dominion Women's Enfranchisement Association, one of the many reincarnations of Emily Stowe's Toronto Women's Literary Society, having staged the first in 1896. However, none before had had such a perfect target, or so charismatic a leading lady.

McClung's approach was simplicity itself: repeat Roblin's arguments of the day before in an environment that would demonstrate their patent absurdity. Thus, she became premier in a world where men were denied the vote. At the climax of the evening, a male delegation arrived, carrying a banner that read, "We have the brains, why not the vote?" McClung replied:

> We like delegations. We have seen a great many and we pride ourselves on treating these delegations with great courtesy and candour. We assure you that we are just as pleased to see you today as we will be to see you at any future day. We wish to compliment this delegation on their gentlemanly appearance. If, without exercising the vote, such splendid specimens of manhood can be produced, such a system should not be interfered with. Any system of civilization which can produce such splendid specimens of manhood as Mr. Skinner is good enough for me and if it's good enough for me, it's good enough for anybody.

> If all men were as intelligent and as good as the leader of the delegation and his worthy though misguided followers, I would have no hesitation in according them the suffrage. But, such is unfortunately not the case. Seven-eighths of the police court offenders are men and only one third of the church membership. You ask me to enfranchise these?

> Oh no, man is made for something higher and better than voting. Men were made to support families. What is home without the bank account? The man who pays the grocer rules the world. In this agricultural province, the man's place is on the farm. Shall I call a man away from the useful plough and harrow to talk loud on street corners about things that do not concern him? … Politics unsettles men, and unsettled men mean unsettled bills — broken furniture; broken vows … and divorce … When you ask for the vote, you are asking me to break up peaceful, happy homes — to wreck innocent lives.

The evening was a sensation, and not just because of McClung's stellar performance. The Premier's opponents could smell blood. Roblin was in trouble. His government had decided in 1912 that Manitoba's Legislative Building would simply no longer do, and had let a contract for a new edifice that promised to become the envy of North America. The winning bid, from contractor Thomas Kelly, had come in at $2,000,000, a price that doubled within weeks of the contract's award. Now, kickbacks had not been exactly unknown during the Roblin's tenure, but this amount was so outrageous that the Liberal opposition was finally roused to action.

Roblin won his fifth election that summer, but he could do nothing about the scandal. Kelly was convicted of fraud in 1915, (two years in the warden's house at Stony Mountain Penitentiary with weekends out to play cards with friends) and Roblin was forced to resign. The Liberals, under their new leader, T.C. Norris, saw their chance to end almost two decades of Conservative rule, but they needed the organization of the WCTU and suffrage groups to put them over the top.

The women's groups, which had worked for the Liberals in 1914, were ready. McClung, who had moved to Alberta, came back to campaign. Norris had promised prohibition and suffrage if the Liberals won, and in January 1916, he delivered. Manitoba became the first province in Canada to give women the vote. Moreover, because the federal Liberals had given control of the voters' list back to the provinces, Manitoba women were also now eligible to vote federally.

Saskatchewan and Alberta soon followed, and by the middle of 1917, all women west of the Québec border had the franchise, a situation that provided Prime Minister Sir Robert Borden with a major headache.

By 1917, the war was not going well. Neither side's initial plan had worked, resulting in a stalemate along the trench system of the Western Front, which offensive after offensive — Ypres, the Somme, Verdun — had failed to breach. The brutal mathematics of war dictates that soldiers take years to grow and seconds to kill, and one thing the Western Front was very good at was killing soldiers, millions of them.

Now, after more failed offensives in the spring and summer, the French army was on the verge of mutiny and the Americans were nowhere in sight, having declared war only in April. The Allies were running out of bodies, while the ongoing Russian revolution was threatening to free up dozens of German divisions for fighting in the west.

With the failure of all attempts to induce more Canadian men to volunteer, there was only one option left. If Canada was to maintain the independence of the Army Corps it had worked so hard to create, and achieve Borden's goal of becoming a more equal partner in the prosecution of the war, there had to be more soldiers. That meant conscription.

There was very little support in Québec for what was seen as an English war, so for the government to force men to fight threatened to play directly into the hands of Henri Bourassa and his Nationalists. The idea would also receive little support from farmers or trade unions. But most of middle-class English Canada now accepted that the war was a crusade that had to be won.

Laurier turned down Borden's offer of a coalition government, calculating that his Liberals could win an election fought on conscription. Many of his MPs disagreed. Trickling over to the Conservative side, they allowed Borden to form a union government and pass the Military Service Act, which mandated conscription.

Borden now had to call an election, but he faced a huge problem. Because women could now vote provincially from Ontario to British Columbia, they would also be able to vote federally. This would mean a large group of new voters added in the West, voters who, because of massive non-English immigration and farm families wanting to protect their sons, were more likely to vote Liberal.

Borden's radical solution was female suffrage. After taking back control of the voters' list from the provinces, his government would extend suffrage to all Canadian women who met certain criteria. The most important, though unstated, of these was that they would be women likely to vote for the government. First, the Military Voters Act extended suffrage to any British subject who was an active or retired member of the armed forces, without regard to property requirements, residency, or even age. This meant that two thousand military nurses became the first Canadian women eligible to vote federally.

Second, the War-time Elections Act gave the vote to the spouses, widows, mothers, sisters or daughters of anyone who had ever served in the military, while removing the right from anyone who had immigrated from an enemy country since 1902. Interestingly, Nellie McClung had approached Borden with the same idea — giving the vote to British women while taking it away from "foreigners"— in 1916.

That was just the opening gambit in what has to have been the dirtiest election in Canadian history. With the Germans by this time having become equated with Beelzebub himself, conscription was sold as the only means to support our boys in their noble Crusade. Protestant ministers across the country preached on their congregations' sacred duty to vote Union. The Liberals, Québec and anyone else who disagreed with conscription were branded traitors.

The tactics worked. On December 17th, Borden and the Unionists won, aided by judicious distribution of the overseas military vote, which could be applied in whichever ridings the government deemed necessary. Women finally had the vote. Bills introduced in 1918 and 1920 made female suffrage universal, and if, in the end, Canadian suffragists had to share the credit with crooked politicians, French mutineers, Russian revolutionaries, Québec nationalists and incompetent British generals, well, when the future of civilization is at stake, God is always on our side and the end justifies the means. It was a victory. It just seemed a little … anticlimactic, somehow.

Led by Louise McKinney, women started to take advantage of their new rights even before the federal campaign had begun. McKinney and prohibition were synonymous in Alberta. She'd headed the successful Alberta campaign in 1915, her only regret being that the plebiscite hadn't also banned cigarettes and tobacco products.

It was therefore no surprise that she would seek public office at the first opportunity, in order to further the causes in which she believed. She was fiercely opposed by representatives of the liquor interests, who knew their income would drop significantly if the prohibition law of 1915 were truly enforced in the province. They tried to use the work she'd done in preventing the shipment of cigarettes and tobacco to the men in the trenches against her.

The first election to be held after women received the vote provincially took place in Alberta in 1917. McKinney ran in the constituency of Claresholm on a platform of prohibition. Her campaign took her throughout the constituency, travelling by buggy and cutter. Her easy win meant that she, along with Roberta MacAdams, became the first women elected in the Empire.[3] Since MacAdams was a military nurse serving overseas, McKinney and MacAdams were sworn in together on February 1, 1918.[4]

McKinney immediately went to work, vigorously criticizing the government for its lack of enforcement of the prohibition law, working actively on public health issues and becoming the force behind the establishment of proper institutions for the mentally handicapped.

She also urged the Government of Canada to take over the operation of the coal mines of Alberta, because it would provide greater employment opportunities and force the government to treat the miners more fairly. Indefatigable, she worked for the establishment of laws to help new immigrants, particularly in the area of language training and aided the formation of the United Farmers of Alberta, whose purpose was to enhance the opportunities for farmers and farm families in the province.

---

[3] Women in New Zealand received the vote in 1893, but could not stand for election until 1919.

[4] Roberta MacAdams was born in Sarnia, Ontario in 1881. Educated at the University of Guelph, she moved to Alberta to join her brother, who wrote of the excitement of the West. In 1916, she joined the Canadian Medical Corps as a Lieutenant and served as head dietician at the Canadian Military Hospital in Orpington, England. The Alberta election that returned Louise McKinney was held on June 7, 1917, but the elections held to choose three Armed Forces members, including MacAdams, were held in August of that year. McKinney and MacAdams were sworn in together the following February, but a year later MacAdams married and moved to the Peace River district. From there the couple moved permanently to Calgary and MacAdams did not run in the 1921 election. She died in 1959.

However, because of what she saw as the unjust legal status of widows and separated wives, the issue to which she dedicated her greatest efforts in the Legislature was the passage of the Dower Act of 1917 and its amendments of 1918 and 1919. Indeed, her son said this was the major reason for his mother's participation in politics, and when the act was amended she was prepared not to run again. As a result of her efforts, wives were required to consent to the disposition of the family property and widows were allowed to remain in the family home until their deaths.

In 1918, she attended a national conference on education in Winnipeg and made a strong plea for the relationship between home, church and school, stating that the three were "the inseparable trinity of democracy". She attacked the Alberta government for the pitiable amount it put into mothers' pensions; the $50,000 it designated was, she said, the same amount it spent on institutions for wayward children. Clearly, Louise McKinney was well ahead of her time in seeing prevention and treatment as being equally important.

Considered by some to be the best debater in the Alberta Legislature, she was also an expert on parliamentary procedure, knowledge she had gained during her many years in the WCTU. Despite these abilities, McKinney lost her seat in the election of 1921. Her defeat was ironic. Though she'd been active in the foundation of the United Farmers of Alberta, the group that swept the province that year, she didn't agree with its founder, Henry Wise Wood, that the UFA should be a political party.

Believing that political parties were representatives of special interest groups and didn't represent the common people, she'd run as a Non-Partisan in 1917. She was particularly offended when she learned that the main-line parties accepted donations from the liquor companies and in 1921 she refused to run under the UFA banner, a move that probably caused her defeat. She lost by only forty-six votes.

She never ran again, preferring to dedicate her efforts to the WCTU, serving as president of the Alberta local for twenty-seven years. During the 1920s, she joined Nellie McClung and three other Alberta women to initiate the Person's Case. She died on July 10, 1931 at the age of sixty-two.

The great irony of the WCTU, and there was plenty of irony to go around in the new, post-war world, was that its greatest achievement involved the cause it had been so reluctant to embrace — suffrage. As for prohibition, so dear to Louise McKinney's heart, she lived to see its ignominious end.

The federal Prohibition Act that became law when Borden won the 1917 election was an Order-in-Council, passed under the War Measures Act. When the war ended and the War Measures Act was repealed, the liquor law had to be

reintroduced; it was immediately obvious to Borden's government that strict prohibition was a non-starter.

Canada was in a very different mood in 1919. Trying to come to terms
with what had been lost since 1914, in the grip of a post-war recession, and with
not nearly enough jobs for the over 600,000 soldiers returning from overseas,
few people were prepared for more self-denial. It also didn't escape notice that
the one province that was experiencing a boom was the one that had immediately
repealed prohibition at war's end. Québec was enjoying increased tourism from
south of the border as the United States prepared to ratify the eighteenth amendment to its Constitution — prohibition.

So, in terms of the battle against demon rum, after almost a half-century
of dedication and effort, the final achievements of the WCTU were these: first,
while the sale of alcohol was once again legal, it passed to government control.
The first government liquor store opened in British Columbia in 1920 and by
1930, every province except Prince Edward Island had repealed prohibition. And
second, as late as 1960, some United Church ministers had to take the temperance
pledge as a condition of their ordination.

It could easily be said that Louise McKinney's own achievements were
considerably more significant and that the wider women's movement had also fared
far better. Their obvious skill at reform in the years before 1914, and the enormous
war effort put forth by women of all classes, had changed many men's opinions
about female capabilities. Not only had they knitted and held bond drives, but
thousands of them had served as nursing sisters, worked on assembly lines and
laboured in munitions plants. Borden even held a Women's War Conference in
1918, something that would have been unthinkable only four years earlier, and
then actually implemented some of the ideas he heard, including the creation of
a federal Department of Health in 1919.

But far from a being shining example of Progress and growing enlightenment, suffrage was really only a political quid pro quo, a simple expense to be
written off like any other as a cost of winning the war. Very few people's minds,
male or female, had been changed about woman's role in society, as all those
assembly line workers were about to find out. Even the churches that were most
supportive of suffrage could find no room for women in their own councils.

So now, at the pinnacle of their achievement, in possession of not only
the right to vote, but the right to stand for election, first-wave feminists found
themselves, their ideas — indeed feminism itself — out of fashion. Social reform
would go on, but the world their approach was designed to impel toward that
City on the Hill — the world of Empire, of Honour, and, most especially, of
Progress — was gone.

I am a Person

(1919–1929)

◆

Scene: 1925

SOCIAL NARRATOR: (*in full flapper costume, dancing*):

Charleston, Charleston, made in Carolina … You know, my overwhelming impression of the Twenties is how downright silly they were. I mean, we cut off our hair, hiked up our skirts, bound up our breasts and went flagpole sitting. Of course, we had just survived the worst disaster in the history of the species. It seemed like everybody had a father, a son, or a brother whose blood had watered the fields of France — a euphemism for being converted to Swiss cheese by machine guns, suffocated by poison gas, or just blown into unrecognizable chunks. It's no wonder everybody seemed a little crazy. It was time to do something — anything — different.

So, we piled into phone booths, swallowed goldfish and walked on airplane wings. We girls had plenty of time for these activities, since companies that were still begging us to come to work for them on Armistice Day, started sending pink slips on November 12th. The federal government even banned married women from the civil service. "Oh, I know he has no arms or legs, my dear, but he's a man. I'm sure you understand."

Now, you know that these were the crazy years when an otherwise reasonably serious country like the U.S. — we won't talk about the Scopes Monkey Trial — a serious country, as I say, goes and bans booze to improve the "moral fibre of the nation". And this went on for fourteen years. It did have its up side, though. How could the Bronfmans have become millionaires if they hadn't been able to smuggle Canadian Club into the States?

A lot of the things that make Canada the country it is today started in the 1920s. Radio, for example. Beginning with CFCF in Montreal — the world's oldest commercial station — radio created Canada's first mass audience — for American programming. By 1929, the Yanks already had eighty per cent of our airwaves. Radio also revolutionized our leisure time. No more free form, what do you feel like doing tonight for us. No siree. "Eight o'clock tomorrow night? Oh, I'm so sorry dear. That's Amos 'n Andy."

Mind you, at least all those soap operas and variety shows gave women something to occupy their time now that they'd been booted from the work force. And Marx thought religion was the opiate of the masses. If he'd only known …

POLITICAL	SOCIAL / TECHNOLOGY

T I M E L I N E

1919

POLITICAL	SOCIAL / TECHNOLOGY
• Mussolini founds Fascism in Italy	• Prohibition in the U.S.
• Sir Wilfrid Laurier dies	• Hugh John Lofting publishes first *Dr. Doolittle*
• Winnipeg General Strike	• Auguste Renoir dies
• Civil War in Russia	• Short wave radio invented
• **Women get the vote in New Brunswick**	• Mass spectroscopy developed
• **Canadian women given the right to be elected**	• Group of Seven formed
• CNR incorporated	
• Treaty of Versailles	

1920

POLITICAL	SOCIAL / TECHNOLOGY
• League of Nations created	• **Joan of Arc achieves sainthood**
• Britain takes over Palestine	• Spanish flu runs its course: up to forty million die
• **American women get the vote**	• Rorschach inkblot test invented
• Russian civil war ends	• Tommy gun patented
• RCMP formed	• World population: 1.8 billion
• Unemployment Insurance in Britain	• **Esther Hill becomes first female architect**
• Sir Robert Borden resigns, Arthur Meighen PM	• Olympics held in Antwerp, Belgium

1921

POLITICAL	SOCIAL / TECHNOLOGY
• Germany owes $33B, Hitler forms the SA	• DH Lawrence writes *Women in Love*
• William Lyon Mackenzie King elected Canadian PM	• Charlie Chaplin stars in *The Kid*
• J.S. Woodsworth first socialist elected	• Canadian population: 8.78 million
• **Agnes Macphail elected**	• Albert Einstein wins Nobel Prize for Physics
• Irish Free State founded	• BBC founded in England
• **Mary Ellen Smith, Empire's first cabinet minister**	• Maurice "Rocket" Richard born
• **Nellie McClung elected in Alberta**	• *The Bluenose* launched
• **No married women in Canadian civil service**	• Banting and Best discover insulin in Canada

1922

POLITICAL	SOCIAL / TECHNOLOGY
• Gandhi jailed for civil disobedience	• James Joyce writes *Ulysses*
• Mussolini takes power in Italy	• King Tut's tomb discovered in Egypt
• Turkey becomes a republic	• Alexander Graham Bell dies
• The U.S.S.R. formed	• White blood cells discovered
	• Bombardier builds first snowmobile
	• **Emily Post writes *Etiquette***

1923

POLITICAL	SOCIAL / TECHNOLOGY
• Tokyo earthquake leaves 120,000 dead	• Felix Salten (Siegmund Salzmann) writes *Bambi*
• 1 US$ = 4.2 trillion Deutsch Marks	• George Gershwin writes "Rhapsody in Blue"
• Hitler's Beerhall Putsch in Munich	• *Time* magazine founded
• Chinese barred from immigrating to Canada	• Jell-O introduced
	• Electric razor patented

POLITICAL	SOCIAL / TECHNOLOGY	
T I M E L I N E		
• Vladimir Lenin dies • Herbert Hoover heads FBI • Woodrow Wilson dies • Red Ensign adopted as the Canadian flag • RCAF established	• Authors Josef Conrad and Franz Kafka die • First Winter Olympics held in Chamonix, France; Summer Olympics in Paris • Popsicle invented	**1924**
• **First female Governor elected in Wyoming** • United Church founded in Canada • **Canadian women can file divorce for adultery**	• *Mein Kampf* published • Scott Fitzgerald writes *The Great Gatsby* • First TV transmission takes place in Britain • The Charleston dance invented • Art Deco design developed • Electrical recording invented	**1925**
• **Queen Elizabeth born** • Hirohito becomes Emperor of Japan • Canada earns right to sign its own treaties • Mackenzie King re-elected	• Canada bans marijuana • Book of the Month Club started • Earnest Hemingway writes *The Sun Also Rises* • Rudolph Valentino, Harry Houdini die • Duke Ellington, Jellyroll Morton cut first records • Permanent wave invented • Pop-up toaster invented	**1926**
• Old Age Pension legislation passed (Canada)	• Charles Lindberg flies solo from New York to Paris • Big Bang Theory developed • First talking picture show: *Jazz Singer* • *Show Boat* plays on Broadway • Kool-Aid invented • Pavlov proposes theory of conditioned reflexes	**1927**

• **Persons Case rejected by Supreme Court**
• **British women allowed to vote at twenty-one**
• **War outlawed (Kellog-Briand)**
• **Women's Liberal Federation of Canada founded**
• Joseph Stalin becomes sole leader of U.S.S.R.
	• **Eileen Vollick becomes the first female Canadian**
	  to obtain a private pilot's licence
	• **Amelia Earhart flies solo across the Atlantic**
	• Alexander Flemming discovers penicillin
	• Vitamin C isolated; Geiger counter invented
	• D.H. Lawrence writes *Lady Chatterley's Lover*
	• Disney introduces Mickey Mouse in *Steamboat Willie*
	• George Gershwin writes *American in Paris*
	• Velveeta, Rice Crispies invented
	• **Summer Olympics held in Amsterdam; Winter**
	  Games held in St. Moritz, Switzerland; women
	  compete
		1928

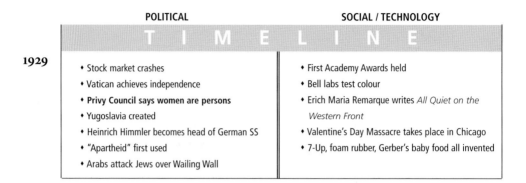

1929

POLITICAL	SOCIAL / TECHNOLOGY
• Stock market crashes	• First Academy Awards held
• Vatican achieves independence	• Bell labs test colour
• **Privy Council says women are persons**	• Erich Maria Remarque writes *All Quiet on the Western Front*
• Yugoslavia created	• Valentine's Day Massacre takes place in Chicago
• Heinrich Himmler becomes head of German SS	• 7-Up, foam rubber, Gerber's baby food all invented
• "Apartheid" first used	
• Arabs attack Jews over Wailing Wall	

I am a Person

(1919–1929)

The **1900s began** with enormous promise for Canadian women. With federal suffrage finally achieved in 1918, and the right to stand for election following a year later, these were heady days for early feminists. Anything seemed possible, which must have made the next five decades very trying.

"Feminism has become a negative term for the modern young woman. Feminists are old fashioned, unattractive and out of touch." Statements like that have become depressingly familiar to modern feminists, but that paraphrase is from a 1927 *Harper's Magazine* article, and it sums up what started to happen almost as soon as the new Elections Act was passed. Feminism just seemed to disappear. The most popular explanation put forward might be summed up as the "they've made their point" argument:

> The woman question … was pressing enough, heaven knows, before the war. We all remember the activities of the militant suffragists — the burnings, breakings and hungerstrikings which used to form a regular part of our daily news … No one could be certain of escaping the violently feminist woman. She caught one everywhere — at the dinner table, in railway carriages, in church. And there was no way of knowing beforehand whether a particular woman was devoted to the cause or not. The most unexpected woman developed the enthusiasm … friends or enemies of the sex, we all suffered.
>
> Of course, women, or some of them, now have got the vote. But, that can scarcely be the reason they have stopped fussing … the cleverest and most farseeing suffragist always said that the mere vote

was a small matter, little more than a symbol; that she wanted much more … not only did she want men to stop thinking of women as inferior creatures. She wanted women to cease thinking of themselves as inferior creatures, to discover that they can do nearly everything that men can. It was not enough for women to earn men's respect. It was necessary for them to establish their own self respect.

George Binghampton
Maclean's, 1921

Nice, neat and nostalgic. Now, things will get back to the way they were. Only they couldn't, of course. There were far deeper reasons for the "disappearance" of feminism after suffrage was achieved — the same reasons that drove so much of what happened in the 1920s.

World War I was Armageddon — fifty bloody months that washed away ten million lives, four empires and a hundred years of social and political certainties. It was immediately followed by the worst pandemic since the Black Death. The Spanish Flu may have killed as many as forty million people worldwide. In six horrible years, nearly three per cent of the world's population was gone, and with it, the nineteenth century.

Something else died on those battlefields and in those hospital beds — optimism. Before the Great War, people believed in the inevitable March of Progress. The question wasn't whether society was perfectible; it was simply a matter of method. Reformer or revolutionary, jingoist or cynic, the underlying assumption was the same — Utopia was achievable.

When Kipling chided the United States for failing to take up the white man's burden in the Philippines, he wasn't criticizing Americans' lack of stomach for empire. What he took exception to was their reluctance to do their duty as an advanced society and help a "lesser" people better themselves. Even as detached an observer as Oscar Wilde remarked, in all seriousness, that "a map of the world that doesn't include Utopia isn't worth even glancing at." The direction of History was clear; the tide, unstoppable.

And then, the unthinkable happened; instead of Utopia, we created the worst disaster in the history of humanity. The loss, disillusionment and sense of dislocation were, for many people, overwhelming. So, what happens when an entire society unknowingly suffers from post-traumatic stress disorder? In this case, you get the 1920s.

> We cannot but lament the morbid restlessness which has
> spread among people of every age and condition in life, the general
> spirit of insubordination and the refusal to live up to one's obligations
> which has become so widespread as almost to appear the customary
> mode of living.
>
> Pope Pius XI, 1922

Many of the trends that came to their modern form in the 1920s were
discernible before World War I. What drove their development after the war was
the enthusiasm, if not frenzy, with which they were embraced. The labour movement, Communism, the avant-garde, scientific management, consumerism —
for many people, it didn't seem to matter as long as it was modern. As long
as it was different. As long as it didn't recall what had been lost.

In Europe, dealing with the physical devastation of the war, as well as
its psychological effects, this rejection of the old meant political instability, if
not outright collapse. Nationalism, fascism, communism: all rushed into the
vacuum created when damaged people could no longer summon the political
will to defend their civilization. The Treaty of Versailles established the conditions for World War II because the negotiators couldn't bring themselves to do
what they knew was right for the greater good; that is, not punish Germany.
The League of Nations didn't fail just because the Americans wouldn't join.
Ultimately, it failed from lack of interest.

In North America, embracing the new often meant rejecting Europe and
shifting focus from the international to the parochial and even the personal. The
effect on women was immediate. For the Canadian government, more than 100,000
dead had provided a new and sobering appreciation of where the tide of History
might actually lead. Still smarting from the huge uproar over conscription, and
worried about the revolutionary potential of demobilized armies returning to no
jobs, Ottawa was soon encouraging women to stop working and start making babies,
just in case the war to end all wars, hadn't.

Much to the displeasure of both the government and the church, many
women did neither. The federal government forced virtually all married women to
resign from the civil service, but the percentage of women in the workforce continued to rise throughout the decade. Most of these jobs were factory, sales and secre-
tarial, which led to the great servant crisis for the upper middle class, and, in turn,
drove the sale of household appliances. And rather than doing their part to save
the race, as many commentators put it, women were actually having fewer babies.
Part of the drop was purely demographic — working women marry later and
have less time to raise children. Part of it was a decreased ability, for many people,

to think about the long term. Part was pessimism about the kind of world into which a new child would be born. And part was an accumulation of economic decisions generated by urbanization.

By the end of the '20s, the urban population was larger than the rural for the first time in Canadian history. Moving to a town or city completely changes the economics of having children. On the farm, each new child represented another set of hands to help with the work; in the city, child labour laws and compulsory schooling meant a new child was simply another mouth to feed, especially as wages bore no relation to family size.

As a result, despite a complete ban on birth control — even publishing information about birth control was a criminal offence — the fertility rate dropped 22.3 per cent in Canada during the 1920s. This presented families with choices not available to their parents.

During the Great War, enormous sacrifices had been asked of Canadians. In the aftermath, people were looking to sacrifice a little less and live a little more. Especially for the growing middle class, once the inevitability of large families was questioned, people began to identify other priorities for their rising incomes. Instead of meeting the constant challenge of "What do we need?", they could begin to wonder, "What do we want?"

Five foot two, eyes of blue,
oh, what those five feet could do:
has anybody seen my gal?

Turned-up nose, turned-down hose
Flapper? Yes sir, one of those
Has anybody seen my gal?

It started with the skirts. As we've already seen, the world discovered women have legs in the 1890s. In the 1920s, people actually got to see those legs, as skirts started their inexorable ascent. The pleas of overwrought parents, fire and brimstone from the pulpit, proposed legislation to establish a female dress code — nothing could stop it.

But it wasn't just the skirts. Women's clothes in general were disappearing before society's scandalized eyes, and along with them, that womanly S curve silhouette — from bosom to bustle — that defined femininity to the prewar eye. Corsets and petticoats were abandoned for brassieres and step-ins. The amount of material in a normal outfit dropped from around seventeen yards before World War I, to under nine yards by the end of the '20s, causing panic in the textile industry. Bare legs! Bare arms! Where would it end?

Of course, this march to complete nudity, set to arrive, according to one wag, on March 12, 1927, wasn't going to happen without a fight. Science was invoked in defense of foundation garments. No less an authority than Havelock Ellis, the English sociologist, opined in the journal, *Current Literature*, that female humans required corseting because the evolution from "horizontality to verticality" was more difficult for females than for males. Ellis had pointed out as early as 1910 that "Woman might be physiologically truer to herself if she went always on all fours. It is because the fall of the viscera in woman when she imitated man by standing erect induced such profound physiological displacements … that the corset is morphologically essential."

Then there was the fear of aging argument, so familiar to modern women. Leonard Florsheim, writing in *Corset and Underwear Review* in 1921, mixed in more than a bit of racism as he described the fate of the uncorsetted female form:

> The Indian girls are known for shapely body lines in their youth, despite the fact that they never get a chance to enjoy the protection of corset or brassiere. They grow and develop 'wildly', but at the age when they acquire the sobriquet of squaw, what a transformation! Squaws, especially those who have become mothers, are well known for their grotesque bodies. Nature has given them in youth well developed, shapely lines, muscles that withstand the first score and ten, but then nature changes her course and begins to add weight that gradually rounds out and converts form into the well known 'mattress-tied-in-the-middle' proportions.

But, this earthquake in fashion went beyond clothes. Hair was disappearing, too — all those flowing tresses sheared away to produce what one school principal derided as "that barbarian bob". Parents sued hairdressers and hair net manufacturers quickly joined corset companies and cloth makers in the propaganda war.

When the fashion industry dubbed the new look *garçonne*, or boy/girl, rumours swirled about sexual perversion, or at least confusion. The young women, most of whom had no doubt about who they were and what they were doing, blithely ignored it all and got on with the party. The gentle Gibson girl was gone. In her place was born the flapper; an unrecognizable creature who smoked in public (cigarette sales increased 265 per cent between 1920 and 1929), wore make-up and was sexually aware if not downright forward. The flapper explained to all and sundry how Freud had shown that repression of the sexual urge was not only unnatural, but unhealthy. So let's do away with all that Victorian claptrap. What was needed now was frankness, especially when dealing with the opposite sex.

Nowhere was this rejection of the old sexual attitudes more publicly expressed than in dancing. No waltz for these kids. It was the Blackbottom, the Charleston, or, worst of all, the Foxtrot. As Frederick Lewis Allen observed in *Only Yesterday*:[1]

> The current mode in dancing created still more consternation. Not the romantic violin but the barbaric saxophone now dominated the orchestra, and to its passionate crooning and wailing the fox-trotters moved in what the editor of the *Hobart College Herald* disgustedly called a 'syncopated embrace'. No longer did even an inch of space separate them; they danced as if glued together, body to body, cheek to cheek.

It was all too much. Even the pope of the time, Pius XI, was so aghast at the whole business that he addressed flapperdom in his very first encyclical:

> We lament, too, the destruction of purity among women and young girls as is evidenced by the increasing immodesty of their dress and conversation and by their participation in shameful dances, which sins are made the more heinous by the vaunting in the faces of people less fortunate than themselves their luxurious mode of life.

By the end of the decade, there was a new piece of furniture usurping the piano's pride of place in living rooms across the country. Radio changed public communication for ever. Using it, a single person — politician, performer or pitchman — could speak into a microphone and know that thousands, even millions of people could hear every word. Along with movies, radio created the mass audience, a manifestation that politicians from "Bible Bill" Aberhart, the Alberta founder of the Social Credit Party, to Adolph Hitler were to recognize and use so effectively during the next decade.

Of course, a mass audience also meant a mass market — just the thing to absorb the huge increases in production being generated by Henry Ford's assembly line techniques. So, for example, by 1925 there were already 724,000

---

[1] *Only Yesterday: An Informal History of the 1920s.* by Frederick Lewis Allen, Harper Collins. 1931

automobiles in Canada, or one for every thirteen people. Most of them had been bought using that other necessary requirement for mass marketing, the newly invented installment plan, which was based on the revolutionary idea that lack of cash should be no impediment to ownership.

People were buying everything on the installment plan. Since science, in the persons of sociologists and home economists, told marketers that it was women who controlled the family budget and women who were most susceptible to a sales pitch, women became a primary target of advertising. Thus, manufacturers joined more reactionary forces like the church and political establishment in the effort to confine women to their traditional roles. One of the best known home economists of the 1920s, Christine Frederick, left little doubt about this convergence between academe and hucksterism. After running an independent test kitchen for most of the decade, Frederick wrote the advertising bible, *Selling Mrs. Consumer*, in 1929.

Science and scientific management were all the rage. The Twenties saw the invention of time-motion studies aimed at producing more efficient, if more robotic, workers. The home wasn't immune to this trend, as strict scheduling for feeding, toilet and play were preached from a multitude of child-rearing guides. It couldn't have escaped the notice of business leaders that this sort of regimentation was just the thing to produce assembly line personnel.

There was, mercifully, some improvement in the lot of the child. Penicillin began to cut down on infection deaths, a vaccine for tuberculosis was developed, and of course, Banting, Best and McLeod discovered insulin. Though thumb sucking was still frowned upon, it was harder to find aluminum mittens. And since Freud had pronounced masturbation to be natural, parents could finally throw away the leg spreaders.

Especially where women were concerned, the other major consumer product of the '20s — and since — was youth. Even as their elders despaired of them, the post-war generation held a strange fascination. As we've seen, after the twin catastrophes — war and the influenza epidemic — everyone wanted to be different somehow. But many young people were actually doing it — adopting a lifestyle that seemed more in tune with the times, more modern.

Thus modern and young became synonymous — to be the first, you had to at least aspire to the second. So young and not-so-young women spent their extra dollars at dress shops, made hairdressing a profession, and were assisted by marketeers to discover bodily shortcomings they'd never known existed. When Gillette needed to sell more razors, suddenly "the underarm must be smooth as the face" for "the lady of fashion". To be "still the girl he married", Lehn & Fink recommended a Lysol — yes, Lysol — disinfectant douche to protect "her zest for living, her health and youthfulness", and her ability to "stay young with him".

Young people and people dealing with stress share another important characteristic — they're more likely to engage in what appears to be irrational behaviour. That's the '20s to a T. In addition to dancing and stock market speculation, fads like flagpole sitting, mah jongg and crossword puzzles swept North America. This was also the decade of Charles Ponzi, inventor of the pyramid scheme, and Émile Coué, the autosuggestion guru who gave us the immortal, "every day, in every way, I'm getting better and better".

People became fixated on sports heroes like Babe Ruth and risk-takers like barnstorming pilots. The best known of these was American Charles Lindbergh, whose popularity rose to Lady Diana-like heights after his solo crossing of the Atlantic in 1927, followed by live coverage of his return on the first network radio broadcast ever. In Canada, we did our bit by electing, and re-electing a Prime Minister, William Lyon Mackenzie King (whom we now know held séances in order to communicate with his dead mother). Even Jesus had a second coming as a leader with God-given business skills in the 1926 bestseller, *The Man Nobody Knows*. It's not surprising that the author was Bruce Barton, the father of modern advertising.

In a description of surrealist art, Eric Hobsbawm notes that "what counted was to recognize the capacity of the spontaneous imagination, unmediated by rational control systems, to produce cohesion out of the incoherent." It's a description that could also characterize the European version of hero fixation in the 1920s. Hitler, Lenin and Mussolini were bit players in that other, older world, and probably would have stayed that way, if not for the Great War. In the new world of the twentieth century, however, they were embraced by people who were, in retrospect, thinking about as clearly as one of Ponzi's victims. The consequences of their collective delusions shaped the rest of the century.

The coalitions of women's groups that had achieved suffrage across Europe and North America had always been shaky at best. In the aftermath of war and epidemic, the focus of activists shifted away from big picture ideas like equality, and back toward local concerns and single issue politics. In Canada, a good example of this trend was the fate of the National Council of Women, formed in 1893. By World War I, it had become very influential across the country, but the pressures within were never fully resolved, and it went into steep decline in the '20s. As Veronica Strong-Boag notes in *The New Day Recalled*:

The WCTU criticized [the Council's] early failure to endorse prohibition. The IODE doubted its patriotism and suspected its internationalism as a cover for pacifism. The YWCA condemned its failure to endorse a more evangelical Protestantism ... western farm women were increasing unhappy with the Council's urban, pro-business and Central Canadian sympathies. Working class women never felt comfortable at the Council's overwhelmingly middle class meetings. Radicals always censured the length of time it took to consider any issue, and its failure to take direct action.

But if failure to maintain a united front caused concern, it paled before the movement's inability to communicate with younger women.

If we want to hold our position, to justify those women who worked hard to obtain the franchise, and those men who were generous enough to give it, we have to do a great deal more and give a great deal more. It isn't the lack of time, or lack of money, which handicaps us, it is apathy — throw it off, and ... influence those around you.

This kind of appeal, which Strong-Boag quotes from the *1928 Annual Report of the National Council of Women*, illustrates just how out of touch with the times the first-generation feminists had become. War and pestilence had changed the world, and it's clear the traumatized survivors weren't ready for more sacrifice. The fact that the leaders of the movement had been prominent before the war, and thus tainted by the disaster, only served to strengthen the intensity of rejection.

The older generation had pretty well ruined this world before passing it on to us. They gave us this Thing, knocked to pieces, leaky, red-hot, threatening to blow up; and then are surprised when we don't receive it with the same attitude of pretty, decorous enthusiasm with which they received it way back in the 1890s ... My generation is disillusionized, and, I think, to a certain extent, brutalized by the cataclysm which their complacent folly engendered ...
[And now] the oldsters stand dramatically with fingers and toes and noses pressed against the bursting dykes. Let them. They won't do any good. They can shackle us down and still expect us to repair their blunders, if they wish. But, we shall not trouble ourselves very much about them anymore. Why should we? What have they done? They have made us work as they never had to work in all their padded

lives — but we'll have our cakes and ale for a' that.

> John Carter Jr.
> These Wild Young People
> *The Atlantic Monthly*, Sept. 1920

Age itself became suspect. Youth culture dictated less deference to elders to begin with, and by 1920s standards, most of the leaders of the suffrage movement were certainly mature. In 1920, Nellie McClung was already forty-seven, Louise McKinney was fifty-two, and Henrietta Muir Edwards, a legal expert who became one of the principals in the Persons Case, was seventy-one. F. Scott Fitzgerald may have summed up post-war youth's attitude toward the older generation most succinctly in his short story collection, *Flappers and Philosophers*:

> People over forty can seldom be permanently convinced of anything. At eighteen our convictions are hills from which we look; at forty-five they are caves in which we hide.

The suffragists, their organizations and their causes, had committed the ultimate cultural crime — they weren't modern. Flapper Jane simply stopped listening.

That's not to say there was no advance in women's rights in the 1920s. If the WCTU lost the fight for prohibition and its members went back to their church groups, other efforts were more successful. Married women's property rights and equal custody of children were recognized in a number of provinces. Maternity leave was introduced in British Columbia. And in 1925, the federal government finally revised the Divorce Act so that grounds were the same for men and women — simple adultery. While appearing more equal, this change had little effect on the divorce rate. In 1929, there were only 817 divorces granted in the entire country. For most women, it was clear that "til death do us part" still meant exactly what it said.

Nevertheless, women had shown, and were continuing to show, that they were effective at wielding influence. However, the move from lobbyist to legislator proved more problematic. Consider the turnout for the 1921 federal election, the first in which all women twenty-one and over were eligible to vote. Despite the addition of nearly 2.5 million mostly female names to the voters' list, percentage turnout actually dropped nearly seven-and-a-half points and stayed down for the entire decade. In fact, by percentage, the 1920s had the lowest voter turnout of the century.

Faced without even the façade of a united front, and with no apparent consequences at the ballot box, the male establishment stiffened its resistance to further political change. Federally, there were four elections between 1921 and 1930. A total of nineteen women were nominated during that period (compared with 2,265 men) and only one was elected. Agnes Macphail became Canada's first female MP in 1921, then sat alone in the House of Commons for the next fourteen years.

She was clearly up to the challenge. "Don't you wish you were a man?" a Member of Parliament shouted to the lone woman in the chamber. "Don't you?" she shouted back.

Though many women who have achieved success were born to wealth and privilege, Agnes Macphail was certainly not. Hers was a family of poor farmers and her determination to escape life as a drudge not only caused her to set her horizons high, but was also one of the reasons she never married. Agnes dedicated her life to politics, believing that through politics she could enhance the life of farmers and more particularly farm women. Yet she neither sought nor achieved affluence; instead, hers was a life of service to her constituents. She truly deserves a prominent place in Canada's history.

Agnes Macphail was born on March 24, 1890 to Henrietta Campbell, known as Etta, and Dougald MacPhail. (Agnes dropped the capital P in her name during the 1930 federal campaign in order to make it easier to spell.) As teenagers, her parents had both left their native Scotland with their families in the mid-nineteenth century and settled in western Ontario. After their marriage, they farmed in Grey County, south of Georgian Bay, where Agnes was born. Their home was a three-room dwelling with a summer lean-to kitchen. Watching her mother labour at farm and household chores left Agnes unimpressed with the equality of opportunity of men and women on the farm. "In farming," she is purported to have said, "women break fifty-fifty with the men, but if this is true, it is fifty dollars to the men and fifty cents to the women."

Agnes hated everything about the day-to-day life of farm women — particularly the laundry. Instead, she excelled at school and determined almost from the time she began her education that she wanted to be a teacher. At thirteen, she announced to her family that she wanted to go to Europe when she grew up. As she often did, her mother accused her of dreaming. She wanted Agnes to espouse the womanly virtues of cleanliness, tidiness and quiet disposition. But Agnes was her father's child, moody with a quick wit and an equally quick temper.

Despite her parents' lack of funds, and in contradiction to their wishes and beliefs that primary school was sufficient, she was determined to complete her education. That resolve led her to place enormous pressure on her mother and grandmother. After two years they finally relented and she was allowed to go to high school in Owen Sound, where she was quickly recognized as an outstanding student and athlete. Completing her junior matriculation in two rather than the normal four years, she moved to Stratford, Ontario, where she received her senior matriculation. The following year, she completed her teaching certificate at Owen Sound Teacher's College.

Agnes began teaching in 1910 in Gowanlock, near Port Elgin, then moved to Kinloss, a hamlet in Bruce County. It was customary practice at the time for the teacher to board with a family in the community during the school year and Agnes found herself living with Sam Braden, the local storekeeper. Hours were long and the store often acted as a drop-in centre in the evenings, where the men sat around the pot-bellied stove and discussed the affairs of the nation. Politics absorbed much of the debate. This was not usually a place where women were found, but the young school teacher, freed from the usual domestic duties and encouraged by her landlord, participated eagerly in these daily sessions.

Braden encouraged her to read the Liberal point of view expressed in the *Globe* and the Conservative view expressed by the *Mail and Empire,* both Toronto papers. The debates were fierce and ranged from trade to women's suffrage, with Macphail giving as good as she got.

After two years in Kinloss, she'd worked herself into a state of exhaustion and was forced to leave, but it was around that stove where her social and political activism was born.

Following a year of recuperation on the family farm, Agnes returned to teaching, this time in Alberta, where she first made contact with a new political movement, the United Farmers. Dismayed by the primitive conditions in the rural west, she returned to Ontario, where she taught in Boothville and Sharon, and became engaged to be married.

World War I began while she was in Sharon and her fiancé, Robert Tucker, went off to battle. Though he survived, when he returned they were no longer engaged. In the years that followed, Macphail never made any references to her broken engagement and though there were other love interests over the years, she seems to have made a decision not to marry each time the opportunity arose.

It was also during the war years that she joined the United Farmers of Ontario. The UFO's position was that the political parties were in the hands of big business and that the farmer, the original small business owner, was being held captive to the interests of those same concerns. Macphail saw the plight of women in a similar light — women were being put down by the establishment. Her political work with the UFO took her to many communities, where her job was organizing farmers' clubs. With much trepidation she gave her first public speech in 1919.

Her political interest was kindled further when she caught smallpox in 1920. This brought home to her the plight of all people who are hit with the

AGNES MACPHAIL

financial burden brought on by poor health. She began to submit articles for the *Farmer's Sun* and her name became well known throughout the community.

The first federal election in which women were eligible to run was held in 1921. Agnes Macphail accepted the nomination for the United Farmers in the constituency of Southeast Grey. Supported by the thirty-nine farm clubs and the union in Hanover, she campaigned in earnest. She gave fifty-five speeches, some of them more than an hour in length. She won with a plurality of more than 2,500 votes. Not surprisingly, given the times, the issue that garnered the most publicity during the campaign was that she refused to wear either hats or gloves; she believed they were society's way of placing limits on the activities of women.

The United Farmers of Ontario took twenty-four seats in the province, enough for them, along with those elected as United Farmers from Manitoba and Alberta, and "progressives" from other parts of the country, to form the Official Opposition. However, the new parliamentarians rejected this as "old time" politics. Instead, each elected member acted as an independent, rather than part of a caucus. Macphail was one of the members who fought hardest for this idea. Unfortunately, all this position accomplished in the end was a lack of cohesion, and power, in the House.

Parliament was called into session in March 1922 and, as the first woman elected to this chamber, Macphail was met with curiosity, excitement and in, some quarters, antagonism. The opening shots were taken by the Speaker, who made a point of addressing the assembly as "Madame and Fellow Members of the House of Commons", as if somehow she was not quite one of them. Flowers on her desk were first interpreted as a kindly gesture, until she learned that they were there as a result of a lost bet, the bet having been that she would lose the election. One of the headlines of the day — "Even Agnes Donned the War Paint for State Drawing Room" — quickly made it apparent that she was to be subjected to special treatment. She reported that she could often hear people in the gallery pointing her out as if she were part of a freak show. Like many women who have held political office, Macphail complained about the loneliness of the job. In speaking to the Ottawa Ladies College in 1924, she said, "Do not rely completely on any other human being. We meet all life's greatest tests alone."

There were three main themes of Macphail's activism. She wanted a better life for farmers and particularly farm women; she wanted greater political economic and social equality for women, and she wanted world peace. Most of her speeches, both in and out of the House of Commons, related to these three themes.

The desire for greater equality for women was the topic of her first speech in the House of Commons. She indicated her opposition to the amendment to the Elections Act, which would have extended the right to vote to women who were not citizens, but who were married to Canadian citizens. Her argument, clearly put, was that this was special and not equal treatment. After all, men married to Canadian citizens did not have the vote unless they too were Canadian citizens. Macphail believed that if women were given special status in acts such as these, they could then be given special status, that is, inferior status, in other acts. She wanted women to be treated as men were treated. Only then did she believe true equality would be achieved.

As part of her equality fight, she forced the Speaker to relax the rule that women had to wear hats in the gallery of the House of Commons, since she was definitely not going to wear one. A token gesture perhaps, but again significant to her because she believed that special rules implied inferiority.

The United Farmers of Ontario, which had such an influence in the early part of the decade, was losing support. Membership had declined from a high of 46,000 members in 1921 to 18,000 in 1925, which must have given Macphail some concern about her re-election chances. However, she saw the United Farmers not so much as a political party, but as a social force; to that end, she believed membership to be less relevant than programs. She particularly saw this as a role for women. She worked with them on such issues as public education on childbirth and introduced iodized pills to counter goitre at a meeting of the UFWO. She encouraged the children of farm families to participate in public-speaking contests and debates. As a result of all these activities, her political support was increasingly based, not on ideology, but rather on the personal approval rating of Agnes Macphail.

Running as a Progressive, she was returned to office in the 1925 election, though with a reduced plurality. Ontario elected only one other Progressive and nationally, the Progressives were reduced to twenty-four seats, a significant decline from sixty-four members in 1921. However, neither the Liberals nor the Conservatives had a majority, although the Conservatives, with 116, had more seats than the Liberals' ninety-nine. Normally the Liberals would have resigned, thereby passing the reins of government to the Conservatives. However, Prime Minister Mackenzie King decided to try to form a government and therefore sought the support of the Progressives, who held the balance of power.

The Prime Minister sent a representative to ask Macphail if she'd consider a cabinet post, but Macphail was not interested in joining a party she thought to be hypocritical. It has often been said that Liberals campaign on the left and govern from the right. Macphail believed this to be the case, particularly after the 1919 election in which they had discussed significant reform, including a publicly supported health care system, and then turned their backs on such ideas.

The session was a raucous one. The government went from day to day not knowing if it would have the support of enough Progressives to survive.

Finally, Mackenzie King decided to go to Rideau Hall and ask that an election be called. Governor General Viscount Byng refused, stating that the Conservatives had to be called upon to form a government, and precipitating what has been called the King Byng Crisis.

King was furious, but had to stand by as Arthur Meighen was asked to form a government. It was to be short-lived, as Macphail and the Progressives, having brought down the Liberal government, now proceeded to do the same thing to the Conservatives. Macphail found herself in another election campaign.

During the campaign, she was labelled a Bolshevik by the Conservatives, who were desperate to take her seat and return to power. But the slights were for naught. Her plurality increased in 1926; the voters seemed to understand that they had a representative who put their interests first. The Progressives, on the other hand, were reduced again, this time to twenty seats nationally.

The Liberals were returned to power with a majority and a constitutional issue had been decided. The Governor General would no longer be able to use his discretion in determining who would form a government. The Canadian people, by choosing to re-elect the Liberals, sent a clear signal that the Governor General had been wrong in asking Meighen to form a government. Henceforth, the Governor General must abide by the advice given by the Prime Minister. [2]

During her years as a Member of Parliament, Macphail wrote a weekly letter to fourteen newspapers in her constituency. Increasingly, as the decade came to a close, she wrote on international issues. She wrote of the unrest in China following the death of Sun Yat-sen in 1925. She wrote of the opium trade and of the need for Canada to end its colonial status. It was clear her political interests were becoming broader.

In 1929, she was appointed Canada's first female delegate to the League of Nations. On her way to Europe, she began by attending the congress of the Women's International League held in Prague. Disarmament was the major topic and Macphail shone. She was elected to the international executive. In Geneva, at the League of Nations meetings, it was assumed Macphail would attend the sessions on issues affecting women and children, but she refused, attending instead the committee meeting on arms reduction.

She was somewhat dismayed at the lack of information that had been given to her and the other members of the Canadian delegation on the issues debated at the conference. On her return to Canada, she informed the Prime Minister of the need to better prepare delegates for meetings where they were to represent the nation. She also stressed the need for better language training. Then, as now,

---

[2] This question was raised again in the run-up to the 2004 election.

the real work was meant to be done by professional civil servants. The Members of Parliament were simply window dressing, but Macphail didn't see it this way.

Her communications skills, honed by three election campaigns, were now proving invaluable as she crossed the country. She was paid $200 a week, no mean sum for the times, when on a speaking tour and often used the money on clothes. Though she was regarded as something of a fashion plate, she seems to have had little concern for the future and put no money aside for a rainy day. This habit was to cause her great financial difficulties, particularly in her old age.

♦♦ ❖ ♦♦

Despite the underwhelming electoral results of the attainment of suffrage, there was one political question that eventually generated widespread interest among women during the 1920s. Women's groups had been petitioning prime ministers to appoint a female senator since 1919. But there was a slight problem. It appeared to some legal experts that, as defined by the British North America Act, even though she could be elected to Parliament a woman wasn't, well, a person. The person largely responsible for correcting this oversight was a reforming judge from Edmonton named Emily Murphy.

Emily was born to Isaac and Emily Jemima Ferguson in Cookston, Ontario, on March 14, 1868, the third of six children. Her grandfather, Ogle Robert Gowan, was a MP for twenty-seven years and the founder of the Orange Order in Canada. Three of her brothers became lawyers and one, William, eventually sat on the Ontario Supreme Court. Emily was an excellent student, and though she didn't study law, no one was surprised when she showed a flair for it.

In 1887, she married Arthur Murphy, an Anglican divinity student, and they had three daughters. It seemed that Arthur was destined for high office in the church, perhaps even a bishopric someday, until he decided to become a travelling or mission preacher instead. Leaving his family in Toronto, he was so successful in the Huron Diocese that he was invited to continue his mission work in Britain. The family lived in England for two years, returning to Canada in 1900. By this time, Emily had become an accomplished author. She wrote about her English experiences in *Impressions of Janey Canuck Abroad.*

Back in Canada, Arthur continued his missions across the country, but Emily spent more and more time in Toronto, where she contributed to the periodical *National Monthly* and devoted time to her family and the writing of novels.

The missionary society that had supported Arthur went broke, but rather than despairing, he decided he'd had enough of preaching and, in a rather breathtaking turnabout, became an entrepreneur instead. The family first moved to Swan

River, in Manitoba, and then, in 1907, to Edmonton, where Emily was to live until for the rest of her life.

She spent her first years in Edmonton gathering material for her now very popular novels. *Janey Canuck in the West* was published in 1910 and was followed by *Open Trails, Seeds of Pine, The Black Candle* (which many believe was largely responsible for modern Canadian anti-drug laws), *Our Little Canadian Cousins of the North West* and, in 1929, the last, *Bishop Bompas.* Always a devout Anglican, she was deeply involved in church organizations, particularly those that provided help for destitute women and children. She also worked with native families and recent immigrants who spoke no English.

The chain of events that led to her involvement in what became the Persons Case began in June 1916. Members of the Law Committee of the local Council of Women were sent by the council to observe the trial of a group of ten women charged as vagrants and prostitutes. The committee members were asked by the Crown counsel to leave the court because, in the magistrate's view, the cases were unsuitable for the delicate ears of ladies (though not those of the accused, presumably). Though angry at being treated like children, after consultation with Murphy, the observers did as requested. As a result of the experience, however, they launched a crusade for the establishment of a women's court.

As is often the case, the person who had the idea was quickly drafted to do the work. Murphy was asked by the local council to take her idea directly to the Attorney General, the Honourable C.W. Cross. It must have come as a bit of a shock when he not only agreed with her, but offered to seek government approval for the immediate appointment of a female magistrate. The next logical step in his mind was to ask Murphy to fill the position. Her acceptance made her the first female magistrate in the British Empire.

Members of the Local Council of Women and others involved in justice issues applauded the appointment. Members of the Law Society, including members of the judiciary, weren't quite so enthusiastic. Her right to preside was challenged during her very first sitting. Defence Counsel Eardley Jackson, angered by the harsh sentence she had just handed down to his bootlegger client said, "You're not even a person, you have no right to be holding court." Judge Murphy asked him to present his argument. He responded that under British common law, in a decision handed down in 1876, women are persons in matters of pain and penalties, but not in matters of rights and privileges. Therefore, he argued, since the role of magistrate was a privilege, Judge Murphy was not eligible and the decisions of her court, not binding.

The British North America Act, which created the provinces, and therefore provincial courts, stated that "persons" could be appointed to such positions.

EMILY MURPHY

❖ ALICE JAMIESON ❖

The question remained as to whether women could be considered persons. The concept was raised frequently during the early months of Judge Murphy's court. Usually, she simply acknowledged the remark and continued trying the case. But she did demand respect.

When Jackson audibly remarked, in court, "To hell with women magistrates. This country is going to the dogs because of them," he received the following terse note: "Unless I receive from you an unqualified apology in writing, I shall regretfully be obliged to henceforth refuse you admittance to this Court in the capacity of Counsel." She got the apology.

No one actually mounted a legal challenge until December, and even then, it wasn't aimed at Murphy, but at Alice Jamieson, who had been appointed a magistrate in Calgary after serving two years as a juvenile court commissioner. [3]

The case was quickly settled when Mr. Justice Scott of the Alberta Supreme Court ruled that there was no legal disqualification from holding public office on the basis of sex. This raised an interesting question. If women were persons in this case, what about other areas where the BNA wasn't specific? What about the Senate?

Shortly after the decision on Judge Jamieson, the Federation of Women's Institutes, of which Murphy was president, petitioned the Prime Minister to appoint a woman to the Senate. Murphy began her assault by using both the media and a letter-writing campaign. She persuaded the editor of *Women's Century* to support the appointment of women to the Senate and she personally wrote 700 letters to influential people. She rallied the delegates at the annual meeting of the Women's Institutes by stating "The world loves a peaceful man, but gives way to a strenuous kicker." The National Council of Women also added its voice.

Arthur Meighen was Prime Minister in 1920, the only Manitoba MP ever to hold the position. In his reply, he stated that he had been advised by the Department of Justice that such an appointment was impossible. The Persons argument had been raised again. He did promise during the 1921 election campaign he would try to have women appointed to the Senate. Alas, he lost the election.

The new Prime Minister, William Lyon Mackenzie King, he of the séances, renewed the promise of support for female senators in a 1922 letter. Senator Archibald McCoig actually gave notice in the Senate of an amendment to the British North American Act which would have permitted women to be appointed. But somehow, it never got beyond the notice stage.

---

3 Which, depending on your definition of "judge", could make Alice Jamieson the first female judge in Canada and the Empire, rather than Emily Murphy.

The National Council of Women sent delegations to Ottawa in 1924, 1927 and 1928 urging the appointment of a female senator, but to no avail.

The only recourse was legal action. As we've seen, the British North America Act was ambiguous. Though many parts of the Act specifically used the male pronoun, other parts, like Section 24, which describes qualifications for the Senate, did not.

> The Governor General shall from Time to Time, in the Queen's Name, by Instrument under the Great Seal of Canada, summon qualified Persons to the Senate; and, subject to the Provisions of this Act, every Person so summoned shall become and be a Member of the Senate of Canada and a Senator.

Clearly, there was no male pronoun. Justice William Ferguson, Murphy's brother, suggested that the government could simply appoint her, as Attorney General Cross had done in making her a magistrate, then wait and see if anyone initiated a challenge. This, however, did not appeal to the government. Justice Ferguson then suggested the use of Section 60 of the Supreme Court Act, which allowed any five persons to petition for an order-in-council directing the Supreme Court of Canada to rule on a constitutional point.

Murphy decided to put together the group of five. The four women she chose all lived in Alberta, but all had a national profile. Two of them — Louise McKinney and Nellie McClung — have appeared earlier in these pages. The others were Henrietta Muir Edwards and Irene Parlby.

After women won the vote in 1916, the Alberta Council of Women created the Provincial Laws Committee to help women take full advantage of enfranchisement. Henrietta Edwards, who had begun compiling information on women, children and the law in 1908, was appointed the chair of the committee. She published *The Legal Status of Women in Alberta* in 1916. Even though the work had not been compiled through a government initiative, it was reissued five years later under the authority of the Attorney General. In 1924, Edwards added to the work she'd done by publishing *The Legal Status of Women in Canada*.

Irene Parlby had begun her political career as a member of the United Farmers of Alberta, serving as president of the Women's Auxiliary from 1916 to 1918. She ran and was elected to the Alberta legislature in 1921 as part of a UFA majority. She was immediately appointed Minister without Portfolio, a position she held for the next fourteen years. She was the only one of the five who was sitting in a legislature when the Person's petition was presented to the Supreme Court.

The "Famous Five", as they came to be called, represented the major political parties of the day. Parlby and McKinney were members of the United Farmers of Alberta. McClung was a Liberal and Murphy and Edwards, Conservatives. They made a formidable group.

The petition signed by the five was sent to Ottawa in August 1927. The signatures were placed in alphabetical order, so the case became known as Edwards v. Attorney General of Canada. It wasn't until March 14, 1928, Murphy's sixtieth birthday, that the Supreme Court heard the case. The group of five was represented by the Honourable Newton Wesley Rowell, who, as the leader of the Liberal opposition in Ontario, had strongly supported the cause of suffrage. The Department of Justice was represented by the Honourable Lucien Cannon, K.C. (King's Counsel) The Province of Québec lent its support to the Department of Justice, whereas the Province of Alberta made clear its support for the group of five.

The argument put forward by the Department of Justice was that the British North America Act, the written constitution of Canada, must be interpreted as written; clearly, women were not included as persons in 1867. Rowell argued that the constitution had been reinterpreted when women were given the federal vote in 1920 and must be reinterpreted again, this time to welcome women to the Senate.

The justices deliberated for more than a month. Then on April 24th, Chief Justice Anglin delivered the court's unanimous decision:

> There can be no doubt that the word 'persons', when standing alone *prima facie* includes women … It connotes human being — the criminal and insane as well as the good and wise citizen, the minor as well as the adult. Hence the propriety of the restriction placed on its use in the sections which speak of 'qualified' persons, and 'fit and qualified' persons. [Therefore], the question being understood to be 'Are women eligible for appointment to the Senate of Canada,' the question is answered in the negative.

The muted reaction across the country was a demonstration of just how far the subject of women's rights had faded from public view. The *Manitoba Free Press* accorded the decision 300 words on page six. The accompanying editorial was even more blunt:

> The Supreme Court of Canada, in full robes and without dissent, has ruled that a woman is not a person within the meaning of the British North America Act … what we will have to do now is to

obtain an amendment to the British North America Act. Canada, of course, has no power to change the act; we will have to ask the British government to do it for us. The House of Commons will have to move, the Senate will have to approve, and the provinces, we suppose, will have to be consulted … we suggest that these persons who have been clamouring about status keep their foul hands off the [BNA] Act.

Judge Murphy, however, was as determined as ever:

While we regret that the decision of the Supreme Court of Canada was not favourable to our cause, I am sure we agree that their decision was a sincere one, and should not be adversely criticized by any of us. Of the ultimate results, I have not the slightest doubt. Nothing can prevent us winning.

Mackenzie King's Minister of Justice had promised action as soon as the decision was announced, but faced with possible resistance, both from Québec and within the Senate, the government did nothing. There was, however, one avenue left.

As the *Free Press* editorial suggested, Canada was still at this time subject in some respects to the authority of Great Britain. The group of five requested an order-in-council giving them the right to appeal the decision of the Supreme Court to His Majesty's Privy Council in London. Arguments began on July 22, 1929 and lasted four days. This time deliberations took three months. Finally, on October 18th, Lord Chancellor Lord Sankey, arrived at Temple Bar to deliver the verdict:

Their Lordships have come to the conclusion that the word 'persons' includes members of the male and female sex, and that therefore the question propounded by the Governor General must be answered in the affirmative; and that women are eligible to be summoned and to become members of the Senate of Canada.

There was jubilation among women across the country, although McClung, as she usually did, put things in perspective.

It's wonderful news, no doubt, though we Canadian women had no idea we were not persons, until we were told we were.

The Person's Case was a tremendous symbolic victory for Canadian women. But at the time, few people outside the women's groups directly involved seemed to be paying much attention. Coverage across the country was distinctly uneven. The editors at the *Manitoba Free Press* considered the story so unnewsworthy that they placed it in a section called "News of Interest to Young Men and Women", right beside "Boy Scout Notes".

Everyone's focus appeared to be elsewhere. Perhaps that's because so many people could sense that the party that had been the 1920s was winding down. In fact, on the afternoon of Lord Sankey's announcement, there were just six days left. Because, of course, October 1929 is far better remembered for something other than the Person's Case. October 24th, otherwise known as Black Thursday, saw the start of the biggest stock market collapse in history, and marked the beginning of the Great Depression.

•• ❖ ••

Canada's first female Senator was summoned in 1930, but it wasn't Emily Murphy. To no one's real surprise, Mackenzie King appointed Cairine Wilson, a Liberal. And when the Conservatives returned to power later that year, Prime Minister Richard Bennett chose to summon only male senators.

Murphy continued to serve as a magistrate until 1931. In addition, she remained active in the Federated Women's Institutes of Canada, the National Council of Women, the Canadian Women's Press Club, the Canadian Council on Child Welfare, the Women's Canadian Club and the Social Service Council of Canada. She was decorated by King George V and was made a Lady of Grace of the Order of St. John of Jerusalem.

Throughout, she continued to push for legislation that would impose social change on society. In 1926, Murphy had been appointed by the Province of Alberta to investigate property laws affecting women. Not surprisingly, her report calling for greater control by women made enemies. Along with Nellie McClung, she was instrumental in the passage of the 1928 Alberta Sterilization Act. Although a backward step for the mentally disabled by today's standards, at the time it was considered on the leading edge of social reform.

With the dedication of Famous Five monuments in 1999 in Calgary and 2000 in Ottawa, came reminders of that support for sterilization and other less admirable opinions. In her writings, Murphy was an unabashed supporter of the Anglo-Saxon majority — that "bright browed race", as she called them in *The Black Candle*. As for other groups, a reading of the *Maclean's* articles based on *The Black Candle* yields terms like "blackamoor" and "boy", used to describe black railway porters, and the implication that the "sallow, unsmiling Oriental" is invariably a drug smuggler, addict and corruptor of innocent young white women. Add to that some rather tasteless illustrations in what's otherwise an interesting series on the drug problem of the time, and the overall impression isn't terribly favourable to modern sensibilities.

Of course, this was a time when racism was pretty much taken for granted. Black men were regularly lynched in the United States and the Klu Klux Klan was expanding into Canada. Restaurants in B.C. could post signs that stated, "No dogs or Chinamen allowed". Saskatchewan passed a law that barred white women from working in any establishment owned by a Chinese person and people talked seriously about the Yellow Peril, an idea invented by William Randolph Hearst and personified by Fu Manchu.

Was Emily Murphy a racist? By any modern definition, probably. Were her attitudes any different than the vast majority of white Canadians of the period? No. Does that in any way diminish Murphy's contributions as a suffragist and legal reformer? Not likely. If one of the requirements for a statue on Parliament Hill was divine infallibility, the Hill would be a statue free zone.

On October 26, 1933, Murphy visited the public library and stopped in at the police court to assure herself that women were not being neglected. In a bit of irony, Eardley Jackson, the man who had challenged her on her first day on the bench, was present. She must have been surprised when he stated before the court, "We are honoured today by the presence of Mrs. Emily Murphy, Police Magistrate and Judge. A feminine note missing from this building is brought back by the kindly, smiling countenance of this beloved lady."

She did some shopping, returned home and retired. She died just before midnight at the age of sixty-five.

♦♦ ❖ ♦♦

The old political guard had cause to be reasonably smug at the end of the 1920s. Though they'd lost the suffrage battle and there would now be women in the Senate, to their relief, it appeared that the power equation hadn't really changed at all. Moreover, the feminists, who had put such fear into the breasts of men everywhere, appeared to be a spent force.

In fact, far from being a swan song, the '20s were actually an incubator. Twentieth-century women may have rejected their mothers' world, but they had not abandoned the principles they espoused. Feminist ideas, particularly the idea of equality, were firmly planted, if dormant. The only question was, how long till spring? The answer, unfortunately, would be quite some time. Social debate would continue, but the attention of the majority was about to turn to something a little more pressing: survival.

MARY ELLEN SMITH

Canada's First Female Cabinet Member

MARY ELLEN SMITH was born Mary Ellen Spear in Tavistock, Devonshire, England. She was the eldest child of Richard Spear and Mary Ann Jackson and their only daughter. In the Spear family, children were encouraged to take part in lively discussions of current affairs, and Mary Ellen contributed to the fullest.

On February 3, 1883, she married a Methodist student minister, Ralph Smith. When Ralph's ill health dictated a move away from England, they chose Canada, settling in Nanaimo. Mary Ellen became involved in political work almost at once. She was a founder of the Laurier Liberal Club, a member of the Suffrage League of Canada and president of the Women's Canadian Club and of the Women's Forum, as well as a regent of the Imperial Order of the Daughters of the Empire.

Ralph was also involved in politics and became Finance Minister in the provincial Liberal government. When he died in 1917, Mary Ellen ran as an Independent on the slogan "Women and Children First", and won the resulting by-election by more than 3,500 votes. It was proof that she'd became a potent political force in her own right. She kept her seat in the general election campaigns of 1920 and 1924, increasing her majority each time.

In her maiden speech on March 1,1918, she stated, "I have faith in the intelligence, honour and integrity of every member of this House. Not only do I come to ask for legislation in the best interests of women and children, but also legislation for the protection of the best interests of all the people of this province." She immediately set about delivering on that promise, piloting a minimum wage law for women through the house in her very first session. Over the next ten years, she was responsible for legislation that included the Juvenile Courts Act, the Deserted Wives Maintenance Act, the Equal Guardianship Act, the Nurse's Act, the Act Regulating Night Employment for Women, and the Mother's Pension Act.

She joined the Liberals in 1920. In late 1921, after turning down an offer to become speaker, she accepted an invitation to join the cabinet as a Minister without Portfolio, making her the first female cabinet member in the Empire. However, she discovered that the rules governing both cabinet secrecy and discipline so interfered with her ability to represent her constituents, that she resigned after only eight months.

"For some time ... I have been in the unfortunate position of having to assume the responsibility for acts of the government without being in a position to criticize or advise. I am, after all, primarily interested in women and children and no matter what government has the power, as long as I can serve the people whom I have the honour to represent, then I shall find the happiness that public life gives."

Despite that decision, she stayed with the Liberals. She chaired the party convention of 1927, in what also appears to have been a political first for a woman. And on assuming the chair in the B.C. Legislature for two days in 1928, she achieved yet another first. The term "Madame Speaker", had never before been heard in an Empire legislature.

Defeated in the 1928 election during a Conservative sweep, Mary Ellen Smith remained active in her party, and her community, until her death on May 3, 1933. The unreserved sense of duty she displayed throughout her career might best be summed up in a quote from one of her final speeches. She said, "We can't all contribute to Canada in ways which will be nationally recognized, of course. But we can all serve Canada just the same".

Depression and War
(1930–1945)

◆

Scene: 1936

SOCIAL NARRATOR: The stage is bare except for a battered plank table and chair DS and a small cabinet UL. There's an empty water glass and an old thermometer from some local business on the table.

A woman at the table is wearing a faded gingham dress that's clearly soaked under the arms and down the back. She's hunched over, laboriously writing a letter. She pauses occasionally to blot the sweat that drips from her face and seeps from her hands. She's twenty-nine years old, but the pain and weariness in her face make her look at least forty-five.

She stops writing, and leans back, wiping her brow with the back of her forearm. Then she picks up the letter and begins to read.

Sunday, July 12th, 1936

Dear Enid,

Already 93 and it's only 10 in the morning. Who'd have thought back in February we'd ever miss all those weeks of 40 below? I'd give anything for just an hour of bein' cool.

I had Ed Rainey take the kids to Aunt Harriet's in Estevan last night. She still has the electricity so there's a fan. I didn't know what else to do.

Jerry didn't want to go. I had to slap him 'fore he'd get in Ed's car. I feel real bad about that. Another sin on my head, I guess. I'm pretty sure he knows. He's always been the one that notices things.

Still haven't heard from Isaac. Can't really blame him for leaving. Not that much, anyhow. Said he was going up north to find us some land that wasn't droughted out, but, deep down, I guess I always knew he wasn't coming back. Too proud, that's his problem. Just couldn't abide the idea of the neighbours knowing he was a failure. That he had to beg for relief.

(She looks up from the letter and her voice begins to rise) As if most of them wasn't in the same boat. Course, the government just makes it worse, accusing people who never missed a day in 20 years of being too lazy to work. What work? *(she's screaming now)* There ain't no work! Do they really think I'd be watching my kids starve if there was any work? *(She stops, panting)*

Oh. Thought I was past that.

(She begins to read again) I think it's the dust that's finally done me. I sweep and I scrub and I stuff the windows and under the doors with old catalogues, but it just keeps coming in. Little dunes on the floor like something out of the *National Geographic*. Even the grasshoppers don't seem to

bother me as much as the dust. In '34 we shoveled them into piles big as the fall leaves back in Kingston when we was little girls, remember? Piles taller than we were? Leaves never moved like dying hoppers, though. And they don't stink near as bad when they burn.

I need to tell you I finally figured out what's happening. God has turned His face from me. That has to be it, don't you see? I pray till my knees bleed, but everything just keeps getting' worse. I tried to be a good wife and mother. Tried my very best, but somehow I sinned instead and this is God's punishment. Can't be anything else.

They made us sell everything 'fore we could get relief, but there's ten dollars under a loose board in the girls' bedroom. I was saving it for … well, that doesn't matter now. I know it's not much for five kids, but it's all that's left. I'd give you and Billy the house, but the bank took it.

(She glances at the thermometer, then puts down the letter and writes):

Ninety-six now. I have to go.

Your sister,
Annie

She carefully folds the letter and puts it in an envelope. She prints Enid Walyschuk on the outside in block letters, then leans the envelope against the empty water glass. She stands and looks around the room. She's very calm now.

She exits R. We hear the creak of an old bedstead, then nothing for a moment. The silence is shattered by a single gunshot.

	POLITICAL	SOCIAL / TECHNOLOGY
	T I M E L I N E	
1930	• Constantinople becomes Istanbul • Haile Selassie becomes Emperor of Ethiopia • Occupation of Germany ends • The Depression begins • **Cairine Wilson become first female Senator** • Richard B. Bennett elected Canadian PM • War Veteran's Allowance created	• Plexiglas invented in Canada • Pablum invented in Canada • Jean Brébeuf achieves sainthood • *Blondie* comic strip appears • Flashbulb invented
1931	• Statute of Westminster marks Cdn independence • Industrialists support Nazis • Japan invades Manchuria	• Maple Leaf Gardens built • Empire State Building opens • Jehovah's Witnesses formed • Star Spangled Banner becomes U.S anthem • Canadian population: 10.38 M; birth rate dropping • **Ten per cent of working women married**
1932	• Nazis win German election • India's Congress Party outlawed • Gandhi arrested • CCF founded in Canada	• **Hamilton, ON, opens first family planning clinic** • Aldous Huxley writes *Brave New World* • The neutron discovered • Zuider Zee drained in Holland • Lindberg baby kidnapped • Summer Olympics held in Los Angeles; Winter Games in Lake Placid, N.Y.
1933	• Hitler becomes Chancellor of Germany • Franklin Roosevelt becomes President of U.S. • **Frances Perkins becomes first female cabinet member in U.S.** • First concentration camps in Germany • Newfoundland reverts to the Crown • Regina Manifesto (CCF)	• Prohibition repealed in U.S. • Canadian unemployment reaches 26.6 per cent
1934	• Purges begin in U.S.S.R. • Long March begins in China	• Wallace Carothers (Du Pont) invents nylon • Dionne quintuplets born • **Marie Curie dies in France**
1935	• Anti-Semitic Nuremberg Laws passed • Italy invades Ethiopia • Persia becomes Iran • Mackenzie King becomes PM again • **Martha Black becomes second female MP** • Bank of Canada opens	• Uranium 235 discovered • First radar station in Britain • Lawrence of Arabia dies • Clark Gable stars in *Mutiny on the Bounty* • Alchoholics Anonymous founded • Rumba in vogue

POLITICAL	SOCIAL / TECHNOLOGY	
T I M E L I N E		
• George V dies, Edward VIII abdicates • George VI becomes King of England • Spanish Civil War begins • CBC founded • Maurice Duplessis becomes Premier of Quebec	• Summer Olympics held in Berlin; Winter Games in Garmisch-Partenkirchen, Germany • Rudyard Kipling dies • BBC begins television broadcasting	**1936**
• Trans Canada Airlines founded • Japan invades China	• John Steinbeck writes *Of Mice and Men* • Pablo Picasso paints *Guernica* • Disney releases *Snow White* • Jet engine developed by Frank Whittle in Britain • *Hindenberg* disaster • Golden Gate Bridge opens • Amelia Earhart lost over the Pacific	**1937**
• Germany occupies Austria • Chamberlain speaks about "Peace in our time" • Germany occupies Czechoslovakia • Famous Five Plaque mounted in Ottawa • Quebec Liberal party supports suffrage	• Royal Winnipeg Ballet founded • Fission demonstrated in Germany • First *Superman* comic • Thornton Wilder writes *Our Town* • Orson Welles produces *War of the Worlds* on radio • 32,000 people die in car crashes in the U.S.	**1938**
• Germany and U.S.S.R. sign non-aggression pact • Germany invades Poland • WW II begins • Spanish Civil War ends • U.S.S.R. invades Finland • Pan Am begins transatlantic air service	• James Joyce writes *Finnegan's Wake* • *Gone With the Wind, Wizard of Oz* open • Polyethylene, DDT invented • First helicopter • FM radio broadcasts begin • Nylon stockings invented • National Film Board established	**1939**
• Germany invades Norway, Denmark, France • Churchill becomes British PM • Dunkirk, Battle of Britain • Blitz begins in London • **Quebec women get the vote** • Mackenzie King re-elected as PM • **Dorise Nielsen elected as MP** • Unemployment Insurance instituted in Canada	• Ernest Hemingway writes *For Whom the Bell Tolls* • Summer and Winter Olympics cancelled • Lascaux Caves discovered in France • Pressurized flight suit invented in Canada • Paint roller invented in Canada • Carbon 14 discovered	**1940**

	POLITICAL	SOCIAL / TECHNOLOGY
	T I M E L I N E	
1941	• Battle of the Atlantic • Fighting in North Africa • Germany invades U.S.S.R. • Japan attacks Pearl Harbour • Japan attacks Hong Kong, Philippines • Internment of Japanese Canadians begins • Siege of Leningrad begins	• Lorne Green becomes CBC's first newsreader • James Joyce, Virginia Wolf die • Manhattan Project begins • Plutonium discovered • Joe DiMaggio hits in fifty-six straight games (record still stands)
1942	• Battle of Midway • Battle of El Alamein • Dieppe • Holocaust begins • **Women admitted to bar in Québec** • **PC Women's Association formed**	• Disney releases *Bambi* • Enrico Fermi constructs first reactor to achieve a chain reaction
1943	• Battle of Guadalcanal • Battle of Stalingrad • Italy surrenders • **Agnes Macphail elected in Ontario**	• Rogers & Hammerstein create *Oklahoma!* • The Zoot Suit fashion rage • Jitterbug craze begins
1944	• D-Day • Battle of the Bulge • Family Allowance Act passed • Germany launches V-2 rocket attack	• George Orwell writes *Animal Farm* • First Family Allowance payments • Canadian birth rate: 24.3/1,000 • Summer and Winter Olympics cancelled again
1945	• World War II ends • Franklin Delano Roosevelt dies; Harry S. Truman becomes U.S. President • United Nations formed • Republic of Yugoslavia proclaimed	• First atomic explosion, Alamagordo (U.S.) • **Women's suffrage in France**

Depression and War
(1930–1945)

Black, black Monday and the market drops, but
We keep on dancing, dancing, we can't stop.
Marathon, marathon, mara, mara, marathon…

Jacques Brel

If the **1920s** were the giant keg party following the disastrous final exam of WW1, the '30s were the grim morning after — the unbearable hangover, the smashed furniture and, a little later, the surprise phone call from your gynecologist. Only in this case, what was smashed was the economy and the voice on the other end of the line was your broker with another margin call. It had taken more than ten years to realize it, but unlike more recent claims, this time the world really had changed.

You might think, that as the scope of the catastrophe became clear, people and governments would pull together and start to look for solutions. After all, it wasn't just the usual victims — the poor and middle classes — who were affected; this time not a few rich people were being beggared as well.

What actually happened, of course, was precisely the opposite. It was every man for himself and the Devil take the hindmost. Trade barriers went up immediately and government spending was slashed to maintain balanced budgets, a move that was very popular with the banks. Both tactics invariably had a contrary effect to that intended. Canada was already in transition to a consumer society, while still depending on exports for much of its national income.

Trade barriers are nineteenth-century tools intended to protect developing local industries from foreign competition. With twentieth-century consumers suddenly having difficulty paying for the washing machines and cars they'd bought on time in the 1920s, there was soon much less industry to protect. And what reciprocal trade barriers do to an economy that exports eighty per cent of what it produces, doesn't need much explaining.

Unemployment skyrocketed as businesses failed, and there was enormous downward pressure on wages in those that survived, which meant still less spending, which led to more bankruptcies in an ever-steepening spiral. Unemployment in Canada was only 4.2 per cent in 1929. (Compare this with a rate of 7.3 per cent in June 2004). By 1933, it had risen to 26.6 per cent — and that figure excluded agricultural workers. In the same period, per capita income dropped forty-eight per cent.

All of this was only exacerbated in the West, where drought was turning Canada's bread basket into a northern Sahara. The drought actually started in 1928 and lasted ten years. Topsoil became so dry that it simply blew away, drifting like snow, filling wells, closing roads, burying buildings. In high winds, it formed great yellow-gray walls of dust that moved relentlessly across the landscape — summer blizzards that blotted out the sun.

Hot summers and dry winters made perfect conditions for another plague: grasshoppers. In 1933 and 1934, they appeared in biblical numbers, devouring everything in their path.

> I was travelling toward CPR Napinka [Saskatchewan] … and we ran into a plague of grasshoppers. Those in the Bible never had it worse. Millions of 'em, smashing and splashing against the coach … I was wearing glasses and I noticed they were fogging up. I couldn't see and I took them off and there was oil on them. Now, this is the funny part. I didn't catch on right off, but that oil was the mist from the juices of thousands of grasshoppers which the train's wheels was crushing and sending up as spray. I wouldn't have believed it. Grasshopper oil mist, penetrating right into the car, and it was all over everything, ruining ladies' dresses, well, everything.
>
> "The Splash of Hopper Juice"
> Barry Broadfoot's *Ten Lost Years*

When winter finally came, there was still no relief. In many places on the prairies, the winter of 1935–36 was the coldest on record, with temperatures regularly reaching -40°C and lower. The final snow of the year fell in June, and was followed by the hottest summer ever experienced in Western Canada. On

July 11th, 1936 the temperature in Winnipeg reached 42.2°C (108 F); in Brandon, 43.3 (110 F) — records that, global warming or not, still stand. Weather, as Pierre Berton wrote, had become the enemy.

> I could walk, say in August, when you couldn't have grown Russian thistle in a creek bed, I could go about ten feet beyond the house fence and pick up a clod of dirt as big as this fist. I'd lay it on my hand and you could see the wind picking at it. Pick, pick, pick. Something awful about it. The dry dust would just float away, like smoke. ... If I tightened my grip ... then it would blow faster and right before your eyes in a few minutes that hunk of dry dirt would just blow away, even to the bits of dust which collected in the wrinkles of your hand. I used to say the wind would polish your hand shiny if you left it out long enough. You've got to understand, this was no roaring wind. It was just a wind, blowing all the time, steady as a rock.
>
> That dirt that blew off my hand, that wasn't dirt, mister. That was my land, and it was going south into Montana, or north up toward Regina or east or west and it was never coming back. The land just blew away.
>
> "A Hot Sucking Wind"
> Barry Broadfoot's *Ten Lost Years*

In these conditions, farming became practically impossible in many areas of the West. For the relatively few who managed to harvest anything, wheat that had sold for $1.24 a bushel in 1929 was fetching forty cents or less by 1932 — below the cost of production. Cattle that didn't die of starvation froze to death in the ferocious winter cold. Farms were simply abandoned and small towns died as rural people began to join the tens of thousands of urban unemployed who were already riding the rails in search of work.

To call the government response to these conditions ineffective is a massive understatement. The new Prime Minister, R. B. Bennett, had been elected in 1930, just as the depth of the economic pit into which the Western world was sinking was becoming clear. Independently wealthy, Bennett had been the law partner of Senator James Lougheed (whose grandson, Peter, would become Premier of Alberta) before winning the Conservative leadership, so his economic views were what J.K. Galbraith has called "conventional wisdom"; he believed that business cycles are a natural part of the capitalist system, and interfering with them causes more suffering than letting them run their course.

The main concern of Bennett's government, at least early in its mandate, was international credibility, which, in practical terms, meant meeting its railroad

and war debt payments before anything else. Since fiscally responsible governments of the period did not run deficits, it followed that, as revenue continued to
fall, taxes had to be raised — as usual, for workers rather than corporations —
and spending had to be cut.

This was an approach that, however brutal the short-term pain for the
working and middle classes, had always resulted in long-term gain for governments
and their business elite backers — the fruit of the conventional wisdom. This
time, however, the Depression economy proved immune to belt tightening, and
the pressure to provide relief money for the unemployed mounted relentlessly.

The discussions among the three levels of government about who would
pay will be depressingly familiar to anyone who read this morning's newspaper.
The federal government, frantic to balance the budget, insisted that relief was a
provincial affair. The provinces were equally insistent that the primary responsibility
lay at the municipal level, where, since revenue was most directly affected by failing
businesses, there really was no money. While they argued, the lines at soup kitchens
and churches kept getting longer.

Bennett and Mackenzie King, when he returned to power in 1935, were
forced to establish and maintain a relief program, known derisively as "the dole"
for its overwhelming inadequacy. But even after the money became available, there
were still problems. As hard as it might be to believe, looking back from the "welfare"
state of the twenty-first century, there were many people in 1930s Canada who
would rather starve — literally — than accept the stigma of a government handout.

Of course, since many of the bureaucrats administering the program
agreed that only someone too lazy to work would go on relief, actually getting
any money was made as difficult and demeaning as possible. After you'd exhausted
your life savings, sold everything that wasn't nailed down and proven it to the
proper authorities, an inspector would arrive to search your home, just in case
you were hiding anything of value. Only then would you receive the pittance that
would keep you and your family alive.

Since the biggest unemployment problems were in the cities, all kinds of
schemes were floated to move the problem out of urban areas. Families that had
never even seen a farm animal were encouraged to move to the country to home-
stead, where as one observer noted, they could starve quietly, out of the public eye.

The army set up relief camps in the wilderness where single men were
poorly housed, badly fed and paid twenty cents a day to do nothing particularly
useful. While the camps did make the problem of unemployment less visible for
a couple of years, the only lasting effect was to take a group of ordinary citizens
who were desperate to work, and turn them into potential revolutionaries.

The unemployed could be forgiven for coming to the conclusion that their government wasn't much interested in them or their plight. Their frame of mind wasn't improved when it turned out that, should they find jobs and become taxpayers again, they'd likely face the same indifference.

The report of the Price Spreads Committee, chaired by H.H. Stevens, Bennett's Minister of Trade and Commerce, shocked even people who had assumed that big companies were gouging, as well as ignoring labour regulations, to maintain profit margins. Lowlights included Woolworth's, which declared a $1.8 million profit in 1932 while demanding and getting a ten per cent wage reduction from its employees; Eaton's, which paid seamstresses just over nine cents for a lot of a dozen dresses that sold for $1.59 each, a price 212 times more than cost, and the president of Imperial Tobacco making $25,000 a year plus bonuses, while the average clerk in one of his cigar stores was taking home $11 for a 44.5-hour week.

During the Depression, it was a very brave person who would quit a job over a pay cut or extended hours — something employers understood all too well. As a result, in the restaurant business, eighty-hour weeks at starvation wages weren't uncommon. Women were particularly vulnerable in this regard, as the minimum wage law applied only to them. One company in Toronto was found to have fired all its female employees and replaced them with males, including under-age boys who were paid as little as ten cents an hour.

It should be pointed out, however, that if you had even a modest income and could ignore the breadlines and hoboes at your kitchen door, the '30s were a great time to live in North America. Falling prices meant that you actually had more to spend than before the Crash. How else to explain that from 1929 to 1933, when unemployment increased by 533 per cent and per capita income dropped forty-eight per cent, car registrations only dropped twelve per cent and had completely recovered by 1935?

There was plenty for employed Canadians to spend their money on. Radio was entering its golden age and for many people, owning a receiver was even more important than the aforementioned car. Nineteen thirties radio introduced Jack Benny, Bing Crosby, Bob Hope, Edgar Bergen and Charley McCarthy, Dick Tracy and Superman to a continental audience.

In Canada, the government finally decided that there might actually be something to this radio[1] business — and established the CBC in 1936. Canadian radio stars included the Happy Gang and Don Messer, but the biggest audiences were reserved for sportscaster Foster Hewitt and William "Bible Bill" Aberhardt, who used his fame to build radio audiences bigger than Jack Benny's and to

---

[1] After all, Reginald Fessenden, a Canadian, had been the first person to broadcast voice and music. The date was December 24th, 1906.

become Premier of Alberta in 1935. Meanwhile, in Britain, the BBC took advantage of a 1926 English invention, and began to broadcast wireless with pictures — television — in 1936.

Movies now had sound, and every village and crossroads in North America was rushing to build a theatre so they could see and hear Charley Chaplin and the Marx Brothers, Fred Astaire and Ginger Rogers, Errol Flynn and Douglas Fairbanks, Clark Gable and Katherine Hepburn. The *Wizard of Oz* made Judy Garland a star in 1939 and that same year, people got to experience the American Civil War in living colour, in *Gone With the Wind*. An animated mouse, who had made his debut in 1927's *Steamboat Willie*, was making his creator, Walt Disney, very wealthy. Disney created an entirely new category of entertainment when he released *Snow White*, the world's first full-length animated feature, in 1937.

Despite the Depression, travel was more popular than ever, for those who could afford it. While maritime disasters like the *Titanic* had no effect on ocean voyages, the same can't be said for air travel. Airships, or Zeppelins, as their German inventors called them, offered the same class of luxury as ocean liners and were much faster. But one crash, broadcast live on radio and shown over and over again in movie house newsreels, demonstrated beyond a doubt the power of the new media on the public imagination. The 1937 *Hindenberg* disaster guaranteed that passenger travel would be in planes, and that airships would become blimps — reduced to serving as camera platforms for sporting events.

The biggest sporting event of the decade was the 1936 Olympics, held in Berlin. Adolf Hitler, the German Führer, was determined that the games would demonstrate German superiority to the entire world, and spared no expense on the spectacle. The Germans invented the torch run for these games and Leni Riefenstahl's film, *Olympia*, is probably the most famous sports movie ever made. While Germany did win the most medals, German athletes being anything but amateur, the Master Race was upstaged by a black American runner. Jessie Owens won four gold medals — the 100- and 200-metre sprints, the 4x100-metre relay and the long jump. Not surprisingly, Hitler refused to shake his hand. Of course, Owens' own coaches weren't much better, suggesting that his prowess stemmed from the fact that "the negro is closer to the primitive".

As much as the Germans spent on entertaining the social elite during the Olympics — and it was a lot — the place to be in 1936 for anyone who was anyone was not Berlin, but London. The serious partying had actually started the year before with George V's Silver Jubilee. His death early in 1936 meant a state funeral followed by the passing of the crown to Edward VIII, whose love for a divorced American commoner, Wallis Simpson, meant an abdication and the coronation of George VI, the future Queen Elizabeth's father, in 1937.

BARBARA HANLEY

Canada's First Female Mayor

IT'S A COMMON MISCONCEPTION that Charlotte Whitton was Canada's first female Mayor. That honour actually belongs to Barbara Hanley, who was born Barbara McCallum Smith on March 2, 1882 in Magnetawan, a small farming community south of North Bay.

After graduating from high school, Barbara attended the Normal School in North Bay. In 1908, she moved to Webbwood, Ontario, to teach in their brand new four-room school house. Webbwood was a railroad town, and eligible bachelors included the CPR foreman, Joseph Hanley. They were married on August 27, 1913, and had one child, an adopted daughter named Ella.

Like all women of this era, she was required to leave teaching upon her marriage. But in 1923, when Ella had entered school full time, Hanley ran for and was elected a school trustee, a position she held for the next twelve years.

Her dismay at the way the town of Webbwood handled relief during the Depression led her to run for town council in 1935. As a councillor, she did her best to increase welfare payments to the hardest hit families and also urged her fellow councillors to work at creating jobs. After a year of frustration with council's lack of action, she decided to run for Mayor.

Only 151 property owners voted on January 6, 1936, but eighty-two of them voted for Barbara Hanley and she became Canada's first female Mayor. For the next few days she was an international personality, with newspapers across Canada and the United States writing stories about her, often describing her as "prominent in Northern Ontario education circles". The New York *Sun* included her on its list of fourteen outstanding international women for that year. In interviews with *Chatelaine* and the *Toronto Star*, she made it clear that being a female Mayor was no different then being a male Mayor. "It's the office that counts and not the holder", she said.

Her work on behalf of the citizens of Webbwood occupied her full time. She demanded the council drop the custom of advertising outside the town when positions became vacant. She demanded they look first to the unemployed in Webbwood to fill these vacancies in the town administration. "Some of our smartest men are on relief," she insisted when the male councillors — and they were all male — argued they hadn't done it that way in the past. She also suggested that all members of the council, including the Mayor, give up their salaries for the year in order to purchase Christmas turkeys for the poorer citizens of the town.

She lobbied the provincial government for more money for public works and used it to hire the unemployed for municipal projects. She ran for re-election in 1937, and when success-ful, turned the entire town council into a relief committee. She thought that there had been too much buck-passing between the councillors in her earlier administration and she was deter-mined the town would get as many people back to work as possible, while looking after the remainder as best it could.

Barbara Hanley was re-elected six more times before retiring in 1944. But even out of office, she continued her advocacy of social issues such as old age pensions, retirement homes and family allowance. Canada's first female Mayor died in Sudbury on January 26, 1959. She's buried in the town of Burk's Falls, Ontario.

These glittering affairs with their medieval pomp and ceremony and enormous conspicuous consumption only served to point up how little the Depression had really affected the ruling classes. The same couldn't be said of many others.

> On the day when King George V's body passed through London on its way to Westminster, I happened to be caught for an hour or two in the crowd in Trafalgar Square. It was impossible, looking about one then, not to be struck by the physical degeneracy of modern England. The people surrounding me were not working-class people for the most part; they were the shopkeeper-commercial-traveller type, with a sprinkling of the well-to-do. But what a set they looked! Puny limbs, sickly faces, under the weeping London sky! Hardly a well-built man or a decent-looking woman, and not a fresh complexion any-where. As the King's coffin went by, the men took off their hats, and a friend who was in the crowd at the other side of the Strand said to me afterwards, "The only touch of colour anywhere was the bald heads."
>
> George Orwell
> *The Road To Wigan Pier*, 1937

Such huge gaps in standards of living simply added to the tension and uncertainty the Depression engendered throughout the '30s. But 20/20 hindsight notwithstanding, there was never any chance of revolution in North America or England. In the rest of the world, however, the story was quite different.

◆◆ ❖ ◆◆

> Since I arriv'd with my triumphant host,
> Millions of souls sit on the banks of Styx,
> Waiting the back-return of Charon's boat;
> Hell and Elysium swarm with ghosts of men
> That I have sent from sundry foughten fields
> To spread my fame through hell and up to heaven.
>
> Christopher Marlowe
> *Tamburlaine the Great*, 1590

More than any other decade of the twentieth century, the 1930s was about "isms". In the English speaking world, consumer-based capitalism had become the choice to fill the gap left by the death of Progress. However, as successful as capitalism has turned out to be in economic terms — and this was not obvious during the Depression — as a philosophy of life, it left a lot to be desired. A self-mediated system, capitalism had no moral dimension, no ethical underpinning. It also favoured the individual over the group. These characteristics alone provided something for everyone to hate, regardless of their place on the political spectrum.

In the end, capitalist democracy proved resilient enough, in enough places, to weather the chaos of the post-war world, but just barely. As Eric Hobsbawm points out, there were only ten countries in the world that remained consistently constitutional and non-authoritarian between 1918 and 1945.

With the exception of Switzerland, none of those countries was in continental Europe. There, dealing with the physical devastation of World War I, the destruction of their political systems and the failure of the Versailles Treaty, people were exploring other ideological options.

First out of the gate was Russia. The 1917 revolution, aside from almost changing the outcome of the Great War, scared the bejeezus out of private property owners around the world. Lenin and his band of intellectuals and thugs were actually transforming a Great Power in an attempt to make Marx's predictions come true.

By the 1930s, when it had become fairly obvious that the Soviet brand of communism wasn't going to sell beyond its own borders, the commissars turned their attention to dragging Russia into the twentieth century and exterminating anyone who disagreed with them.

Head exterminator, by virtue of being last man standing in the fight to become successor to Vladimir Ilyich Lenin, who had died in 1924, was Joseph Vissarionovitch Dzhugashvili, better known as Stalin — or "man of steel". In the service of communism and his own paranoia, Stalin became the greatest Asian mass murderer since Tamerlane (or Tamburlaine the Great, as Christopher Marlowe put it), the fourteenth-century iron man of the steppes, who built pyramids from the skulls of his victims.

Of course, Stalin's form of communism had far more to do with power and the cult of personality than Marxist dialectic, the rise of the proletariat or, especially, the withering away of the state. Stalin's Russia in the '30s was a totalitarian paradise where everything and everyone served the state and people who disagreed or just got in the way were purged. This meant a quick show trial followed by a one-way ticket to the gulag or a bullet in the back of the head. One or the other was a fate shared by most of Stalin's Bolshevik colleagues and twenty million, or even more, of his fellow citizens.

Stalin's overall goal, other than becoming a secular god, was the industrialization of Russia before the next war. He and his acolytes proved that miracles are possible — if cost really is no object. Needing food for armies of industrial workers, as well as foreign currency to buy technology that Western countries, despite their misgivings about communism, were only too happy to sell, Stalin decided the state had more need of Kazakh and Ukrainian grain than the children of the farmers who grew it.

The resulting famine had the felicitous side effect of ridding Mother Russia of the kulaks, peasants who clung to the bourgeois notion that they worked for themselves, and thus had resisted the collectivization of agriculture.

The result of this socialist realism approach to governance was industrial output that increased at an astonishing rate — and at least five million dead Ukrainians. By 1933, the posters around Kiev sternly warning survivors that "Eating Dead Children is Barbarism", seemed to be having little effect.

It's instructive that, while the purges, famines, gulags and show trials were, even at the time, pretty clear evidence that Stalin's Russia was anything but a worker's paradise, true believers in the West could still write about the birth of a new civilization. If the belief in Progress had ended, the desperate search for Utopia hadn't.

Communism was not the only "ism" on the rise. West of Russia were even more ambitious thugs who lived, most conspicuously, in Italy and Germany. Both were young nations in which the roots of liberal democracy did not run deep. In fact, much of the elite of both countries — the Catholic Church in Italy and the Prussian aristocracy in Germany among others — were profoundly, committedly reactionary, not withstanding the soaring prose of their new constitutions. So, with little support from the powerful, with the trauma engendered by the war and the flu epidemic, as well as the chaos caused by the return of the armies during a severe recession, the post-war governments in Italy and Germany were vulnerable to revolutionary forces of both the right and left.

◆◆ ❖ ◆◆

The fascist conception of the state is all-embracing, and outside of the state no human or spiritual values can exist, let alone be desirable.

Benito Mussolini

Much of Germany was occupied immediately after the war, which gave the new government there a little breathing space. In Italy, there were eight governments between 1919 and 1922, none of which appeared to have any stomach for opposing Benito Mussolini and his fascist bullies. In fact, Mussolini became

Prime Minister at the invitation of the King, not because of his soon-to-be mythologized March on Rome, but because, by October of 1922, nobody else wanted the job.

Once in power, Mussolini set about creating a new Roman Empire, with himself, Il Duce, filling in for Caesar. Unfortunately for Italians, he modelled himself more on Nero than Marcus Aurelius. It was Mussolini who pioneered many of the techniques and trappings that Hitler later made famous — a rejection of political norms, street violence, mass rallies, grandiose architecture and references to a glorious past that was mostly invention.

Fascism was a uniquely twentieth-century phenomenon — a mass movement, mobilized from the bottom up, which is, as Eric Hobsbawm argues, what set it apart from other reactionary forces like the Catholic Church or various aristocracies. Their rejection of democracy and anything modern, though similar in spirit, was imposed from above in traditional fashion.

Another attribute shared by fascism, reactionary forces and Stalinist communism, was a profound anti-intellectualism, except where technology was concerned — a thug with a gun is always more useful than one without. The fascist version sought to replace actual thought with a mix of hero worship and mysticism designed to keep the rank and file from asking too many pertinent questions. The Italian approach was explained by Giovanni Gentile, Mussolini's court philosopher.

> Often Il Duce, with his profound intuition of fascist psychology, has told us the truth, that we all participate in a sort of mystic sentiment. In such a mystic state of mind we do not form clear and distinct ideas, nor can we put into precise words the things we believe in. But it is in those mystic moments when our soul is enveloped in the penumbra of a new world being born that creative faith germinates in our hearts … The fascist spirit is will, not intellect … Intellectual fascists must not be intellectuals.

Il Duce's "profound intuition" resulted in reduced technological innovation, overpopulation, high infant mortality due to a drop in agricultural production and real wages lower than those of Spain, a country where many peasants were still living in the Bronze Age. Governance seemed remarkably unimportant in a country where the rich stayed rich and the rest were urged to live by the motto, "believe, obey and fight".

This motto — Article 4 in the party constitution — reflects another of the key precepts of fascism: the glorification of violence. As Mussolini put it, "perpetual peace would be impossible and useless. War alone brings all human energies to their highest state of tension, and stamps with the seal of nobility the nations which dare to face it." Under Il Duce, noble Italy would so dare, by bestowing the honour of joining the new Roman Empire on Ethiopia.

Ethiopia, or Abyssinia, as it was known at the time, was selected for two reasons. First, it was the only independent country left in Africa, which lessened the chance of the Duce's legions having to fight anyone with a modern army. But second, and far more important, Ethiopia and Italy had fought before, at Adowa in 1896. The Italian Army had left 10,000 dead on the field, and Mussolini was determined to wash away the stain with Ethiopian blood.

Superior technology rather than military prowess secured the victory, with air raids on non-combatants and poison gas attacks among the favourite weapons. All the while, the rest of the world, assembled at the League of Nations, did nothing. Collective security was stillborn and one might argue, as would the dictator to the north, that democracy was a spent force, destined for the ash heap of history.

> Political parties are inclined to compromises; philosophies, never.
> Political parties even reckon with opponents; philosophies proclaim
> their infallibility.
>
> Adolf Hitler
> *Mein Kampf,* 1925

Germany, straddling east and west, never really embraced the liberal democracy that accompanied industrialization in the rest of northern Europe and North America. So, when the monarchy fell as a result of defeat in WW1, the new regime, known as the Weimar Republic, as well as the German people themselves, had no experience with true representative government.

It's fair to say that the majority of power brokers had no interest in it, either. The army duped the Social Democrats into signing at Versailles, thereby ensuring that the Republic could be blamed for the defeat. Weimar had to deal with a Communist coup attempt in 1919, a right-wing putsch in 1920 and a number of military coups against state governments. The country swarmed with *freikorps*, groups of demobilized soldiers armed by the Reichswehr (the German armed forces) and funded by big business.

Unable to pay the enormous reparations demanded by Versailles on top of its war debt, the government started to print money, which ultimately led to the worst inflation ever recorded. By November 1923, one U.S. dollar would buy you 4,200,000,000,000 marks. The pensions and life savings of the middle and working classes disappeared, as did, not coincidentally, the debts of the Junkers, the large landowners who formed the backbone of the officer corps and big business. Their debt was in Deutschmarks while much of their income was in dollars, francs or pounds. For millions of Germans, this was the last straw. Democracy was destroying the Vaterland! Something must be done!

The Weimar Republic actually lasted until January 30, 1933, which is the day Adolf Hitler became Chancellor of Germany and the Third Reich was born. A lowly corporal during the Great War, Hitler had come to public attention in 1923 while leading the abortive Beer Hall Putsch in Munich. In jail afterwards, he wrote his manifesto, *Mein Kampf*, and when he was released, he, his National Socialist or Nazi Party and his "Brown Shirt" enforcers, began their inexorable rise to power, using and elaborating the techniques Mussolini had pioneered in Italy.

Throughout the '30s, governments and business leaders around the world remained convinced that the real threat to world order lay in communism, not fascism. So, while Hitler rearmed Germany, annexed middle Europe and began to implement his Final Solution to the Jewish "problem", Canada and other Western countries consistently soft pedalled extremists on the Right, while demonstrating an almost pathological fear of the Left. After all, the argument went, the methods employed by Herr Hitler, Signore Mussolini and their followers may be somewhat brutish, but they do make the trains run on time.

Although Canadian Nazis (there were actually three separate parties based in Winnipeg, Toronto and Québec) actually got a photo spread in *Life Magazine* in 1938, there were never any brownshirts on the European scale in Canada. This didn't stop communists and other activists on the Left from arguing that the government used the RCMP in a Nazi-like fashion to interrupt meetings and break strikes. And there were plenty of the latter. Between 1930 and 1939, there were 1,410 strikes and lockouts across Canada, as workers began to protest that the government wasn't inclined to do much about the conditions they were enduring.

It has to be said that many of these stoppages were organized by the Worker's Unity League, a front for the Communist Party of Canada. The party itself was illegal until 1936 under Section 98 of the Criminal Code, which had been rushed through Parliament after the Winnipeg General Strike of 1919. Section 98 made it against the law to advocate "governmental, industrial or economic change within Canada by the use of force, violence or physical injury to persons or property, or by threats of such injury". In practice, Section 98 was a very effective tool in suppressing dissent, because it could be, and sometimes was, interpreted as making it illegal to even talk about political change.

But while Section 98 had a chilling effect on the activities of the Left, it couldn't stop them entirely. Conditions were too bad, and government policies too clearly insufficient. The communists themselves were not a political force in Canada because, like their doctrinaire cousins in Europe, they had no interest in the political process or even democracy itself. Thus the role of organizing a political alternative fell to a group of progressive farmers, industrial workers and academics who made very strange bedfellows, but who managed to create something most observers thought impossible.

During her early years in the House of Commons, Agnes Macphail had become a friend of James Shaver Woodsworth (better known as "J.S."). Woodsworth had been elected as an Independent Labour member from Winnipeg and Macphail greatly admired the stands he took on behalf of the less fortunate. Many Canadians believed that the representatives of labour were socialists — this was certainly true in Woodsworth's case, though social justice didn't necessarily equal socialism — and since Macphail didn't see herself as a socialist, this is probably the reason she didn't formally join them at this time.

Perhaps her major area of disagreement with Woodsworth was his support for the Liberals. Throughout their history the socialists, later the CCF and still later the NDP, have often entered coalitions with the Liberals in order to stop the Tories. Macphail felt this to be a betrayal of those who elected her as an independent thinker, not a representative of the established parties. She often voted with the socialists — sometimes in opposition to other members of the United Farmers — but never on issues of coalition. However, she had a deep friendship with Woodsworth and later with his daughter, Grace MacInnis. These friendships would eventually draw her into membership in the Canadian Co-operative Federation, or CCF.

Her move to the left began as early as 1924, when she formally broke with the Progressive caucus. Shortly thereafter, she and nine other former Progressives began to meet with members of the Labour Party, becoming known as the Ginger Group.

Then in 1925, she visited a coal mining town in Cape Breton and discovered that poverty wasn't limited to farm families. She returned to Parliament to give a scathing speech on the conditions of the people in Glace Bay. She was criticized by her opponents for not touring the mine offices and meeting with the owners, preferring instead to visit the homes of the workers. And so her reputation as an advocate for the downtrodden was secured and she was drawn even closer to the Labour Party.

Like most Canadians, Macphail was deeply affected by the Depression. The conditions endured by farmers and all other working Canadians were, in her mind, unconscionable, and she insisted that Bennett's government must respond. The government, in the meantime, was becoming increasingly disturbed at the anger and frustration of the people, often expressed in boisterous public meetings. Bennett used the full force of the law and banned such public demonstrations. Macphail herself was prevented from speaking at one such meeting.

This kind of hysteria led to violence. The RCMP shot and killed three men during a strike at a coal mine near Estevan in 1931. That same year, eight communists from Toronto were convicted under Section 98, and their leader, Tim Buck, was the subject of what appears to have been an officially condoned assassination attempt by guards at Kingston Penitentiary. Deportation of non-citizens even suspected of encouraging civil disobedience became commonplace. Incidents like these led Macphail to believe a new political order was necessary and she wanted to be a part of it. The Ginger Group was revived and members of the Labour Party, Progressives, United Farmers and left wing academics worked to find common ground.

At about the same time, the United Farmers of Ontario organized a demonstration in Ottawa. Four thousand people, including many from Québec, gathered on Parliament Hill. The Prime Minister refused to meet with them directly, grudgingly agreeing to see a small delegation while ignoring the main assembly. The crowd was ready to riot, but at Macphail's urging, cooler heads prevailed.

However, this demonstration prevented her from attending a meeting in Calgary where the Ginger Group and the League for Social Reconstruction — a group of academics guided by Fred Underhill of the University of Toronto and Frank Scott of McGill — put together a movement in principle. They also gave themselves a name: the Co-operative Commonwealth Federation.

This early CCF movement faced enormous problems which made the development of cohesive policies very difficult. Some members, mainly the Progressives, were farmers, opposed to high tariffs that prevented them from buying cheaper equipment in the U.S. Others, members of the Labour Party, had close links with the socialist movements (though real communists were not invited to join), and were in favour of high tariffs, which tended to keep wages up. What bound them together was a focus on social justice issues. For the most part, members still saw themselves as a loose political movement on the model of the United Farmers. It was when they decided to become a political party, with the discipline required in such an organization, that the inherent political differences once again became an impediment.

However, Macphail persuaded the United Farmers of Ontario to affiliate itself with this new movement, although the UFO was to maintain its separate identity. But she couldn't keep them from internal dissention. When the Ontario Farmers arrived at the founding convention of the CCF in Regina in July of 1933, the divisions were clearly drawn.

A compromise was reached on the floor of the convention allowing this disparate group of farmers, unionists and socialists to forge a new political party, but even Macphail was at odds with much of the debate. She became furious, for example, when addressed as "comrade". She also opposed the request that women have representation by regulation on every committee, believing it smacked of special status. She insisted that the CCF was not a political party, but a federation. For all intents and purposes, however, it was a political party, and her participation was to hurt her in the years to come. She was able to win her election in 1935, but her affiliation with the CCF led to her defeat in the wartime election of 1940.

Despite the depth of the Depression and inability of governments to deal with it, the alternative presented by the CCF in their Regina Manifesto — nationalization of industry, trade unions as partners in management, unemployment insurance and universal health care are among the highlights — failed to excite the electorate. The CCF's 8.8 per cent of the vote yielded only seven seats in the 1935 election, none east of Manitoba. Macphail herself, though re-elected, didn't run for the CCF, preferring to stand as a United Farmers of Ontario/Labour candidate.

The CCF was unable to field a single candidate in the Maritimes, and polled a dismal 0.6 per cent in Québec. It's always an uphill battle for a new party, but in a province like Québec where the ruling élites considered new ideas an abomination and only half the adults were allowed to vote, the task became positively Sisyphean.

$$\cdots \diamondsuit \cdots$$

Women themselves have not really evolved. Created to be the companions of men, women are always, and above all, wives and mothers.
Dorian Commission on the
Civil Rights of Women, 1929

In light of the observation above, it's interesting to note that a "new" party did win a Québec election during the Depression. It was 1936 and the party was the Union Nationale, formed from the old Conservatives and disgruntled refugees from the Liberals, a party that had become staid and uninspiring after forty years in power.

New the Union Nationale may have been; an advocate for change, it was not. The UN prescription for Québec, fully supported by church and business, was ultramontanism, which might be summed up as "Forward to the Past".

Ultramontane literally means "over the mountains", a reference to the power of the Pope in Europe and the rest of the world outside Italy. On matters of faith and morals, the Popes had, in 1870, declared themselves to be infallible.

So, if the Pope said atheistic communism, including socialism, is not to be tolerated, then it wasn't. If the Pope said the role of women is to be wives and mothers and nothing else, then that's what they would be. Pope Pius XI (1922-1939) and his predecessors had indeed said these things, so in Roman Catholic Québec, that's largely how things were.

Popes beginning with Pius IX (1846-1878) had also declared that progress, liberalism and modern civilization, including industrialization and the idea of temporal power administered by a secular state, were "errors" in the eyes of the Church. This worldview coincided with the opinions of many French Canadian nationalists who, considering that virtually all economic power in Québec lay in English and American hands, felt that Catholicism and the traditional agrarian way of life were the only way to achieve "*la survivance*" — the preservation of French culture and language.

> Farming was the natural economy of the people and when you farmed you inevitably communed with the forces of nature and with God. The rural areas were steeped in tradition and were the backbone of the fight for survival of the nation (i.e. the French Canadian people.) By contrast, the cities were the work of 'les autres'. It was a vast impersonal and godless universe, a place full of dangers for one's soul and nationality, an occasion for sins.
>
> Claude Bélanger
> *Québec Nationalism*, 2000

Despite this pressure, by 1920 the Liberals, led by Alexandre Taschereau, had finally begun to industrialize in earnest. Of course, as Québec was a largely agrarian society, there was a shortage of capital inside the province. The Liberals had solved this problem by luring outside investment with extremely laissez-faire policies.

> Taschereau firmly believed that taxes must be kept at the lowest possible level so as not to 'paralyze progress and stop initiative'. The various forms of social legislation must be avoided as much as possible, not only because they increased the financial burden of the taxpayer, but also because they were a form of 'state paternalism' which destroyed the initiative and sense of responsibility of the individual.
>
> Herbert F. Quinn;
> *The Union Nationale:*
> *A Study in Québec Nationalism*, 1963

The result was rapid industrialization, but with control of resources and utilities in private, non-French hands. This meant that the struggle between capital and labour was, if anything, even more bitter in Québec than elsewhere in Canada because the class struggle also became a cultural struggle — virtually all of management was British, English-Canadian or American, and virtually all the workers, French.

Despite this growth in industry, and the urbanization that went with it, the attitudes prevalent in French Canadian society changed very little. On social questions such as the nature of civil liberties or the rights of women, the bishops still had the ear of the politicians, and therefore, the last word.

All in all, Québec between the wars was not a promising place to live for an independent French-Catholic woman of strong views and a political bent. But, then, the Québec Establishment had never encountered anyone quite like Thérèse Casgrain.

Thérèse was born in Montréal on July 10, 1896. Her mother was Blanche MacDonald and her father Sir Rodolphe Forget. She was educated by Les Dames du Sacré Coeur at their convent in Sault-aux-Recollets, a boarding school where she was sent at the age of eight. Separated from her parents from September to June of each year, except for parlour visits on Thursdays and Saturdays and short holidays at Christmas and Easter, she later spoke happily about her experiences with the nuns. During the time she did spend at home, the house was often filled with politicians. Her father was a Conservative Member of Parliament and politics was part of her upbringing.

Thérèse had a great desire to attend university. Her father, however, believed that the role of young women was to marry, raise children and be gracious hostesses. Indeed, when she told her father of her desire to undertake further studies, he told her "to go to the kitchen and see if Cook can teach you something".

Upon graduation from the convent school, she did as her father requested, only to find that the cook considered the kitchen her private domain and wasn't the slightest bit interested in having Thérèse mucking about. She did some travelling, adding Italian to the list of her linguistic skills, and entered society.

She had first encountered Pierre Casgrain at a tea dance when she was fifteen, an age at which she was still considered a child. The two had clearly noticed one another however, for he attended her coming-out party at the Deaf and Dumb Institute in Montréal. Run by the Sisters of Providence, the Annual Debutante Oyster Supper was the institute's major fundraising activity and an important event on Montréal's social calendar. It was important for Thérèse as well, for the following day a bouquet of roses arrived at her home and her courtship with Pierre began.

THÉRÈSE CASGRAIN

Though he was ten years older than she, and though Thérèse was only nineteen when they were married on January 19, 1916, it seems they were an almost perfect match. The union not only produced four children and a deep love and affection; more importantly, it created an abiding respect and encouragement that went both ways. In an era where women were not expected to have a public profile, Pierre Casgrain openly supported his wife in her very political activities.

Madame Casgrain's father, still a Conservative MP during WWI, chose not to run in the 1917 election. Perhaps as a result, Pierre decided to seek nomination in Sir Rodolphe's former constituency of Charlevoix, but as a Liberal, believing as former Prime Minister Wilfrid Laurier did, that conscription was unnecessary. Pierre was elected, though the Liberals failed to form the government, and in January 1918, the Casgrains took up residence in Ottawa. It wasn't until three years later, however, that Thérèse was herself bitten by the political bug.

Nineteen twenty-one marked the first federal election in which most Canadian women could vote. During the campaign, Pierre became seriously ill with pleurisy and was confined to bed. Ernest Lapointe, also a Member of Parliament, was asked to campaign on his behalf and Lapointe, in turn, persuaded Madame Casgrain to address the audience and explain why her husband was unable to attend. It was Thérèse Casgrain's first political speech and it launched a career that would continue for the next fifty years.

Her first political cause was the right to vote for women in the province of Québec. Though Québec women voted in federal elections beginning in 1921, they were still denied the right to vote provincially. The battle was fought in the province over the next nineteen years, with Thérèse Casgrain always in the front lines.

When the first large delegation, comprising some 400 English- and French-speaking women, went to Québec City on February 9, 1922, Casgrain was among them. The meeting was held in the dining room of the National Assembly. Casgrain, with acerbic wit, pointed out to Premier Taschereau that it was a fitting room to have been chosen, since it was so close to the kitchen where women were generally relegated. Taschereau responded that "if the women of Québec ever get the right to vote, they will not have got it from me."

The Catholic Church was equally opposed to the idea. Cardinal Bégin, Archbishop of Québec, in a letter to the Archbishop of Seleucie, also in Québec, wrote:

> The entry of women into politics, even by merely voting, would be a misfortune for our province. Nothing justifies it, neither the natural law nor the good of society. The Roman authorities endorse our views, which are those of the entire episcopacy. Our teachers in their instruction should take account of this directive.

Despite her devotion to the Catholic Church, Casgrain found herself at odds with it on this issue; her disagreements with church teachings would increase over the years.

In February 1927, Victor Marchand, with the encouragement of many Québec women, introduced a bill in the National Assembly to grant the vote to women. It was defeated by a vote of fifty-one to thirteen, despite the fact that women by then had the vote in every other province. This was followed by fourteen court appearances — all unsuccessful — in an attempt to get the judiciary to do what the legislature would not. It was decided that a single voice must represent women across the province and Casgrain became the President of La Ligue des Droits de la Femme, the League of Women's Rights, a position she would hold for the next fourteen years.

In 1929, Casgrain again went before the National Assembly to present amendments to the Civil Code that would enhance the equality of women. She demanded that the code be changed in the following ways: a married woman should be given control over her own wages, women should be able to become the guardians of their own children and married women should be protected from the squandering of the family property by their husbands, particularly when that property was brought to the marriage by the wife.

Taschereau appointed a commission to study the civil code in light of the league's proposals. Despite recommendations that women should be represented on the commission, four male members, all members of the judiciary, were selected. The chair was Mr. Justice Dorion. The Dorion Commission was presented with chapter and verse concerning the inequities of the civil code with respect to women in the province of Québec. Much of it fell on deaf ears.

However, some successes were achieved. When the commission tabled its report in 1930, it included sixteen amendments to the civil code, the most important of which was that the proceeds of personal work of the wife were to be administered solely by the wife. But the commission refused to recommend changes to the law on marital separation.

At this time, it was still the case in Québec that a husband could demand a separation on the basis of his wife's adultery, while a wife could demand separation only if her husband kept his mistress in their common habitation. The commission, while agreeing that adultery was always an injury, stated that the wound to the heart of the wife is not as severe as the wound to the husband and therefore the law should not be changed. Along with most Québec women, Casgrain was thoroughly disappointed. But she wasn't defeated.

Throughout her husband's career as a Member of Parliament, one in which he served as Speaker and as a Secretary of State, she was supportive not only on the campaign trail and in his constituency, but also in the Liberal Party itself. She served for a time as vice-president of the National Federation of Liberal Women. Following World War I, she served on the Minimum Wage Board, but her interests always returned to the needs of women in society.

She recognized that many women, with the luxury of full-time help in their homes, had a great deal of time on their hands. They were discouraged from working outside of the home, universities were reluctant to admit them and families even more unwilling to have them attend. She had noted that in the United States and English Canada many of these women had turned to the Junior League as a means to direct their unused talents and abilities. Along with a group of older women, well known for their charity work, Casgrain helped found the Ligue de la Jeunesse Feminine, The League of Young Women. They decided not to have a chaplain — an act they knew would be controversial.

At this time almost all organizations of French-speaking women in Québec were in some way affiliated with the Catholic church. It was therefore reasonable to expect that the LJF would have a chaplain to provide them with guidance and advice. Casgrain and her colleagues believed they could provide their own guidance and advice and were, therefore, considered quite scandalous in some circles. Their purpose was the promotion of more effective social action and among their works was the establishment of a school for crippled children. However, as they were for the League of Women's Rights, the vote and the ability to practice law were never far from the top of their agenda.

In 1930, Oscar Drouin introduced a new bill to grant the franchise to women and admit them into the legal profession. Once again, it was defeated. Following this vote, Casgrain sent the Premier a bouquet of sixty-three red roses on his birthday. She clearly believed that you keep all avenues of communication open and gracious gestures were never out of place. Of course, she did recall in her memoirs that she had chosen flowers with thorns!

By 1935, the question had been introduced and defeated nine times. Madame Casgrain decided that a new route must be taken. As 1935 was the silver jubilee of King George V, it was decided to petition the king. Ten thousand signatures were gathered and, when the Québec government refused to present it, the League of Women's Rights sent it by private courier. It's not clear whether it ever reached the king, but the publicity garnered from the collection of signatures and the media coverage of the refusal of the government to send it, certainly made the effort worthwhile.

Though Casgrain believed that the vote was essential for equality, it was not the only concern or cause for which she worked. The Depression had a profound effect on her. As she observed the destitution of the people, she grew to believe that Québecers were far too docile. For generations they had accepted the dictates of church and government; reform, she felt, was impossible unless the people were prepared to act.

Her husband Pierre was also concerned at the lack of government action. Along with a number of other more progressive members of the Liberal party, a group calling itself Action Libérale Nationale was formed. Frequently, the meetings took place at the Casgrain home, with most wives playing bridge while the men held their discussions. Thérèse, on the other hand, sat and listened to the men's debates. Premier Taschereau demanded that the group be dissolved, but was ignored.

On July 28, 1934, the manifesto of ALN appeared in the press. It encouraged the development of small business, the opening of new areas of Québec for settlement, assistance to agriculture, and economic control of the province by French Canadians. In the area of social reform it urged the regulation of hours of work, minimum wages, old age pensions (something that had happened in the rest of Canada in 1927) and sickness and disability insurance. It also called for complete reform of the electoral system. Along with B.C., Québec was the most gerrymandered province in Canada — Montréal had forty per cent of the population and ten per cent of the seats.

They were bold demands, but the cabinet wasn't listening. Frustrated by its inability to influence the Liberal leadership, the ALN formed a strange alliance. Despite the views of the Casgrains, who believed the ALN should solely be a means of reforming the Liberal Party, it instead affiliated itself with Maurice Duplessis, the Conservative leader, and formed the Union Nationale.

The Liberals won the election of 1935 with forty-eight seats. However, the Union Nationale had elected forty-two members of which twenty-six were from the ALN. Officially, Madame Casgrain was still a Liberal. Her husband, after all, was still the Liberal MP for Charlevoix. But, she was already looking for a new political home. After all, how could she continue to support a party that let one of its MNAs table a bill in the National Assembly prohibiting women from any form of employment other than farming?

Things only got worse when Duplessis managed to bring down the Liberals in less than a year, and then won seventy-six of ninety seats in the ensuing election. Despite its pledges to implement the ALN reform platform, the Union Nationale turned out to be even more reactionary than the Liberals.

For instance, when Mackenzie King repealed Section 98 in 1936, Duplessis passed an "Act Respecting Communistic Propaganda", which

> was supposedly aimed at preventing the spread of Communism and the printing of Communist literature. The Attorney-General of the

province was given the authority, upon evidence that satisfied him and without any court action, to close or padlock any premises suspected of being used to spread the doctrines of Communism. ... The danger of Communism should not obscure the main significance of the 'Padlock Law' — that it gave the provincial government an arbitrary power which infringed basic liberties and that it was a denial of due process of law. A member of the Canadian Bar Association reported in 1937 that 'possibly it is under such laws as this that in other lands the homes of respectable and law-abiding citizens are ransacked simply because their owners do not wear a brown or a black shirt.'

John Saywell
How Are We Governed, 1977

The ultimate chilling power of the Padlock Law was that, in practice, even to object to it, was to break it. Not that there was much objection. Such was the revulsion toward communists in Québec that, outside of the target groups and a few intellectuals, this "loi de cadenas" enjoyed almost universal support.

Given the alternative, someone like Casgrain, who eventually did find a new political home as leader of the Québec CCF — making her the first woman to head a political party in Canada — had little choice but to continue working with the Liberals. Out of power for the first time since 1896, they had replaced Taschereau with the more progressive Adélard Godbout. At the instigation of the Ligue des Droits de la Femme, the Liberals opened their 1938 convention to the participation of women. The female delegates not only proposed compulsory education with free textbooks and a uniform curriculum throughout the province, they also succeeded for the first time in having a resolution passed in support of women's suffrage. Finally, a Québec political party had committed to this essential right for women.

In 1939, Duplessis called a provincial election and the women launched a new publicity campaign. Both the Ligue de Droits de la Femme and the Alliance pour le vote des femmes supported the Liberal Party because of its support for suffrage. The Liberals won the election and Godbout become premier. Constantly reminded by letters, telegrams and visits of his commitment to women, the government indicated in the Speech from the Throne, read on February 20, 1940, that a bill would be introduced giving women the vote. Sixteen days later, the church weighed in.

We are not in favour of female political suffrage because:
1. It is contrary to the unity and authority of the family;

2. It exposes women to all the passions and intrigues of electoralism;

3. In truth it appears to Us that the very large majority of the women of the province do not want it, and

4. The social, economic, hygienic, and other reforms that are brought forward as recommendations for granting the suffrage to women could just as well be achieved though the influence of female organizations outside politics.

When Madame Casgrain met with Godbout, he appeared stunned and actually discussed the possibility of resigning. After their meeting, however, he'd obviously recovered. He contacted Cardinal Villeneuve and informed him he was prepared to request that the Lieutenant Governor ask T.D. Bouchard, a man of strong anti-clerical views, to form a government. Since it was clear that a government led by M. Bouchard would not be likely to act in the best interests of the church in Québec, the cardinal relented and the objections of the church were withdrawn.

The bill was finally introduced on April 9, 1940 and, after considerable debate, was passed nine days later. The vote was sixty-nine to nine. In those days, Québec still had an Upper House and so the bill went there. These stalwarts made one last attempt to block the bill, but failed. On April 25, 1940, the women of Québec finally had the right to vote in provincial elections. Madame Casgrain was in the Assembly as Royal Assent was given to the bill to which she had committed nineteen years of her life.

❖

The political momentum that Casgrain and her colleagues generated during the 1930s was not matched outside Québec. In 1935, Agnes Macphail was finally joined in the House of Commons by another woman. But since Martha Black's reason for running was to hold the seat for her husband during his illness, it's hard to claim new ground was being broken.

Even in wider society, arguments that seemed to have been laid to rest by the success of first-wave feminists and the independence of their flapper daughters, were rearing their ugly heads once more. "Working women are just marking time till they get married." "Women are actually harming children by taking jobs men need to support their families." "Women are biologically unsuited to working in (insert industry here)."

There's no doubt that the economic pressures of the 1930s were partly to blame. With so many men out of work, it became harder to justify hiring female employees, and so much easier to let them go if you hadn't agreed with the idea in the first place. It's equally true that some people saw the Depression as an opportunity to turn the clock back. For instance, despite the existence by this time of female university professors, doctors, lawyers — even a few engineers — the question of how or whether women should be educated was being raised again, even in reputable publications.

> The teacher will not fail to notice certain differences in the reactions of his mixed classes to the various tasks that he gives them. He [though the vast majority of teachers were women] will see the girl, patiently, laboriously, painstakingly spend hour after hour imitating some work of art or committing to memory something that someone else has written. He will see her dismiss as silly a simple experiment in physics, or an exercise in geometry, learning by rote 'mercuric chloride' and 'potassium iodide' and admiring the pretty colours, while her brother sneaks into the laboratory, heats a little potassium chlorate with sulphur and sugar and hopes for the best.
>
> A. M. Pratt
> *Maclean's*, October 1934

> We have far too many courses in history and economics, in social and natural science. They could all be abridged without any cultural or scientific loss. If a student wanted to become an expert in any field, that would be her privilege in the graduate school.
> A department of cosmetics and beauty culture should be created. Women use makeup. Why not do it as artistically as possible? A woman who graduated with competent knowledge of how to take care of her face and hair and how to make herself as attractive as possible would take out into life with her training that would, it seems to me, be as advantageous as her grasp of geo-synclines. There should be a professor of style. Every effort would be made to show girls how to dress as becomingly as possible.
>
> Willis Ballinger
> *The Forum*, 1932

One male bastion where women were beginning to make serious inroads was sports. The modern Olympic Games, which had begun in 1896, finally admitted female track and field athletes in 1928. Canada soon had new sports heroines, as sprinters Florence Bell, Myrtle Cook, Bobbie Rosenfeld and Ethel Catherwood, who also won the high jump, took the gold in the 400-metre relay. Not surprisingly, there were men who still preferred heroes, thank you very much.

> … take the Galloping Ace, I mean you take her; I'll take a cup of coffee. She can run the 100 yards in better than 11 seconds, as indeed can many a schoolboy. Not that there's any sense in comparing men and women on an athletic basis, for there isn't any comparison. But Ace is a big, lanky, flat-chested girl with as much sex appeal as grandmother's old sewing machine that we stuck up in the back of the attic. The sewing machine and Ace both run well. So what?"
>
> Elmer Ferguson
> *Maclean's*, August 1, 1938

In writing about the "Galloping Ace", Ferguson was probably referring to Stella Walsh, the Polish sprinter who took the gold medal in the 100 metres at the 1932 Olympics, beating Canadian champion Hilda Strike in a photo-finish. Interestingly, when an autopsy was performed on Ms. Walsh after her murder in 1980, she turned out to be a man. Despite this revelation, Hilda Strike still has not been awarded her gold medal.

◆◆ ❖ ◆◆

The Depression and Mackenzie King's careful focus on domestic politics, particularly relations with Québec, ensured that world peace and humanitarian causes were not major policy concerns. So activism in these areas throughout the 1920s and '30s was left largely to women. In this regard, one of the main instruments was the League of Nations Society; Agnes Macphail and Thérèse Casgrain were active members, as was Nellie McClung. The national organization was chaired by a well-connected mother of eight who also happened to be Canada's first female Senator. Her name was Cairine Wilson.

Cairine Reay Mackay was born on February 4, 1885 in Montréal. Her parents were Jane Baptist, daughter of a lumber baron from Trois Rivières, and Robert Mackay, a wealthy Montréal businessman and Liberal Senator.[2] This was a family where young ladies were expected to be much more than decorative. Her parents believed firmly that privilege carried with it responsibility and this responsibility went beyond the family.

---

[2] Though there have been many father-son combinations to serve in the Senate, Cairine Wilson and co-author Sharon Carstairs are, thus far, members of the only two father-daughter combinations. To date, a mother and daughter have never been named to the Upper Chamber.

Cairine Wilson

In 1909, at the age of twenty-four, Cairine married Norman Wilson. The marriage was presumed to be a love match since she gave up a life of travel and activity in a large city in order to settle with her husband in the small hamlet of Rockland, where Norman was the secretary treasurer of a lumber firm. She certainly described her marriage as having brought her great happiness. Norman Wilson soon added politics to his resumé, thus seeming to fulfill Sir Wilfred Laurier's prediction to the young Cairine. On visits to the family home in her childhood, the Prime Minister would state that someday she would be the wife of a great politician. In fact, though Norman served several terms as the Member of Parliament for the constituency of Russell County, it was Cairine who would become the famous politician.

In the early years of her marriage, Wilson was busy with child rearing — there were eight children, five girls and three boys, born during the first sixteen years. For the first ten years she devoted herself entirely to this quickly growing brood and to running the family homes in Montréal, Ottawa and St. Andrews-by-the-Sea in New Brunswick. After the birth of her fifth child, her doctor informed her that he had never seen anyone deteriorate mentally as much as she! It was the jolt Wilson needed to become active in her community once again and she never looked back.

Her first outlet for this newly regained energy was politics. Wilson had been raised in a Liberal family where the philosophies of British Prime Minister William Gladstone and reformer John Bright were topics of frequent discussion and debate, and Christian duty was taken for granted. Her family connections with Sir Wilfrid Laurier, considered by Wilson to be Canada's greatest national statesman, and to Mackenzie King, led her to look to politics for enrichment and contribution.

She became an active party worker in 1921 and was recognized not only for her efficiency in electoral organization, but as someone committed to expanding the role of women in politics. She was instrumental in establishing the Young Liberals, in which her older daughters became active. She founded the Eastern Ontario Liberal Women's Association, the Ontario Women's Liberal Club and the National Federation of Liberal Women. This federation gave encouragement to women candidates, insisted on roles for women in the policy making processes of the party and generally brought the party rules in line with the new suffrage granted to women in Canada.

Politics was not the only venue for her activities — in fact, she was at a committee meeting of the YWCA when her appointment to the Senate was announced. However, the interest to which she ascribed her greatest public passion was the League of Nations Society of Canada and its derivative the

Canadian National Committee for Refugees.

Immediately after World War I there was great public interest, particularly among women, in seeing that organizations be put in place to ensure there would be no more wars. These organizations also had the goal of providing aid to those who had been made refugees during the conflict. Wilson believed that women needed to take up the cause of world peace, because war grew from men's greed and ambition and only women could change history's direction. She even took on armament manufacturers, accusing them of making war for profit's sake.

It should therefore have been no great surprise that she was chosen to be the first female Senator. She had a long history of contribution to the Liberal Party, was wealthy and not particularly radical. These were the established criteria of the day for male appointments, so why would they be any different for the first female appointee?

For Canadian women struggling for political equality, it would have seemed just that one of the "Famous Five" should have received the appointment. Senator Wilson herself was reported to have stated "You are going to make me the most hated woman in Canada" when Prime Minister Mackenzie King first proposed the idea of her appointment. She quickly let it be known that she was indebted to the five women from Alberta who made it possible for her to be in the chamber and to all other Canadian women who had struggled to achieve more equality for women.

The Senate was an institution where Wilson could continue the peace and refugee work to which she had dedicated herself prior to her appointment. This has always been a characteristic of the Senate, and one which receives little comment. Senators, freed from the necessity of supporting popular causes because they do not have to face the electorate, can frequently bring new support and insight to significant matters affecting our nation.

Wilson used her position in the Senate to openly campaign for causes like world peace. Because of the inability of the League of Nations to deal with the crises confronting it, the League of Nations Society fell into disrepute and was eventually labeled as an extreme pacifist group. Though Wilson didn't agree with the label, she knew that another outlet for her work had to be found.

The establishment of the Canadian National Committee on Refugees in 1938 became her outlet. As chair, she helped lobby the federal government for policy changes which would enable a larger number of Jewish refugees to enter Canada. She also tried to educate the government and the Canadian people about the atrocities going on in Nazi Germany, but was dismayed at the blatant racism of both the public and some members of government.

She tried to change the focus to children in the hope that the maternal instinct of Canadian women could be mobilized to at least help these younger refugees. However, Canadians were more sympathetic to the British children desirous of evacuation to Canada, a movement organized in part by Charlotte Whitton. Senator Wilson was not opposed to helping these children, but understood that the needs of Jewish children were much greater. Sadly, her pleas fell on deaf ears. In all, Canada admitted only 100 Jewish orphans, all of whom were already in Britain.

◆◆ ❖ ◆◆

On the evening of October 30, 1938, radio listeners across North America were shocked to discover that the United States was under attack. The first wave had landed at Grover's Mill, New Jersey, and was rapidly advancing on New York. The Army and Air Force were helpless in the face of the enemy's overwhelming military superiority. Panic began to spread along the American east coast as the extent of the defeat became clear …

Even if you're a student of military history, you're probably unfamiliar with this particular campaign. That's because what people were listening to that evening was a radio play presented by Orson Welles' Mercury Theater of the Air, and the invaders were fictitious beings from Mars.

But, if the invasion was fiction, the panic was not. It says something about the *zeitgeist* of the times that thousands of otherwise rational people actually believed the Earth had been invaded by Martians and conquered in, as it turned out, about fifty minutes.

By the end of 1938, the international situation was such that, even in America, the Western country farthest removed from possible war, it was easy to convince people that something bad was about to happen. It was the ninth year of the Depression. The brief rally of 1937 had ended in another market crash, when, John Maynard Keynes [3] be damned, governments immediately cut spending. Even the end of the drought wasn't enough to turn things around. In Europe, Hitler seemed the personification of Leni Riefenstahl's other famous film, *Triumph of the Will*.

Hitler had reoccupied the Rhineland while the Western democracies dithered about Ethiopia. He absorbed Austria in the spring of 1938 with barely a ripple of international comment. He then turned his attention to Czechoslovakia, demanding the Sudetenland, a German-speaking province. This is where democratic

---

[3] Keynes was an English economist whose theory of full employment dominated government policy into the 1970s.

diplomacy reached its nadir, with England and France abandoning the Czechs to their fate at Munich, and then celebrating the result as a great victory — "peace in our time", in Prime Minister Neville Chamberlain's famous phrase.

Finally, in the spring of 1939, Hitler went too far. At Munich, England and France had guaranteed the borders of what was left of Czechoslovakia. Hitler occupied it anyway, calculating that the West would, again, do nothing. He was right, but the public outcry was so loud and sustained that Western governments finally had to admit the obvious — Hitler wasn't going to stop. Anyone who'd read *Mein Kampf* knew what the next target would be. On March 31st, England and France pledged to defend Poland in case of attack, thereby guaranteeing there'd be war.

In the end, what the appeasement of the 1930s demonstrated was that the leaders of England, France, Canada and the United States never fully grasped the fundamental change that World War I had wrought, and the Depression distilled. That the Great Game of the twentieth century would be about ideology rather than empire was something that Hitler, Mussolini and Stalin, for all their expansionist ambitions, understood all too well. But dark as the days to come would be, they did open doors for Canadian women.

Is it only under the stress of war that we are ready to admit
that the person who does the job best is the person best fitted for it?
Must we always treat women like Kipling's common soldier?

It's vamp and slut and gold-digger,
And 'Polly, you're a liar!'
But it's 'Thank you, Mary Atkins'
When the guns begin to fire.

Dorothy Sayers
Are Women Human? 1946

It's always interesting to discover how the impossible can be transformed into the necessary when priorities change. On September 10, 1939, when Canada declared war on Germany, there were still more than 300,000 men on the unemployment rolls. By the fall of 1942, demand from the military and war industries had reduced unemployment to near zero and showed no sign of slowing down. As was the case during the Great War, there was only one way to expand the labour pool.

On September 8, 1942, all single women aged twenty to twenty-four were ordered to register under the National Selective Service (NSS) program. By the summer of 1943, this had been extended to all single women from sixteen to sixty-five, and by 1944, to married women, first for part-time work and later full-time. It should be pointed out that not all of these women were being trained as Wanda the Welder — many of them were being asked to fill the low-paying service jobs that the Wandas had left.

Regardless of the importance of the work being done — which included everything from handling explosives to building aircraft   women were universally paid less than men doing the same job. Of course, it was unpatriotic to point this out.

In addition to working in war industries, ("the women behind the men behind the guns", was one recruiting slogan) women took a large role in the administration of the Home Front. The Associate Director of the NSS was Fraudena Eaton, and her Assistant in Charge of Day Nurseries was Charlotte Whitton's companion, Margaret Grier. Elsie MacGill, Canada's first female electrical engineer, ended up in charge of production of the Hurricane fighter — an indication, given the attitudes of the time, of her truly remarkable ability.

In an admission that many of these women already had full-time jobs — mother, wife, homemaker — the government set aside money for public daycare; a first in Canada. Only three provinces agreed to the idea, however, and less than fifty centres were actually opened, mostly in Ontario. The ones in Montréal were established despite being attacked in the Catholic press as a communist plot aimed at undermining the family. The government also tacitly admitted that its pre-war tax structure had been designed to keep married women out of the work force — admitted it, by changing it. The $750 limit on spousal income was eliminated, so that a wife's employment would not cost the family at tax time.

By the end of 1944, there were over a million women in the labour force and 45,000 in the armed forces, up by well over twenty-five per cent since war's beginning and much more widely distributed across the economy than during WWI. But any hope that this female demonstration of competence in traditional male areas would lead to an upsurge in demands for greater equality, and or a change in societal attitudes, were soon dashed.

The vast majority of women weren't working for feminist ideals or even, as it turned out, from patriotic fervour. Surveys showed that only ten per cent of working women had taken a job out of a sense of national duty. No, most women were working because, after ten years of Depression, they and their families needed the money.

Though support for the war effort was practically universal outside Québec, there were no white feather campaigns during WWII, and no white-scarved pilots gallantly saluting their vanquished foes. The war against Germany, and later Japan, was a grim necessity, an industrial process and, for many, an opportunity. But, with few exceptions, it was never a crusade. Poland was not, and never could have been, Brave Little Belgium, because the idealism of 1914 no longer existed. By war's end, more than 30,000,000 civilian dead, including the 6,000,000 of the Holocaust, had proven that beyond the shadow of a doubt. Somewhere, Tamerlane was smiling.

Unlike the aftermath of the Great War, there was no chance of the losing side spinning the result of WWII. Germany was in ruins. Japan had experienced the future of warfare at Hiroshima and Nagasaki and wanted nothing more to do with it. Italy had ended up on the winning side through the brutal, through poetically just, expedient of putting a bullet through Il Duce's brain, hanging his body from a meat hook and declaring the whole Fascist experiment had been a mistake.

On the winning side, it was immediately clear that the population had had enough of war and sacrifice, as well. Even before the Japanese surrender ended the conflict, British Prime Minister Winston Churchill, the man regarded as the saviour of England, lost an election to an unapologetically socialist Labour party. In the United States, Roosevelt was dead, and his party won the 1948 election only by the skin of its teeth, before being dispatched in 1952.

Canadians, on the other hand, decided to stay with the feller what brung 'em, and elected Mackenzie King for the fifth time. Canada was now the fourth-largest military power in the world, with the third-largest navy, but that status didn't last long. Now that the job was done, most of the boys had no more interest in being in the military than the cabinet had in financing it. This, of course, faced the government with the same problem as in 1918 — what were a million servicemen going to do when they got home?

Well, they were going to take the majority of the jobs women had been doing in their absence, of course. As Dorise Neilson, Canada's third female MP sarcastically put it, "well girls, you've done a nice job; you looked very cute in your overalls, and we appreciate what you've done for us, but, just run along. Go home. We can get along without you very easily."

To encourage them to go home, the daycare program was terminated, the limit on spousal earnings was reinstated, this time set at $250, and married women were once more invited to leave the federal public service.

Among the post-WWII female unemployed was Thérèse Casgrain. Pierre had accepted an appointment to the Québec Supreme Court, so, in 1944, Thérèse decided to run to replace him in Charlevoix.

The seat had first been held by her father and then by Pierre for forty years, but, in the end, it made no difference. She and three men ran as Independent Liberals, no one daring to run on a straight Liberal ticket for fear of being tarred as a conscriptionist. None was endorsed by the provincial party. As a result, it couldn't have been much of a surprise that the Conservative candidate won the seat. It was this lack of support from Godbout's Liberals that ultimately led to Casgrain's break with the party, and eventual rise to leadership of the Québec CCF in 1956. In the meantime, electoral defeat, made especially bitter by the almost total lack of support from women in the riding, did nothing to stifle her activism.

In an attempt to head off the economic crisis he feared the end of the war would bring and under pressure from the CCF, which by 1945 held twenty-eight seats in Parliament, Mackenzie King had started to propose social reform legislation as early as 1943. One of these proposals, which became law in July 1945, proposed establishing a family allowance of five to eight dollars per month per child.

The payment was to be made to mothers, who, it was believed, would be more willing to see the benefits used directly for their children. Even in English Canada many opposed the legislation, thinking it a sop to Québec families that were traditionally larger.

Duplessis opposed the legislation for two reasons. He was automatically against any direct payments made by the federal government to Québecers. And he was against a payment to mothers, believing the father to be the head of the family, and therefore the decision-maker on finances and expenditures.

Madame Casgrain was informed at an Ottawa dinner party that Québec mothers were in danger of being treated differently than those in the rest of Canada. She went to see the federal Minister of Justice, Louis St. Laurent, for an explanation. He informed her that the Civil Code of Québec still declared women to be minors and therefore the payment would have to made to the fathers. This was clearly not acceptable.

On her return to Montréal, she established a committee that immediately began to lobby the government through the media and bombard it with letters and telegrams. During the battle, she heard directly from Mackenzie King. He told her he would settle the matter on his return from the founding meeting of the United Nations.

On Dominion Day, July 1, 1945, the cheques were sent to mothers throughout English Canada. Québec mothers did receive their cheques — some three weeks later. One can only assume the delay was to change the recipient from father to mother. Casgrain had won again.

The CCF, however, never won a seat in Québec under Casgrain's leadership. She resigned in 1957 and went on to found the Québec branch of the Voice of Women, an organization dedicated to world peace, and the Fédération des femmes du Québec, which focused its efforts on coordinating women's groups throughout the province. Pierre Trudeau appointed her to the Senate in 1970 and she continued to lead an active public life until her death in 1981.

She wouldn't have had it any other way. As she said near the end of her life, "I am no longer satisfied to be an old lady sitting serenely on the sidelines. I see myself now as a black sheep with grey hair, a rebel who shudders at the thought of any kind of a fence, gilded or otherwise, and who wants active involvement." Thérèse Casgrain was quite a wonderful rebel.

In Ontario, meanwhile, Agnes Macphail had won a seat in the Ontario legislature after her defeat in the 1940 federal election, establishing another first. But for her, it wasn't the same as serving at the federal level. When she lost in 1951, she knew it was the end of her political career.

Canada's first female MP was always a feisty politician. She stood firm for causes in which she believed, even when they were unpopular. She had male and female friends across the country, mostly associated with the work to which she devoted herself, but she had no close ties to her family and no family of her own. She sacrificed a great deal for her constituents and her country, and handled the burden of being first and only with great aplomb. For that alone, she's earned our deepest respect. Agnes Macphail died at the age of sixty-three on February 13, 1954.

In 1950, France recognized Cairine Wilson's work on behalf of Jewish refugee children in Europe by making her a Knight of the Legion of Honour, the country's highest award. It's ironic that, personally, she was dismayed at how little she had been able to accomplish. That disappointment didn't stop her from continuing her refugee work even after the Second World War. She chaired the Senate Standing Committee on Immigration and Labour from 1946-48.

Senator Wilson lived by her principles. She was a Christian woman who believed in the virtues of hard work and devotion to those less fortunate. She made her mark, quietly and with dignity. In doing so, she made it much easier for other women to be appointed to the Senate. By the time of her death in 1962, she'd put to rest the fears of those who might have said, "well, we tried one once and look what happened." Cairine Wilson was very, very good at what she did and women have benefited tremendously from her legacy.

◆◆ ❖ ◆◆

Though WWII officially ended on September 2, 1945, the actual date is, of course, August 6th. It's fitting, somehow, that a war that caused the greatest destruction since the mythical Flood should end with the obliteration of a largely civilian target by nuclear whirlwind.

In the three decades after 1914, there were only ten years when at least one of the major powers wasn't involved in a war. Now, one branch of totalitarianism had been defeated, and with the semifinals over, capitalism and communism faced each other uneasily across the ruins of Europe.

Soviet Russia's alliance with the West had been just as much a marriage of convenience as its non-aggression pact with Germany, and all the major players knew it. So, the fight to be the last ism standing was already taking shape — it was a matter of when, not if. The United States, and, briefly, only the United States possessed the means to destroy any army, any city, any country. So, what to do? Nuke Russia and end it now, before the Commies could get the bomb (which was Churchill's solution[4])? Or, step back and enjoy the fruits of a hard-won victory, while hoping to contain Stalin's ambitions?

The West opted for curtain number two, with mixed results. The explosion of material wealth following World War II was truly astonishing — but Russia had the bomb by 1949. It's safe to assume that most people found eating lunches under their desks (the *Duck and Cover* program) took a bit of the lustre off the post-war economic boom. As for women … Well, let's just say that Elmer Ferguson[5] and the Pope can't have been all that unhappy with the way things were going.

---

[4] Trachtenberg, Marc, "A Wasting Asset", *International Security*, Vol. 13, Issue 3 (Winter 1988-89), pp. 9-10
[5] See page 121

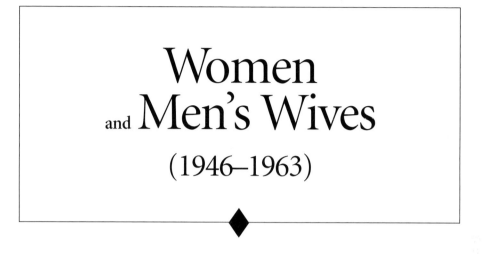

Women
and Men's Wives

(1946–1963)

◆

Scene: 1956

Stage dimly lit. Just off centre, SL, a classic psychiatrist's couch. An ashtray on a stand is beside it. Just off centre, SR, a chair. A woman, dressed as Mrs. Anderson from *Father Knows Best* enters, SL. She stops halfway to centre.

Thank you for seeing me, John. I… *(he's interrupted her. She glances at the couch)* Oh. Yes. Of course.

She lies down on the couch, awkwardly trying to smooth down the full skirt. Suddenly, she sits up and looks sharply at the chair.

John, before you go into Freud mode, just stop for a second. I majored in psychology, so I understand the game. I just needed someone to talk to, all right? All right?

She takes a cigarette from a pack in her purse, lights it and lies down again.

I … Where do I begin? With Dave, I suppose. I do love him, you know. Really I do. But, it's … penis envy, I'm sure dear old Sigmund would say. And, he'd be half right. I do envy Dave — truly envy him.

He's so … fulfilled. He's doing important work and he loves it. He just loves it. When he comes home, he glows. Every night. Glows.

He just can't wait to tell me what problems he's solved or what insight he's had. And then, he asks me what I did today, and, I want to … I want to scream, John. Because I did nothing! *(bitter)* Nothing!!

Summa cum laude at McGill. Dean's honour list. And where did it get me? Playing nanny in a three-bedroom bungalow built on a cow pasture. Reading article after article telling me I'm the luckiest, most blessed woman ever to walk the face of the Earth.

How is that possible, John? How?

Hell, I understand everything he tells me. Everything! I could run his department better than he could ever imagine. Except, there's not one of them who'd work for a woman.

And, who can blame them? *(voice changes to "blonde")* Why am I at university? Well, that's where the best husbands are, silly. Mmmm, fourth year and still haven't found Mr. Right. What's wrong with you? Too picky? I mean, you're not exactly Marilyn Monroe.

So, when I met Dave, I turned down grad school. Out of gratitude. I mean, it's a zero sum game, John. Career or family. Either or. Celibate shrill or model mother. No wait, I take that back. There are actually three choices. We mustn't forget slut. I chose Dave.

I'm dying, John. Here *(taps her temple)* It's just drying up and blowing away. I try to keep up. I really do. I force myself to read — articles on science or Suez or Diefenbaker's chances at the convention. But all the while, there's this little voice in the back of my head saying, "why are you wasting your time on this? The children will be home soon and you haven't even begun to think about dinner."

I can't go on like this, John. I just can't. I'll go mad. *(He says something. She reacts)*

I'm not hysterical! *(She sits up)* My prescription? Well, I ran out of mother's little helper last week, no thanks to you. *(petulant now, she stubs out the cigarette)* Hell of a time for a convention.

Even as she crushes the cigarette, she's watching the chair intently — he's writing her prescription for meprobamate, an early antidepressant known popularly as Miltowns, after Milton Berle.

It's not just anxiety, John. *(her hand is out.)* I know it's not. But, I can't … By myself, I can't …

She mimes taking the slip of paper, then stands and puts the prescription in her purse. She stares at the chair, but is finally forced to look away.

No. Nothing else. Thank you, John. *(Head down, she exits SL)*

	POLITICAL	SOCIAL / TECHNOLOGY
	T I M E L I N E	
1946	• First United Nations session • Nuremberg verdicts • Canadians no longer British subjects • Juan Peron becomes President of Argentina • **Federal-provincial daycare program ended**	• Doctor Benjamin Spock writes: *The Common Sense Book of Baby and Child Care* • Chester F. Carlson invents first photocopier
1947	• Canadian Supreme Court becomes final authority • India and Pakistan independent • First Canadian peacekeeping mission (Korea) • Tax law amended to encourage women to quit working	• Carbon dating invented • *Diary of Anne Frank* published • Sound barrier broken • First audio tape recorder developed • Dead Sea scrolls found • **Baby Boom officially begins**
1948	• Mahatma Gandhi assassinated • Marshall Plan (U.S.); war recovery program • Organization of American States founded • Founding of Israel • First Arab/Israeli War • Declaration of Human Rights (UN) • Harry S. Truman elected U.S. President • Mackenzie King resigns, Louis St. Laurent becomes PM	• Transistor radio patented • Laurence Olivier performs in *Hamlet* (film) • Mount Palomar observatory opens • Birth of Prince Charles • Canada's Roger Lemelin (Cdn) publishes *Les Plouffes*, definitive Québecois radio play • Kinsey report (on males) • First LP released • Olympics resume in London and St. Moritz, Switz.
1949	• Chinese revolution (Mao) • **Nancy Hodges (BC) is first female Speaker in Commonwealth** • Newfoundland joins Canada • NATO formed • St Laurent elected in a landslide • Apartheid established in South Africa • West Germany created • U.S.S.R. tests A bomb	• Samba in vogue • AVRO tests first jetliner in North America • George Orwell writes *1984* • Donald O.Hebb (Cdn) writes *The Organization of Behaviour*
1950	• Korean War begins • China occupies Tibet • McCarthy hearings begin (U.S.) • **Ellen Fairclough elected** • Red River Flood • Mackenzie King dies • First American advisors in Vietnam	• World population passes two billion • World's largest city is London at 8.3M • Antihistamines become available • George Bernard Shaw dies • Charles Schultz comic strip *Peanuts* debuts

POLITICAL	SOCIAL / TECHNOLOGY	
TIMELINE		
• Churchill re-elected PM in England • **Charlotte Whitton becomes Mayor of Ottawa** • Old Age Security (Cda) available to citizens at 70	• **No treaty rights for Aboriginal women** **married to whites (repealed 1985)** • Radiation treatment for cancer (Toronto) • J.D. Salinger: writes *Catcher in the Rye* • Heart-lung machine • Colour TV released (US) • Penicillin generally available	**1951**
• Vincent Massey becomes first Canadian Gov. Gen. • George VI dies, Elizabeth becomes Queen • U.S. explodes H bomb; U.K., the A bomb • **Women allowed to serve on juries in MB** • **Equal pay for women in ON, co-sponsored by** **Agnes Macphail** • Dwight D. Eisenhower becomes U.S. President • **Charlotte Whitton re-elected Mayor of Ottawa**	• First jet passenger service (BOAC) London-Rome • *The Mousetrap* opens in London (still running) • Eva Peron dies • Fashion designer Christian Dior gains fame • First Canadian TV stations • *Hockey Night in Canada* begins • Summer Olympics in Helsinki; Winter Games in Oslo	**1952**
• Stalin dies • Korean War ends • Winston Churchill knighted • U.S.S.R. explodes H bomb • St. Laurent re-elected Canadian PM • **Margaret Aitken, Sybil Bennet, Ann Shipley elected** • **First female Senator from Quebec**	• Structure of DNA described (double helix) • Mount Everest conquered • Ian Fleming writes *Casino Royale* (first Bond book) • Arthur Miller writes *The Crucible* • CinemaScope introduced • **Kinsey Report (female)** • First link between smoking and cancer revealed • First shopping mall in Canada	**1953**
• U.S. Supreme Court bans school segregation • Senator McCarthy censured in U.S. • **Charlotte Whitton re-elected Mayor**	• Tennesee Williams writes *Cat on a Hot Tin Roof* • *On the Waterfront* makes Marlon Brando a star • Four-minute mile broken in Victoria • **The Pill invented (not legal in Canada untill 1969)** • First Canadian subway opens in Toronto	**1954**
• Churchill resigns, Peron overthrown • **Unwed mothers, deserted wives get support (ON)** • **Married women allowed in public service** • Warsaw Pact • **Fairclough proposes equal pay legislation**	• Rock Around the Clock: first rock hit • Merger creates TD bank • Montreal hockey riot • Disneyland opens • First optical fibres produced	**1955**
• Second Arab-Israeli War • Suez Crisis, Lester B. Pearson mediates • Hungarian uprising • Eisenhower re-elected U.S. President • **Equal pay for federal employees**	• Martin Luther King becomes civil rights leader • First Elvis Presley hit • Springhill mine disaster No. II (No. I in 1891) • Grace Kelly marries Prince Rainier of Monaco • Transatlantic cable telephone laid • Olympics in Melbourne and Cortina d'Ampezzo, Italy	**1956**

	POLITICAL	SOCIAL / TECHNOLOGY
	T I M E L I N E	
1957	• European Common Market begins • U.K. explodes H bomb • Sputnik launched – Space Age begins • John George Diefenbaker elected Canadian PM • **Fairclough becomes first female cabinet minister**	• *Front Page Challenge* begins on CBC • Canada Council established • Dr. Suess writes *The Cat in the Hat* • The Beat generation (beatniks)
1958	• Diefenbaker re-elected PM • Khrushchev in power in U.S.S.R. • **Margaret Meagher first female ambassador** • **Charlotte Whitton runs federally and loses** • Charles De Gaulle becomes President of France	• First transatlantic jet service (British Airways) • AVRO Arrow's first flight, cancelled following year • NASA established • Leon Uris writes *Exodus*
1959	• Fidel Castro takes power in Cuba • Tamils assassinate Sri Lankan President • St. Lawrence Seaway opens	• Microchip invented • *Lady Chatterley's Lover* banned in U.S. • First photos from far side of moon (U.S.S.R.)
1960	• Kennedy/Nixon debates • Congo independent from Belgium • John F. Kennedy elected U.S. President • French explode A bomb • **Charlotte Whitton re-elected Mayor of Ottawa** • Treaty Aboriginal Canadians given the vote	• William L. Shirer writes *Rise and Fall of Third Reich* • TIROS launched: first weather satellite • Echo 1 launched: first communications satellite • Druggist arrested for selling condoms (Toronto) • First pacemaker • Olympics in Rome (summer) and Squaw Valley, U.S.
1961	• Bay of Pigs crisis in Cuba • Berlin Wall is built • South Africa tossed from Commonwealth • **Judy Lamarsh elected in Canadian by-election** • **Five female MPs now in House of Commons** • **Claire Kirkland-Casgrain is first Québec MNA**	• Joseph Heller writes *Catch 22* • Cosmonaut Yuri Gagarin is first man in space • Canadian population passes 18M • CUSO formed • First James Bond movie: *Dr. No*
1962	• Last execution in Canada • China/India war • **Charlotte Whitton re-elected Mayor of Ottawa** • **Claire Kirkland-Casgrain is first Quebec Minister**	• John Glenn orbits the Earth • **Rachel Carson writes *Silent Spring*** • Thalidomide introduced to treat morning sickness; results in birth defects
1963	• Kennedy assassinated • Nuclear test ban treaty (atmosphere) • **Fairclough defeated** • **Judy LaMarsh is first Liberal cabinet minister** • First FLQ bombs in Quebec	• **Valentina Tereshkova (U.S.S.R.) is first woman in space** • Quasars discovered

Women
and Men's Wives
(1946–1963)

The structures of a society — modes of life, social relations, norms and values — are not reversed overnight. The structures of power may change quickly: new men arrive, new routes of social ascent opened, new bases of command created. Yet such dramatic overturns are largely a circulation of elites. Societal structures change much more slowly, especially habits, customs and established, traditional ways. Our fascination with the apocalypse blinds us to the mundane: the relations of exchange, economic and social; the character of work and occupations; the nature of family life. Even when a political order is toppled by war or revolution, the task of building a new societal order is a long and difficult one, and must necessarily use the bricks of the old order. If the intention of any science is to show us the structures of reality underlying appearances, then we have to understand that the time-dimensions of social change are much slower, and the processes more complex than the dramaturgic mode of the apocalyptic vision, religious or revolutionary, would have us believe.

Daniel Bell
The Cultural Contradictions
of Capitalism

While we've argued that the nineteenth century ended with World War I, that observation in no way suggests that a coherent new age began immediately after 1918. In fact, political chaos and incoherence were the order of the day throughout the 1920s, '30s and '40s. But beneath the economic disasters and practically constant war, social attitudes and behaviours, especially with regard to women, were barely changing at all. Agnes Macphail, sitting alone in Parliament all those years, serves as a constant reminder of this reality.

By any measurement, the period from the late '40s to the early '60s was the absolute nadir for twentieth-century feminism, especially in the political arena. The country had nine female MPs between 1945 and 1963 — an improvement to be sure, but still a hollow victory, as it brought the grand total for the century to a depressing thirteen. And, like the first three post-war prime ministers, most of these women had been born before WWI — the last echoes of the first wave.

Now, one would think that, no matter how glacial the pace of social change, the rising tide of transformation in practically every other area of human endeavour would eventually weaken this inertia — especially since, by the 1950s, the tide was becoming a torrent.

We learned that the basic stuff of the universe was not an atom, but rather, a strange particle called a quark. And that the continents were not permanent features of the Earth's surface, but islands adrift on a sea of magma, as mutable as the maps of fading empires.

The Leakeys showed us that our tenure on earth must be measured in millions of years, not thousands; and Watson and Crick, Wilkins and Franklin, that the code of our entire physical being was written in the double helix of DNA. With Sputnik, we proved that the heavens themselves were not beyond our grasp. And the discovery of the Dead Sea Scrolls suggested that the hand of man was at least as important as the hand of God in choosing what was in the Bible.

Alfred Kinsey demonstrated that, far from being the chaste, faithful, churchgoing folk of popular tradition, both men and women, at least in private, were in fact intensely sexual beings who had desires and acted on them, social conventions notwithstanding.

Another new world was dawning. For better or worse, it was only a matter of time before social structures began to show the effects of these seismic shifts. And yet our reaction to the biggest change of all, the discovery of a power with which we could utterly destroy ourselves and leave the planet to the cockroaches, seemed to impell us to do just the opposite.

The Bomb, and the fact that the godless Communists had it, hung like a pall over the 1950s. Air-raid sirens were erected in cities that had never imagined an aerial attack, air-raid drills became a normal part of school life and terms like fallout shelter and radiation sickness entered everyday speech.

If the fear of nuclear annihilation in a world that seemed less comprehensible by the day wasn't enough to give the idea of change unpleasant connotations, the association was magnified by the fact that an entire generation was

MURIEL MCQUEEN FERGUSSON

Canada's First Female Speaker of the Senate

"YOU CANNOT HAVE THE POSITION because the competition is only open to men." So Muriel McQueen Fergusson was told in 1947 when she applied to be the regional director of Family Allowances and Social Security. She immediately contacted all the women she knew. They proceeded to bombard the Minister of Health and Welfare, the Honourable Paul Martin, Sr. with letters and calls until the rules were changed. Henceforth women, and therefore Muriel, were eligible for the job.

Muriel McQueen was born on May 26,1899 in Shediac, New Brunswick, a small community about twenty-five kilometres from Moncton. She was educated at the Shediac High School, Mount Allison Ladies College and Mount Allison University, graduating with a B.A. in 1921. She wanted to study law, but her parents argued it would be a waste of time since she was engaged to be married and therefore, they believed, would never practise. She persevered, however, reading law at her father's firm and was admitted to the bar of New Brunswick in 1925.

She married Aubrey Fergusson in 1926. They had no children, but during the first ten years of her marriage she led a typical young married woman's life. However, in 1936 she began to assume Aubrey's practice, due to his failing health. Her clients believed that she was getting advice from him and she never disabused them.

In 1943, Muriel left her legal practice to become the assistant enforcement counsel for the Wartime Prices and Trade Board in St. John; the only woman in Canada to hold this position. During her tenure at Family Allowances and Social Security (1947–53), she became the first alderwoman in the City of Fredericton and then, the first female Deputy Mayor. But this promising career in civic politics came to an end on May 15, 1953 when she was appointed to the Senate by Prime Minister Louis St. Laurent.

Her career in the Senate over the next twenty-two years was a continuous record of advocacy for the poor, the underprivileged and women. In addition to her work on prison reform, she was instrumental in modernizing the divorce laws, particularly in extending grounds beyond adultery to include cruelty, desertion and marriage breakdown. She was an active member of the Senate Committee on Poverty, and counted her contribution to its report to be one of her finest achievements. No one was surprised, therefore, when Pierre Elliott Trudeau made her the first female Speaker in the history of Parliament, appointing her Speaker of the Senate on December 14, 1972.

Though her appointment to the Senate was for life, Senator Fergusson chose to resign on May 23, 1975 at the age of seventy-six. She'd supported the legislation providing for mandatory retirement at seventy-five, and therefore thought it appropriate to step down. When she returned to Fredericton, the city threw a party in her honour — not a retirement party, but a welcome home party, because they knew she'd continue to lead an active life in the community.

They were right. For many years afterward, she remained a trustee for the Forum of Young Canadians. She was a patron of the Lester B. Pearson College of the Pacific, and lent her name and her efforts to the New Brunswick-based Muriel McQueen Fergusson Foundation on Family Violence. A recent recipient of the foundation's annual award, which recognizes those who work to prevent family violence, is co-author Senator Sharon Carstairs.

In recognition of her many contributions to this country, Muriel McQueen Fergusson was appointed an Officer of the Order of Canada in 1976. She died in Fredericton on April 12, 1997, just short of her ninety-eighth birthday.

simultaneously assuming the responsibilities of parenthood. So, when it came to human relations — social, sexual or otherwise — the parents of the baby boom weren't interested in anything but the tried and the true.

Operating in a self-satisfied political climate and benefiting from an economic boom, these factors not only enhanced the natural resistance to social change — they actually inspired a concerted effort, at least for a time, to turn back the clock. Call it the last gasp of the Old World.

The tone was set at the top. The Prime Minister through most of the '50s was "Uncle" Louis St. Laurent, already sixty-six when he came to power in 1948, and a man even less likely than Mackenzie King to be comfortable with change. Complacently sure that Liberals were the natural party of governance, St. Laurent and his "Minister of Everything", C. D. Howe, saw no reason to rock the boat, and didn't. With the post-war economic boom in full swing, the status quo looked pretty good.

So, the Liberals were happy to wait on the St. Lawrence Seaway (1954) until the Americans decided to participate, and let American entrepreneurs try to build the Trans-Canada pipeline (1956). True, they did establish CBC Television (1952), though mainly because Howe wanted to promote the electronics industry, and only created the Canada Council (1957) because a couple of Maritime millionaires had had the good grace to die and provide the money through estate taxes.

Meanwhile, business maintained a very cozy relationship with the Liberals. Though the explosion in demand for consumer goods meant that substantial return on investment was practically guaranteed, there were still public "incentives" involved in the locating of any new plant. And the government, in the form of the RCMP, could always be depended upon in case of an industrial dispute.

During the 1946 Stelco strike in Hamilton, even the Governor General got into the act — authorizing the temporary nationalization of the steel industry and thus making striking an offence against the government [1]. The union eventually won, probably because jail didn't seem like much of a threat to a veteran who was working a fifty-five hour week for thirty-four cents an hour, got no vacations and had a better chance of being killed on the job than during the war.

This relationship with government is just one of the tools corporations used to achieve the stability they too craved. Because, although they talked a great deal about entrepreneurship and how there can be no reward without risk, what the captains of industry were actually doing was quite the opposite, as J. K. Galbraith points out in *The Affluent Society*:

---

[1] Canada was still being governed under the War Time Measures Act in 1946.

The riskiness of the modern corporate life is, in fact, the harmless conceit of the modern corporate executive, and that is why it is vigorously proclaimed. Precisely because he leads a careful life, the executive is moved to identify himself with the dashing entrepreneur of economic literature … Nothing has been more central to the purpose of General Motors or General Electric than to encompass and eliminate the perils to which the one-time entrepreneur was presumed to be subject.

The rapid expansion of both the private sector and the civil service, where the post-war ban on hiring married women was finally discontinued in 1955, meant there was plenty of opportunity for these attitudes to permeate downward through every organization. They didn't meet much resistance.

Anyone who has ever watched television has a vivid mental image of the post-war years. It was Pleasantville — a golden time when the economy boomed and everyone lived in cozy, detached homes in the suburbs. Dad drove to work in the family's late model car while mom, spotless apron always in place, effortlessly managed home and children.

After dinner, the family would gather in the living room to watch their favourite programs before retiring for a good night's sleep. The only problems seemed to be on the order of that broken window from Billy's baseball game, or what Jane was going to wear to the prom. It was as though the world had returned to an imagined pre-1914, only with electric appliances and indoor plumbing.

This picture is traditionally presented as evidence of tremendous progress for the middle class and those aspiring to it. The war had been won, the Depression was a fading memory, the good times were now a permanent feature of life, and things were only going to keep getting better. And, if things getting better was defined by a new, improved car model being rolled out every fall during the World Series, well, is this a great country, or what?

Of course, this picture represents an alternate universe, as do most things presented on television or in the movies. But it does contain a few small nods to reality — chief among them the fact that it's almost completely static.

The growing prosperity of both the middle class and unionized workers resulted in a much larger segment of the population with a serious investment in the status quo. So, as a world where nothing changed, Pleasantville met the aspirations of its inhabitants perfectly.

There was a turtle by the name of Bert
And Bert the turtle was very alert.
When danger threatened him he never got hurt,
He knew just what to do.
He'd duck and cover. Duck and cover.
He did what we all must learn to do.
You and you and you and you.
Duck and cover.

Civil Defense Film, 1950

At a superficial level, one reason people yearned for safety and stability was pretty obvious — there really was a threat. Regardless of your politics, the Bomb itself was a horrifying reality, as were its aircraft and missile delivery systems. No one who has seen photographs of Hiroshima or Nagasaki can keep from imagining what their own town would look like, smell like, be like, after such an attack; from imagining how they would feel if all that was left of their children were shadows seared into concrete.

One of the great morale boosters for Allied soldiers during WWII (Britons excepted, of course), was that, at least their families were safe. No more. If the death of Progress had introduced the idea that the world is a dangerous place, the advent of the Bomb confirmed it — now, no one was safe.

The nuclear threat was pervasive in popular culture. Best sellers like Nevil Shute's *On the Beach* dealt with the aftermath of global nuclear war and most science fiction writers of the period treated World War III as future fact rather than possibility (Robert Heinlein and E. E. "Doc" Smith are representative). Monster films like *Godzilla, The Blob* and *Them* gloried in showing what might be possible in a nuclear world. Even *Spiderman* was originally created by a radioactive arachnid.

Of course, the sense of threat didn't emanate from the Bomb alone. For business leaders, as well as the military and political elite who were planning to win a nuclear war (we might lose 20,000,000 people, but we'll bomb our enemies back to the Stone Age), the real threat came from Communism. If this sounds familiar, this time, there were reasonable grounds for fearing communists.

After Stalin orchestrated a brutal coup in Czechoslovakia 1948 and followed up with the blockade of Berlin, it became apparent to Western leaders that the Soviet Union had become a serious adversary. They responded with the formation of NATO in 1949, only to be upstaged when the Soviets exploded their first A-Bomb and Mao's Communists took over China the same year.

But if the international response was fairly rational, domestically, it was a little closer to the xenophobia that had led to the internment of citizens of

Japanese descent during WWII. So, we had Joe McCarthy spreading paranoia in the U.S. by accusing everyone and his or her dog of being a Communist, and Igor Gouzenko assuring Canadians that the really dangerous Commies were, in fact, here in the Great White North.

The world situation continued to provide little relief. The division of the world into East and West had begun before the war ended, and every regional conflict thereafter had Cold War overtones — Korea, the Arab-Israeli wars, Suez, the Hungarian uprising, the Berlin Wall, the Cuban Missile Crisis. This last was the most heart-stopping of all, with the United States literally hours away from declaring war on the Soviet Union after the Russians started building nuclear missile bases on the Caribbean island. Happily, by this time, Stalin was safely in his grave. Otherwise, the outcome might have been somewhat different.

Given this situation, Communists inevitably took their place in the pantheon of popular villainry. Many books and films of this period were straightforward potboilers, with the always vaguely Eastern European commies filling the roles occupied by gangsters in the '30s and Nazis in the '40s. But the message about the threat of and fight against Communism appeared everywhere. Even a Biblical epic like *The Ten Commandments*, where the script transforms the Egyptians into thinly-veiled Commissars, and Charlton Heston plays Moses like a cross between Dwight Eisenhower and Jesus Christ, wasn't immune.

Backyard bomb shelters became the latest real estate selling feature, and, while no one can say exactly why people started seeing UFOs, it's instructive that the sightings began in the late '40s, followed quickly by tales of alien abduction and government conspiracies. Plainly, people were spooked, and in times of uncertainty, astute people will pull in their horns a bit. The threat of a subpoena from Joe McCarthy or a visit from the RCMP (the Padlock Law was still in effect) was enough to dissuade many from exhibiting behaviour or expressing opinions that might make them stand out. But while the perceived need to be careful would result in a certain amount of conformity, it still doesn't explain the legions of Man in the Grey Flannel Suit and Betty Crocker clones that characterized the middle class during this period. There's still more to this story.

◆◆ ❖ ◆◆

By social ethic, I mean that contemporary body of thought
that makes morally legitimate the pressures of society against the
individual … I think the gist can be paraphrased thus: Man exists as

a unit of society. Of himself, he is isolated, meaningless; only as he collaborates with others does he become worthwhile, for by sublimating himself in the group, he helps produce a whole that is greater than the sum of its parts.

William H. Whyte
The Organization Man, 1956

All we're trying to do is take that mindset that, 'I'm the most important thing and everything else revolves around me,' and switch it right around into, 'I'm an important part of this team. This team needs me, and I need this team, so that we can go and perform the mission that's been given to us.'[2]

MCpl. Tony Hayes
Basic Training Instructor, CAF

In the 1950s, North America was in the midst of one of the greatest sociological experiments ever conducted. During WWII, over a million Canadians served in the armed forces, and almost all of them underwent the sort of "re-programming" Master Corporal Hayes describes above. That includes as much as half the entire male cohort that would become the fathers of the baby boom. These are people who grew up during the Depression, were exposed to the trauma of war and then returned home to the cultural milieu already described.

If Whyte and many others — including David Riesman in *The Lonely Crowd* (1950) — are to be believed, it appears that the Depression and war experience, with basic training as a significant component, helped to convert an entire generation into the people that Riesman called "other directed" and Whyte termed "organization men". People for whom "the group was the centre of creativity and belongingness is the ultimate need of the individual." In other words, people who aspired to Pleasantville.

This prevailing social ethic was so strong that companies were able, with little complaint, to transfer young white-collar workers — those occupying the lower rungs of the corporate ladder — and their families on a regular basis. That meant these couples had to work even harder to belong, both within the organization and in each new neighbourhood to which they moved.

The economic boom ensured that most of these people, when they arrived in a new city, could afford better than an apartment for their first home. But fifteen years of depression and war had rendered the existing housing stock completely inadequate to the demand created by this burgeoning middle class.

---

2   Quoted in *Into the Blue*, DND recruiting video, 2003.

In a capitalist society, when a great mass of people are all looking for the same thing and has money to spend, there will always be suppliers who are only too happy to deliver it. Hence, the suburb, with its four styles of bungalow, each surrounded by its own lawn; a standardized bit of paradise far from the noise, dirt and crime of the city.

It was the perfect place to raise the children who were beginning to arrive in unheard of numbers — a bastion where security and predictability came from the knowledge that you were surrounded by people just like you — familiar backgrounds, same socioeconomic status, shared view of the world.

Without sounding too much like Herbert Spencer, one could argue that this was yet another environment that tended to select for a mental pattern already present in the population — the desire to fit in, to belong — and make it the norm. So, out in suburbia, if you were anything less than a full participant in communal life — the barbecues, the afternoon bridge games, the school meetings and church activities, dinner parties with the boss and his wife — you were met with subtle but effective peer pressure that soon saw you back on the straight and narrow. Or, as Johnnie Cochrane (O.J. Simpson's celebrated lawyer) might have put it, "to be part of the norm, you must conform".

Of course, part of the norm — a large part of it — involved the role of women. If the stability and predictability these people prized so highly can be paraphrased as a place for everybody and everybody in their place, then the suburbia in the 1950s clearly had no place for so quirky an individualist as a feminist.

◆◆ ❖ ◆◆

Probably no man has ever taken the trouble to imagine how strange his life would appear to himself if it were unrelentingly assessed in terms of his maleness; if everything he wore, said or did had to be justified by reference to female approval; if he were required to regard himself, day in day out, not as a member of society but as a virile member of society. If the centre of his dress consciousness were the cod-piece, his education directed to making him a spirited lover and meek paterfamilias; his interests held to be natural only in so far as they were sexual. If he were vexed by continual advice how to add a rough, male touch to his typewriting, how to be learned without losing his masculine appeal, how to combine chemical research with seduction, how to play bridge without incurring the suspicion of impotence …

"Professor Bract, although a distinguished botanist, is not in any way an unmanly man. He has, in fact, a wife and seven children.

TILLY JEAN ROLSTON
Canada's First Female Cabinet Minister with a Portfolio

THE PUBLIC WAS NOT IN ATTENDANCE at the meeting of the City of Vancouver Parks Board. Tilly Rolston didn't smoke in public, but now she was free to do so and lit up. She didn't just light the cigarette, however. The veil on her hat also caught fire. Just as the chairman of the board threw a glass of water at her to douse the fire, a newspaper reporter walked into the room. She begged him not to write about the incident. He refused, saying it was simply too good a story to pass up. It was to be the first of a long list of stories that would give Tilly Rolston her well-deserved fame in the province of British Columbia. As she grew in experience, she wasn't the least bit reluctant to have the media write about her.

Tilly Jean Cameron was born in Vancouver on February 23, 1887. She attended public schools, spent two years at Vancouver College, which was to become the University of British Columbia, and then earned her teaching certificate at the Vancouver Normal School.

Her teaching career ended in 1909 when she married Fred Rolston. Tilly had very strong views about working mothers with young families. For example, she publically opposed the establishment of government nursery schools, stating, "It is an insult to suggest that a mother can't bring up her own children better than some parched, dried up, cultured academician."

Though she didn't work outside the home while her children were small, Rolston did engage in the volunteer work that paved the way for her political career. She was a member of the B.C. Council of Women when her presentation to the 1938 Rowell-Sirois Royal Commission on Federal Provincial Relations brought her to public attention for the first time. By 1939 she was sitting on the Vancouver Parks Board and in 1941, she entered the B.C. Legislature, winning a Vancouver area seat for the Progressive Conservatives.

Between 1943 and 1950, she was chair of the legislature's Standing Committee on Social Welfare. She investigated lack of employment opportunities for the able-bodied unemployed and ordered studies on drug addiction and juvenile delinquency, as well as old age and mother's pensions. She was also an advocate for family courts and free maternity benefits.

Frustrated at being kept out of cabinet, she left the Tories in 1951 to sit as an independent, then joined the Social Credit Party in 1952 on the promise of a cabinet post. When Social Credit won the '52 election and she was returned with the biggest plurality in the province, W.A.C. Bennett kept his promise and made her Minister of Education. She was sworn in on August 2, 1952, the first woman in the British Commonwealth to be given a department to run.

Bennett's minority government fell after little more than a year, largely over the "Rolston Formula", her plan for the redistribution of education financing. In the ensuing provincial election, the Social Credit won a majority, and though Rolston lost her seat, Premier Bennett chose to keep her in the cabinet, this despite the fact that during the campaign, it had become clear she was seriously ill.

She died of cancer on October 12, 1953, and as a Minister, became the first woman in British Columbia to receive a state funeral. But, as was often the case with Tilly Jean Rolston, the eulogist didn't get the last word. A few days after her funeral, the B.C. Legislature passed her final bill — The Equal Pay For Women Act. It was a fitting tribute.

Tall and burly, the hands with which he handles his delicate specimens are as gnarled and powerful as those of a Canadian lumberjack, and when I swilled beer with him in his laboratory, he bawled his conclusions at me in a strong, gruff voice that implemented the promise of his swaggering moustache."

Dorothy Sayers
Unpopular Opinions, 1946

Much satire has been inspired by the classic image of the 1950s housewife — house-proud, child-oriented, deferential — a woman who is her role, and seems thrilled about it. Of course, the best satire works because it builds from a solid base of truth, and there's more than a little of that here.

The pressure to conform began for young women long before they arrived at the split level on the secluded cul-de-sac. They felt it in home ec class at school. They were bombarded by it in magazine articles and the new mass medium of television. They saw it in movies. And when they got to university, they were confronted by courses like Mate Selection, Adjustment to Marriage and Education for Family Living:

> Let us even suggest for a moment that a woman's mind, in general, may lack those qualities which produce great books, great works of art. Perhaps her more subjective, sentimental nature stands in the way of masterpieces. At a glance, say, literary achievement might force one to concede that Jane Austens and George Eliots are not only fewer in number among the great novelists than their rivals, but that their work, at its best, lacks the scope and strength of the Fieldings, the Flauberts and the Dostoyevskys of the world.
>
> But, if this is true, and I am not at all prepared to grant that it is, what about those masterpieces that a woman can create, and she alone? A well-ordered home, a secure and reasonably happy household, a contented and proud husband, an atmosphere within her family of intelligent companionship in those values which at once delight, amuse and nourish the human mind and spirit. All these accomplishments call for the distinctive talents of women. They are beyond those of men.

Professor Mary Ellen Chase,
Smith College, 1960

The message was clear. Your future didn't lie in intellectual pursuits. You must embrace your role in society. To do otherwise was to deny your essence, to reject your femininity, and that was not normal — a mortal sin in this society.

Being single was abnormal, so you were less likely to go to graduate school or into a profession — you got married. And the premium on finding the right husband meant you couldn't afford to wait. The average age of marriage for women dropped from 25.3 to 24.4 between 1947 and 1966, which meant more women were marrying in their teens. So, it's not surprising that, while female university enrollment during this period was the highest recorded to date, the number of women graduating was lower than in 1920.

Being childless was not only abnormal — it made you an object of pity. So you had lots of children. Canadian women added at least 400,000 new citizens to the population in almost every year of the boom, which in Canada lasted from 1947-1966. These babies now make up close to a third of our population.

A married woman who worked wasn't normal. It was bad for her husband, bad for the children, and it would look very bad at the office. It might also indicate (shades of hysteria) mental unbalance:

> The career woman may well have been raised in a household in which the mother directly or indirectly rejected her own female role. Directly, perhaps, by choosing to go to work outside the home. Indirectly, perhaps, by her dissatisfaction at staying home, reflected in remarks about the dullness of housework, the trials of giving birth, being a mother, and so on … The little girl, then, very early formed the idea that womanly occupations are unpleasant. She grew up in a culture that put a higher value on getting and spending than on conceiving and bearing. So, she was naturally inclined toward a career, toward independence, toward 'self-expression' … She would acquire attitudes of aggression, exploitation and dominance, and to that degree become masculinized.
>
> … The masculinized mother and feminized father produce girls who are even more masculine and boys who are even more feminine. [So there has been] a considerable increase in impotence and frigidity … and an increase in male homosexuality.
>
> Dr. John Cotton, psychiatrist
> *Life Magazine*, 1960

So, to preserve your marriage, and save your entire family from going gay, apparently, you didn't work. And finally, your husband's income made it possible (just) to buy a house; if he were looking for career advancement, that house would be in the suburbs. You were a partner in his career — head of the dinner party department if nothing else. So out to the former cow pasture you went.

Once there, you and many of your sisters were introduced to the problem with no name, identified by Betty Friedan in her groundbreaking 1963 book as *The Feminine Mystique*:

> I've tried everything women are supposed to do — hobbies, pickling, canning, being social with my neighbours, joining committees, running PTA teas. I can do it all and I like it all, but it doesn't leave you anything to think about — any feeling of who you are. I never had any career ambitions. All I wanted was to get married and have four children … I love the kids and Bob and my home. There's no problem you can even put a name to. But I'm desperate. I begin to feel I have no personality. I'm a server of food and a putter on of pants and a bedmaker, somebody who can be called on when you want something. But who am I?

This quote is just one example of what Friedan discovered as she talked to middle and upper middle class women, including many of her college classmates. It became clear to her that these women had been trapped by the mystique of femininity — the societal belief, especially strong in the '50s for reasons already discussed — that all a woman needs, or should need, to be totally fulfilled, is husband, home and family (the echoes of *kinder, kirche, küche* are unmistakable.)

Now, in suburbs around the continent, women were painfully rediscovering what their grandmothers — the first-wave feminists — could have told them. The mystique is a lie, and for most women, no amount of peer pressure or advertising or therapy or tranquilizers will make it truth. Because a woman is not a role — wife, mother, lover. She's a human being with interests and needs in her own person. But in this society, there was very little recourse. Divorce was still difficult to obtain and the stigma of failure attached to it, unpalatable, to say the least. Besides, even before Friedan put a name to it, most women knew the problem wasn't their husbands or children per se.

The lack of birth control (in a famous 1960 case, a Toronto pharmacist was actually sent to jail for selling condoms) meant that sex outside marriage could be social suicide. The fact that, according to Alfred Kinsey (1953), a quarter of women were having affairs anyway, was just one more indicator of the depth of the problem. But we have to remember that the problem with no name was a problem because the women affected had bought the mystique hook, line and sinker. This was partly because society offered no viable alternative. But it also stemmed from the desire that affected both men and women in this time and place: the desire to belong, to do what was expected.

❖ CHARLOTTE WHITTON ❖

Clearly, this state of affairs presented a challenge for the educated women who would have been the next Agnes Macphails or Emily Murphys. So it's not surprising that the few prominent female politicians of this period, and many of their supporters, weren't really of this period at all.

•• ❖ ••

Whatever women do, they must do it twice as well as men to be thought half as good. Luckily, this is not difficult.
Charlotte Whitton

In the first meeting of the Ottawa City Council following the election of 1951, one of the councillors remarked that his colleagues should be more careful of their language now that there was a lady in their midst. Charlotte Whitton, in the acerbic tongue which was to characterize her political life, announced to those assembled, "May it please the board, whatever my sex, I am not a lady!"

Charlotte Whitton was born in Renfrew, Ontario on March 8, 1896. Her father, John Edward Whitton had been born in Belleville, Ontario, but his family was originally from Britain and had deep Methodist roots. Her mother, Elizabeth Langin, however, was of Irish Roman Catholic stock. The marriage was to be a difficult one from the beginning. The young couple eloped and were married in the Anglican Church, against the wishes of both parents. When one of Charlotte's siblings died, her mother seemed to feel this was a sign from God and returned to her church, insisting that the younger children be raised as Roman Catholics. Charlotte, ever the individualist, refused and was confirmed in the Anglican Church when she was thirteen.

Whitton was educated at the Renfrew Collegiate Institute. A gifted student, she'd won six scholarships by the time she graduated in 1914. Her university career at Queen's was exemplary. During her first years, women were in the minority on the campus, but as World War I progressed, the ratio of men to women changed dramatically.

Eventually, women made up sixty-eight per cent of the student body, which required female participation in areas not earlier contemplated. Whitton took full advantage of the opportunity. She became an athlete of merit; she earned her letter in basketball, but also became an outstanding member of the field hockey team. She was the first female editor of the *Queen's Journal*, a member of the debating team and president of Levana, the Women's Society.

As valedictorian of her graduating class in 1917, she praised the opportunity she'd been given to participate in campus activities. In addition to receiving her M.A. in 1918, she was awarded gold medals in English and history, as well as the Governor General's Medal in pedagogy (though she was, despite her earlier intentions, never to teach).

Immediately following graduation, Whitton moved to Toronto where she was hired as assistant secretary of the Social Service Council of Canada and editor of its monthly publication, *Social Welfare*. When she began at SSCC, social work was in its infancy. By the time she left social work in 1940, it was a well recognized profession and Charlotte Whitton deserves a great deal of the credit.

She was particularly responsible for changing the way in which children were treated by social service agencies in Canada. Much of her influence derived from the surveys of child welfare policy and attitudes she conducted as part of her job, and the position papers she wrote based on the results.

In 1922, Whitton left the SSCC and accepted a position as secretary to Thomas Low, a Liberal Member of Parliament. On the surface, this looked to be a strange career move as she was a Conservative, but the handwriting at the SSCC was already on the wall. The organization's financial difficulties made it vulnerable to takeover by church interests, while she was a firm believer in a secular approach to social service.

She also knew that by moving to Ottawa she could become actively involved with the Canadian Council on Child Welfare and she was immediately appointed its honorary secretary. She worked days for Low, and devoted her evenings and weekends to her work with the CCCW. In 1923, Low was appointed Minister of Trade in Mackenzie King's first government, and as his secretary Whitton was given the opportunity to learn how government worked from the inside. She frequently travelled with her Minister, making contacts across Canada and throughout the world.

Meanwhile, she continued her work on behalf of the CCCW, including fundraising. In 1926, when the organization was financially stable, she accepted the position of permanent executive secretary at a negotiated salary of $3,600 per year. Her salary was raised to $4,000 two years later, very good pay for anyone in that era. It was a mark not only of her capacity, but also her strong conviction that women should be as well paid as men.

It was also during this time that she seems to have made the decision never to marry. She believed that to combine work with the raising of a family was an impossible task. "A woman has to choose. No woman's job or woman's home can be balanced or subdivided. One or the other is short changed."

Instead, she moved into a house in New Edinburgh, a section of Ottawa close to Rideau Hall, with civil servant Margaret Grier. Their home seems to have been administered and decorated by Grier, except the library, which was Whitton's domain. It was filled with more than 1,000 books, a tenth of which were dedicated to the formidable Elizabeth I — certainly a revealing choice in heroines.

The two had what was euphemistically called a Boston Marriage — a relationship between two women who had a deep and abiding friendship but no sexual intimacy. They lived together until Grier's death in 1947. Margaret Grier's tombstone not only gives her birth and death dates and her parents' names, but also says "dear friend to Charlotte Whitton".

Whitton's years at the CCCW were active ones. Under her leadership, the organization became the foremost lobby group and advocate for social welfare in the country. She produced a series of exposés and surveys of child welfare in Canada, believing the more lurid the stories, the greater the rage they would engender. She was not the least bit worried about whose toes she might step on.

Saturday Night said of her, "She has elevated social welfare from the abyss of common charity to the standards of a profession." In recognition of her work, King George V invested her into the Order of the British Empire in 1934.

In her success, of course, lay the seeds of her downfall. Her take-no-prisoners approach to management didn't help, but in raising social work to a profession, she also made it an acceptable career choice for men. By 1940, the majority of the board of the Canadian Council of Child Welfare was male, and it was a group that had little interest in working for a woman — even one of her formidable qualifications. She refused to resign at first, but by the end of 1941, she was without a job for the first time since she'd left university.

The next ten years were difficult ones. Whitton's close association with the Conservatives under Bennett made her unpopular with the governing Liberals. She might have received an appointment on the basis of reputation alone, but her outspokenness had earned her a large number of enemies. She also found herself in competition with the many women entering or returning to the work force because of the war. She bitterly resented this competition, particularly from married women.

To earn a living, she began to write a weekly column for the *Ottawa Gazette*, accepted speaking engagements in Canada and the United States, and took contracts to do research with various organizations and governments.

Whitton had strong views that were quite representative of her class and time. She believed that families often received far too much on social assistance and this made them dependent on the state. Her views had significantly informed R.B. Bennett's domestic economic policies, which had regularly denied benefits to those left destitute by the Depression and the prairie drought. As well, she opposed family allowances based on the number of children, because she believed this simply encouraged women to be breeders.

NANCY HODGES
Canada's First Female Speaker of the House

"THINK OF THE FUN YOU'RE MISSING", the young man said to Nancy Hodges. "My friend", she replied, "I've had fun when you didn't know what you were having — fun or anything else." That was Nancy Hodges' comeback on her habit of never having drunk anything stronger than tomato juice. Her quick wit was a definite asset in the male-dominated British Columbia provincial legislature. In fact, her reputation was such that few men were willing to challenge her rulings when she became the first woman in the British Commonwealth to be addressed as Madame Speaker in a full-time capacity.

Nancy Austin was born in London, England on October 28, 1888, the ninth of ten children. She attributed her strength in debate to her placement in the family. She noted that, with six older brothers to tease her, it became necessary for what she said not only to be heard, but to be clear.

After graduating from King's College, University of London, in 1910, she married Harry Percival Hodges, a newspaperman. They emigrated to Canada, eventually settling in Victoria in 1916. Both worked as editors for the *Victoria Times*, and Nancy's column, "A Woman's Day", appeared in the paper 2,550 times through to 1943.

Soon after her arrival in British Columbia, she met Mary Ellen Smith, Canada's first female provincial cabinet minister, and joined her in the suffrage movement. Nancy believed in full equality for women, including their right to work. She and her husband were childless. However, she recognized her own need to work to fulfill herself and wanted that right extended to all women regardless of the number of children they had.

In 1937, she was asked by the Victoria Liberal Association to run as a candidate in the provincial election. She was defeated, but once bitten by the political bug, she was hooked. She became a powerhouse in the Liberal Party in British Columbia, serving for a time as president of the National Federation of Liberal Women. She let her name stand again in 1941 and this time, she was successful. She was re-elected in 1945, 1949 and 1952.

A skilled and respected debater, she was instrumental in preventing the layoff of single women after World War II and worked hard to have women included in the Workman's Compensation Act. At the 1949 leadership convention, her speech helped Byron Johnson become Liberal Leader and Premier. Later that year, Johnson announced that Nancy Hodges would be appointed Speaker, the first woman to hold the position anywhere in the Commonwealth.

She was deeply honoured at being chosen. "I look upon the Premier's decision not so much as a tribute to myself, but as to the place women now occupy in the public life of our country." The former Social Credit Premier of B.C., W.A.C. Bennett, said of her, "She was a fair and courteous Speaker. Certainly her example encouraged me greatly to assign major responsibilities to women from the moment the Social Credit government was formed in 1952 … [Her] qualities of a brilliant and constructive mind should rightly earn her the admiration of all women — and indeed all the people of British Columbia."

Nancy was defeated in the 1953 election, but her retirement was short-lived. On November 5, 1953, Prime Minister St. Laurent appointed her to the Senate, where she was able to keep working on womens' issues. She took an active role in changes to Canada's divorce laws and also sat on the committee that recommended abolition of the death penalty.

In failing health, she resigned from the Senate in 1965. Nancy Hodges died in Victoria on December 15, 1969.

Her preference for the values of British immigrants versus those from Eastern Europe won her few non-British friends in Western Canada. She rushed to the aid of children from Britain during the war, but appears to have worked actively to deny Jewish and Armenian children a chance to escape the Holocaust by being accepted as refugees here.

In 1947, she was hired by the Edmonton Chapter of the IODE — the Imperial Order of the Daughters of the Empire, an influential women's organization — to investigate welfare practices in Alberta. This was bound to be a problematic assignment, for she was not a favourite of Premier Ernest Manning, due to attacks she'd made on the province's child welfare system during her days with the CCCW.

When she exposed a cross-border traffic in black market babies, Manning's government decided she'd gone too far and sued her for conspiracy to commit criminal libel. However, before the case came to court a Royal Commission was appointed to investigate. It proved that Whitton was right and the government was forced to drop its legal action.

During the latter part of the 1940s, Whitton began to give speeches about the need for more women in politics. In October 1950, after one such appearance in Ottawa, she was challenged by the *Ottawa Journal* to run in the upcoming civic election. She accepted the challenge and gathered a group of women at the Chateau Laurier ballroom. Women from all walks of life arrived wearing the needle and wisp of thread that was to become her campaign symbol. Whitton met them in fighting form:

> The nation that fails to enlist the magnificent resources of its women is flying on one wing and bound for a crash landing … There are 25,000 members on the elective boards in this country, and how many are women? Not 200 … There is hard, slogging, unpleasant work ahead. If you're not ready for it, go back to your vacuum cleaners and mops.

By the time they left the Chateau that day, each energized woman had agreed to convince ten more to support Whitton. Coordinated by her Ladies' Committee of 100, Whitton's "Let This Be A Women's Campaign" proved to be a steamroller. When the counting was over on election night, she had defeated her nearest rival by 7,000 votes. Charlotte Whitton had a new career and Ottawa politics would never be the same.

She demanded the title of Deputy Mayor, since custom dictated that the councillor earning the most votes be given that title. After refusing to chair the fire department portfolio — "the firemen have ladders and hoses and I may have ladders in my hose but that is all we have in common" — she was offered the newly-created post of social utilities chair. Since this new department had control of health, housing, child care and community agencies, it was right up her alley.

Within the year she had the top job. The elected Mayor died in office and, on October 15, 1951, Charlotte Whitton became the first female mayor of a major Canadian city.

Remarking that, "I have never had a man or a Cadillac in my life", one of her first actions was to get rid of the mayor's car and chauffeur. This is not to say that she didn't like pomp and ceremony. She designed an ornate set of mayor's robes trimmed in beaver, over which she wore the medal of office.

In 1952, when she campaigned for a term of her own, the women turned out again, this time wearing darning needles as the symbol. She won by a margin of 3,923. In 1954, her plurality increased to 10,305.

As she had in her earlier career, once in charge, she stirred the waters and demanded reform. She forced the federal government to contribute a much fairer share for the operation of the city, demanding they pay taxes for buildings occupied by crown corporations. Because of her belief that gambling was both addictive and a tax on the poor, she banned bingo in Ottawa. She had Ottawa property assessed and, because of the new taxes, was able to lower the overall rate. With these additional funds, she built a new City Hall and police headquarters.

When she decided to retire in 1956 to run federally, there was a long sigh of relief from the male councillors whom she had browbeaten over the years — she'd once even left the mayor's chair to sit in the gallery so she could heckle them. But many of them obviously gave as good as they got. Once, after the Queen Mother asked her what Canadians called their mayors, she replied, "Your Majesty, deference to the presence of royalty prevents me from being explicit."

She won the Conservative nomination in the riding of Ottawa Vanier West in 1957, but lost the election. Unable to secure the nomination in 1958, she returned to writing her weekly column for the *Ottawa Gazette*.

Then, in 1960, she decided to come out of retirement. It didn't seem to bother her that none of the Ottawa papers, the *Gazette*, the *Journal* or *Le Droit*, supported her candidacy, though in the days before TV ads, newspaper support was usually vital to political success. The *Journal* had actually styled their City Hall reporters "war correspondents" during her previous tenure as Mayor.

She was also undeterred by the opposition candidate, Sam Berger, a distinguished Ottawa businessman and owner of the Montréal Alouettes. However, she knew that she would have to broaden her support base. She maintained the women's committee that had worked so tirelessly before, but added men known in both business and legal circles.

Most in the know were convinced she'd have the devil's own time even

competing, but true to a favourite motto, *Ce que Diable ne Peut Femme le Fait* —
a woman does what the Devil can't — she not only won in 1960, but again in 1962.

Then, shortly after the 1962 election, she managed to offend even her
most loyal supporters — she became involved in a fist fight with the senior con-
troller, Paul Tardif. Actually the fight was all on her side. Whitton had made a
comment about being kept awake half the night worrying over city business.
When Tardif replied that it was too bad she didn't have other things to keep her
busy, she kicked him in the shin and punched him in the face.

This was too much for the citizens of Ottawa. She was defeated at the
polls in the 1964 election campaign and was no longer in charge of her "dear
boys", as she called the controllers. The loss didn't end her political career, however.
She continued to serve as an alderman until her retirement in 1972 at the age of
seventy-six. She died of a heart attack on January 15, 1975.

Charlotte Whitton enjoyed a remarkable career, but it's unlikely that she
inspired large numbers of younger women to consider politics during her tenure
as Mayor of Ottawa. There's not much in her fierce individualism that victims of
the feminine mystique would recognize in themselves. So Whitton is actually an
ending, part of the legacy of McClung and Macphail, rather than a precursor of
the feminist resurgence. That would have to wait, though not much longer.

◆◆ ❖ ◆◆

The saplings planted by the inhabitants of the new suburbs had barely
begun to take root when the societal changes initiated by the collapse of the old
order after WWI finally began to gather pace. It was happening in schools, in
music stores, and in the living rooms of Pleasantville itself.

Before WWII, the final year of school for the general population was
usually Grade 8 — high school was reserved almost exclusively for the tiny minority that was going on to university. As a result, teaching in the higher grades
focused on delivering a classical education and building character in the British
public school tradition. Think of Kevin Kline's *The Emperor's Club*. This was
education for the governing class.

By the end of the war, it was already apparent to educators that early
school leaving was going to have to change. The advances in science and technology meant the country was going to need all the well-educated workers it could
get if the economy were going to continue growing. But, what would be the
content of this new mass education? The imminent arrival of the baby boomers
in the classroom made the question particularly pressing.

Since it was assumed that the vast majority of these new graduates still wouldn't be attending university, producing good citizens seemed more important than turning out classical scholars. This went well with the progressive education theories that were in the ascendant after the war; the idea that the classroom should be more child-centric, with active participation on the part of the students. As one can see from the sample report card, in this environment, personal development was deemed more important than measurement against some arbitrary standard.

GRADE I

195 6 - 195 7

NAME Timmy Higgins

Key – Satisfactory . – Yes
Improving – Imp.
Unsatisfactory – No

HABITS AND ATTITUDES	1	2	3	4
1. Works and plays well with others	Yes	Yes	Yes	
2. Is courteous	Yes	Imp	Imp.	
3. Is clean and neat in appearance	Yes	Yes	Yes	
4. Completes work promptly	Imp.	Imp.	Yes	
5. Listens to & follows directions	Yes	Yes	Yes	
6. Works neatly and carefully	Imp	Yes	Yes	

The de-emphasis on producing competitive individualists in favour of students who got along well with others suited the group-oriented parents of suburbia just fine, as did the idea of having separate classes for each grade (a minority practice before WWII and an organizational necessity afterwards). So before long, Canadian schools were successfully turning out class after class of other-directed, age-sorted children who were constantly assured that what they wanted, mattered.

At the same time, the second of the century's three great techno-social revolutions was coming to maturity with the mass introduction of television. Here was a medium with the ability to deliver the entertainment value of the movies in the comfort and security of your own home — not an unimportant consideration when practically every household had young children. By 1963, Canadians were buying nearly half a million sets a year and radio and reading had begun their long declines.

In television, marketers quickly realized they had a new way into parents' pocketbooks — advertise directly to children and let them do the selling. This was a generation of parents that were young, intensely focused on children and quite permissive, historically speaking. The result was a gold mine, as Ruth Handler discovered when, in 1959, she purchased one of the first TV spots aimed directly at kids. It ran during the Mickey Mouse Club show and it was for a doll named Barbie.

The kids did more than bug their parents until they got what they wanted. They took word of their new acquisitions to school, and soon every other

Grade 4 student was also bugging their parents. Not only did this multiply sales of popular toys tremendously — it showed that the peer group was becoming increasingly important for young people, who were spending year after year with kids the same age — often the same kids.

In addition to being the best-selling toy of all time, Barbie was a watershed in another way. Earlier dolls had been babies; a chance for young girls to practise for their future roles as mothers. Barbie, and of course, Barbie's unending wardrobe, let these same girls practise being their big sisters, or admired older girls at school. (This trend has since been formalized as Aspirational Marketing.)

This kind of behaviour — the tendency to emulate your peer group instead of your parents — was already firmly established by the time Barbie was introduced, and helps explain her astounding popularity. The equivalent for boys might be GI Joe. The point is that these influences — advertising, peers, older kids — were external to the family.

These were boomer kids, so the urge to conform, to belong, was pretty strong. They got it at home, at school, at church (there was a temporary resurgence in church membership throughout North America during the '50s — Sunday School was seen as a good influence for the kids), so the peer group only intensified what was already present. Add in the fact that, unlike any past generation of children, these kids had been brought up convinced that their opinions mattered — that they were special, and you had all the ingredients for the birth of a true youth culture. The only thing needed was a spark.

Of course, the spark was already there. Boomer children weren't old enough to join the throngs that screamed when Elvis sang *Blue Suede Shoes* or Paul Anka crooned *Diana*, and they weren't the ones who started buying millions of the new LPs and 45 RPM singles (first released in 1948 and 1949 respectively). The teenagers whose devotion set off the rock and roll revolution were born in the late '30s or early '40s.

Too young for war, unburdened by the Depression and more likely to be influenced by *Rebel Without a Cause* or Beat writers like Allen Ginsberg and Jack Kerouac than anything that emanated from Pleasantville, this is the group that became the role models for boomer kids. That their "rebellion" made them the very image of the juvenile delinquent so feared in '50s society only increased their currency with their younger admirers. It's more than a little ironic that many of them would quickly turn in their black leather jackets and poodle skirts to become the parents of the last half of the baby boom.

So, by the late 1950s, you had organization men focused on their careers married to women who increasingly felt trapped by society's expectations. The couple was raising children who were spending more and more of their extended adolescence with people their own age and emulating a group that didn't share Mom and Dad's values. If there was ever a formula for social change, this was it.

In this charged atmosphere, it seemed that even staid old Ottawa wasn't immune. The Prime Minister, "Uncle" Louis St. Laurent, was now seventy-five and visibly tired, while the Conservatives' performance during the recent Pipeline Debate had energized the entire party. The time to strike was now, while the iron was hot. But then, just as victory seemed assured, disaster loomed.

One can just imagine the scene. The high nobility is gathered round the monarch's sickbed. His palsied hand reaches out to take the pen and then, slowly, painfully, he signs. In a moment, it's done. He's abdicated. He lies back, then gestures that all come closer. His counselors lean in to hear his final words of advice. His voice, weak at first, quickly rises to a bellow. "Now find someone to stop that Prairie yokel from Taking Over MY PARTY!!"

It was September 18, 1956 and George Drew had just resigned as leader of the Conservatives. The gathered party heavyweights, including Ellen Fairclough, knew there would be an election call soon; for the first time since 1935, the Liberals were looking vulnerable.

There was just one small problem. With Drew out of the running, the leading candidate to replace him was a lectern-pounding spellbinder from Saskatchewan, of all places — John George Diefenbaker. The party Old Guard was not amused.

Dief the Chief, as he came to be called, was sure evidence that the youth movement was still just an undercurrent. He was a year older than Charlotte Whitton, and had been an MP since 1940. His two previous defeats at leadership conventions (he was judged too provincial or too progressive) had not discouraged him, because he believed he was destined to be Prime Minister.

Now, while no one would ever confuse John Diefenbaker with Elvis Presley, they did share one very effective trait — an ability to get people on their feet, get them shouting, stomping, focused and ready to be led. This ability, of course, allowed Elvis to sell millions of records. For Diefenbaker, it finally propelled him to a first-ballot victory at his third Conservative leadership convention, despite resolute opposition from the party establishment. On June 10, 1957, it helped make him Prime Minister of Canada.

Diefenbaker has always been a difficult figure for historians. He won three elections and almost pulled out a fourth, yet seemed at times to be Canada's Peter Principle made flesh. He's been called the greatest opposition leader in parliamentary history, but his superb skill at dissecting opponents, honed during his years as a defence lawyer, was ill suited to defending government positions.

In introducing the Bill of Rights, he acted on his firm convictions about civil liberties, but he also used the weight of the government to hound the Governor of the Bank of Canada from office when the latter displeased him. He was a strong anti-Communist, but dithered during the Cuban Missile Crisis.

He believed that the Liberal policies had turned Canada into a U.S. branch plant, yet by cancelling the Avro Arrow supersonic fighter, guaranteed that our military would be buying American. He passionately proclaimed a vision for the entire country, but his "One Canada" had no place for two founding nations. Yet, such was the power of his personality, that there are still people across the West who believe he was Canada's greatest Prime Minister.

Diefenbaker had a phenomenal memory for faces and names. He also never forgot or forgave a slight. This placed him in an awkward position in the days after the 1957 election. One of his promises during the campaign had been that he would be the first Prime Minister to include a woman in his cabinet. Unfortunately for him, the obvious candidate was someone who had failed to support him at any of the leadership conventions. He delayed as long as he could, but in the end, he really had no way to avoid appointing Ellen Fairclough as Secretary of State. That didn't mean he had to like it.

Ellen Louks Cook was born on January 28, 1905, in Hamilton, Ontario. Her parents, Norman Ellsworth Cook and Nellie Bell Louks were of modest means, but they gave their daughter both ambition and an appreciation that education was a means to achieve that ambition. Her father had started out as a farmer in Delhi, Ontario, but soon joined the migration away from the land, moving the family to Hamilton where he become a carpenter and later a contractor.

Ellen had a traditional upbringing, learning to play the piano as many young girls did in those days. She attended Ryerson Public School and, in her final year, studied typing and shorthand. She took her first job at the age of twelve, carrying the change to the cashiers at a Hamilton department store. Her first permanent position was as a stenographer for a rubber company, a post she won by lying about her age. But at night, she was studying accounting:

> When I was young, to say that you were going to be a chartered accountant, they'd say, 'Oh yeah? Ha. Ha. Ha. You might become a bookkeeper … if you can add.' If a girl wanted to go into one of those professions, it was not at all unusual for a professor to tell her, 'Go home and wash the dishes. That's where you belong. You belong in the kitchen.' It was quite the usual thing. [3]

---

[3] The quotes in this section are excerpted from an interview conducted by Tim Higgins and Darlene Mulligan in 1995.

Ellen married David Henry Gordon Fairclough in 1931 and they had their only child, Howard, a year later. She'd met Gordon at a church social when she was sixteen and they dated for a decade before they married. It was obvious to her husband and all who knew her that her career was always going to be an important part of her life — on evenings when he wanted a date and she had to study, she sent him out dancing with her sister.

She was by now a competent accountant and an auditor, but tradition and the Depression dictated she remain at home and raise her son. This arrangement had lasted less than a year when she agreed to work nights for a broker who promised wages sufficient for a baby sitter. She looked after Howard and did the housework during the day and then went off to her job, often staying until three or four in the morning. She would then snatch a few hours of sleep and be up with her son. Her competence was such that she was soon hired full time at a salary that paid for a housekeeper.

She became a certified public accountant and established her own accounting business, receiving her office furniture in lieu of back wages from an employer who had gone bankrupt while owing her money. Fairclough became a tax expert with a practice that was distinguished by the fact that she hired only women.

Work and family weren't all that filled her life. She'd been an active member of the Imperial Order of the Daughters of the Empire since she left school. She also served on the executive of the Dominion Council of the United Empire Loyalists. She extended her business contacts by becoming the secretary-treasurer of the Canadian Wholesale Grocers Association and she was chair of the Zonta Club, a women's service organization.

She ran for Hamilton Council for the first time in 1946, losing by three votes, but then gained the seat anyway when the man who beat her took a job with Ontario Hydro. Her political ambition grew through successive electoral victories in 1947, 1948 and 1949.

She had been active in the Progressive Conservative Party even as a young woman. In 1931, she and Gordon had founded the Young Progressive Conservative Club of Hamilton. In 1949, after her successes at City Hall had been duly noted by the party, she paid her dues by running (and losing) in Hamilton West against Colin Gibson, a cabinet minister in both the Mackenzie King and St. Laurent governments. After her defeat, she decided to increase her political profile by running for the position of city comptroller. Early in 1950, she became vice-chair of the Hamilton Board of Control and Deputy Mayor.

Meanwhile, Gibson had been appointed to the Ontario Court of Appeal. Fairclough was now a political force in Hamilton and, in the ensuing by-election,

ELLEN LOUKS FAIRCLOUGH

held in May 1950, she was successful in her bid to become the Member of Parliament for Hamilton West.

She made a strong appeal for the women's vote. Her slogan was "Canada Needs a Woman's Voice". The fact that no women had been returned in the 1949 federal election gave her the opportunity to be blatant and she used it. She actually bought radio ads telling women if her vote was low on election day, it would be because women had failed her. One newspaper, in proclaiming her election, sardonically remarked that, "Canada is saved. We now have a woman in Parliament."

Her husband lent his support, not only to the campaign, but to her political ambitions. Both Gordon and Howard were in the House of Commons when George Drew and her friend Frank Lennard, MP for Wentworth, escorted her up the aisle of the Chamber to make the traditional bow to the Speaker. Lennard had actually taken a seat in the back row of the House of Commons so the newly elected female member could sit in the second row, an honour usually reserved for backbenchers of some years of experience.

Gordon Fairclough seems to have maintained his sense of humour throughout his wife's political career, finding invitations addressed to him suggesting he wear a cocktail frock to be amusing rather than insulting. At a Government House reception in 1955, then Governor General Vincent Massey brushed past Gordon to say he had to speak to Mrs. Fairclough about a little party he was giving for the members' wives. "Just a minute sir," Gordon said, "that's me you're talking about".

She was only the second female Progressive Conservative to sit in the House of Commons, as well as the first businesswoman and the first woman to represent an industrial riding. She was also the only woman in the 21st Parliament, which put her in the unenviable position of being a bit of a side show for the public in the galleries. Her status did have one advantage, however. She got her own office.

In the 1950s, the offices of all the Members of Parliament and the Senate were located in the Centre Block of the Parliament Buildings. Because there were only so many offices and the numbers of members had increased over the decades, many of the parliamentarians had to share offices, particularly the newly elected ones. However, none of the men wanted to share with a woman and, therefore, she was on her own. On the downside, there were still no washrooms for female MPs.

Her early years as a Member of Parliament were busy. She had great energy and was often described as always being in a hurry. She continued running her business, returning to Hamilton nearly every weekend when Parliament was in session, and attending as many of her beloved Tiger Cats' games as she could manage.

In addition, she undertook a number of caucus responsibilities. She spoke more than seven hundred times during her seven years in opposition, on issues ranging from the sloppy dress of postmen to a suggestion that the Canadian Army use more female cooks. However, it was as labour critic that she made her mark, particularly on issues of discrimination against women in the workplace. Many of her recommendations were included in the labour legislation passed by the Liberals in 1956.

She also represented Canada abroad. She was part of the Canadian delegation to the United Nations in October 1950, and she attended the Conference of NATO parliamentarians in Paris in 1955.

Her partisanship was clear — she could heckle with the best of them. One of the best known examples of this skill came in 1956 during the Pipeline Debate, which was about the wisdom of C.D. Howe's plan to get Alberta natural gas to eastern Canada by selling seventy-five per cent of the proposed pipeline to American interests.

Donald Fleming (who would become Finance Minister under Diefenbaker), had refused to take his seat because the committee chairman wouldn't recognize him, that is, allow him to speak. The Speaker had "named him", which is a form of discipline invoked prior to expulsion from the House. Fleming then shouted, "this isn't the way to run a peanut stand, let alone Parliament", and was expelled.

In a stunt worthy of Sheila Copps and the Rat Pack of the 1980s, Fairclough immediately draped the expelled Fleming's seat with an eight-foot Canadian flag — in those days the red ensign — as her own statement on the perceived abuse of parliamentary rules by the government. She always denied this was a planned move, arguing it was a spontaneous gesture of respect for Fleming and disrespect for the government of the day. It would, however, be somewhat unusual for a Member of Parliament to keep an eight-foot flag in her desk.

Despite the government's poor performance during the Pipeline Debate (it eventually had to invoke closure) and the fairly obvious fact that after twenty-two unbroken years in power, the Liberals were out of ideas, no one really thought Diefenbaker and the Conservatives could win the 1957 election. When the Tories defied expectation and formed a minority government, electing 109 against 105 Liberals, twenty-two CCF, nineteen Social Credit and four independents, there was shock both across the country and inside the party.

By crafting a campaign that focused almost exclusively on the Chief, a man the Old Guard had been rejecting since 1942, the party had been delivered to the promised land. As events would prove, the messiah-like aura created by this victory and the unprecedented landslide of a year later gave Diefenbaker far more sway inside the government than was advisable for so inexperienced a leader. It also led insiders to excuse his paranoia. So, while no one questioned Fairclough's ability, and many thought she should have received a more prominent portfolio than Secretary of State, they also accepted that Diefenbaker was unlikely to trust anyone who had opposed his desire to become Prime Minister:

> Dief had very little respect for women. As women, yes, but, in the world where things get done, no. We respected each other, I think. I respected his ability — he was quite an orator, you know — but I didn't always respect his judgement. If a difficult matter came up regarding labour or the Steel Company of Canada, did he call anybody from [Hamilton]? No! He'd call some farmer from the backwoods and say, 'What do you think?'

There was also, it has to be admitted, some relief that she hadn't received the post most suited to her experience — Minister of Labour. Management considered her far too pro-worker. This was a reflection of the constituency that elected her, as well as the fact that she'd subjected both her own party and St. Laurent's government to repeated speeches insisting on equal pay for female employees.

However, Fairclough understood you have to start somewhere and was delighted with her appointment. Her responsibilities included patents, trademarks and copyrights, communications between federal and provincial governments, ceremonial decorations and custody of the Great Seal of Canada. Under no circumstances could her duties have been considered onerous. However, it did give her a seat at the cabinet table, and therefore a position of influence. It also gave her the opportunity to speak across the country to women's groups, which she used to conduct a personal crusade to get more women into Parliament.

She was regarded as a good public speaker, competent though not particularly passionate. She was told over and over that she thought like a man and, for the most part, she considered this to be a compliment. She made it clear to anyone who asked that she was not a feminist. Apparently, she thought this was the wrong message to give, despite her work on behalf of greater equality for women.

In her speeches, she was often critical of women for not trying hard enough. She believed that, since she'd made it, so could other women and she demonstrated little acceptance that others' circumstances might have been quite different from her own:

> I can't see [equal representation] as a goal. I have no way of assessing a situation where a man is more qualified than a woman, or a woman is more qualified than a man. To me, they're individuals. [It's]

their background, their education … their experience, more than anything else. I don't think you can just pick somebody off the street and
say, 'You're going to be Prime Minister. It'll take a few years, but …'
You don't do that.

In a speech to the Empire Club in 1957, she stated, "I have long held the
view that there is no difference in one's approach to the problems of business of
state because of one's sex." Yet, she clearly encouraged women and believed that
a woman would become Prime Minister one day, though she knew it would not
be her and never seriously considered running for the leadership of her party.

The only inkling that perhaps she thought there was some inequity
toward women in politics came in 1958 during an interview with Doyle Klyn in
Weekend Magazine. "You know, men think it's a compliment when they say 'she
thinks like a man'. I accept it as the compliment they intend. But sometimes I
wonder if they would feel flattered if a woman said admiringly, 'He thinks like
a woman.'"

Like Agnes Macphail before her, she was regarded as an oddity. The public
was interested and the media wrote and discussed in great detail the appearance,
clothes, personality traits, physical attributes, and hairstyle of the new minister. It
was invasive and immaterial, but all women holding office for the first time seem
to be subject to this desire for copy. In the case of Fairclough, even her shoe size
and the sheerness of her stockings were topics to be discussed.

At the same time, there was the general suspicion and resentment surrounding a wife and mother who worked, especially at something as high profile
and time consuming as politics:

You have no idea. I'd meet people on the street who'd say, 'Why
don't you go home and look after your house?' Well, I didn't make any
obscene gestures, but I felt like it. Ah, anybody as small as that, just brush
them off.

A minority government like Diefenbaker's in 1957 is often an indication
of uncertainty among the electorate. There was no such uncertainty on March 31,
1958. The Tories scored an incredible electoral victory, winning 208 of the 265
seats in the House of Commons. The Liberals were reduced to forty-eight members, the CCF to eight and the Social Credit party was completely wiped out.

Fairclough was in great demand during the campaign. Her speaking
engagements were second in number only to those of the Prime Minister. She
gave more than sixty speeches in two separate cross-Canada tours. It was on one

of her trips back to Ottawa to ensure her department was functioning properly, that she was actually made acting Prime Minister for the day, another first for a woman.

Following the election, the Prime Minister gave the now, as he believed, supportive Fairclough a much more senior portfolio. She became the Minister of Citizenship and Immigration. She'd handled her previous portfolio with distinction, representing Canada abroad in Trinidad at the birth of the West Indies Federation and at the inauguration of the President of Argentina, Arturo Frondizi. Indeed, she was given the title of Ambassador when she made these visits and so became the first woman to hold the title "Your Excellency" in her own right. She was ready for more responsibility and she was given it.

However, her tenure at Citizenship and Immigration proved to be contentious. On the positive side, she was the minster who, in 1960, finally gave First Nations people the right to vote, a just and long overdue act. As for her main area of responsibility, let's just say her United Empire Loyalist roots showed.

Immigration declined steadily during the Diefenbaker mandates as part of a deliberate policy. In 1957, 282,164 immigrants arrived in Canada. By 1962, this number had dropped to 74,586. Then in April 1959, Fairclough announced an Order in Council that placed severe new restrictions on the admission of relatives of non-British immigrants.

The announcement was met with a storm of protest. She appeared to have forgotten, at least for the moment, that among her most fervent supporters in Hamilton West were Italian-Canadians whose relatives would not qualify under the new rules. She rose in the House a few days later to announce that it had all been a mistake and the regulations were being withdrawn, blaming the whole thing on the "propagandists of the Liberal Party". The matter seemed to blow over, but her constituents wouldn't forget.

In 1962 Canadians again went to the polls. There was now widespread dissatisfaction with the Diefenbaker government. The Conservatives had the largest majority ever given to a political party, but seemed unable to get anything done. The situation was exacerbated by the first interruption in the postwar economic expansion, which had caused a significant rise in unemployment.

The electorate showed its annoyance by reducing the Conservatives to 116 seats. The Liberals won ninety-eight, Social Credit thirty and the CCF, rebranded as the NDP, nineteen. It was a minority Conservative government and trouble was brewing within the Tory caucus. For Fairclough, part of the fallout was her demotion to Postmistress General, primarily as a result of the immigration fiasco.

The conflicts within the caucus and cabinet came to a head during the Cuban Missile Crisis. American President John F. Kennedy delivered an ultimatum to the Soviet Union over its attempt to base missiles in Cuba. The penalty, if his order was ignored, was war.

Douglas Harkness, a Calgary MP and the Minister of Defence, assumed that Canadian support for the American plans would be a simple formality. Unlike Fairclough, Harkness had backed Diefenbaker during the 1956 leadership race and was considered one of his insiders. But to Harkness' astonishment, support from Diefenbaker for the American position was anything but automatic. The cabinet wrangled for three days before the government finally announced it would stand with the United States. From this time on, the rift in the cabinet was permanent. Fairclough, for her part, lined up with Harkness.

In February 1963, Doug Harkness resigned. The final straw had been the Bomarc affair. When Diefenbaker cancelled the Avro Arrow, it was to be replaced with the American-made Bomarc nuclear missile. But, despite what Harkness believed to be a commitment to NATO, he was unable to get Diefenbaker's approval to put nuclear weapons on Canadian soil. So Canada was left with a weapons system that had no weapons. Harkness had once again demonstrated the Prime Minister's indecisiveness for all to see. Within the cabinet, the knives were being drawn.

The opposition soon brought down the government on a non-confidence vote and Canadians went back to the polls for the fourth time in six years. This time the Tories lost an additional twenty-one seats. The Liberals now formed a minority government with 129 seats. Among the seats lost by the Tories was Fairclough's in Hamilton West.

She had never been forgiven by some of her constituents for the order-in-council on immigration in 1959. She proceeded to remind them of it during the campaign when she pledged she would do all in her power to keep the seat from "aliens". She said she meant she wanted the seat to remain Conservative, but as the names of her opponents were Chertkoff and Macaluso, her remarks were once again interpreted as anti-immigration, particularly non-British immigration.

Nineteen sixty-three was Fairclough's last election. She returned to Hamilton and to her business career. In 1965, she was elected a fellow of the Institute of Chartered Accountants of Ontario. She became vice-president and secretary of the Hamilton Trust & Savings Company and was appointed to the Hamilton Hydro Commission in 1974. She involved herself in many charitable projects, including work for the Council of Christians and Jews and the Rehabilitation Foundation for the disabled.

She disappeared from political view until June 1993, when she appeared at the leadership convention of the Progressive Conservative Party. She was there to second the nomination of Kim Campbell as leader of the party and Prime Minister. She had obviously decided it was time for a woman to take control of her party.

❖

The Conservatives lost to Lester Pearson's Liberals again in 1965. John Diefenbaker stayed on as leader of the opposition until 1967, when Dalton Camp organized the putsch that deposed him in favour of the Premier of Nova Scotia, Robert Stanfield.

The 1967 leadership convention was clear evidence that the Conservatives, in their determination to get rid of Diefenbaker, had forgotten the lesson of his success. The Chief had shown that, in the age of television, mass consumption and rock and roll, image and performance were already becoming more important than message. Politics had started its journey toward entertainment.

The evidence was all around them. If any of the delegates had left Maple Leaf Gardens for a few minutes and taken a stroll over to Yorkville to meet some of Canada's next generation of voters, alarm bells might have started ringing. The tactics the "hippies" were using in their running battle with City Hall would have been a dead giveaway. Apparently, no one thought to go.

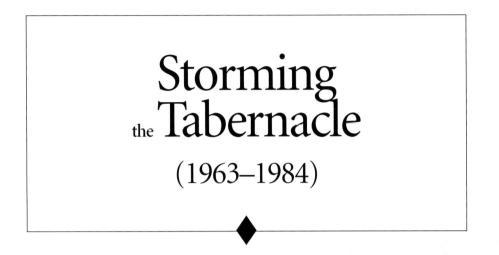

Storming
the Tabernacle
(1963–1984)

♦

Scene: 1967

A woman is dressed in jeans and a tie-dye T-shirt. She has long straight hair, held back by a bandana. She's sitting cross-legged on the floor. The record player on the wooden crate beside her is playing the Beatles' *Lucy in the Sky with Diamonds*. The air seems hazy throughout the scene.

Deborah Boretsky: (*She's singing along with the record till she notices us. She lifts the needle and waves her hands as if to get rid of the smoke.*)

Hey, peace and love, man. Well, there was a whole lotta love in the '60s, thanks to these little babies (*picks up birth control pills*). But peace, well ... peace was a little scarce. You gotta remember, war was a television event now — Vietnam, Israel, Biafra. Supper in the '60s was a TV dinner in front of the tube, served with a side of starvation, death and destruction. Is it any wonder a lot of us decided to turn on, tune in and drop out?

For the more energetic, the '60s were about revolution, man. Student demonstrations all over the planet. Everybody in China denouncing everybody else while they all played the cultural revolution version of "Chairman Mao says". And the white establishment in the U.S. finally figuring out that blacks were mad as hell, and they just weren't gonna take it any more.

The length of men's hair and women's skirts moved in opposite directions at about the same rate. Events were replaced by happenings and love-ins. There wasn't a single taboo or social norm that somebody didn't take a whack at. And if it involved sex or drugs, you name it, somebody tried it — usually in a group and in public.

In addition to Baby Boomers, we gained 20,000 well-educated young men from south of the border who decided that visiting the jungles of South East Asia was a bad career move. They were welcomed to Canada by our very own flower child, Pierre "lock up your daughters" Trudeau, who became Prime Minister in 1968.

This is the decade when Canadian scientists and engineers helped put a man on the moon. Unfortunately, they were working for the Americans at the time, job prospects being somewhat limited north of the border after cancellation of the Arrow. And people laughed at Laurier when he said this would be Canada's century.

As for women, the '60s was the so-called decade of liberation. Many of us started as June Cleaver clones — trapped with the Beav and his 3.1 siblings in a lovely split level on a secluded cul-de-sac. Then along comes the pill and Betty Friedan and suddenly it's, "throw off your shackles, girls. You have nothing to lose but your hairdresser and attached garage." But that VW bus with the floral paint job took a weird turn on the way to Woodstock. While the boomer generation was dedicating itself to sex, drugs and rock and roll, our mothers ended the decade pretty much the way they started — except way more of them were divorced and working, as well as keeping house and raising kids. Ain't progress great?

	POLITICAL	SOCIAL / TECHNOLOGY
	T I M E L I N E	
1964	• Martin Luther King wins Nobel Peace Prize • Malta becomes independent nation • Lee Harvey Oswald found responsible for killing JFK • Arafat gains leadership of guerrilla force Al Fatah	• Satellites take close-up images of moon's surface • Summer Olympics held in Tokyo; Winter Games in Innsbruck, Austria • Race riots erupt in Harlem • Gallery of Modern Art opens in NYC
1965	• Malcolm X shot in New York • KKK shootings in Selma, Alabama • Gambia, Singapore, Maldive Islands join UN • Lester Pearson re-elected Canadian PM	• Soviet astronaut floats in space for ten minutes • Momentum grows for anti-pollution laws • First flight around world over both poles
1966	• Charles De Gaulle re-elected President of France • Forty-eight-hour Christmas truce observed in Vietnam • Cultural Revolution in China begins	• Unmanned Soviet rocket lands on the moon • Miniskirts • Canada's Charles.B. Huggins wins Nobel Prize for Medicine for hormonal treatment of prostatic cancer
1967	• Hanoi attacked by U.S. bombers • Six-Day War (Israel & Arab nations) • Che Guevara dies • Anti-war riots across U.S.	• Soviet cosmonaut killed during re-entry • Synthetic DNA produced by biochemists • China explodes its first H-bomb • Dr. Christian Barnard performs first human heart transplant in South Africa • Expo '67 Montreal: Queen Elizabeth's centennial visits
1968	• Martin Luther King Jr. assassinated • Pierre Elliott Trudeau elected Canadian PM • Senator Robert F. Kennedy assassinated in U.S. • Rchard Nixon promises end to Vietnam War, wins U.S. election	• Unmanned Soviet satellites make contact in space • Apollo 7 and 8 spacecraft launched • Foundations of Temple of Herod discovered • Summer Olympics in Mexico City; Winter Games in Grenoble, France
1969	• Northern Irish violence between Protestants and Catholics • First U.S. troops withdrawn from Vietnam • De Gaulle resigns as President of France	• Mario Puzo writes *The Godfather* • Concorde aircraft makes first test flight • Apollo 11: Neil Armstrong first man to walk on moon • Research links food additives to cancer • Woodstock concert takes place in U.S.
1970	• Gambia proclaimed a Republic • Israel and U.A.R. declare ninety-nine-day truce • Four student protestors killed in U.S. (Kent State) • Assassination attempt on Pope Paul VI • Salvador Allende elected President of Chile	• Unmanned Soviet spacecraft lands on Venus • Priestly celibacy reiterated to be principle of the Roman Catholic Church
1971	• President Nixon travels to China • **Women granted right to vote in Switzerland** • India and Pakistan go to war	• Sylvia Plath writes *The Bell Jar* • Cigarette ads banned from U.S. television • **Billie Jean King: first female athlete to earn $100,000**

POLITICAL	SOCIAL / TECHNOLOGY	
TIMELINE		
• Bangladesh becomes sovereign state • Beginning of Watergate affair • Nixon re-elected U.S. President • Britain imposes direct rule on Northern Ireland • Ceylon becomes Sri Lanka, independent republic • Pierre Elliot Trudeau re-elected Canadian PM	• 2.5 million-year-old human skull discovered • World Hockey: Team Canada defeats U.S.S.R. • Arab terrorists kill eleven Israeli Olympic athletes at Summer Olympics in Munich • Winter Olympics held in Sapporo, Japan	1972
• Watergate: Nixon denies Involvement • Arab-Israeli War • East and West Germany establish diplomatic ties • Bahamas granted independence from Britain • Elected Chilean President Allende killed, replaced by Augusto Pinochet	• Bernardo Bertolucci directs *Last Tango in Paris* • U.S. Skylab astronauts spend twenty-eight days in space • Energy crisis: petroleum product shortage	1973
• Trudeau re-elected in Canada • Terrorism in Northern Ireland spreads to England • Watergate: Nixon found to be co-conspirator; resigns	• Britain, China, India, France conduct nuclear tests • Smallpox epidemic in India kills thousands	1974
• Cambodia: Khmer Rouge rises to power • Islamic nations vote to expel Israel from the UN • Portugal grants independence to Angola and Mozambique	• Junko Tabei (Japan) first woman to climb Mt. Everest • Boston: abortion doctor found guilty of manslaughter • Steven Speilberg directs *Jaws*	1975
• U.S. and U.S.S.R. sign treaty to limit nuclear arms • Jimmy Carter elected U.S. President • **Flora MacDonald makes bid for PC party leadership** • Rioting in South Africa against apartheid • East Germany limits emigration to West Germany	• **Episcopal Church approves ordination of women** • Disco • U.S. unmanned spacecraft travels to Mars • **U.S. Air Force Academy admits women** • Summer Olympics in Montréal; Winter Games in Innsbruck, Austria, after Colorado refuses Games	1976
• First black mayor elected in Los Angeles • Nobel Peace Prize goes to Amnesty International	• George Lucas writes and directs *Star Wars* • Genetic structure of first living organism determined	1977
• Camp David peace talks btwn Israel, Arab nations • U.S., China establish diplomatic relations • Military junta gains power in Afghanistan	• Gutenberg Bible auctioned for $2 million • First human test-tube baby born in England	1978
• **Margaret Thatcher first female British PM** • White minority rule in Rhodesia ends; now Zimbabwe • Joe Clark elected Canadian PM • **Flora MacDonald first female Cdn. Secretary of State for External Affairs** • Cambodia: Khmer Rouge and Pol Pot overthrown • Soviet invasion of Afghanistan begins	• **Mother Teresa wins Nobel Peace Prize** • First gay rights march in U.S. • ESPN television debuts	1979

	POLITICAL	SOCIAL / TECHNOLOGY
	T I M E L I N E	
1980	• Civil War in El Salvador • Iran-Iraq War begins • Solidarity trade union established in Poland • Ronald Reagan wins U.S. Presidential election • Pierre Elliott Trudeau re-elected Canadian PM • **Robert Mugabe elected in Zimbabwe**	• U.S. team defeats Soviets in Olympic hockey in Lake Placid, NY. • U.S. boycotts Summer Olympics in Moscow • Mount St. Helen's erupts in Washington State • John Lennon shot and killed
1981	• Cold War: discussions to reduce nuclear capacity • Gulf Cooperation Council is created • Egypt's Anwar al-Sadat assassinated	• First MTV music video aired • Xerox invents computer mouse • First launch of space shuttle
1982	• U.S. embargo on Libyan oil for terrorist links • Spain joins NATO • Lebanese civil war	• U.S.: first execution by lethal injection • *Time*: Man of the Year award to the computer • Film *Gandhi* portrays extraordinary Indian pacifist
1983	• France launches its first nuclear-powered sub • Suicide bomber destroys U.S. Embassy in Beirut • Korean commercial aircraft shot down by Soviets on entering Soviet airspace: 269 die • Reagan calls Soviet Union an "Evil Empire"	• Internet officially created • **Sally Ride first American woman in space** • **Vanessa Williams: first black Miss America** • M*A*S*H*: final episode
1984	• **Indian PM Indira Gandhi assassinated by Sikhs** • Spain & Portugal enter European Community • Reagan re-elected U.S. President; signs international ban on chemical weapons • U.S. and Vatican establish full diplomatic relations • Brian Mulroney elected Canadian PM	• 1984 Winter Olympics in Sarajevo • Summer Olympics in L.A. boycotted by Soviet-bloc athletes • South Africa's Desmond Tutu awarded Nobel Peace Prize

Storming
the Tabernacle
(1963–1984)

Oh when I look back now
That summer seemed to last forever
And if I had the choice
Ya — I'd always wanna be there
Those were the best days of my life.

Bryan Adams & Jim Vallance
Summer of '69

It **can be** argued that there were four iconic events in the second half of the twentieth century. That two of these — *Apollo 11* and Woodstock — occurred within a month of each other in the summer of 1969 says a lot about the juxtaposition of forces at work during the 1960s [1]. It's difficult to imagine two more disparate undertakings than travelling to an extra-terrestrial body and staging the concert that came to epitomize sex, drugs and rock 'n' roll. In fact, their very disparity sums up what's probably the defining feature of the sixties — the Generation Gap between the boomers and all who went before.

The manned space program was the ultimate achievement of the organization man. Thousands upon thousands of engineers, administrators, technicians and support staff working together, all single-mindedly committed to "achieving the goal, before this decade is out, of landing a man on the moon and returning him safely to earth," as John "Camelot" Kennedy put it in 1961.

---

[1] The Kennedy assassination and the fall of the Berlin Wall were the others.

That much of the motivation involved demonstrating to the Soviets (and everyone else) that the United States had the right stuff (and, in the context of the Cold War was willing to do just about anything to prove it) in no way diminishes this extraordinary achievement. This was technological and bureaucratic civilization at its finest — rational, firm in its belief that for every problem, there is a solution; the devoted grandchild of Progress and the Enlightenment.

Three weeks later and 400,000 kilometres away from where the Eagle had landed, the offspring of these technocrats were gathering at Max Yasgur's farm in upstate New York for a quite different purpose. While their parents had been helping build the military-industrial complex (or the Diefenbunker, to add a Canadian twist), they had been constructing a youth culture based on their alienation from everything Pleasantville, their self absorption and their firm belief that there was only one problem, and it had many possible solutions.

So they came to Woodstock with their long hair and flowers, beads and LSD, convinced that the alternative to the society they'd rejected could be found in communal living or women's liberation or pacifism or altered consciousness or free love or eastern spirituality or violent revolution — all to a soundtrack by Bob Dylan, Jimi Hendrix, the Who, the Doors, the Stones, the Beatles, the Guess Who and on and on.

These are two groups of people who had lived together for two decades or more. Yet in the end, they often had little or nothing meaningful to say to each other, and scant common language to express it if they did. Is it any wonder then that the '60s and '70s were, as the Chinese curse has it, interesting times?

◆◆ ❖ ◆◆

It's April 9, 1963 — the kind of morning that's become depressingly familiar to female politicians in Canada. In the previous day's election, the Diefenbaker government had been defeated and Ellen Fairclough had lost her seat. As Fairclough prepares to move back to Hamilton, Liberal Judy LaMarsh from Niagara Falls is about to replace her as the lone female cabinet minister in the new Pearson government.

In yesterday's election, 1,023 candidates presented themselves to the voters. Only forty were women. After forty-six years of suffrage, four elected means fifty per cent of the population has achieved 1.5 per cent representation. This is not how first-wave feminists imagined the twentieth century progressing.

That same morning, Betty Friedan, then a forty-two year old (not just a) housewife, was most likely sitting at a table in the New York Public Library, putting the finishing touches on *The Feminine Mystique*. The book was an immediate sensation, selling more than a million copies in its first year of publication. Because, as it turned out, the reason the problem had no name was that not enough people were actually talking about it. Every cue in Pleasantville told a woman that the problem, if there was one, was within her, and certainly not something worth burdening anyone else with. Remember your duty to your essence, your husband and your kids.

By the early '60s, even the media had picked up on the fact that there was dissatisfaction in suburbia. But for all the litres of ink spilled on the subject and all the cures suggested, Friedan was the first to actually attempt an explanation beyond the old bromides. Once a woman realized that it wasn't just her problem — that millions of women across North America felt more or less the same — the groundwork was laid for the second wave of feminism.

Of course, it wasn't just *The Feminine Mystique*. By the middle '60s, many boomer mothers were watching their precious children transform into Pleasantville's worst nightmare, and in the light of rising consciousness, asking themselves, is it really so bad? It may seem like they spend all their time screwing, dropping acid and listening to rock and roll, but isn't there an idealism there too; a desire to change things for the better?

> We are people of this generation, bred in at least modest comfort, housed now in universities, looking uncomfortably to the world we inherit …
>
> … First, the permeating and victimizing fact of human degradation, symbolized by the Southern struggle against racial bigotry, compelled most of us from silence to activism. Second, the enclosing fact of the Cold War, symbolized by the presence of the Bomb, brought awareness that we ourselves, and our friends, and millions of abstract "others" we knew more directly because of our common peril, might die at any time. We might deliberately ignore, or avoid, or fail to feel all other human problems, but not these two, for these were too immediate and crushing in their impact …
>
> from the Port Huron Statement
> Students for a Democratic Society, 1962

If these so-called "drugged out hippies" of the New Left could come up with something like that, and work to make it happen, couldn't women do the same?

North of the 49th parallel, it started with the Committee for the Equality of Women in Canada and La Fédération des Femmes du Québec, headed respectively by Laura Sabia and Thérèse Casgrain. Their goal was to convince the Pearson government to establish a Royal Commission to study and report on the status of women.

The Liberals, who had twice failed to win a majority against Diefenbaker, were proving somewhat reform minded — with the NDP holding the balance of power, they had little choice. They'd already established the Canada Pension Plan and were moving toward Medicare, (adopted in Saskatchewan in 1961, it became a national program with the passage of the Medical Care Act in 1966) so Sabia and Casgrain decided the time was ripe to push them on feminist issues.

When the government was slow to respond, Sabia made her now famous threat to march 2,000,000 women to Ottawa. Though she later hyperbolized she'd have been lucky to turn up three, the climate of protest across the country was such that she was believed, and the commission was established in February 1967.

It was chaired by broadcaster Florence Bird and consisted of five women and two men, one of whom was diplomat John Humphrey, the Canadian who drafted the Universal Declaration of Human Rights for the United Nations (a fact not widely recognized until the 1990s). They held well-attended hearings in fourteen cities and across the North. The 468 briefs and more than a thousand letters of opinion they received are an indication of the nationwide interest in their project.

The commission published its report in September 1970:

> Explicit in the terms of reference given us by the government is our duty to ensure for women equal opportunities with men. We have interpreted this to mean that equality of opportunity for everyone should be the goal of Canadian society. The right to an adequate standard of living is without value to the person who has no means of achieving it. Freedom to choose a career means little if the opportunity to enter some occupations is restricted.

> Women and men, having the same rights and freedoms, share the same responsibilities. They should have an equal opportunity to fulfil this obligation. We have, therefore, examined the status of women and made recommendations in the belief that there should be equality of opportunity to share the responsibilities to society as well as its privileges and prerogatives.

> In particular, the Commission adopted four principles: — that women should be free to choose whether or not to take employment outside their homes. The circumstances which impede this free choice have been of specific interest to our inquiry. Where we have made recommendations to improve opportunities for women in the work world,

our goal has not been to force married women to work for pay outside of the home but rather to eliminate the practical obstacles that prevent them from exercising this right. If a husband is willing to support his wife, or a wife her husband, the decision and responsibility belong to them.

The second is that the care of children is a responsibility to be shared by the mother, the father and society. Unless this shared responsibility is acknowledged and assumed, women cannot be accorded true equality.

The third principle specifically recognizes the child-bearing function of women. It is apparent that society has a responsibility for women because of pregnancy and child birth, and special treatment related to maternity will always be necessary.

The fourth principle is that in certain areas women will, for an interim period, require special treatment to overcome the adverse effects of discriminatory practices. We consider such measures to be justified in a limited range of circumstances, and we anticipate that they should quickly lead to actual equality which would make their continuance unnecessary.

> from Criteria and Principles
> *Report of the Royal Commission on*
> *the Status of Women in Canada*

Anthony Westell, writing in the *Toronto Star*, called the report "a time bomb primed and ticking … packed with more explosive potential than any device manufactured by terrorists." [2] He was right.

The 167 recommendations covered everything from amending unemployment insurance legislation and tax laws, to inclusion of women in the armed forces; from liberalizing abortion laws to establishing public daycare; from redefining prostitution to establishing affirmative action programs (i.e.: quotas) in the public service and Senate.

The commissioners were unable to fully agree on everything in the report, and the questions that fuelled their disagreement are still with us today. On abortion, two were against any liberalization, and one thought the recommendations didn't go far enough. Two had problems with daycare (who pays?). And on the question of affirmative action (women will, for an interim period, require special treatment to overcome the adverse effects of discriminatory practices),

---

[2]   The reference is to the FLQ crisis in Québec

John Humphrey disagreed so strongly that he refused to sign and wrote a minority report instead (he argued that special treatment is discrimination).

Still, as the authors of *Canadian Women: A History* point out, "the second wave of feminism now had its agenda, an agenda that could transform Canadian society."

The transformation had begun even before the report was tabled. In 1968, the divorce laws were modified to include rape and marital breakdown as grounds[3] and students at McGill published (illegally) the first edition of *The Birth Control Handbook*. The next year, the laws banning birth control and homosexuality were struck down, the government finally deciding it had no place in the bedrooms of the nation, as the new Prime Minister, Pierre Elliott Trudeau, so succinctly put it.

The Catholic Church, on the other hand, saw the bedroom door a little differently. Despite the collapse of its power in Québec during the Quiet Revolution, (attendance at Mass dropped from eighty per cent to twenty per cent of the population in just six years) the Vatican had no intention of abrogating what it saw as its moral responsibility for what happened between the sheets:

> Responsible men can become more deeply convinced of the truth of the doctrine laid down by the Church on this issue if they reflect on the consequences of methods and plans for artificial birth control. Let them first consider how easily this course of action could open wide the way for marital infidelity and a general lowering of moral standards. ... Another effect that gives cause for alarm is that a man who grows accustomed to the use of contraceptive methods may forget the reverence due to a woman, and, disregarding her physical and emotional equilibrium, reduce her to being a mere instrument for the satisfaction of his own desires ...
>
> We are obliged once more to declare that the direct interruption of the generative process already begun and, above all, direct abortion, even for therapeutic reasons, are to be absolutely excluded as lawful means of regulating the number of children.
>
> Pope Paul VI
> *Humanae Vitae*, 1968

It should be pointed out that, elsewhere in *Humanae Vitae*, His Holiness did allow, reluctantly, that saving the life of a woman with, say, uterine cancer might justify the resulting infertility.

---

[3] As a result, the divorce rate went from 54.4/100,000 in 1968 to 124/100,000 in 1969.

As opposed to the general feminist activism represented by Sabia and Casgrain, the women's liberation movement arose when young women began to realize that the idealism of the New Left, expressed in statements like the Port Huron Statement, didn't necessarily extend to them. Like their sisters south of the border, women in the Student Union for Peace Action (SUPA) and Company of Young Canadians (CYC) found that all too often, their roles were limited to making coffee rather than policy decisions and typing manifestos rather than writing them.

As for free love, being the concubine of a radical leader wasn't much different in 1960s' Canada than it had been in 1930s' Spain, or World War I Europe, though the pill made the physical consequences less bleak. From the female perspective, Black Panther Stokely Carmichael may have summed up the situation best when he infamously remarked that the only position for a woman [in his organization] was prone.

So in 1967, a group of SUPA women issued a manifesto of its own, stating in part, that "until the male chauvinists of the movement understand the concept of liberation in relation to women, the most exploited members of any society, they will be voicing political lies." The New Left was thus exposed as a tool of the "patriarchy", and Canadian Women's Lib was born.

One of the reasons that student radicals appeared so successful during the '60s was that these boomers, having grown up with television, understood the medium in ways that their government and university administration opponents never could. And whatever their complaints about the underuse of their talents as student radicals, the women's movement had learned the language of the sit-in and publicity stunt as well as any of its male counterparts.

Take, for example, the Abortion Caravan. It traveled from Vancouver to Ottawa in the spring of 1970 and managed to make history when thirty-one of its members, after entering the building with forged passes, successfully chained themselves to seats in the visitors' galleries of Parliament, closing down the House of Commons for the first time ever:

> Thirty-one shouting, chanting women activists took the disorder and chaos of street demonstrations into the House of Commons and shut it down. They were the 31 members of the self-styled Women's Liberation Groups who at 2:45 p.m. took over the galleries of the House with a well planned and coordinated disruption, shrieking and screaming for free abortions ...
>
> *Victoria Daily Colonist*
> May 12, 1970

Wallace Nesbitt (PC—Oxford) said, "It was something like the tactics the Nazis used in the thirties to break the German parliamentary system.

Ottawa Citizen
May 12, 1970

"Where does this sort of thing end?" said [Solicitor General] McIlraith when questioned by reporters. "How do you keep Parliament an open forum free of violent minority groups and its galleries available to the public?" Carried to its ultimate extreme, it could force Parliament to close its doors to the general public, he pointed out.

Winnipeg Free Press
May 12, 1970

By 1972, Sabia's Committee on Equality for Women had become the National Action Committee on the Status of Women (NAC), and was advocating expanded daycare, the end of any discrimination on the basis of sex (raising among men nightmares of unisex bathrooms), and complete decriminalization of abortion (my body, my choice).

Under Trudeau, the federal government had already established a Ministry for the Status of Women, though curiously headed by a man. Now, the Prime Minister turned his attention to the courts. If, as feminist analysis claimed, the justice system was hopelessly biased with respect to gender, perhaps it was time to introduce a little counterbalance.

With some trepidation, the thirty-one-year-old woman met with the learned dean of the Dalhousie University Law School, Horace Reid. She had decided to study the law. He, however, was less than receptive. Why couldn't she be content with her life as a minister's wife, he wondered. When she replied that the study of law seemed to her to be a good way to pick up a liberal education, he barked "Madam, we have no room for dilettantes. Why don't you just go home and take up crocheting." Fortunately for all Canadians and particularly disadvantaged Canadians, Madame Justice Bertha Wilson ignored the dean's advice. Her decisions on the Supreme Court of Canada are landmark in establishing that in the highest court of this land, issues of equality and equity are of paramount importance.

Bertha was born on September 18, 1923 in Kirkcaldy, Fife, Scotland to Archibald Wernham and Christina Noble. Her parents were working class — both had dropped out of school to enter the work force — but like most Scots, they firmly believed that the only way to be upwardly mobile in the very structured class system of the United Kingdom was through education. All of their three children, two sons and a daughter, not only went to university, but obtained post-graduate degrees.

Bertha attended the University of Aberdeen to read philosophy, completing her M.A. and a year of teacher training. While there, she met John Wilson, who was studying to be a Church of Scotland Minister. He was the only boyfriend she ever had.

Soon after their marriage in 1945, John accepted his first call in the small fishing village of Macduff located between Aberdeen and Inverness. Though it was her husband's ministry, Bertha, as in all minister's families, was equally involved. She became the head of the women's guild, captained the Guide Company, entertained the ladies of the parish at tea and along with her husband, acted as counselor for many of the thousand people living in the community. She also showed a somewhat independent streak when she scandalized the little hamlet by riding a bicycle, a man's bicycle, to tote her groceries from store to home.

Among those she counselled was a young shop girl, unhappy that her employer was passing off shoddy merchandise to his customers, pretending it was regular goods on sale. The young clerk was quietly steering the customers to the quality goods as best she could, but was concerned with the ethical dilemma.

Wilson knew the young woman needed the job and the time was not right to stand on principle and be fired. She told her to continue to do the best she could to direct the customers to the genuine sale articles and to keep her job. This practical approach was to form a significant part of her later judgements. Wilson believed in ethics and principles, but she also recognized people had to protect themselves.

In 1949, the Wilsons decided to emigrate to Canada. Being strangers in a strange land gave another dimension to their life experience — insights that would also play a role in Bertha's future judgements. John became the Presbyterian minister in Renfrew, in the Ottawa Valley, and for three years they ministered together, learning the customs of their new country.

The Korean War began during their time in Renfrew, and the chaplain of the navy fleet was in need of padres to serve the men at sea. John believed he could be of service and Bertha urged him to go. It meant they'd be separated for at least a year, but in this marriage, neither was held back from new challenges.

For the first time in her life, Bertha was on her own. She took a position as receptionist for two dentists in Renfrew. As her first paying job, it not only gave her a sense of financial independence, but a greater understanding of her own

BERTHA WILSON

abilities. She learned to type and drive a car. Though it wasn't employment in keeping with her academic skills, it started her down a new path. The following year, she joined her husband in Halifax, where he was now stationed, and made the decision to study law.

Not unlike politics, there were few women in law schools in the mid-Fifties. Her class of 1957 was somewhat unusual in that it included six women — in the class of 1958, there was only one among fifty. The professors were not accustomed to women in their classes and sexist stories and jokes, including many told by the dean, were commonplace. Wilson had the advantage of being an older member of the class. She was also married and, while it was clear she was bright and knowledgeable, she was consequently not considered a threat to the men.

She graduated near, but not at the top of her class, winning several prizes and the opportunity to take a Masters in Law at Harvard. Once again the dean put the damper on any thoughts that she might like to teach law by stating, "A woman on faculty! Not in your time!"

Predictably, Wilson had great difficulty finding a place to article, a necessity for any lawyer wanting to practise. She was finally accepted by Fred Bissett, considered by some Haligonians to be a bit of an eccentric. On the basis of her grades, she should have been accepted into one of the senior Halifax firms, but they still hadn't opened their offices to female lawyers. Though she was given some experience in the police courts, most of her articles were spent on titles and mortgages.

John's service in the Canadian Navy came to an end early in 1958 and the couple moved to Toronto. Bertha deliberately applied to large law firms because she knew the smaller ones would not have a ladies' washroom and use it as an excuse for not hiring her. She was offered a position with Osler, Hoskin and Harcourt. Even here she was lucky to be hired, as the suitability of women for the law was still discussed at the meeting of the partners making the decision.

Wilson created a special niche for herself within the firm. She became a lawyer's lawyer. She rarely dealt with clients, and even more rarely went to court. Instead, she became the member of the firm that her colleagues sought out when they needed a legal opinion or analysis. If they required first-class research they turned to Wilson, knowing they would get the best available.

She was finally made a partner after ten years with the firm, but even after seventeen years still hadn't become a senior partner. Then in 1973, she was made a Queen's Counsel — a strange appointment in some ways because Wilson had not been politically active and wasn't well known outside her own firm. However, as we've seen, governments were becoming more cognizant of the need to recognize women and Wilson was a beneficiary of this new consciousness raising.

In fact, Wilson would be the first to recognize that her appointment as a member of the Ontario Court of Appeal was as a result of the government's need to appoint a woman. She hesitated, talking it over with John for two days before accepting. Part of her reluctance was based on the appearance (to some) of tokenism, but she was also concerned about her lack of courtroom experience. In her opening remarks to the court on her appointment, she acknowledged that, other than on the day she received her call to the bar, this was the first time she'd worn a legal gown.

Indeed, she admitted she had not practised the law as had most solicitors. She then went on to make an almost prophetic statement. She said:

> When one becomes immersed in the pressures of daily practice there may be a tendency to emphasize the form over the substance, and the letter of the law over the spirit and to lose sight of that larger dimension … Perhaps the unusual nature of my practice has helped me to retain this perspective, and to remember that people and the law are inextricably intertwined, and the role of the profession is essentially to serve the needs of the people.

One can only imagine the chagrin with which these comments were received by those who'd hoped to get the appointment. After all, they'd played the political game, paid for the expensive lunches at Winston's, and golfed with the right people. Wilson knew that she was not the high-profile establishment candidate the other members of the court expected. She was there because the Prime Minister had decided a woman was required on the bench and she was the best qualified one they could find. It's perhaps just as well that Horace Reid, her dean at Dalhousie, didn't live to see her appointment — it probably would have killed him.

Wilson was determined to make her mark. She set out on a personal fact-finding tour of Ontario prisons, seeing the conditions and opportunities first hand. She wanted to know where she was sending people. She undertook to learn as much as she could about criminal law, using all her academic expertise. Two new fields of the law were growing rapidly in the seventies — human rights and family law. Wilson established herself as an expert in both.

Her most famous judgement while on the Ontario Court of Appeal was *Bhadauria* v. *the Board of Governors of Seneca College of Applied Arts and Technology* (1981). Pushpa Bhadauria was a mathematician who said she had been denied interviews at the college because of her race. Instead of turning to the Ontario Human Rights Act for relief, Bhadauria chose to go directly to the courts, arguing that she should be afforded protection from injury by discrimination and

Pauline McGibbon

Canada's First Female Lieutenant Governor

"GOVERNMENT CANNOT DO IT ALL ... [it] should not do it all". These words, spoken by Pauline McGibbon, were an affirmation of her belief in the importance of voluntarism. Her first full-time paying job was Lieutenant Governor of the Province of Ontario, but her life was one of full-time achievement on behalf of the citizens of her province and country. The fact that she did it all for free doesn't diminish the value of her remarkable work.

Pauline Emily Mills was born on October 20, 1910, in Sarnia, Ontario. She attended Sarnia Collegiate Institute and Technical School, then Victoria College, University of Toronto, where she graduated in 1933 with a B.A. in modern history. She married her childhood sweetheart, Donald McGibbon, in 1935.

The marriage was childless, but the social pressure against married women taking a paying job was so strong at that time that Pauline decided to contribute through full-time volunteer work instead. She began with the Imperial Order of the Daughters of the Empire, of which she'd become national president by 1965.

When the couple moved to Toronto in 1940, Pauline had the opportunity to pursue her interest in education. She was president of the University of Toronto Alumni Association and served on the university senate before eventually becoming chancellor in 1971. In all these positions, she was the first woman to serve.

Her long-time commitment to theatre led her to the presidency of the Dominion Drama Festival in 1957. She was awarded the Canadian Drama Award for Services to Canadian Theatre in the same year. In the late 1960s, she became the first female chair of the National Theatre School of Canada, and vice-president of the Canadian Conference of the Arts. She also served on the Advisory Council of the Order of Canada, of which she'd become a member in 1967, as well as on the Canada Council.

During the '60s, the business community had become sensitized to the need for female board members — both IBM Canada and IMASCO recognized her lifetime achievements and made her their first female director. So in 1974, when Prime Minister Trudeau decided it was time for a female Lieutenant Governor, and the vacancy was in Ontario, no one was really surprised that the honour went to Pauline McGibbon. She attributed her appointment to her love of people and her sense of humour, but acknowledged that it wouldn't have been possible without the women's movement. She was surprised, however, when feminist commentators expressed dismay that she had talked it over with her husband before accepting. Having realized that the position would require a great deal of his time and invasion of his privacy as well as her own, it was obvious to her that Donald should be part of the decision-making process.

She knew from experience that being the first woman to do anything was a two-edged sword. She said, "When I am first I'm always terribly conscious of the fact that if I do a good job, it makes it easier for the other women, and if I fail it's probably going to be quite a while before they take a chance on another woman."

She didn't fail. When she left office at seventy, the Province of Ontario struck a medal in her honour, and the Honourable Pauline McGibbon Award in Theatre Arts is a $7,000 prize, awarded annually.

Of course, leaving office didn't mean retirement. Pauline McGibbon continued to actively serve her community until her death in December 2001.

the court should provide a remedy for her.

Wilson wrote the opinion supporting Bhadauria's right to use the court. By virtue of this ruling, Bertha Wilson and her fellow judges had developed a new tort — the right to sue for discriminatory practices. Though the case was later overturned by the Supreme Court of Canada in a ruling written by Justice Bora Laskin, this judgement took place prior to the entrenchment of the Charter of Human Rights and Freedoms in the Canadian Constitution, and is therefore considered a landmark. Clearly, with regard to human rights, she was also willing to take the court in bold new directions.

She was equally bold in family law. In the case of *Pettkus* v. *Becker* (1978), Wilson argued firmly in favour of a doctrine called constructive trust. This concept was normally applied to business relationships, but had been extended to marriages by Bora Laskin in an earlier Supreme Court case. In his dissent in *Murdoch* v. *Murdoch* (1974), he'd basically argued that marital and business relationships were one and the same. Though he had been on the losing side of the case, Wilson chose to develop his principles further.

Rosa Becker, as the common-law wife of a beekeeper, had worked beside her partner in the development of their business. When the couple separated, she wasn't entitled to anything under the law then current, so she was forced to sue Pettkus for what she regarded as her half. In her judgement, Wilson said that they had worked side by side and that Rosa Becker had made it possible for them to acquire their first piece of property. This time the Supreme Court of Canada upheld Wilson's judgement. Family law and the rights of married women had entered a new age, due in no small part to Wilson's courage and convictions.

What was clear from this judgement, and from others she would subsequently make, was that Wilson believed the courts must reflect changing societal attitudes. She believed judges lived within society and their judgements must reflect that. Despite the fact that she could build on the common law to achieve this, Wilson was always cognizant that her position was an unelected one. She remained convinced that first responsibility for changing laws rested not with the courts, but with Parliament and legislatures throughout the country.

She was, for example, unwilling to reopen a number of cases in which maintenance payments were the dispute, arguing that they had been legally entered into and therefore, in order to affect redress, the law, not the judgement, needed to be changed. And despite considering herself a feminist, she refused to use her position to advance women's rights. "If I went around making speeches and displaying a bias, it would make me totally useless as a judge."

On March 4, 1982, Prime Minister Trudeau announced that Bertha Wilson had been appointed the first female member of the Supreme Court of

Canada. Her appointment was significant not only because of her gender, but because it coincided with the entrenchment of the Canadian Charter of Rights and Freedoms in the repatriated constitution.

The Charter has changed the direction of law in Canada, and Wilson used this new constitutional provision to a greater degree than any other justice on the court. She gave that signal at her swearing-in ceremony when, in reference to the new charter and the expectations it raised, she said she felt "excitement because we are about to come of age; anxiety that we shape our future with sensitivity, imagination and flair."

> I get unbelievably annoyed at this notion of activist judges. In the behind the scenes meetings, the non-public meetings, there was a very extensive debate between the Prime Minister, the Premiers, the Minister of Justice federally and the Attorneys General over the supremacy of legislatures versus the supremacy of the courts. And in the end, everyone understood that they were transferring some power from the legislatures, from Parliament, to the courts. Now, you may decide thirty years later that you don't like that, but it's not fair to blame judges for using power that we consciously gave them.
>
> Senator Michael Kirby
> Secretary to the Cabinet for
> Federal-Provincial Relations (1980-82)
> June 21, 2004

In April 1985, the Supreme Court of Canada, in a judgement written for the majority by Wilson, gave an indication of how the Charter would be used. In the case of *Harbhajan Singh et al* v. *the Minister of Employment and Immigration*, the court stated that, under Sections 1 and 7 of the Charter, refugees had the right to appeal their status in person and not only in writing, as the law stated. Wilson wrote:

> It seems to me that it is important to bear in mind that the rights and freedoms set out in the Charter are fundamental to the political structure of Canada and are guaranteed by the Charter as part of the supreme law of our nation. I think that, in determining whether a particular limitation is a reasonable limit prescribed by law which can be 'demonstrably justified in a free and democratic society', it is important to remember that the courts are conducting this inquiry in light of a commitment to uphold the rights and

freedoms set out in the other sections of the Charter. The issue in
the present case is not simply whether the procedures set out in the
Immigration Act, 1976, for the adjudication of refugee claims are
reasonable; it is whether it is reasonable to deprive the appellants
of the right to life, liberty and security of the person by adopting
a system for the adjudication of refugee status claims which does
not accord with the principles of fundamental justice …

Certainly the guarantees of the Charter would be illusory if
they could be ignored because it was administratively convenient to do
so. No doubt considerable time and money can be saved by adopting
administrative procedures which ignore the principles of fundamental
justice but such an argument, in my view, misses the point of the exercise under s.1.[4] The principles of natural justice and procedural fairness
which have long been espoused by our courts, and the constitutional
entrenchment of the principles of fundamental justice in s.7, implicitly
recognize that a balance of administrative convenience does not over-
ride the need to adhere to these principles.

For those who believed the charter was just a group of pious phrases
designed to make Canadians feel warm and fuzzy about their wonderful democracy, this was a rather rude awakening.

It is for her decision in the case of Dr. Henry Morgentaler that she will
perhaps best be remembered by women. In *Regina* v. *Morgentaler* (1988), the court
unanimously agreed that the conditions that Section 251 of the Criminal Code
imposed on access to abortion were unconstitutional. However, the court left the
door open for the politicians to pass a new law the limits of which would be constitutional. Wilson disagreed. She strongly hinted that, in her opinion, no such
legislation would be possible under the Charter:

The Charter is predicated on a particular conception of the
place of the individual in society. An individual is not a totally independent entity disconnected from the society in which he or she lives.
Neither, however, is the individual a mere cog in an impersonal
machine in which his or her values, goals and aspirations are subor-
dinated to those of the collectivity. The individual is a bit of both. The

---

[4] **Section 1 (s.1)** states: The Canadian Charter of Rights and Freedoms guarantees the rights and freedoms set out in its
subject only to such reasonable limits prescribed by law as can be demonstrably justified in a free and democratic society.
Section 1 (s. 7) states: Everyone has the right to life, liberty and security of the person and the right not to be deprived
thereof except in accordance with the principles of fundamental justice.

Charter reflects this reality by leaving a wide range of activities and decisions open to legitimate government control while at the same time placing limits on the proper scope of that control. Thus, the rights guaranteed in the Charter erect around each individual, metaphorically speaking, an invisible fence over which the state will not be allowed to trespass. The role of the courts is to map out, piece by piece, the parameters of the fence.

I believe … that the flaw in the present legislative scheme … [is that it] asserts that the woman's capacity to reproduce is not to be subject to her own control. It is to be subject to the control of the state. She may not choose whether to exercise her existing capacity or not to exercise it. This is not, in my view, just a matter of interfering with her right to liberty in the sense (already discussed) of her right to personal autonomy in decision-making, it is a direct interference with her physical 'person' as well. She is truly being treated as a means — a means to an end which she does not desire but over which she has no control. She is the passive recipient of a decision made by others as to whether her body is to be used to nurture a new life. Can there be anything that comports less with human dignity and self-respect? How can a woman in this position have any sense of security with respect to her person? I believe that s. 251 of the Criminal Code deprives the pregnant woman of her right to security of the person as well as her right to liberty.

This was (and continues to be) completely unacceptable to the antiabortion movement, which by this time included conservative Protestants as well as Catholics. But it's interesting to note that, when the government did try to introduce a further abortion bill, it was defeated; there is at present no abortion legislation in the Criminal Code of Canada [5].

However, it was not only through judicial decisions that Wilson let Canadians know her view on the law. In a speech to the students and faculty at Osgoode Hall Law School in 1990, she said that some laws in Canada discriminate against women and that gender bias existed in Canadian courts. "A distinctly male perspective," she said, has led to "legal principles that are not fundamentally sound."

She further stated that "some aspects of the criminal law in particular cry out for change since they are based on presuppositions about the nature of women and women's sexuality that, in this day and age, are little short of ludicrous." These comments resulted in REAL (Real, Equal, Active, for Life) Women, a traditionalist

---

[5]   See pages 277-278 for more on why this is the case.

group, demanding in a letter of complaint to the Canadian Judicial Council, a judicial review of her comments and her removal from the bench. In a convincing indication on how far the country had moved on the role of women in society, the complaint was dismissed.

As with many human beings, Bertha Wilson reserved the right to become more outspoken with age and Canadians interested in equality issues cheered as she became more and more willing to air her views in public.

On November 21, 1990, citing diminished energy, she retired from the Supreme Court of Canada. While only sixty-seven years of age and with another eight years of eligibility, she made the decision that she could no longer continue with the heavy burden she had accepted. She wanted time for herself and her husband. Had she not been such a prodigious worker, her energy might have lasted, but Wilson accepted a work load equalled by no other justice. In her last years on the court she wrote eighty-one judgements. Chief Justice Antonio Lamer was second with fifty-eight.

Bertha Wilson was an outstanding jurist, not only because of her thorough knowledge of the law, but because of her understanding of the human dynamic and the evolution of social change. Canada is a different country because of her.

American woman, stay away from me,
American woman, mama let me be.
Don't go hanging around my door,
I don't wanna see your face no more.
I don't need your war machine,
I don't need your ghetto scene.
Coloured lights that hypnotize,
Sparkle someone else's eyes.
Now woman, stay away from me,
American woman, mama let me be.
The Guess Who, 1970

The Swinging Sixties (we're speaking of *zeitgeist* as well as the physical decade) came to a rather ugly end in Canada as peace and love gave way to increasing acrimony on campuses across the country. It culminated with the destruction of the computer centre at Sir George Williams University (now Concordia) in February 1969 — the first time students on a Canadian campus had actually resorted to violence.

Until this point, moderate students (and faculty, it should be said) had been giving radical activists across the country at least passive support. But the image of those millions of computer punch cards fluttering down while the main frame burned gave everyone pause. This wasn't San Francisco or New York or Chicago — this was Montréal, for godsake. If our young people looked to an American example, it was Martin Luther King, not the Weathermen or the Black Panthers, wasn't it? Or maybe not.

Even the Old Left — the classic CCFers — wasn't having any of this:

> In the 1930s, German students denounced, threatened and manhandled professors who would not preach the Nazi doctrines to which they themselves had been converted. In 1969 — after university administrators in Europe and North America had suffered abuse, man-handling and even kidnapping by malcontents — a Canadian student leader proposed at the University of Toronto that undergraduates should have the power of veto not only over what a professor might teach in the classroom, but also over the research he did in private. As reported in the *Toronto Star*, Robert Rae, [the future NDP Premier of Ontario, as it turned out] with the humourless arrogance of his kind, explained himself thus: "We mustn't confuse academic freedom with academic license."
>
> Following on the events at McGill and the University of Montréal, at Simon Fraser and Sir George Williams, this is one of the more recent in a series of episodes which show that, in Canada, we are not behind the rest of the world in a type of radical activism that pre-tends to be libertarian but is in action authoritarian and in prospect, totalitarian.
>
> Because this development has appeared on the "left", and among the young, we have been reluctant to recognize its true charac-ter, and especially its disturbing resemblances to the formative stages of fascism.
>
> George Woodcock, poet, anarchist
> *Saturday Night*, July 1969

Woodcock was no friend of the establishment, and while he was over-stating the case, he certainly wasn't alone in pointing out how much the student movement had changed since those idealistic times of just a few years before. Across the country (Québec excepted), university student unions and newspaper editors began to distance themselves from radical direct action, and even as permanently troubled a campus as Simon Fraser began to settle down.

Civil rights and the Vietnam War inspired continuing protests in Canada throughout the '60s. But, without any visceral domestic issues to drive dissent, the vast majority of students north of the border were, by the end of the decade, coming to the conclusion that projects like landing on the moon were more productive than burning computer centres. They were also more likely to provide a career path now that the post-war boom seemed to be coming to an end.

Come to an end it did, decisively, in 1973. In the wake of the fourth Arab-Israeli War, OPEC (the Organization of Petroleum Exporting Countries) cut the supply of oil and quadrupled its price, setting off the economic equivalent of a global car bomb.

Over the next decade, interest rates peaked at over twelve per cent (and some mortgages at more than twenty per cent), unemployment rose to almost twelve per cent and inflation soared to the thirteen to fourteen per cent range. Under these circumstances, the economy encountered a condition dubbed stagflation (low growth, high inflation) that economists had previously thought impossible. Deficits exploded as governments struggled to pay for the social programs introduced in the '60s.

Added to all this, the boomers had not died before they got old, as The Who had begged in *My Generation*. In fact, by the middle of the 1970s, the leading edge was approaching the magical age beyond which no one was to be trusted. That old commie baiter, Richard Nixon, was in the White House, declaiming "I am not a crook," as he and his country sank into the morass of Watergate.

Here at home, we did as we were told, and then just watched Pierre Trudeau age before our eyes as he discovered how little currency sheer brilliance and cool rationality have in political life, especially when it comes to the old Canadian parlour game of federal-provincial relations. (The War Measures Act, wage and price controls, the National Energy Policy — it was a tough time for the feds.)

For many, after the promise of Flower Power, the disco-balled, platform-shoed, afro-haired '70s seemed superficial and cynical. Timothy Leary's LSD-fuelled altered consciousness had no effect on reality, activism seemed a dead end, leaders turned out to have feet of clay, and the creators of the first great youth culture were rapidly losing the *sine qua non* of membership. What was a boomer to do?

Well, for people who had been told from birth that they were important; who had been endlessly bombarded by media messages reinforcing that importance; who had seen entire institutions redesigned to reflect that importance, the answer was obvious. What society was really about — what really mattered — was Me!

Tom Wolfe coined "The Me Decade" in his famous 1976 essay. He noted that the '70s saw the rise of movements like est[6] and Arica and Scientology and dozens of others, each with a goal was to help its "acolytes" strip away all the shams and excess baggage of society and her or his upbringing in order to find the "Real Me". So you had hotel ballrooms full of people confessing and screaming away for hour after hour, and communes where nudity was *de rigeur* and the sex non stop as these Me spelunkers groped their way toward the spark within that represented their true essence. It should come as no surprise that it was during this time that fundamentalist and charismatic Christianity began to re-enter the mainstream.

The quest for Me presented real problems for the women's movement, as feminists tried to communicate what they were about and what needed to be accomplished. NAC might claim to represent 5,000,000 women across the country, but the reality was that many of these adherents were newly divorced working mothers who had more practical problems than the patriarchy to deal with, and many, many more who were most likely in Women's Lib for the Me.

Wolfe uses Shirley Polykoff's 1961 advertising catchphrase, "If I've only one life to live, let me live it as a blonde!" to sum up the dilemma. In a single slogan, she had captured what might be called the secular side of the Me Decade. "If I've only one life, let me live it as a _____!" (You have only to fill in the blank):

> This formula accounts for much of the popularity of the women's liberation or feminist movement. "What does a woman want?" says Freud. Perhaps there are women who want to humble men or achieve equality or even superiority for themselves and their sisters. But for each such woman, there are nine who simply want to fill in the blank as they see fit. If I've only one life, let me live it as a ... free spirit! (Instead of ... a house slave, a cleaning woman, a cook, a nurse maid, and stationwagon hacker, and an occasional household sex aid.) But even that may be overstating it, because often the unconscious desire is nothing more than: Let's talk about Me. The great unexpected dividend of the feminist movement has been to elevate an ordinary status — woman, housewife — to the level of drama.

---

6 Werner Erhard's "est" [Erhard Seminar Training, as well as Latin for "it is"], is described in *The Skeptic's Dictionary* as: "One of the more successful entrants in the human potential movement, est is an example of what psychologists call a Large Group Awareness Training program."

One's very existence as a woman … as Me … becomes something all the world analyzes, agonizes over, draws cosmic conclusions from, or, in any event, takes seriously.

> Tom Wolfe
> *The Me Decade*
> *and the Third Great Awakening*

Even if women's liberation and radical feminism didn't convince the public that the patriarchy exists or that women should adopt, say, lesbian separatism as a way of dealing with a hopelessly male-biased society, it's fair to say that consciousness was raised. What Betty Friedan started was taken seriously from the 1970s on. And, if part of the credit has to go to the quest for Me, so be it. Even in the ideological twentieth century, for most people, it's the results that count.

◆◆ ❖ ◆◆

The term "the Me Decade" might imply that social and political activism died with the '60s. Far from it. Not with people like Rosemary Brown around.

The woman loved to dance and was dancing up a storm. Her partner, a guest at the same party, was clearly intrigued by her. He asked her name. "Rosemary Brown," she replied. He found this hilariously funny. "Don't be silly," he said, "You couldn't be that man-hating battleaxe. You're wonderful," and he went on dancing. Of course, it was Rosemary Brown and, once again, she had to deal with the conflict between the public persona and the real person whom this gentleman had just met. This is a common experience for so many female politicians, particularly those who are breaking new ground.

Rosemary Wedderburn was born on June 17, 1930, in Kingston, Jamaica, in the home of her maternal grandmother. Her mother Enid had married Ralph Wedderburn when she was only fifteen and was widowed at nineteen. Ralph had died of pneumonia, leaving her with three children — Gus, Rosemary and Grace.

Enid Wedderburn married four more times, but though their mother moved back and forth between Jamaica and the United States, the children did not live with her until their late teens. Instead, the stability in their lives was provided by their maternal grandmother, Imogene Wilson-James, and their uncle and aunt: Dr. Karl Wilson-James and Leila James Tomlinson.

Imogene Wilson-James was an accomplished woman and a property owner in her own right. Her husband, Walter James, had been a pharmacist and left the family in comfortable economic circumstances on his death. In addition, Imogene was a political activist and a member of the PNP, the Peoples National

Party founded by Norman Manley (whose son, Michael, became Prime Minister in the 1970s and '80s).

This was a socialist party determined to end colonial rule and put political power in the hands of black Jamaicans. One of Rosemary's earliest political memories was of the riots of 1938, sparked by the lack of franchise for blacks who did not own property, as well as the unfair labour practices of the day. She wanted to grow up to be a politician in Jamaica in order to right these injustices.

Her life as a child was an enriching one, which was not a given for a black Jamaican. Raised by her extended family with the help of a nurse, she attended private as well as public schools — whichever her grandmother decided was most necessary for her development at the time. She loved school and was a very good student. She was particularly adept at games of mental arithmetic. In fact, when her own children were in elementary school they liked to bring their friends home in order to show off their mother's talents by having her compete with a calculator.

She was taught at an early age that cleanliness was the mark of both class and status and was kept at home until the last possible moment so that she would arrive at school as neat as a pin. The importance of education was instilled daily along with her grandmother's religious and political principles — Grandmother apparently believing that God favoured her political point of view.

Rosemary's Uncle Karl had attended medical school at the University of Edinburgh and opened a practice in Kingston when he returned to the island. He was dismayed at the lack of appropriate treatment for his mother when she was diagnosed with cancer — the family was forced to take her to New York. As a result, he established a Cancer Treatment Centre in Jamaica and was ultimately awarded an MBE (Member of the British Empire) by Queen Elizabeth II in recognition of his work.

Rosemary's Aunt Leila had attended the University of London. On her return to Jamaica, she established the welfare system for the island. She, too, was honoured by the Queen and given an OBE (Order of the British Empire.) It was simply assumed that, like the rest of her family with the exception of her mother, Rosemary would attend university, probably in Britain, and would, like them, become a professional woman.

Rosemary, however, from the time of the 1938 riots, resented the British and was not interested in attending university in their country. The family — her brother, aunt and uncle — decided her mouth would probably get her into trouble in England, so they chose Canada and more particularly McGill to further her education. On August 10, 1950, with her family all at the airport to see her off, she left for Montréal.

This was not a young woman who had experienced racism and discrimination and she was not prepared for the experiences she would soon encounter. On the other hand, she had been raised in a family that encouraged her sense of self-worth and she was not prepared to accept what many others, because of generations of put-downs, were. Her instinct was to fight back.

She was given a room at the Royal Victoria College, a women's residence. Her double room quickly became a single when she was told they could find no one willing to share with a black girl. She learned that this was not uncommon; each year many Jamaican students played a game of applying for a double room, knowing they would always be given the single room rate because no one would share the double with them and the university was too embarrassed to admit it.

She also learned that unless she found other black women or the few white students she had been able to befriend in the dining room, eating could be a very lonely experience.

At the end of her first year of university, Rosemary returned to Jamaica for the summer holidays. She had left a young man at home, but now found herself unsure that he was the right life partner for her. She was drawn to Bill Brown, a black American chemistry student she'd met at McGill, and she was determined that marriage for her, unlike her mother, would be for life.

After her second year, she decided to remain in Montréal for the summer. It was illegal for foreign students to work in Canada, but most of them did anyway because it was the only way they could afford the tuition and living expenses. Rosemary had some support from her family, but she also wanted to pay her own way as much as she possibly could. Finding summer employment was a challenge. She was told by the university employment office that she should apply to be a child care worker or a domestic. Employers wouldn't hire black women for other jobs.

Finally through her friendship with Gretchen Weston, whose family owned Weston Bakeries, she was able to find a clerical job at the Weston plant in Longueil, where she worked through the rest of her university years.

Locating accommodation was even more difficult. The student residence closed for the summer and it was impossible for a black woman to find accommodation except in the poorer parts of the city. Rosemary was a young woman who had always lived well. She said, "I never lost the rage at the injustice, stupidity and blind cruelty of prejudice."

She wanted to return to Jamaica after graduation, but Bill didn't. As an American he found the prejudice in Canada much reduced from that he experienced in the United States and he wanted to go to the University of British Columbia to attend medical school. They agreed that he would do his first year at UBC while she finished her B.A. at McGill. She would then join him and work

ROSEMARY BROWN

until he completed his medical education. After that, it would be her turn to attend graduate school, probably in law.

On August 7, 1955, Rosemary arrived in Vancouver and five days later she and Bill were married. Her original impressions of Vancouver and British Columbia were positive compared to Québec, but changed somewhat when, following a honeymoon in Victoria, they once again experienced accommodation difficulties. They were finally forced to settle for a bachelor suite — one room with cooking facilities and a bathroom down the hall shared with two other tenants.

And again, finding employment was difficult. She finally applied for a clerical position with the Registered Nurses Association of British Columbia. The woman who conducted the interview explained that with her B.A she believed Rosemary was over-qualified for the position. When Rosemary explained that her colour was making it impossible for her to find appropriate employment, she was hired immediately at a salary of $130 a month. She remained there for two years until she found a position at the library at UBC for $181 per month.

Their daughter, Cleta, was born a year later and was followed, in 1959, by their son Gary. Rosemary still dreamed of raising her children in Jamaica, where the majority of the population was black. This dream was reinforced when she took Cleta to Jamaica, for the astonished child told her mother that she'd thought her parents were telling fairy tales when they'd spoken of a place where white people were the minority.

With the children, the young couple returned to Montréal in 1959 to allow Bill to take a one-year residency in psychiatry and while there she experienced racism yet again. A friend made an appointment for Rosemary, who had a toothache, to see a dentist. When she arrived, the dentist began berating her, apparently mistaking her for the maid of one of his patients. Why had she not told her employer about her toothache earlier in the day? he demanded to know. She would have saved him the bother of having to work late.

She demanded to see another dentist, but by the time she arrived at his office, the toothache had disappeared. The first dentist called with an apology the following morning, but the apology was based on his concern he had mistaken her for a maid. He clearly didn't understand that Brown's anger was in having been mistreated because of her colour and not her occupation.

Despite genuine concerns over the quality of life available to her children, Rosemary and Bill took out Canadian citizenship on their return to Vancouver in the fall of 1959. As planned, she returned to school but instead of law, she decided to study social work. On graduation, she went to work for the Vancouver Children's Aid Society and was soon dismayed by her realization that children in

Canada did not seem to be valued for themselves. Her experience in Jamaica had been very different. She and her siblings were the children of the family in the broadest sense. When her father had died her grandmother and aunt and uncle had simply taken over their care. In Canada, the extended family had largely vanished and children often fell between the cracks.

Following two years as a social worker she returned to UBC to take a Master of Social Work, graduating in 1964. By this time, the family, now with three children, was well established in Point Grey, an affluent community in Vancouver. Her husband's medical practice in Vancouver was prosperous enough that the family employed a housekeeper. Rosemary felt it was time for her to make a contribution beyond her profession.

Working part-time as a counselor at Simon Fraser University, she had become interested in the work of the Royal Commission on the Status of Women. Now she agreed to become the ombudswoman of the British Columbia Advisory Council on the Status of Women. This unpaid part-time position involved monitoring progress on implementation in British Columbia of the recommendations of the Royal Commission and Rosemary soon made her mark as the group earned a national reputation for being on the forefront of the demand for change.

In 1971, Brown joined the New Democratic Party and began to consider becoming a candidate. She believed that change to the status of women was most likely to take place under the NDP. Besides, like her grandmother, she had always been a socialist.

A year earlier, two events had led her to look more closely at a political career. The first came when she had run and been defeated in a bid to become a member of the Board of Governors at UBC. She was considered too radical. In addition, she had applied and been denied entrance to law school as a result of a mediocre LSAT (Law School Admission Test) result.

At forty-one, she qualified as a mature student, and the test could have been waived, as it had been for two male businessmen that year. Since that didn't happen, she decided to pursue other avenues. She sought the NDP nomination in the provincial riding of Vancouver Burrard, having been persuaded by colleagues at the Advisory Council that the constituency was winnable and she was the person to win it.

At this time, British Columbia was still following the unusual practice of double ridings [7], and Vancouver Burrard was such a constituency. It became clear that Ray Parkinson, who had run for the NDP and lost in the previous election, wanted the nomination again as one of the two candidates. Parkinson and Bill

---

[7]   In double ridings, there were two elected members in each constituency.

Brown shared a medical practice and he urged Bill to persuade Rosemary not to run. Bill said it was not his decision to make.

Bill had his own misgivings about Rosemary contesting the nomination — he simply didn't want her to lose — but he was supportive of her efforts. When Parkinson told Rosemary she would lose, implying that a black woman had no chance, she gave his comments short shrift, pointing out that he had been less than successful himself in the past election. Norman Levi, a fellow social worker, also wanted to run and the nomination battle was hard fought. In April 1972, Levi and Brown were nominated and six months later, the medical practice of Brown and Parkinson was dissolved.

Success at the nomination meeting meant the hard work was just beginning, however. The August election campaign was tough, partly because the Levi and Brown campaigns were not well coordinated, though they shared the same headquarters. But the NDP had the issues going for them. The public was tired of the Social Credit government and when the NDP called for public automobile insurance and improved benefits for the poor and seniors, they struck the right note, as did their slogan "Enough is Enough".

The NDP was elected, and among their MLAs were two black candidates — Emery Barnes and Rosemary Brown — a first in provincial politics. Lincoln Alexander had been elected to the House of Commons in the 1950s as the first black man to hold that office in Canada. But Rosemary Brown was the first black woman, indeed the first woman of colour, to hold elected office at either the provincial or federal level.

Despite this first and her obvious qualifications, Brown was not invited to join Dave Barrett's cabinet. Instead, he chose her running mate, Norman Levi, and therefore could argue that Vancouver Burrard couldn't have both its members in the cabinet. Levi was also qualified but represented neither of the groups that Brown clearly did, women and visible minorities. One can only surmise that Barrett found her ideas and her persona threatening.

Brown began the weekly treks from Vancouver to Victoria, where the British Columbia Legislature is located, normally travelling on Monday morning and returning Friday afternoon. She found it hard to be away from her family during the week, though they supported her effort. In her biography she recalled that the stress of this absence resulted in her gaining a great deal of weight in her first year. She lost the weight in her second year in the legislature and regained it in the third.

Though Premier Barrett would not establish a cabinet position on women's issues, he did move forward on a number of items important to the Advisory Council of Women. The new government established rape crisis centres and shelters for battered women and increased child care spaces from 2,500 to 18,603 in three years. It also established public automobile insurance, amended the Human Rights Act to eliminate discrimination on the basis of sex and marital status, and established a committee in the Department of Education to eliminate sexism in school curricula. Brown was an activist backbencher and supportive of the government's initiatives.

But her life was soon to take a new turn. David Lewis, the national leader of the New Democratic Party, announced his retirement following his personal defeat in the 1974 federal election campaign. The convention to determine his replacement was slated to take place in the summer of 1975. At an NDP women's convention in Winnipeg the summer before, the delegates had decided that since 1975 would be International Women's Year, the party should have a female candidate to present to the convention.

Brown had been one of the guest speakers at Winnipeg and she'd impressed the delegates not only with her skill as an orator, but also with her dedication to the principles of socialism and equality for women. She was not, however, their first choice. Grace MacInnis was the best-loved female member of the NDP and the odds-on favourite.

MacInnis was J.S. Woodsworth's daughter and had been a Member of Parliament. She declined the offer, partly because of failing health, but mainly because she did not accept the concept of running a woman candidate just to have one. She believed all members of the party should be working to get the best person elected, regardless of gender. Nancy Eng, an active member from Alberta, also rejected the advances of the women's group. They then turned to Brown.

Once again her family was supportive, but she had serious reservations about running for a position she didn't believe she could win. However, when Ed Broadbent announced he would not be a candidate, the situation changed. Brown announced her candidacy on February 12, 1975.

Two days later, her provincial leader, Dave Barrett, announced that the party needed someone of Ed Broadbent's calibre, clearly a snub toward Brown's candidacy. There would be more to follow, for the party establishment was opposed to her from the beginning. Some years later, she asked David Lewis why he had worked so hard against her in 1975. His reply was that she was "a genuinely dangerous threat to the party."

Her supporters came from three distinct groups. The feminists, who would support Audrey McLaughlin's successful bid for the leadership in 1989, were not in the mainstream in the party in 1975, but were firmly behind Brown. She was also supported by the left wing of the party — the Waffle Group, which was made up mostly of socialist academics — and finally, a miscellaneous group that was unhappy with the structure of the party. None of these belonged to the party establishment.

Despite this, it soon became clear that the Brown campaign was picking up steam. To counter her success, the NDP elite persuaded Ed Broadbent to reconsider his decision not to run. Brown and Broadbent were joined by Lorne Nystrom, John Harney and Doug Campbell.

The Brown campaign spent $13,147, not including travel, which was covered by the central committee for all candidate meetings held across the country. Because Brown lived in Vancouver, it was that much more difficult for her to take part in the cross-Canada candidate tour, but her team forced the central campaign to take her travel challenges into consideration.

Brown said her love of Canada grew tremendously during the campaign, as she was able to speak with people from all regions. She was particularly moved by the number of black families who brought their children to meet her. For these parents, she represented a rare opportunity to show their children a role model.

Brown's campaign team operated differently from the others. They didn't track delegates as was normal. They knew she was running from behind and all their energies were focussed on attracting new adherents. They concentrated on her public appearances because her strength as a public speaker was clear — they knew she had the ability to convert delegates when given the chance to speak with them.

When asked on the opening day of the convention how much delegate support they had, they couldn't reply with any authority, though they thought they were running second. Indeed they were. On the first ballot, Ed Broadbent had the support of 536 delegates and Brown was second with 413 votes. Lorne Nystrom was in third place.

After the second ballot, Broadbent led with 694 votes, Brown had 494 and Nystrom, 413. If Nystrom crossed to Brown, she had a chance, but the Brown campaign had been unwilling to play the second support game and he went with the party establishment. Broadbent won on the third ballot 948 votes to 658.

She had lost but, she'd made a tremendous impression. Despite the opposition of all the members of the party establishment, including two provincial premiers — Allan Blakeney and David Barrett — she'd finished with forty-one per cent of the vote.

The media recognized that strength. The headline in the *Winnipeg Free Press* read "Brown Last To Be Defeated — Leadership Race Tight To The End". "Brown Wins Believers In Defeat", read *The Vancouver Province*. And Nick Hills, a reporter with *The Province* wrote, "with Rosemary Brown, the end was full of grace and eloquence, and even some humour; but particularly honour in pledging all her support to the man who had beaten her." It's interesting to note that Brown supported Audrey McLaughlin in the 1989 leadership race. McLaughlin's main opponent was Dave Barrett, who was not nearly as gracious in defeat.

Following the leadership race, she returned to her work as the Member of the Legislature for Vancouver Burrard and found herself immediately at odds with her party over labour policy, particularly back-to-work legislation. She also opposed the government's decision to call an election in December 1975. She thought they were still too early in their mandate and they needed to heal wounds opened by recent policy initiatives. The Premier didn't agree and dropped the writ. The NDP was defeated and Barrett lost his seat. Brown however, was reelected.

It didn't take the new Social Credit government led by Bill Bennett long to rescind some of the NDP reforms. One of their first actions was to dismantle the Vancouver Resource Board, the elected body established to administer welfare services in the city. The minister responsible for its administration was Bill Vander Zalm, the future Premier, and he wanted it abolished. Brown led a filibuster against the legislation, speaking for fifteen hours and forty-eight minutes before she broke.

Her party was less than supportive of her initiative because of the bad press, but even that didn't affect Brown negatively. People expected her to speak out. Her ability to do so was nearly terminated when the Social Credit government gerrymandered the electoral boundaries and caused the constituency of Vancouver Burrard to disappear from the electoral map. However, she wasn't to be eliminated quite that easily. She was elected as the member for Burnaby in 1979 and again in 1983.

By this time, the family had also moved to Burnaby, because Brown believed she should live in her constituency. This had been an unpopular move for the household; the older two children chose to leave the family home and establish separate living quarters over the decision, as did the youngest, Jonathan, as soon as he was able. Bill went along with the move, though he was less than happy about it.

In 1986, Brown chose to retire after fourteen years in the legislature. She was saddened when the NDP lost her seat in the next election, but by then she'd accepted an appointment as the Chair of Women's Studies at Simon Fraser University and she and Bill moved back to Vancouver.

In addition to her political work, Brown was active in other endeavours, including her work as a founding member of the Vancouver Crisis and Suicide Prevention Society. In 1972, she was awarded a United Nations Human Rights Fellowship and went to both Sweden and Cuba to study how two countries with such different historical experiences had achieved socialism. Her autobiography, *Being Brown: A Very Public Life*, was published in 1989.

In April 1993, she was offered and accepted the challenge of becoming Chief Commissioner of the Human Rights Commission of Ontario. In this new position she had a staff of 185 and a budget of $12.4 million. She was chosen at a time when there was a backlog of 250 complaints and 1,800 active cases, many of them complaints of racism and sexual harassment. It was a position for which her skills, temperament and life experience had particularly suited her.

Rosemary Brown died on April 27, 2003. She was a woman who knew what it was like to be privileged in this country, but also one who had also endured discrimination. To this unique combination, she added a very rare gift — the ability to effect real change. With her passing, those whose equality rights have been denied have lost a passionate and determined champion.

•• ❖ ••

Meanwhile, back in Québec … In the period covered by this chapter, there were two "revolutions" in Québec. The first, the Quiet Revolution, is generally regarded to have begun in 1959 with the death of Maurice Duplessis.

In the provincial election the following year, Jean Lesage's Liberals won in a stunning upset, and immediately began to drag Québec into the same century occupied by the rest of Canada. Electoral ridings were redrawn to reflect the fact that, even in Québec, the majority of people now lived in cities. The web of foreign-owned power companies were nationalized as Hydro Québec. New social programs were established that would have been unthinkable under the old Union Nationale regime, including a school system in which the state, rather than the church, had final say.

All of this required money, and, having rejected the method of raising it that had worked for Taschereau in the 1920s (i.e.: selling the patrimony), the only other possible source was Ottawa. This presented a problem. Québec, resurgent under Lesage, argued from the assumption of two founding nations and there-fore expected control of both the money and the programs they funded. Ottawa, which had nine other provinces to deal with as well, was less disposed to treat Québec as a special case. And so, the dance began in earnest.

The Quiet Revolution put paid to *la survivance* once and for all. But, if Québec wasn't a nation of farmers with a mission from God, then what was it? Apart from identification with language and state, Québec had no answer [8] in the

---

[8] While doing research at the National Archives in Gatineau in 1997, one of the authors (Tim Higgins) encountered a small example of this lack of understanding. "My escort was an ex-soldier from a small town in Québec. When he learned I was from Manitoba, he recounted how he'd once been posted to Winnipeg. He told me he'd been terrified because he knew, as a francophone, that he'd be hated in the West. His amazement and gratitude at being treated like any other Canadian, and at his discovery of the French fact outside Québec, were palpable."

'60s, other than it was unhappy with its status inside Canada. So, partly as a bargaining tool and partly out of frustration that, in their view at least, negotiation was taking place without the mutual understanding that leads to real communication, Québec governments began to speculate publicly about independence as an alternative to federalism.

That kind of talk angered Diefenbaker and the many people in English Canada who agreed with his One Canada approach. In Québec, people who went to Ottawa to work were considered by many to be *vendus*, sellouts (if not traitors). In practice, this meant most of the francophone movers and shakers in the Liberal government were strong federalists like Trudeau, a One Canada devotée if ever there was one.

Amid the chaos caused by the redesign of the education system, 1960s Québec was dealing with its own student and other radicals, the francophones among them having embraced the idea of independence from Canada with the full passion of youth. They helped keep the streets empty when the Queen visited Québec City in 1964. They cheered when French President Charles DeGaulle disrupted the euphoria of Expo '67 by shouting "Vive le Québec libre" from the balcony of Montréal City Hall. And they were enthusiastic members of the Québec student union that supported the action at Sir George Williams.

There was an edge of violence to radicalism in Québec that had more in common with events in Europe or the United States than anything that was happening in the rest of Canada. Richard Gywn has blamed much of this atmosphere on what he calls, quoting Québec journalist Adele Lauzon, the "dandy radicals" among the intelligentsia, artistic community, union leaders and parts of the civil service:

> Dandy radicals knew that Fanon had written, 'Violence is a purifying force; it frees the native from his inferiority complex,' and that Marighella had written, 'to be a terrorist is a quality that ennobles.' They pinned Guevara posters to their walls, lent their xerox machines to those whom they suspected of being real revolutionaries; from the safety of tenure, they delighted in embarrassing the Establishment of which everyone else, the terrorists most of all, considered them a part.
>
> Richard Gwyn
> *Northern Magus*, 1980

The situation deteriorated as the Quiet Revolution petered out in the second half of the decade. The St. Jean Baptiste Day parade in 1968 turned into a riot, in part because Trudeau was on the reviewing stand. (Ironically for the separatists, the television images of him sitting calmly as Coke bottles whizzed past his head probably helped ensure that he was Prime Minister in October 1970.) And the bombing campaign of the FLQ (Front de Libération du Québec), a group of disaffected working-class youth whose vision of a new Québec had more in common with that of Lenin (or possibly Bakunin[9]) than anything *pure laine* separatists had in mind, was killing and maiming with distressing regularity.

Then, in the fall of 1970, cells of the FLQ kidnapped James Cross, the British Trade Commissioner, and Pierre Laporte, the Québec Minister of Labour. When, after a general strike, 3,000 students and unionists rallied in Montréal in support of the FLQ, Robert Bourassa, the Liberal Premier of Québec, concluded (or at least claimed) that the province might be facing an insurrection. Responding to his request, the federal government invoked the War Measures Act, the first and only time this had happened while the country was at peace.

Soldiers appeared in the streets of Montréal and police arrested almost 500 people[10] from lists supplied by the RCMP, lists that turned out to be hopelessly inaccurate — the home of Gérard Pelletier, Trudeau's best friend and a member of his cabinet, was among those raided. The FLQ, which had been demanding the release of "political" prisoners, responded by strangling Laporte and leaving his body in the trunk of an abandoned car in downtown Montréal.

The murder killed all support for the FLQ (through not for independence). The crisis ended in December with the recovery of Cross and subsequent arrest of the kidnappers. But many erstwhile federalists were appalled by Trudeau's refusal to negotiate and his unapologetic use of the military. For the dandy radicals who were arrested, (and subsequently, in best witch-hunt tradition, wrote versions of events that featured themselves as martyrs to the cause) the whole affair just confirmed that their Québec had no future in Canada.

Many others agreed. Two separatist parties had already been formed to fight the 1966 Québec election — one socialist, the other more or less ultramontane. They won a very respectable nine per cent between them in a contest that saw the Union Nationale returned to power and the Quiet Revolution period come to an end.

By 1968, both parties had been absorbed into a new organization headed by lapsed Liberal René Lévesque. It was called the Parti Québecois and made no bones about its goal — Québec was to be an independent country in some kind of economic union with the rest of Canada. The PQ won the 1976

---

[9]   Mikhail Bakunin (1814-1876), Russian anarchist

[10]   Of the total arrested, only sixty-two were charged and just twenty convicted of anything.

election, Lévesque became premier, and English Canada held its breath. The eternal Canadian question had suddenly been transformed: "What does Québec want?" became "What will Québec do?"

The answer came in 1980. The PQ had promised that it would not try to take Québec out of Canada without consulting Québeckers first. Lévesque called a referendum based on the following, rather convoluted question:

> The Government of Québec has made public its proposal to negotiate a new agreement with the rest of Canada, based on the equality of nations; this agreement would enable Québec to acquire the exclusive power to make its laws, levy its taxes and establish relations abroad — in other words, sovereignty — and at the same time to maintain with Canada an economic association including a common currency; no change in political status resulting from these negotiations will be effected without approval by the people through another referendum; on these terms, do you give the Government of Québec the mandate to negotiate the proposed agreement between Québec and Canada?

In deciding on a date, Lévesque and the PQ probably thought they had the federal government at a serious disadvantage. Trudeau had lost the 1979 election and retired. The new Progressive Conservative Prime Minister, forty-year-old Joe Clark, was leading an equally inexperienced minority government (remember, the Tories been out of power since the election in which Ellen Fairclough had lost her seat, sixteen years earlier). However, by the time the PQ actually announced May 20, 1980 as the date of the referendum, Clark's government had fallen, Trudeau had been persuaded to return and the Liberals had won the ensuing election, a victory that included triumph in seventy-four of seventy-five ridings in Québec.

One of those seats was Ahuntsic, in Montréal. It was held by a former broadcaster whom Trudeau was about to make the first female Speaker of the House of Commons. She'd reluctantly agreed, on one condition — that she be allowed to take part in the referendum campaign. Her name was Jeanne Sauvé.

◆◆ ❖ ◆◆

The media and guests had gathered for the 1985 Press Gallery Dinner, an annual event in Ottawa. The first speaker, by tradition, was the Governor General. She began her speech by thanking the Prime Minister for allowing her to attend. She then began a parody of a letter to the Queen:

The Irish were at it, the shamrocks were golden,
Mulroney and Reagan don't seem beholden
For the use of the Fort, and the loan of the key;
They were workin', they said, there was no use for me.

The guests were on their feet shouting "Jeanne, Jeanne, Jeanne". It was clear that the Governor General felt she'd been treated with disdain at the so-called Shamrock Summit in Québec City earlier in the year, and she wasn't going to tolerate the insult to either her person or her position. She used this very public event to let the Rt. Hon. Brian Mulroney know that she was not amused. He never tried to one up her again.

The event in question had been the first meeting between the new Prime Minister and U.S. President Ronald Reagan. The Prime Minister's office (or PMO) had informed the Governor General that it was to be a working meeting and not a state function. Therefore, while the PMO requested the use of the Governor's Wing of the Citadel, the official residence of the Governor General in Québec, the actual presence of the (de facto) Head of State, the Governor General, was not required.

However, when the President arrived in Québec City to be greeted by the Prime Minister, it was to a twenty-one gun salute, 101 Mounties in full regalia, a full military guard of honour and a thirty-five piece band. These are honours provided for a state visit and not a working meeting. The Governor General had every right to be angry, but in her usual style, she chose not to get mad, but even.

The fifth of seven children, Jeanne Benoit was born on April 26, 1925, in Prud'homme, Saskatchewan. Her parents, like most of the inhabitants of this small town near Prince Albert, were French Canadian. Her mother, Anna Vaillant, was from Ste. Cecile de Masham, a community located on the Québec side of the Ottawa River a few kilometres outside of Ottawa. Her father, Charles Benoit, was from Ottawa. They'd moved west in the hope of making their fortune. M. Benoit was a carpenter by trade and spent his life in the construction business — he built the belfry of the church in Prud'homme during their time there.

Both parents were concerned that their French heritage be preserved, which led them to move the family back to Ottawa when Jeanne was three. She attended school at the Notre Dame du Rosaire convent from Grade 1 through high school, where she was recognized not only as an excellent student, but some-one with strong oratorical skills — she was often asked to make the opening speech to welcome visitors to the school.

In addition, all the family members liked to write and perform in plays. Their father built a raised platform at the back of the house where the children would stage their productions, charging a button for admission. For a woman who would become a successful broadcaster and then even more successful politician, these skills would be enormously beneficial.

On her graduation from high school, she was awarded a scholarship to attend university. Though her education had been entirely in French, Jeanne, like all Ontario children, was forced to write her matriculation exams in English, a requirement that put many Franco-Ontarians at a major disadvantage. But Jeanne's fluency in both official languages was such that she received first-class honours.

Unfortunately, her father was unwilling or unable to finance her further education. And when she suggested that she work picking fruit in the Niagara peninsula during the summer to raise the money herself, her parents refused to let her go. Instead, she found a job as a translator for the Department of National Defense and went to the University of Ottawa in the evenings.

Jeanne had joined La Jeunesse Étudiante Catholique, or JEC, when she was a student at the convent and had become the president in the Ottawa diocese soon after her graduation from high school. In 1942, she left her position with the Department of Defense and suspended her university studies in order to move to the head office of JEC in Montréal.

Her parents were reluctant to let her go, believing that, as a young Québécoise, she should remain at home until her marriage. However, they'd already refused her the opportunity to go to Washington, D.C., where she'd been offered a job with UNESCO (the United Nations Educational, Scientific and Cultural Organization) and they seemed to understand that they could no longer hold her back.

The position was more volunteer than paid, since the students received seven dollars a week and were given free room and board. The heads of the boys' section of the JEC were Gérard Pelletier and Pierre Juneau, both of whom would later serve with her in the federal cabinet. Soon after her move to Montréal, she became the head of the girls' section.

As a Catholic organization, the JEC was a hotbed of Québec ultramontane nationalism. The Benoits, on the other hand, were federalists, and after a trip across the country, Jeanne had soon returned to the fold. She also had difficulty understanding the fervour of many nationalists on the issue of conscription. Having been raised in Ottawa and with both her brothers, Jean and Armand, serving in the armed forces, she didn't see the English as her enemy. She wholeheartedly supported the desire of the Québecers to preserve their language and culture, but believed they could do these things best within Canada.

In June 1946, the JEC celebrated its fifteenth anniversary, with 25,000 people attending the celebrations. Jeanne was one of the organizers and met a

JEANNE SAUVÉ

young man in charge of the parade, Maurice Sauvé. Initially, she believed him to be her cousin's boyfriend so, though they saw each other during much of the fall of 1946, their first real date wasn't until December. They dated throughout 1947, but Maurice had been elected president of the National Federation of Canadian University Students and he was travelling the country for much of the year. It was during this time that he, like Jeanne before him, became a devoted federalist.

In January 1948, Maurice won a scholarship to the London School of Economics, with his studies to begin in the fall. He decided his courtship must begin in earnest and in February, he and Jeanne decided to marry; she was twenty-five and he, a year older. Their wedding took place on September 24th, the day before they set sail for London on the *Empress of Canada*. Not even the open opposition of his mother, who thought Jeanne much too strong-willed for her son, could prevent the marriage.

They arrived in London with very little money, but Jeanne quickly found a job as the tutor to Diana Wilgress, the fourteen-year-old daughter of the Canadian High Commissioner. For this she was paid £5 a week, plus lunches, and things slowly began to look up financially. They improved significantly when, in 1949, Maurice became president of the World Assembly of Youth, a position he was to hold for the next three years at an honorarium of $1,000 a year.

It was also in 1949 that Jeanne had the first of two miscarriages — the second was in 1954. She and Marcel wanted children, but they were also busy, active people and seem to have been philosophical about whether children came or not. This changed in 1957, when Jeanne gave birth to a son, Jean-François, whom they called J.F. Suddenly, both parents were totally devoted to their new charge.

Meanwhile, in 1950, the young couple had moved to Paris. Maurice had not completed his Ph.D. studies at the LSE, but was able to transfer the credits to the University of Paris. Jeanne, meanwhile, became the assistant to the executive director of the Youth Secretariat of UNESCO.

To Jeanne's dismay, Maurice became involved in the many student protests of the era, but his participation ended when the French government declared that foreign students participating in such events would be deported. Nevertheless, Paris offered a preview of the union activities in which Maurice would engage on his return to Canada.

In addition to working at UNESCO, Jeanne also returned to university, earning a degree in French civilization from the Sorbonne in 1952. The same year, Maurice completed his Ph.D. in economics. It was time for them to return home to Canada.

Over the next three years, Jeanne began to develop her broadcasting career. Maurice became a union organizer, often calling on Jeanne for help in businesses in which most of the employees were female. She found it could be a tough slog; her first attempt, organizing a group of women in St. Hyacinthe, Québec, failed because, with an employer who gave each of them a turkey at Christmas and a Coke every day, they saw no need for a union.

She had greater success in working with the women in Shawinigan, which was later to become Jean Chrétien's riding. She realized that to ensure that wives remained supportive of their striking husbands, it was necessary to ease their financial burdens. She persuaded businesses in town to delay payments on articles bought on time until the strike was over and convinced some of them to extend credit. In alleviating the families' financial pressures, she found a way to ensure that the strike would be settled in a way that was fair to the employees.

In 1955, Maurice accepted a position as assistant secretary to the Royal Commission on Canada's Economic Prospects, chaired by Walter Gordon. While he was busy travelling the country and commuting from Ottawa to Montreal, Jeanne's broadcasting career took off. She began to make regular appearances on *Femina*, a public affairs program for women. Thérèse Casgrain, whom Jeanne saw as a role model, had been an earlier host.

Assured and good-looking, she easily moved into television as host of the program *Opinions*. By 1956, she was working in English radio as a regular contributor to *Trans-Canada Matinée*, a CBC network program. Remarkably versatile, she also appeared regularly in print during the early '60s, writing frequent editorials in both French and English for *La Presse* and the *Montreal Star*.

Meanwhile, Maurice had begun his political career. Following the completion of the Royal Commission, he accepted a position as an assistant to Jean Lesage, at the time still opposition leader in the Québec National Assembly. Following the victory of the Liberals in 1960, Maurice chose to leave provincial politics and became a consultant and organizer on the federal scene.

When he decided to run for the federal party two years later, he couldn't find a seat on the Island of Montréal and ran instead in the Magdalen Islands (in the St. Lawrence River). He won the seat in 1962 with a majority of 535 and was reelected in 1963. Both he and Jeanne were bitterly disappointed that he was not given a cabinet position, but he was not known as a team player. Further, he was considered to be brutally frank — not always an asset in a politician.

When he was finally appointed to cabinet in February 1964, it was to the junior Ministry of Forestry. One of the few controversial aspects of his ministry involved Jeanne, as the Tories tried to prove a conflict of interest with Maurice sitting at the cabinet table supporting funding for the CBC while Jeanne worked for it. The accusations went nowhere.

Maurice seemed to have more influence behind the scenes, for he was influential in persuading Jean Marchand, Gerard Pélletier and Pierre Trudeau to contest federal seats for the Liberal Party in the 1965 election. There were power brokers in the party opposed to Trudeau, particularly because of comments he had made about the party in the past, but as a staunch federalist, Maurice knew that the presence of Trudeau, a recognized intellectual, was very important.

In 1968, before Trudeau was persuaded to run for the leadership of the Liberal Party of Canada, Maurice committed himself to the campaign of Paul Martin Senior. When Trudeau decided to run, Jeanne tried to persuade Maurice to switch candidates, but he refused, stating he had to honour his earlier commitment. Partly as a result of this, he was denied the opportunity to run in the constituency of Outremont in the '68 election and was defeated in the riding of St-Hyacinthe.

Following his defeat, Trudeau offered him a seat in the Senate, and there was talk of Maurice being named Ambassador to Italy. Maurice refused both appointments and left politics, opening the door for Jeanne. He became a vice-president of Consolidated Bathurst and Jeanne became the politician in the Sauvé family.

In 1970, Maurice received a phone call from Robert Bourassa asking if Jeanne would run for the provincial Liberals in the 1970 election. She was incensed that the Liberal leader went through her husband instead of asking her directly. Partly for this reason, but primarily because her son was only thirteen, she refused the invitation. Instead, she accepted the invitation of the federal party in 1972. J.F. was now fifteen and Maurice agreed to take a greater role in his supervision. He encouraged her to run and she became a far more influential politician than he'd ever been.

She ran in the riding of Ahuntsic, in Montréal, winning with a majority of 15,000 votes, a victory which made her the first Québécoise to sit in the House of Commons. When she was appointed to the cabinet a month later, she joined Judy LaMarsh and Ellen Fairclough as the only female cabinet ministers in Canadian history to that point.

Her first ministry was as Secretary of State for Science and Technology. On her appointment, she and Maurice became the only couple in Canada to both have served in the federal cabinet and to be privy councillors for life. Their record still stands.

The government, which had earned only minority status in 1972, was defeated in the House of Commons in 1974 when the NDP withdrew its support. Sauvé increased her plurality to 18,000 in the resulting election. Her campaign office staff was so confident of victory, they were reported to have closed the office and gone swimming the afternoon before the election. The Liberals won and she was made Minister of the Environment when the new government was sworn in. It was under her administration that Canadians were first alerted to the danger of PCBs.

She also began the clean up of the St. Lawrence River and took a very hard line against the Garrison Diversion Project. This brainchild of the U.S. Army Corps of Engineers would divert water from the Missouri River into the Red, with potentially serious consequences for Canadian water quality, particularly in Manitoba. (In 2004, the Americans still haven't given up on the idea.)

But it was in December 1975 that she was appointed to the cabinet position where she would truly make her mark. With all of her broadcast and media experience, the Ministry of Communications was a natural fit. During the next four years, she made a number of lasting contributions to Canada's communications strategy. It was Jeanne Sauvé, for example, who persuaded the cabinet to invest nine million dollars in the launch of Telidon, one of the forerunners of the Internet.

She also persuaded her colleagues to make a $24-million investment in the David Florida Laboratory in Ottawa, to promote Canada's involvement in the satellite industry. She clearly understood the need for Canada to become a high tech leader, and had the intelligence and influence to help make it happen. As Richard Gwyn points out in Northern Magus, Sauvé was one of a very few of Trudeau's ministers who could hold her own with him intellectually.

When Trudeau resigned after the 1979 election, Sauvé, along with many other Liberals, encouraged John Turner to come out of retirement and run for the leadership of the party. But before a leadership race could be planned, Joe Clark's government was defeated on its first budget, which meant yet another election. The Liberal caucus persuaded Trudeau to renounce his retirement and come back to lead them once more.

It was clear to Trudeau's advisors who among his former cabinet ministers were in favour of his return and who were opposed. They knew that Sauvé had encouraged Turner and perhaps this was why she was offered the position as Speaker of the House of Commons when the Liberals once again formed the government in February 1980. Her immediate reaction was "Oh no, not that!"

She asked the Prime Minister for time to consider. The next day, having assured herself that she would still be given a cabinet post if she refused, she listened to his arguments in favour of her accepting the position of Speaker. Trudeau argued that she would be the first woman to hold the position and would therefore be making history. He also stressed the need for complete fluency in both languages, and told her that he believed her skills made her well-suited for the job.

Sauvé imposed one condition on her acceptance. Speakers are expected to refrain from entering debate both in and out of the House of Commons, but she was determined to participate in the Referendum Campaign on the No side. Trudeau immediately agreed, as did Joe Clark. Ed Broadbent, the NDP leader, was at first reluctant to allow the Speaker to take on a public role of this nature, but he too was eventually persuaded that she should be allowed, indeed encouraged, to participate in the referendum campaign.

The results of the 1980 referendum left little doubt as to either the efficacy of the No campaign or, as the country entered the worst recession since the 1930s, the level of uncertainty about the independence project inside Québec; only forty per cent voted yes. But, if the federalists thought that was the end of it, they were wrong. Later that year, the same electorate returned Lévesque and the PQ to power with an even larger majority.

Historically, the role of the Speaker in the parliamentary system of government is an unpopular one. Often those chosen had to be forcibly dragged to the chair. Over the years, Speakers developed a custom of feigned reluctance to take the chair. But when Jeanne took her seat for the first time, having been accompanied to the chair by the Prime Minister and the Leader of the Opposition as custom dictated, she decided not to show the usual reluctance. She thought the friendly dragging of the Speaker unbecoming to her gender.

When she sat down, however, it became immediately apparent that the chair had not been designed with a woman in mind. She often pushed her body into a corner of the chair, because this was the only way she could get any support. Moreover, she had to be provided with a footstool, for her legs dangled well above the floor.

What Trudeau couldn't have told her was that the 32nd Parliament would be the longest and most raucous session in decades. The Conservatives were, understandably, an unhappy group. When they'd formed the government in 1979, it was the first time they'd won an election since 1962. They'd believed that if their minority government was defeated, it would mean they'd simply go back to the electorate and be given a majority, for this had been the pattern in the past.

Instead, the opposite had happened and they were determined to take out their ire on someone. Party solidarity required that they outwardly support their leader, (though they defeated him three years later in a leadership convention). Nothing, however, could protect the new Speaker. Their criticisms were quick to come and vindictive. And like most women who do things for the first time, she was scrutinized far more closely than a man would have been.

She'd never had a great facility for names, which made learning to identify

282 MPs a considerable challenge. In addition, the Clerk of the House of Commons, her chief advisor, entered the hospital with a severe heart ailment just prior to the opening of the session.

Her other staff members were also new and so were unable to give her the benefit of their experience. And again, partly because she was a woman, the camaraderie that other speakers had enjoyed with House of Commons members wasn't a part of her experience. In fact, it probably would have caused a major scandal if the first female Speaker had played poker with the other MPs as her predecessors had done. Looking for an alternate route, Jeanne tried intimate dinner parties, but the usual male bonding simply didn't exist.

The Auditor General had also ensured that she would be placed in a very difficult position by issuing a report stating that the operations of the House of Commons did not meet acceptable standards. It was the Speaker's job to clean up the mess. Jeanne Sauvé was up to the challenge, but in order to accomplish what she felt was required, heads would have to roll, perks disappear and fiefdoms dissolve. None of these things were calculated to increase her popularity.

Despite all this, she did what no Speaker had had the courage to do before. She made the operations of the House of Commons effective and cost efficient. One of the first things she did was to replace opaque garbage bags with clear ones so that staff would no longer be able to remove government property with impunity. She replaced cleaning staff, some of whom spent nearly four hours of their eight-hour days on lunch, coffee and rest breaks. She forced some of them into retirement with pensions, including two cleaning women who were in their eighties. She ordered tendering processes to be put in place and established a human resources directorate, so that employees were hired on merit rather than at the whim of MPs.

There were two major debates in her time in the chair which required all her skill. The first involved the repatriation of the constitution. The Liberal government was determined to bring the Canadian Constitution home from Great Britain, so that amendments could take place in this country. To the Prime Minister, this would be proof of our sovereignty.

The Tories were opposed to the Liberals' plan because they believed unilateral repatriation — that is, without the agreement of the provinces — was itself unconstitutional. They used every parliamentary tactic at their disposal to highjack the constitutional bill and have the repatriation question sent to the Supreme Court of Canada. They eventually succeeded, only to have the court rule that both sides were right — unilateral repatriation was legal, but unconstitutional in the sense that there was no precedent for it. After further negotiations, the federal

CONSTANCE GLUBE

Canada's First Female Justice of a Supreme Court

THERE HAD BEEN A THEFT OF JEWELLERY and other valuables from their home. The Chief Justice of the Trial Division of the Supreme Court of Nova Scotia was called to give testimony against the pawn broker who had been charged with fencing the stolen merchandise. When asked if she knew who had stolen the goods, the Chief Justice told the court it had been her fifteen-year-old son. It would have been easier to have dealt with this matter privately, but that is not Constance Glube's style.

Constance Lepofsky was born in Ottawa on November 23, 1931. She received her B.A. from McGill in 1952, the same year she married Richard Glube of Halifax. Her decision to marry was certainly an indication of the decisiveness she would bring to the bench — they agreed to marry three days after they met!

She didn't let marriage interfere with her education. She immediately enrolled at Dalhousie University Law School, one of only two women in her class. She won the Nova Scotia Barrister's Society Scholarship for the highest standing in second-year law and the Cardwell Prize for the highest grade average in her third year. She graduated in 1955, which was also the year she had the first of her four children.

In 1969, after spending more than a decade in private practice, she accepted the position of Solicitor for the City of Halifax. Interestingly, when she asked her former employer why he didn't try to persuade her to stay with the firm instead of going into city government, his reply was that he didn't think she was serious about the practice of law.

In 1977, after three years as City Manager of Halifax (another first) she became the first woman in Nova Scotia to be appointed to a federal court in that province when she became a member of the Supreme Court of Nova Scotia, Trial Division. And, when approached by Prime Minister Trudeau in 1982, she didn't hesitate to accept his invitation to become Chief Justice of the Supreme Court of Nova Scotia, Trial Division.

As chief justice, she was involved in more than her fair share of controversial cases, but perhaps the most interesting involved her decisions in the case of Donald Marshall. Marshall is a Mi'kmaq from Cape Breton who, in 1971, was wrongly convicted of murder. He was finally released after spending eleven years in prison.

Chief Justice Glube was not on the bench when his case was heard, nor was she engaged in provincial or federal politics. She therefore was the appropriate choice to decide whether appeal court judges would be required to appear before the inquiry into the affair and whether ministers would be required to reveal discussions of the case that took place in cabinet meetings. In both instances, she ruled in the affirmative and in both cases, her decisions were upheld.

As with many women, her one spoken regret is that she didn't have enough time to spend with her children. She readily admits that when she's on the bench she's single-minded and all other thoughts are pushed to the background. She loves the law and equally loves being a judge.

Constance Glube should have no regrets. Her service to her profession, her community and her family has clearly shown that it's possible to handle all three and to do so with dispatch. Since 1998, she has been Chief Justice of Nova Scotia, Appeal Division, yet another first in a distinguished career.

government and nine provinces agreed to repatriation and entrenchment of the Charter of Rights (Québec was odd man out as Trudeau and Lévesque could find no common ground.) The Queen arrived to make it official on April 17, 1982.

While this drama played itself out, there was more uproar in Parliament. In March of 1982, the Tories refused to enter the House of Commons as a way of stopping the passage of the government's omnibus energy bill (the infamous National Energy Policy). The bells rang for fifteen days, calling the members into the chamber. The Liberals wanted to hold the vote even though the opposition was not there. The Speaker refused because she believed it was contrary to good parliamentary practice. She forced the government and the opposition to compromise.

When the crisis passed, her impartiality and integrity finally gained her some media praise. And, after a speech to members of the House of Commons in which she stated that the rules must be altered so that this kind of crisis could be avoided in the future, she basically forced Parliament to examine its own rules and make changes for the first time in decades.

Jeanne Sauvé made a difference as Speaker of the House of Commons in many ways, but perhaps one of her most lasting legacies, and a reflection of her own life experience, was the opening of a child care centre in the Confederation Building for MPs and staff.

In 1982, she was asked to head the United Nations World Refugee Commission, which would have required her to resign from politics. Maurice was opposed to the idea and Trudeau said he needed her as Speaker, so she reluctantly agreed to remain in Ottawa. Then, in December 1983, she was invited to the Prime Minister's residence to discuss her future.

Determined to move on to other things, she thought perhaps she would be made Ambassador to France. She was both amazed and delighted to learn that she was being offered the position of Governor General. She accepted immediately, not even accepting the Prime Minister's advice that she should perhaps consult with her husband.

Canada's first female Governor General was scheduled to be sworn in early in 1984. But in January, a respiratory illness that Sauvé had first experienced in the fall of 1983 suddenly became life threatening. She spent many weeks in intensive care and for a time her condition was listed as critical. On March 3, 1984, as she returned to Montreal from Ottawa by ambulance, she was convinced she would be unable, physically, to become Governor General. The Prime Minister, however, refused to appoint anyone else and, on Monday, May 14, 1984, a still very physically fragile Jeanne Sauvé was sworn in.

To those who watched the ceremony, it was clear that she was still a very sick woman. Her face showed all the puffiness of her cortisone treatments and she clearly stumbled during her examination of the military guard of honour. Photographs show her holding on to her aide-de-camp for dear life. However, she soldiered on and Canadians soon grew to admire their new head of state. They wanted her returned to full health.

The only tarnish on her otherwise unblemished career appears not to have been entirely her responsibility. The National Capital Commission, with responsibility for all government residences, expressed concern for the security of the park surrounding Rideau Hall (the Governor General's official residence). So despite the fact that Ottawa residents regularly used this land for walks, Sauvé ordered the gates at Rideau Hall closed.

This was a most unpopular decision in the capital city and left Sauvé with a reputation for arrogance and haughtiness. However, she did allow the cricketers to continue to play on the cricket field inside the grounds. Someone had given her the message that most of the cricketers were black and that she might be accused of racism if she banned them from their field. She had, after all, been a politician for a long time.

During her five years in office she travelled the country, meeting Canadians from all walks of life. She returned to Prud'homme on one of these visits and the entire town turned out to greet its special daughter. At the end of her term in 1990, she retired to Montréal where she died on January 26, 1993 at the age of seventy.

Ray Hnatyshyn, her successor at Rideau Hall, said of her, "Jeanne Sauvé's career was marked by great achievement and she will long be remembered for her substantial contributions to Canadian society and the immense dedication with which she served her country. For citizens throughout the country, particularly those with whom she worked at Government House, her exceptional talent, professionalism and buoyant good humour will be sorely missed."

By the time Pierre Trudeau took his "walk in the snow" in February 1984, and returned to announce he was retiring for good, there were three women in the federal cabinet, fifteen female MPs, and, of course, Her Excellency, Governor General Jeanne Sauvé. Canada had seen female Speakers in the House of Commons and the Senate; two women, the remarkable Flora MacDonald and Rosemary Brown, run for the leadership of a national party and a woman on the bench of the Supreme Court. Heady days indeed.

The momentum women had built coming out of the 1960s had finally begun to overwhelm the social inertia that had held back their participation in politics. That inertia would at least appear to continue crumbling through the 1980s, but it wouldn't be Liberals setting the agenda. Trudeau's replacement, John Turner, called an election almost as soon as he was sworn in. Unfortunately for Mr. Turner, the country equated Liberal with Trudeau, and by then the country had had quite enough of the man often known as "PET". In the 1984 election, the Conservatives broke Diefenbaker's 1958 record by taking 211 seats.

Whatever else people might say about Brian Mulroney, it was in his mandates that women finally became real political power brokers on the national scene. As for the rest of it, well, it's fair to say he was a man of his time.

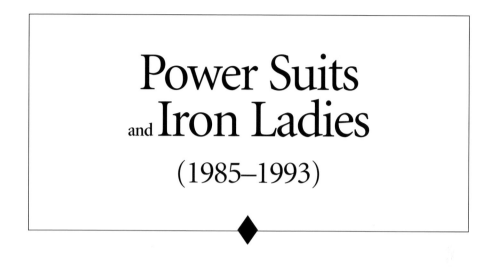

Power Suits
and Iron Ladies

(1985–1993)

◆

Scene: 1985

A bedroom. There is a dressing table, and a large mirror UR and a single bed with a bedside table, DL. There is a telephone and lamp on the bedside table, various creams and makeup on the dressing table.

A woman is standing in front of the mirror, her reflection visible to most of the audience. She's wearing a power suit (dark pinstripes, padded shoulders, short skirt, white blouse). Her hair is shoulder length and done in an understated perm, à la Sigourney Weaver in *Working Girl*. She's humming a k. d. lang tune as she fixes her hair. There's an open briefcase on the bed behind her.

She flips the comb onto the bed and examines her reflection in the mirror for a moment. She takes her glasses out of the briefcase, puts them on, then looks again.

That's better. Serious … *(she suddenly tosses her curls and poses, fists on hips)* … but sexy. Old man Zetterberg doesn't stand a chance.

She sits on the end of the bed, legs crossed, elbow on knee, chin in the palm of her hand.

Debbie … no, Deborah, if that useless ex-husband of yours was still around, he would die. "Whaddaya wanna go back to school for? I ain't gonna be laid off forever. *(pause)* They didn't mean nothin' by it. Guys always try to give the waitress a little squeeze." Yeah. Well, squeeze this, *(she flips a bird at the mirror)* Albert. This *(she pats the briefcase)* is gonna get me promoted and then, you can move every day if you want.

(Phone rings. She answers.) Hello? Oh no, that's quite all right, Mr. Michaels. Yes, everything's on track. I'll drop my daughter at the daycare and meet you in the restaurant at 8:45. We'll go over the pitch one last time and then knock 'em dead at 10. *(listens)* Mr. Michaels, I did the numbers again last night. There is no way Dandier can beat our quote. Believe me, Zetterberg's in the bag. Ah, thanks, Mr. Michaels. I do try. All right. 8:45. Good bye. *(hangs up)*.

Now if you'll just promote me like a man. *(She calls off stage)* Jennifer? Is Laura dressed yet? *(pause)* Why not? You know Mom's got an important meeting this morning. *(pause)* What do you mean, sick? She can't … *(rushes off SL)*

(off) Laura, honey, what's wrong? Oh, shit. No, no, no honey, everything's fine. You're fine. It's just a little fever. Here, you take this aspirin, and then get dressed. Everything's fine.

(*Re-enters from SL and paces. Finally picks up phone and dials*)
Eleanor? It's Deb Wallace. Oh, no, no. She's fine. It's just a touch of fever. Ah, well, that's the thing. I've got a meeting this morning and Mrs. Baldelli's on vacation. I know you're not supposed to … I know, but there's nobody else … Eleanor, I have to get to this meeting. It's … Goddamit, Eleanor, you know she caught it there. It's the least you can … All right. I understand. I'll see you when she's better. Bye.

She hangs up the phone and walks back to the mirror. She stares at herself, her hands fists at her sides. Tears are beginning to make her mascara run.

Christ! (*She picks up a jar of cold cream and hurls it at the wall. Her head snaps round as she hears her daughters react.*)
It's OK. It's OK. Mommy just dropped something. Jennifer, are you ready? The school bus will be here any minute. Laura? You get in your jammies and get back in bed. You're staying home with Mommy today.

She takes off the suit jacket and lays it on the bed. She grabs a kleenex, then sits on the bed near the phone, daubing at her eyes. Finally, she can't put it off any longer. She picks up the receiver and dials.

Nancy? Deb. Look, Laura's got a fever and I've gotta stay with her. Could you send a courier for my pitch notes and tell Bill Reynolds to call me at home? There's still time to brief him. Thanks … No, I better tell him myself. Can you transfer me?
Ah, Mr. Michaels. I'm glad I caught you. My little girl's come down with something so I'm afraid I won't be able to make the meeting after all … I do have alternate arrangements, Mr. Michaels, but they've fallen through. Yes, sir, I know how important this contract is. Believe me, I know. But Bill Reynolds is a good man, and I'll bring him up to speed …
Sir, the daycare won't take a sick child and I can't leave a three-year-old by herself … If you feel you have to, sir, that's your prerogative, but I'm sure … Yes, sir. And good luck this mor … (*he's hung up*) … ning. Asshole. (*She hangs up and caresses the suit jacket*)
Wonder if I can get my money back? (*The phone rings*) Hello. Oh hi, Bill. (*She throws the jacket on the floor, grabs her briefcase and pulls out the notes.*) Yeah, yeah, life's a bitch. Look, there's a courier on the way, but I want to make sure you understand my approach, OK? And Bill? I worked on this for nearly two months. Screw it up and I'll make damn sure you go down with me. Clear? All right, this is how it goes. You start with a summary of …

	POLITICAL	SOCIAL / TECHNOLOGICAL

TIMELINE

1985	• Mikhail Gorbachev elected Soviet leader • Reagan and Gorbachev meet for first time	• *Air India* 185 explodes off coast of Ireland • **Libby Riddles: first woman to win Iditarod dog race**
1986	• Nuclear disaster at Chernobyl in Ukraine • *Challenger* spacecraft disaster • South Africa declares national state of emergency	• Martin Luther King Jr. day celebrated • U.K. and France agree to build "Chunnel" • Prince Andrew marries Sarah Ferguson
1987	• Iran-Contra Affair • Vatican condemns surrogate motherhood, test-tube babies and artificial insemination • Klaus Barbie (WWII): life term for war crimes	• Supernova detected in the Large Magellanic Cloud • Van Gogh's *Sunflowers* sells for nearly $40 M • First heart-lung transplant
1988	• Brain Mulroney re-elected PM • George Bush Sr. elected U.S. President • Estonia declared sovereign state • **Benazir Bhutto elected PM of Pakistan, first woman to be head of an Islamic country**	• **Sharon Carstairs becomes first elected female Leader of the Opposition in Canada** • Nicotine found to be addictive • Winter Olympics held in Calgary • Summer Olympics held in Seoul, South Korea • Ben Johnson stripped of Olympic gold for doping • Pam Am Flight 103 explodes over Scotland
1989	• Tiananmen Square Massacre • Berlin Wall dismantled • Largest anti-apartheid march in South Africa	• Serial killer Ted Bundy (U.S.) is executed • Bounty offered for death of Salman Rushdie (Iran) • *Exxon Valdez* oil spill in Alaska
1990	• Germany: East and West united • Namibia gains independence • Nelson Mandela freed; apartheid ends • Iraq invades Kuwait, leading to Gulf War	• First McDonald's opens in Russia • Hubble Space Telescope launched
1991	• Break-up of Soviet Union; Gorbachev resigns • Operation Desert Storm begins • Warsaw Pact officially dissolved • UN condemns Israel's treatment of Palestine, again	• World Wide Web introduced • Beating of Rodney King captured on camera (U.S.) • Serial killer Jeffrey Dahmer arrested
1992	• Bill Clinton elected U.S. President • Yugoslavia breaks up and erupts into civil war • European Union is formed • Riots in Los Angeles over Rodney King trial • U.S. troops enter Somalia • Charlottetown referendum	• FDA approves Depo Provera as birth control • **Church of England approves women as priests** • **Dr. Roberta Bondar first Canadian woman in space** • Winter Olympics held in Albertville, France • Summer Olympics held in Barcelona, Spain

POLITICAL	SOCIAL / TECHNOLOGICAL
T I M E L I N E	
• Arafat & Israeli PM Itzhak Rabin sign Peace Treaty • Bomb in a van explodes at World Trade Center • Czechoslovakia separates • Brian Mulroney resigns • **Kim Campbell becomes Canada's first female PM** • **Catherine Callbeck is Canada's first elected female Premier (in P.E.I.)** • **Janet Reno: first female Attorney General (U.S.)** • Jean Chrétien elected Canadian PM	• Films: *Schindler's List; Jurassic Park* • Canada's Michael Ondaatje shares the Booker prize for *The English Patient* • Canada's Michael Smith wins the Nobel Prize for chemistry • Political satire *This Hour has 22 Minutes*, airs on CBC television

1993

Power Suits
and Iron Ladies
(1984–1993)

There are no universals in the history of human populations, but there are certainly trends. So what happens when the affluence of the post-war years is rocked by the Oil Crisis and stagflation at the same time that the social activists of the "Thou" generation (Richard Gwyn's phrase) are turning themselves into Tom Wolfe's "Me" generation? Well, if you believe there's more to life than making money, not much good.

On television, M*A*S*H* and *All in the Family* gave way to *Dallas* and *Married … with Children*. Politically, voters in most English-speaking countries moved their governments to the right, electing Margaret Thatcher (1979) in England, Ronald Reagan (1980) in the United States, David Lange (1984) in New Zealand and Brian Mulroney (1984) in Canada. The French, always keen to buck any anglophone trend, elected a socialist, François Mitterrand, in 1981.

Of course, in each of these cases, there were particular, local reasons for a change in government. In the U.K., recession and the perception (not entirely unfounded) that militant unions were trying to take over the country helped propel Mrs. Thatcher to power. In the U.S., it was the Iranian hostage crisis and President Carter's failed rescue attempt, as well as the economy, that elected the "Great Communicator". And in Canada, as we've seen, John Turner was unable to convince Canadians that the Liberals should have yet another term in office, and paid the price at the polls.

But the electors' choice of government was only one symptom of a much broader shift in Western culture. This shift was driven by three major, interrelated themes: rising materialism, identity politics and neo-conservatism.

❖

Capitalism is a magnificent instrument for measuring the price of everything. It is supremely unequipped to identify the value of anything. Values derive from people, institutions, elected legislatures, social organizations and not from entities possessed of no vision but their own bottom line.

Richard Gwyn
Nationalism Without Walls, 1996

Greed is good.

Gordon Gekko,
Wall Street, 1987

When criticized, private sector companies often explain their activities with the hoary old line, "we're simply giving the customer what he (or she) wants". While strictly true, this response ignores the fact that, in order to maintain economic growth in a consumer society, these same companies spend billions of dollars every year creating the very desires they subsequently fulfill.

This focus on marketing has proven to be a very effective investment. Not only has it made many corporate executives and shareholders very wealthy, but the billions of dollars spent have actually helped change the way people think about themselves and their society. It's difficult to explain the Bonfire of the Vanities that was the 1980s without assuming that societal norms were undergoing a radical change.

What the culture of Me was finally beginning to achieve was the breakdown of the kind of community life that had always served as a counterpoint to the isolating forces of twentieth-century urbanization. Even as late as the 1960s, as the post-war pattern of increased mobility and less permanent relationships was becoming firmly established, people were still driven to generate new communities to replace the small towns, extended families and marriages they'd left behind.

Writing about the suburbs he had studied in the '50s, Willliam Whyte noted that though a large proportion of the population was transient, communal services like babysitting clubs sprang up almost automatically. Audiences for public events like lectures, movies and artistic performances were still consistently large. People were active in civic affairs; membership in various societies and professional organizations was robust and attendance at mainline churches, with their message of service (as opposed to salvation), reached an all-time high. In 1965, the

United Church of Canada peaked at over a million members — five per cent of the population[1].

In other words, the level of social capital, which Robert Putnam has described as "connections among individuals — social networks and norms of reciprocity and trustworthiness that arise from them," was still quite high.[2]

When Putnam speaks of reciprocity in relation to social capital, he means reciprocity in the broadest sense — rather than enter into a strict quid pro quo, I'll do something for you because I expect someone will do something for me. I can have that expectation because of my trust of the community and the network of relationships I have within it. In Catherine Ryan Hyde's phrase, "paying it forward" was the norm.

By the 1980s, the culture of Me had begun to create a very different picture. With their sense of entitlement egged on at every turn by the advertising industry, boomers were happily turning wants into needs as they took consumer society to a new level of materialism.

The exemplars of this phenomenon were chardonnay-sipping, Beemer driving yuppies, and the suspender-sporting young investment banker wannabes epitomized by Michael J. Fox in *Family Ties*. These were people whose intense interest in the status provided by acquisition and consumption tended to preclude the kind of community participation that builds social capital. They had neither the time, nor, frankly, the interest.

> The self-made man … owed his advancement to habits of industry, sobriety, moderation, self-discipline and avoidance of debt. He lived for the future, shunning self-indulgence in favour of patient, painstaking accumulation … in an age of diminishing expectations, these Protestant virtues no longer excite enthusiasm. Inflation erodes investments and savings. Advertising undermines the horror of indebtedness, exhorting the consumer to buy now and pay later. As the future becomes menacing and uncertain, only fools put off until tomorrow the fun they can have today.
>
> Christopher Lasch,
> *The Culture of Narcissism*, 1979

Lasch could have added that this more modern man had little interest in public affairs, except as they affected his direct interests, and was likely to tell

---

[1] By 2002, membership in the United Church had dropped to 625,000.
[2] *Bowling Alone: The Collapse and Revival of American Community.* Simon & Schuster. 2000.

an interviewer that television rather than an evening out was his preferred form of entertainment. When asked to name the great people of the age, he might include Lee Iaccoca, Michael Cowpland or Donald Trump.

As Daniel Boorstin points out in *The Image*,[3] Western society has spent most of the twentieth century inventing celebrities, the majority of which have been entertainers and sports figures, to replace the heroes of yore. It says a great deal about the 1980s that the last time members of the public could reliably be counted on to name a business leader was the Gilded Age of Rockefeller, Hearst and Morgan.

Celebrities, people "known for their well-knownness" as Boorstin puts it, are constantly manufactured, and many work extremely hard to stay in the public eye. But celebrity has always been a collaborative endeavour, in that these people are projections of the public's dreams and aspirations. If we were willing to pay good money for Iaccoca's book, admire Trump's over-the-top conspicuous consumption or, as the years passed, read about Cowpland's pampered wife with her diamond-nippled breastplate, it was because that's who many of us wanted to be.

In addition, as youth culture made us ever more aware of the passing years, the old pathways to a comfortable life seemed less and less attractive. The middle class's traditional route — the professions — meant years of penury and hard work, with very little chance of "freedom 55".

The idea of entrepreneurship had a new appeal in the business-oriented '80s, but as any small businessperson can relate, the work is even harder, and the risk of failure, very high. Besides, risk was not what the modern businessman we wished to emulate was about at all. Personal risk, at least, was for suckers.

The middle class is defined by its expertise, its technical skill. If the goal was to attain the wonderful life of the wealthy, why be a doctor or English professor, when you could arrange for the rich to pay you directly (and handsomely) for the relatively straightforward task of making them richer? No, investment banking and corporate law was where the action was.

And if the ethical environment in these fields during the 1980s was but a prelude to the Enron scandal of the '90s, with work that included leveraged buyouts, junk bond scams, fake gold mines and other financial shenanigans that effectively involved getting something for nothing, well, *caveat emptor*.

I met my first mortgage trader after he had persuaded the CEO of a Texas Savings and Loan to sell $70 million of one mortgage bond

---

[3] Boorstin, Daniel J. *The Image: A Guide to Pseudo-Events in America*. Vintage Books. 1961, 1992.

and buy $70 million of another mortgage bond, much like that he had just sold. The CEO, the trader said, was famously ignorant about mortgage-backed bonds … So, the CEO didn't notice that the price he received from the Salomon (Brothers) trader was too low, and the price he paid was too high. Since the CEO had spent his career trying to please his customers — after all, he had to face them on the street from time to time — he couldn't imagine any other approach to business. More to the point, he couldn't imagine how ruthless a Wall Street trader can be. A Wall Street trader behaves as if each trade were his last. This Salomon trader made the $70 million swap and in a matter of seconds netted over $2 million — two million dollars!

Then, he reflected.

That, he said, was why Salomon Brothers was the king.

"Jesus," I said.

"Jesus got nuthin' to do wit' it," he said.

Which was true. Jesus didn't work at Salomon Brothers.

Michael Lewis

The Money Culture, 1991

The middle-class inhabitants of Pleasantville, as well as their downtown contemporaries, will often remark that, despite the constantly growing economy, they were never really well off during the post-war years. But they go on to say that it didn't seem to matter, because everybody they knew was pretty much in the same boat. To the middle class, no personal acquaintances seemed ostentatiously rich, but few were grievously poor, either. (As Barbara Ehrenreich has remarked, real poverty wasn't "rediscovered" until the '70s.)

We can attribute part of this perception to the fact that flaunting one's wealth was still considered extremely déclassé. But economists Claudia Goldin and Robert Margo have argued that this perception also has some basis in fact.[4] Their analysis shows that the gap between rich and poor actually got smaller between the 1940s and 1970s. They've dubbed the American version of this phenomenon "the Great Compression", but many Canadians who grew up during this period will recognize the description.

It's surely no coincidence that the Great Compression started to dissipate just as boomers were entering their accumulation years. But the *zeitgeist* of the 1980s was not all about greed; many middle-class youth still became doctors,

---

[4]   *The Great Compression: The Wage Structure in the United States at Mid-Century.* National Bureau of Economic Research. August 1991.

RITA JOHNSTON
Canada's First Female Premier

RITA MARGARET LEICHERT was born on April 22, 1935 in Melville, Saskatchewan. Her mother, Annie Chyzzy and her father John Leichert were of Ukrainian heritage. Her family was farming when she was born, but when she was six, moved to Vancouver in search of a more prosperous life.

At sixteen, she married George Johnston, a millwright. Following an industrial accident that confined George to a wheelchair, the family, which now included three children, operated a gas station. Then, in 1967, they purchased land in Surrey and decided to open a trailer park. Rita began to attend Surrey council meetings in order to understand what was required of them to get approval for their development.

In 1969, she won a seat on the Surrey City Council. The Mayor at the time was Bill Vander Zalm, and over the next seven years the two became good friends. Vander Zalm left municipal politics in 1975 to run provincially, giving Johnston the opportunity to run for Mayor. She was defeated, but returned to council in 1978.

In 1983, Vander Zalm resigned his provincial Social Credit seat over a disagreement with his own party, and Johnston won the seat in a by-election. When Bill Bennett resigned as leader of the party and the leadership race was called, Johnston was one of only three MLAs who supported Vander Zalm's run. Vander Zalm won, which meant he became Premier of British Columbia. In appreciation of her support, he appointed Johnston Minister of Municipal Affairs and Minister of Transit. In 1989, she became Minister of Highways and Transportation and, in 1990, Deputy Premier.

On April 2, 1991, Vander Zalm resigned over economic improprieties, and the caucus had to choose an interim leader. Several hours and four ballots later, Johnston emerged to inform the media that she was the leader, which made her the first female Premier in Canadian history.

It's often the case in Canadian politics that a party forced to select a new leader near the end of a mandate has problems in the ensuing election. Johnston's Social Credit was no exception. It didn't help that many in the party were only members because they opposed the NDP, especially when the Liberals began to look like a viable alternative.

The twenty-eight-day campaign was a disaster. The Social Credit campaign chair seemed to think the best strategy was to keep the Premier as far away from the public as possible. Some days she made no public appearances at all. When she did emerge, it was often to very small crowds.

The NDP won the election with fifty-one seats and the Liberals became the Official Opposition with seventeen. Social Credit was reduced to seven seats. Johnston herself lost to an NDP candidate, and resigned as leader a month later.

During her last days as Premier, she reflected on the problems that have beset so many female politicians. She stated that when she attempted to speak about serious issues affecting the economy, the media was more interested in where she bought her panty hose. She recalled one incident in which she pulled out a lipstick after an interview only to read the next day in one of the province's papers not only the brand but the price. She pointed out that the triviality of this sort of coverage puts women in politics at a definite disadvantage.

Johnston has retired from public life and now lives in Vancouver and California, where she and George spend time together watching their grandchildren grow.

English professors and entrepreneurs. And while rising materialism will tend to favour parties whose policies value building wealth over building community, yuppie obsessions can't entirely explain the general move to the political right. There was another, even more important factor at work.

The turmoil of the 1970s had left many asking whether the comfortable lives they'd envisioned for themselves might be at risk. What if the modern middle class they'd taken for granted was a temporary condition; an artifact created by the public service, unions and the post-war boom, rather than a natural outcome of twentieth-century progress? This was a very sobering thought, especially for working-class families who'd been able to adopt a middle-income lifestyle.

Having let themselves be persuaded that the good life was defined as much by what they possessed as who they were, the middle class, broadly defined, faced the new age of perceived scarcity with a certain amount of anxiety, if not actual fear.

They built new subdivisions and endless malls because they were afraid of going downtown where they'd be exposed to the effects of disappearing social capital and perhaps even personal danger. As the Japanese model of industrial efficiency gained ascendancy, they were afraid that they were no longer hard-working enough, or smart enough, or young enough.

Members of the professional class were afraid their materialism was leading them to commoditize the very expertise that marked them as an elite (and set them apart from the merely rich). Members of the salaried managerial class were afraid of the resentment displayed by people lower on the economic ladder, including the hourly employees they supervised. And those hourly employees, many of them the first in their families to own a home or send their children to university, were afraid of losing the hard-won gains of the post-war expansion.

People who are successful, even comfortable, soon construct a certain moral justification around their lifestyles; a feeling that theirs is not just a nice way to live, but the right way to live. And, if they feel that way of life is threatened, they will understandably act to maintain the status quo.

In a democracy like Canada's, that act, or at least the first act, is to throw the bums out. So any examination of how Brian Mulroney became Prime Minister has to pay close attention to these people. John Kenneth Galbraith has called them the Contented Majority — not because they're anywhere near a majority of the population, but because they do form the majority of people who vote.

> … individuals and communities that are favoured in their economic,
> social and political condition attribute social virtue and political

durability to that which they themselves enjoy. That attribution, in turn, is made to apply even in the face of commanding evidence to the contrary. The beliefs of the fortunate are brought to serve the cause of continuing contentment, and the economic and political ideas of the time are similarly accommodated. There is an eager political market for that which pleases and reassures. Those who would serve this market and reap the resulting reward in money and applause are reliably available.

J.K. Galbraith

The Culture of Contentment, 1993

That the Canadian Contented Majority was basically of one mind in 1984 is pretty clear — yuppies and investment bankers didn't produce 211 seats for the Conservatives by themselves. It was also people — many people — who were tired of Liberal activism. Who decided that stodgy old Pleasantville hadn't been such a bad place after all. Who thought that Conservative meant conservative.

•• ❖ ••

Ed Broadbent is a very astute politician. When Mulroney and the Conservatives were returned to power in the Free Trade election of 1988, he could clearly see the writing on the wall for the NDP. The country was following the lead of the U.S. and Britain, and moving into neoconservative territory, which meant prospects for a left-of-centre party were likely to be slim for some time.

So, despite the NDP's best showing ever, forty-three seats, Broadbent chose to fall on his sword. This left the party with a dilemma. Did they elect one of their high-profile front benchers to take one for the team and, Moses-like, lead the party into who knew how many years in the wilderness? Or, did they do what every party has done in no hope ridings — run a woman and hope to salvage something from the moral high ground?

Audrey McLaughlin, the newly elected member for the Yukon, arrived at the security desk of the House of Commons and informed the security guard, as she'd been directed by her party whip, that she needed to obtain her security pin. She was sent to the appropriate office, but the young woman there couldn't seem to find her name on the list. McLaughlin said that was perhaps understandable since she was just a very newly elected Member of Parliament.

The staff person had the good grace to blush. She'd been looking for Ms. McLaughlin's name on the spouse list as opposed to the members list. It was 1987, and McLaughlin had just had her introduction to the "Men's Club". Parliament Hill, she was soon to learn, was still considered by many to be the final preserve of

❧ Audrey McLaughlin ❧

the male gender. Ironically, of the three by-elections just held, two had been won by women.

Audrey Brown was born on November 7, 1936 in Dutton, Ontario, a small village in Elgin County. Her mother, Margaret Clark, was diagnosed with breast cancer at the time of her daughter's birth and had an immediate mastectomy. As a result of her mother's hospitalization and recovery, Audrey's first year of life was not spent with her parents but with a family in Port Stanley, the Newkirks. They weren't related to Audrey, but were given the honorary title of aunt and uncle.

The Newkirks wanted to keep the baby, as they had no children of their own. They told Margaret that, since it was clear she was going to die soon, Audrey was better off with them. This was sufficient impetus to get the young woman back on her feet. As soon as Margaret was able, she moved to Port Stanley where she and her husband, William Brown, took custody of their daughter.

As a child, Audrey showed none of the characteristics normally associated with a politician. She was painfully shy and had great difficulty speaking to people. She acquired a devalued sense of her self-worth and report cards and parental visits to schools often resulted in assessments that she was not living up to expectations. After failing to obtain all of her Grade 13 credits, she decided to take a one-year course in home economics at the Agriculture College at Guelph. Her first paid position after graduation was as a junior dietician at the Victoria General Hospital in London, Ontario.

At eighteen, she met and married Don McLaughlin, and two years later, had become the mother of two children, David and Tracy. She and her husband ran a mink farm in Ontario, though in the later years of the operation she did most of the work because Don had accepted a teaching position. It was a hard, time-consuming business that kept her isolated from the community. In order to provide some stimulus in her life, she began to take a series of correspondence courses from the University of Western Ontario.

In 1964, at the age of twenty-eight, McLaughlin graduated with a Bachelor of Arts. Yet this was much more than a piece of parchment. After suffering from a lack of confidence for nearly her whole life, her B.A. was an accomplishment that helped her start to believe in her own ability and potential.

She persuaded her husband to take a position teaching mathematics in Ghana and the whole family moved to West Africa, where they remained for three years. Shortly after their arrival, Audrey accepted a position teaching English. The family travelled throughout most of West Africa during their stay, broadening their cultural and political awareness. However, it also became apparent to both of them that they were drifting apart and shortly after their return to Canada, Don and Audrey divorced.

McLaughlin was now a single mother, and needed a way to support her two teenage children. At sea again, she applied to take a diploma program in social work at Ryerson Technological Institute. Fortunately, she met a counsellor who saw her potential and urged her to apply to the Master's Program in Social Work at the University of Toronto. She was accepted, and despite administration reservations that all of her previous university work had been by correspondence, she graduated with an M.A. She then began her career as a social worker, a career that introduced her to the cause that eventually led her to politics — the culture of poverty. Eventually, because with McLaughlin, the route was never direct.

In 1979, now forty-three and an empty nester, she launched the great adventure of her life. She sold almost everything she owned, purchased a purple half-ton truck, loaded it with the belongings she knew she would need or with which she couldn't bear to part, and drove to Canada's north. She chose the Yukon rather than the Northwest Territories because of the mountains. She had no job prospects. She simply wanted a change, to do something different. With no obligations to restrain her, this was exactly what she did.

After several months of travelling, some of the time with her son David, who by coincidence had also moved to the Yukon, she settled in Whitehorse. She took a part-time position with the Department of Health and Human Resources, while volunteering with the Yukon Educational Theatre, a group that used productions to inform people about alcohol abuse. She found that the shyness that had plagued her as child disappeared on stage. This wasn't her first experience with acting, but it was the first time she was called upon to use her creative skills to write and edit scripts.

She also became active in politics. McLaughlin had joined the New Democratic Party in Ontario because she believed their philosophy to be most in tune with her own. However, it was not until she moved to the Yukon that she began to consider a political career for herself. Her first involvement, like that of so many women, was in support of a male candidate, Roger Kimmerly, who had also become her partner. During their seven-year relationship, she ran two successful campaigns for him and he ultimately became Minister of Justice for the Yukon. During this time, she also ran for city council in Whitehorse but was defeated.

Following the breakup of the relationship, McLaughlin took a volunteer position in Barbados to clear her head and to make decisions about her future. She returned to the Yukon refreshed in body and spirit, which was likely just as well, since her friends had decided on a whole new career path for her. Erik

Nielsen[5], the Conservative member for the Yukon for twenty-nine years, had resigned. A by-election would soon be called and McLaughlin's friends were determined that she should be the next MP for the Yukon.

She finally decided to seek the nomination after a call from Tony Penikett, the NDP premier of the Yukon. He had received pressure from a number of NDP women both within and outside the Yukon, including Pauline Jewitt, an MP from Vancouver. All were dismayed at the lack of a female candidate for the nomination. Penikett evidently encouraged McLaughlin to run mainly in order to get a woman into the race. He didn't expect her to win and his face showed it when the final vote was announced. However, he soon became a McLaughlin fan and a strong supporter of her later bid for the national leadership.

The Yukon has only one seat in Parliament and therefore the constituency comprises the entire territory. The party decided the only way to hold a nomination meeting was to take the meeting to the membership via a travelling ballot box. This meant that the candidates (eventually there were three men in addition to McLaughlin), had to seek support from all parts of the territory.

She had only $5,000 to run the campaign, but she was determined to win the nomination. She took to her faithful pickup and through the summer of 1987, travelled to as many communities as she could, sometimes staying with friends and sometimes sleeping in the back of her truck. When the ballots were finally counted, she had defeated the party establishment candidate, Maurice Byblow, by thirteen votes. She narrowly lost the vote in Whitehorse, but had won a majority in areas outside the capital.

The by-election battle was equally tough. Her Liberal opponent, Don Branigan, was a respected physician. Her Tory opponent was David Leverton. Once again she travelled the Yukon and once again, the strategy worked. On election night, with her mother by her side, she accepted the accolades of victory. She'd defeated Branigan by 332 votes, with her Tory opponent another 500 behind. Audrey McLaughlin was off to Ottawa.

She knew there would be problems ahead. For a member of a third party to win in a by-election is one thing; to win that same seat in a general election, when the majority of the media coverage goes to the two main parties, is quite another.

---

5   Erik Neilsen is the elder brother of actor Leslie Neilsen. He was Deputy Prime Minister durng Brian Mulroney's first government.

To be successful, McLaughlin had to prove she was a different kind of representative than Erik Neilsen, who, particularly in his later years as an MP, had rarely visited the constituency. McLaughlin was determined to return to the Yukon as often as possible. Every second or third weekend, she undertook the trek, which involved seven hours in the air each way with an overnight stop in Vancouver. She wrote a weekly column for the local newspaper and attended to constituency matters, giving Yukoners a sense of both her approachability and her dedication. This went a long way toward her being re-elected in 1993, despite the party's dismal fortunes in the rest of the country.

On her arrival in Ottawa, McLaughlin was assigned responsibilities as critic for Northern Development and Tourism, a natural given her constituency. She later became the critic for Revenue Canada. She began to study French, and though she never became fluently bilingual, she was more than able to hold her own in leaders' debates. Her French became considerably better than that of her predecessor, Ed Broadbent.

When Broadbent decided to resign after the failure of the party to make a breakthrough in the 1988 election, many members of the NDP decided it was time for a woman to lead the party. It would be a first in Canada and, the NDP prided itself in giving that kind of leadership. However, there were few women in the party with the practical political experience many felt was essential. Marion Dewar, elected with McLaughlin in 1987, had been the Mayor of Ottawa for some years, but she had lost her seat in the 1988 general election and believed this disqualified her.

Pauline Jewitt had chosen not to run because of her ill health. Joy Langan and Dawn Black, both elected in 1988, felt they lacked experience and Rosemary Brown, the first woman to run for the leadership of a national political party, believed her time had passed. The only other potential candidates, Alexa McDonough, leader of the NDP in Nova Scotia and Elizabeth Weir, the leader in New Brunswick, decided to stay at the provincial level. The field of female candidates had been reduced to Audrey McLaughlin.

She was encouraged to run by both male and female caucus members. When she announced her candidacy on May 24, 1989, she was surrounded by a large group of current and former MPs, including Marion Dewar, Pauline Jewitt, Svend Robinson, Margaret Mitchell, Dawn Black, Joy Langan, Ross Harvey and John Brewin. Nelson Riis, a long-time front bencher, was still considering a run, but when he made the decision not to seek the leadership, he too joined the team.

The group needed money, workers and a message. The campaign eventually spent $129,000, well below the budgets for leadership races in other political parties. They had only one paid staff member — the rest were volunteers — and the money was spent on travel, brochures and the convention. McLaughlin went

ALEXA MCDONOUGH
Canada's First Elected Female Leader of a Political Party

ALEXA SHAW was born in Ottawa on August 11, 1944. Her mother, Jean MacKinnon, was a feminist and political activist. At the time of Alexa's birth, her father, Lloyd Shaw, was working as the executive secretary of the Co-operative Commonwealth Federation, or CCF, then a relatively new political movement in Canada. Throughout her childhood, giants of the CCF movement like M.J. Coldwell, Tommy Douglas and David Lewis were frequent guests in the family home.

After graduating from a private high school in Pennsylvania, Alexa spent two years at Queen's before returning to Dalhousie University in Halifax to complete her Bachelor of Arts degree in 1965. She took a summer job as a reporter with the Halifax *Chronicle Herald* and *Mail Star* while completing her Bachelor of Social Work at the Maritime School of Social Work. Soon after, she married Peter McDonough, a Liberal lawyer. They had two sons, Justin and Travis.

To the dismay of her family, McDonough started her political career in the Liberal party. However, she became disillusioned with the traditional political patronage system, and soon returned to the NDP. She ran federally in 1979 and 1980, finishing third both times. Although she was a popular candidate, and many Haligonians admired the campaigns she ran, the majority remained unwilling to actually vote for the NDP.

When party leader Jeremy Ackerman resigned to accept a Conservative government appointment, McDonough decided to enter the race to replace him. She took the 1981 leadership convention, held in Kentville, by storm. Not only did she defeat two male opponents on the first ballot; she received 237 of the 320 votes cast, a whopping seventy-four per cent of the vote.

In the 1981 election, she ran in the provincial riding of Halifax Chebucto, and to the pundits' surprise, won the seat. In so doing, she became Canada's first elected female party leader. Unfortunately, she was also the only NDP candidate returned, which meant no official party status, no office and no staff.

Taking her seat in the Nova Scotia House of Assembly, she was surprised at the chauvinism she found. When she asked that legislators condemn the comments of a journalist who'd lamented that men could no longer beat their wives "even when they deserve it", she was answered with shouts of, "No! No!"

McDonough led the NDP through four elections, but was unable to crack the traditional two-party system; during her tenure, the NDP never had more than three elected members. In 1994, after fourteen years as leader, she decided she'd had enough and resigned.

The following year however, dismayed at what she saw as the Liberal's retreat from protection of the social contract and more particularly Medicare, she announced she'd be running to replace Audrey McLaughlin as leader of the federal party. Third after the first ballot, she won when the front runner, Svend Robinson, conceded.

She inherited a party that, by winning just nine seats in the Liberal landslide of 1993, had lost official party status. Though the NDP took a respectable twenty-one seats 1997, it fell back to only thirteen in 2000. Meanwhile, debate about the future of the party was ongoing, with McDonough leading a group that argued for something closer to British Labour's Third Way [6], while another faction wanted to return to the party's socialist roots.

McDonough stepped down as leader in January 2003, but remained an MP. She was re-elected the following year and serves on the front bench of her successor, Jack Layton.

---

[6]   Pioneered by Britain's Tony Blair, who called it "New Labour", this is an attempt to create a more inclusive base for socialist parties.

on the road, taking her message to the membership throughout the country.

Her greatest challenge was to get the support of labour. One-third of the delegates who would eventually vote at the leadership convention would represent the labour unions with which the NDP was affiliated. McLaughlin, unlike her major competitor, David Barrett, and some of the other candidates, had no labour connections. So it was a real coup when she was able to bring Carol Phillips, assistant to Bob White, then head of the Canadian Auto Workers, onto her team.

In the campaign's last days, Phillips was able to persuade White to support McLaughlin. He in turn recruited Leo Gerard of the steel workers. This turned out to be essential, as the race between Barrett and McLaughlin was very close.

Barrett's delayed entry into the campaign was perhaps the ultimate reason for McLaughlin's success. He wanted to make sure that neither Bob Rae, soon to be Premier of Ontario, or Stephen Lewis, the former Ontario leader, and more recently Canada's Ambassador to the United Nations, were going to enter the race. Unfortunately for his campaign, this limited his growth potential — by the time he decided to run, many of the delegates had already been chosen and were committed to other candidates, including McLaughlin.

The media found it difficult to get used to McLaughlin's low-key campaign style. They were used to the fiery oratory of Tommy Douglas, David Lewis and even, as he grew into the leadership, Ed Broadbent. McLaughlin didn't give fiery speeches. Her presentations were thoughtful, but didn't stir the blood.

Nevertheless, it was clear she was winning more and more support from female delegates, who ultimately made up the largest contingent of women ever to attend a national political convention. However, she didn't have the support of all the women. Shirley Carr, head of the Canadian Labour Council and her vice-president, Nancy Riche, announced their support for Barrett during the convention, a serious blow to the McLaughlin campaign.

When the delegates gathered in Winnipeg in December 1989, both McLaughlin's private polling and public polling done by media outlets had McLaughlin ahead in delegates, but without enough support for a first-ballot victory. The perennial question asked of leadership candidates, and particularly the women who'd run in the past — Rosemary Brown and Flora Macdonald — was: did they have growth potential in the subsequent ballots? As the convention began, her campaign had no answer.

McLaughlin continued to do things differently. She wouldn't sit in the stands surrounded by her enthusiastic supporters. She sat with the Yukon delegation on the floor of the convention. She insisted on remaining in the hall when the other candidates gave their speeches. Though she was warned that this could affect her own presentation, she believed it was courteous to listen.

She refused to have a hospitality suite, believing that plying delegates with alcohol was not an example of the new style she wanted to bring to politics. She even refused to allow her supporters to stage a demonstration in her support as she mounted the platform to speak to the delegates. She finally agreed to some music and her campaign committee's selection, Tracey Chapman's "Talkin 'Bout a Revolution", was an inspired choice.

Reaction to her speech was mixed. Some believed it lacked power, others that it was fine, or at the very least, satisfactory. However, whatever the reaction on the floor, Stephen Lewis, who was working as a commentator for the CBC, announced to viewers from coast to coast that the speech was pedestrian and that she simply didn't have the right stuff. It was potentially disastrous news for the McLaughlin camp and might have been the kiss of death.

Fortunately, her campaign team was very practised at "spin". They knew that Lewis's words mustn't remain uppermost in the minds of the delegates. The first thing the next morning the campaign team was out on the floor in full force. They spoke repeatedly and positively about Audrey and the future of their party.

Though she probably had lost some votes overnight, her workers were still expecting a first ballot total of over 700. When the votes had been counted, however, she led the ballot with 646 votes, followed by Barrett at 566. It was crunch time. Could she grow? Ian Waddell dropped off the ballot and went to support Barrett. Howard McCurdy went to Steven Langdon and Roger Lagasse, who had only fifty-three votes, told his supporters to go where they liked. It appeared that an "anybody but Audrey" movement was forming.

McLaughlin still led on the second ballot and, although there were now only fifty-nine votes between her and Barrett, she had picked up 183 additional votes. Two strange things then occurred. McCurdy, who had moved to Langdon on the second ballot, now deserted him and went over to McLaughlin. Howard McCurdy, as a black man, knew first hand what it was like to be trying to do something for the first time.

Simon De Jong, whom Barrett was sure would be coming to him, changed his mind at the last minute and also moved to McLaughlin. When the third ballot was counted, her lead had grown to 125. Now Steven Langdon was dropped from the ballot. It was when he moved to the McLaughlin camp that Shirley Carr and Nancy Riche announced they would be supporting Barrett, but they were too late. McLaughlin won the fourth ballot by a margin of 1,192 to 1,072, and entered the history books as the first Canadian woman to lead a national political party.

Leadership conventions always open wounds. Those who are defeated need to be made to feel important, as do their supporters and McLaughlin knew her first job was healing. Her leadership style was put to the test as she reached out in new ways, choosing to visit members in their offices rather than have them come to hers. She wanted to build an interactive style of leadership — collegial rather than strictly hierarchical. This approach, though highly effective, was often portrayed as gender specific, and misinterpreted as softness and an inability to lead. Her willingness to share the limelight, while it allowed her caucus to grow in self-confidence, ended up being deadly. It blurred her image before a media that had become almost totally leadercentric, always expecting, even demanding that a party leader must be the principal source of comments and sound bites.

Then there were those who wanted to make her over. Like many newly elected leaders, she was subjected to a litany of personal shortcomings — not exactly a confidence-building exercise. She needed a new hairstyle. Her teeth needed straightening. Her voice lacked decisiveness. Her clothes were too colourful, and not sufficiently stylish. Some of these comments were undoubtedly the result of her being female. On the other hand, many Canadians can remember when Ed Broadbent was convinced to cut his hair and give up his corduroy jackets. For the most part, McLaughlin ignored the advice and continued in the style with which she was comfortable.

In the early months, it all seemed to work. The NDP was carried to its highest level ever in public opinion polling. By March 1990, three months after the leadership race, Gallup numbers showed the NDP with forty-one per cent of voter support. It was an astonishing number, though one has to remember Mulroney's popularity was plummeting and the Liberals were just beginning their leadership race. John Turner had resigned, leaving the leadership in the hands of Herb Gray, whom everyone knew would not be a candidate for the position.

It didn't last. Eighteen months later, in September 1991, the polls showed the NDP had dropped to twenty-five per cent and by August 1992, the party was at just sixteen per cent. Was it McLaughlin's leadership? Or the election of NDP governments in Ontario, Saskatchewan and British Columbia, none of which could live up to their election promises because of a serious downturn in the economy? Both factors seemed to play a role.

Ontario was a particular sore point. When Bob Rae, the province's first NDP premier, forced a social contract on labour that reminded many of Ronald Reagan's handling of American unions, the backlash hurt the party across the country. McLaughlin made it clear she thought the former student radical was wrong, but it didn't help.

While McLaughlin was admired for her principled stand against the Gulf War, the majority of Canadians didn't agree with her. She was the only elected leader to debate the Charlottetown Accord on national television when she went head to head with Preston Manning, leader of the new Reform Party. Most observers thought she won the debate, but once again she was on the wrong side of the issue as far as voters were concerned. The country was moving to the right and the NDP appeared to be increasingly out of step. As leader, McLaughlin was blamed for the party's failure to walk with the times. By the eve of the 1993 election, there was little doubt the NDP was facing a disaster.

In June, McLaughlin offered to resign if the General Council of the party thought it was the right thing to do. The council asked her to stay, but this act of selflessness, putting the needs of her party above her own, was once again interpreted in the media as a sign of weakness.

When the election was called in September, McLaughlin and her party had already been written off. Though her appearances in the leaders' debates were consistently judged to be good or very good, and her ability to speak French was celebrated in the Québec media, the minimal coverage of her speeches, statements and events throughout the campaign simply reinforced the party's image as also-rans.

Party policy was largely ignored in the media, with what few questions there were focusing solely on party fortunes. In the end, the predicted disaster came to pass. The NDP lost official party status, dropping from forty-one seats to just nine, though McLaughlin, unlike Prime Minister Kim Campbell, was re-elected.

After the election, McLaughlin dropped out of sight, this time travelling to Nepal to do some soul searching. On April 18, 1994, shortly after her return to Canada, she tendered her resignation as leader of the New Democratic Party. In another act of selflessness, she told the party she'd remain until they chose a new leader, a decision they put off for eighteen months.

Though born in southern Ontario, McLaughlin has become a true northerner, passionately advocating for the north and its peoples. Since her departure from federal politics in 1995, she has continued in public life, serving as a Circumpolar Envoy for the Yukon Territorial Government and a member of the advisory committee to the Northern Research Institute at Yukon College. She was a founding member of the board of governors of the University of the Arctic, and has been elected both vice-president of the Socialist International, and president of Socialist Women International.

There's little doubt that if the party was looking for a leader who could claim the moral high ground, Audrey McLaughlin was their woman. Problem was, in the 1980s, it was so incredibly slippery up there.

There's a constant tension in the NDP between principle and pragmatism that goes right back to its Progressive roots. On one side are the pure socialists and their allies even farther to the left, who seem to believe that electoral disasters not withstanding, the self-evidence of their arguments will eventually bring voters to their senses. On the other side are those who see little chance of changing the country without first forming a government, and so are in favour of a certain amount of compromise. Both groups, however, share the basic belief that the party and the political system are the best vehicles to achieve their goals.

But in the '80s, the traditional Left (and everyone else) was bushwhacked by an entirely new school of thought. Putatively Marxists, these people argued that the entire discussion was irrelevant because neither side was right; couldn't be, in fact, because there was no such thing as right. Or wrong.

One of the great themes of the twentieth century has been the gradual reversal in stature of the sciences and humanities. As early as the 1970s, it was becoming clear that the sciences were providing more useful descriptions of the world around us, as well as our place in it than were the humanities — something that had not been the case before 1939.

For the heirs of Freud, Wittgenstein and Sartre, this simply wouldn't do. And so, the counterattack. It was launched from philosophy and sociology departments, first in Europe and then North America, and was breathtakingly in tune with the uncertain times. Humanities professionals came to the conclusion that their approach to describing reality couldn't be wrong. The problem, therefore, must lie with reality itself.

Postmodernism, that archetypically French explanation of how we live, began its formal existence with a study commissioned, not by Paris, but Québec City. The author was a French philosopher named Jean-François Lyotard. In *The Postmodern Condition*, Lyotard asked why the only knowledge we accept as real is scientific knowledge. In other words, why is scientific knowledge privileged?

His answer — proof positive that reports of Marxism's demise were exaggerated — was that since most scientific knowledge has been produced in universities that are largely supported by the state, this is the knowledge valued by the liberal bourgeois establishment. In other words, power defines knowledge.

The implications of this idea are fairly startling. If knowledge is a description of reality, but knowledge is subject to political, social and economic forces, is it even possible to identify an objective reality? A large group of social scientists have spent the succeeding years building entire careers on answering "Non!" to that question.

To take just two (highly simplified) examples, it's been argued that reality is, in effect, a continuum — since more people agree on what "green" is than on what "justice" is, green is therefore "realer". Michel Foucault concluded that there is no such thing as normal. Sanity, for example, has no objective existence —

it's defined by those in power: psychiatrists, in this case.[7]

Flowing from the same mode of thought is deconstructionism, which asserts that, because of self editing and the baggage that words naturally accumulate over time, what one says must always be more, or less, than what one means. In other words, there's always some deeper meaning in even the simplest communication — nothing is what it seems.

Cultural relativism is the idea that no culture is ethically or morally superior to any other. In this view, right and wrong are social constructs. There are no absolutes.

Whether these ideas offer a better description of the human condition than science is able to provide is still being debated. Whether they've been used to advance other agendas, is beyond dispute.

For example, this general approach (postmodernism) has been successfully employed to cast doubt on the existence of a single understandable history of humanity (metanarrative is the favoured phrase). In other words, my story, my reality, my way of knowing is just as legitimate as yours, and further, just as worthy of respect.

All of this was very encouraging for groups that felt they had been disadvantaged under the metanarrative of white males — nothing brings communities together like a shared grievance. Once consciousness had been raised and these groups came to understand that ideas like "good" music, "moral" behaviour, or even gender and race were someone else's story imposed on the oppressed, the stage was set for the rise of identity politics and the sense of entitlement that goes with it.

Identity politics has been defined as:

> … [the] demand for recognition on the basis of the very grounds
> on which recognition has previously been denied: it is qua [as]
> women, qua blacks, qua lesbians that groups demand recognition.
> The demand is not for inclusion within the fold of "universal
> humankind" on the basis of shared human attributes; nor is it for
> respect "in spite of" one's differences. Rather, what is demanded is
> respect for oneself as different.[8]

Exacerbated by the culture of Me, identity politics has grown rapidly

---

[7] Given some of the conditions psychiatry has historically labelled mental illness – female "hysteria" and homosexuality come to mind – he may have had a point.

[8] Kruks, Sonia. *Retrieving Experience: Subjectivity and Recognition in Feminist Politics.* Cornell University Press. Ithaca, NY. 2000.

throughout North America, and, to a lesser extent, Europe. It's a plague to which Canada is uniquely vulnerable.

Canada has never been the same kind of nation state that the U.S. or England or France are. We have no Uncle Sam or John Bull or Marianne; no simple, monolithic national myth — no metanarrative, if you will. In fact, as John Ralston Saul has pointed out, "the essential characteristic of the Canadian public mythology is its complexity". In that sense, Canada has been celebrated as the first post-modern nation-state. But, our bilingual, multicultural approach to nationhood also made it much easier for people to define themselves as something other than, or in addition to, simply Canadian.

Of course, there have always been hyphenated Canadians — one of our greatest strengths is that we are, and have been, a country of immigrants. It's equally clear that there are groups within the Canadian population, minorities, that through no fault of their own, stand outside what the majority defines as mainstream. The now familiar list is set forth in Section 15 of the Charter [9].

> I think a democracy that has a serious commitment to fundamental rights and freedoms; that makes a Parliament or legislature think and justify before it infringes those; I think that is a richer, fuller democracy which is likely to give more allowance for expression to minorities and other groups. And, given that Canada is an increasingly pluralistic, diverse society, I think this becomes very important for sustaining ourselves as a democracy … the Charter provides a peaceful way for our differences … to be accommodated.
>
> Chief Justice Beverley McLachlin,
> Supreme Court of Canada
> May 28, 2004

> The purpose of the Charter is to protect the rights of minorities, whether it's popular or unpopular. And, by the way, if it was popular, they wouldn't need protection. The reality is that the rights of minorities need to be protected from the tyranny of the majority. That's exactly what the Charter does.
>
> Senator Michael Kirby
> Secretary to the Cabinet (1980-82)
> June 21, 2004

---

[9]   15. (1) Every individual is equal before and under the law and has the right to equal protection and equal benefit of the law without discrimination and, in particular, without discrimination based on race, national or ethnic orgin, colour, religion, sex, age or mental or physical disability.

What was new in the 1980s was the formation of groups with sensibilities centred around self interest — anti-development groups, shareholders rights groups, anti-tax groups, any organization with a name that begins, "Victims of …", — groups that were more than eager to define their difference, and their entitlement by seeking to broaden the definition of oppressed minority.

> For me, feminism is equality between men and women. They often say we must push to get things or we must be stronger than men. No. For me, it has nothing to do with that. Feminism is to be equal with men, and that's all … the new generation say they don't want to be feminists because we are too aggressive. I never crash doors — I open them. It takes more time to open a door than to crash it, but the door [stays] open after that. For me, you have to open doors to women's rights and women's needs.
>
> Senator Lucie Pépin
> June 21, 2004

Postmodernism was a godsend for the postulators of Patriarchy. It provided a theoretical underpinning for the melding of Marxism and gender politics that had come to represent radical feminism's worldview. By successfully selling reality as social construct, it allowed feminist academics to explain the world as one created to reflect an exclusively male reality. The impediments to achieving true equality between men and women (not a universally shared goal among feminists, it should be noted) were not due to mere social inertia. Our entire culture — every part of it — was inherently hostile to women.

> Canada's image abroad is that of a country with a high standard of living — a country dedicated to promoting peace in the world; a country where women have access to post-secondary education, and freedom of expression; a country where women are free to pursue the occupation they choose and move around without constraint.
> But the Panel learned that Canadian women are all too familiar with inequality and violence which tether them to lives few in the world would choose to lead … all women in Canada are vulnerable to male violence. Race, class, age, sexual orientation, level of ability and other objective characteristics, alone or in combination, compound the risk.
>
> Changing the Landscape
> Canadian Panel on Violence
> Against Women, 1993

It's fair to ask, after reading this report, whether the authors have ever actually visited the Canada in which the rest of us live. At one point, they even make the claim that ninety-eight per cent [10] of Canadian women have been abused, a figure so remarkable that it should have generated demands for clarification across the country. The fact that this number, and the report itself, seem to have been accepted at face value by many who are publicly identified as feminists, suggests yet another problem a modern woman might face when running for office.

From a purely practical point of view, it's unfortunate that feminist scholarship took such a resolutely postmodernist approach. By concentrating on the patriarchy, feminism's focus was shifted away from issues that concerned women in wider society — income equity, child care, glass ceilings — to be replaced by what many potential supporters might consider extreme — even dangerous — cant. For example:

1. Woman are victims …

Feminism['s] … project is to uncover and claim as valid the experience of women, the major content of which is the devalidation of women's experience. [11]

2. The Western canon is a product of patriarchy …

Feminist scholarship begins with an awareness that much previous scholarship has offered a white, male, eurocentric, heterosexist, and elite view of "reality". Often feminist scholars seek to uncover and examine the way this bias has operated in their own discipline. These projects involve showing how certain groups, lifestyles, methodologies, categories, metaphors, symbols, or art forms were devalued or rendered invisible by the previous biases and distortions of the field. [12]

3. Scientific knowledge is a specifically male way of knowing ...

If we are to believe that mechanistic metaphors were a fundamental component of the explanations the new science provided,

---

10 "When all kinds of sexual violation and intrusion are considered, ninety-eight per cent of women reported they personally experienced some form of sexual violation." The figure is derived from The Women's Safety Project, a study based on interviews with 420 women from the Toronto area. See *Moral Panic: Biopolitics Rising* by John Fekete for one analysis of this study's methodology.

11 Catherine MacKinnon. *Feminism, Marxism, Method and the State: Toward Feminist Jurisprudence.* "Signs: Journal of Women and Culture in Society." 8: 635, 638.(1983).

12 *Feminist Scholarshhip Guidelines*, the New Jersey Project, 1991.

why should we believe that gender metaphors were not? A consistent analysis would lead to the conclusion that understanding nature as a woman indifferent to or even welcoming rape was equally fundamental to the interpretations of these new conceptions of nature and inquiry … In that case, why is it not as illuminating and honest to refer to Newton's laws as 'Newton's Rape Manual' as it is to call them 'Newton's mechanics'? [13]

Rather than participate in elected politics — a patriarchal system — followers of this brand of feminism have generally concentrated their energies in other areas. They work to reform education curricula, build women's studies departments and produce government-supported studies like the one quoted earlier; studies that are often quietly shelved because no cabinet minister who wants to be re-elected, male or female, would dare be associated with them.

Whatever the quality of the research produced (like postmodernism itself, the jury's still out), this kind of feminism seemed to have little practical effect, other than this: it provided (and continues to provide) convenient targets for people who have no interest in seeing women and men as equals, and it produced ever more highly educated female graduates who saw politics as a patriarchal conspiracy and declined to become involved.

The final irony was that, having helped open Pandora's Box, radical feminism proved no more immune to identity politics than the rest of Canadian society. The demand for "respect of oneself as different" soon saw women oppressed by the patriarchy atomize into women of colour oppressed by white, middle-class women; lesbians oppressed by heterosexual women; women of different abilities oppressed by able-bodied women, and on, and on. The National Action Committee on the Status of Women (NAC), so successful at advancing women's rights in the 1970s, imploded in the '90s, largely on this issue alone.

So, as its discussions became more esoteric, and its proposed interventions to correct society's oppression of women ever more excessive, feminism was once again becoming an epithet. Worse, outside university campuses, it was becoming irrelevant.

Given all this, what was an old-time equality feminist, who had a firm grasp on reality, who didn't think society was a vast patriarchal plot and was definitely not a victim to do? Well, she could run the Northwest Territories.

[13] Sandra Harding, *The Science Question in Feminism*, Cornell University Press. 1986.

✦ NELLIE COURNOYEA ✦

Walking home in Yellowknife late one cold January evening, Nellie Cournoyea came across one man beating up another. After yelling at passers-by to call the police, she kicked the attacker in the groin, then broke his nose. He ran away, yelling, "Leave me alone!" She yelled at him to come back. "I haven't finished with you yet." The following day, with a black eye and bruised ribs, she took her usual seat in the NWT Legislature. This and many similar stories back up her reputation as one tough lady!

Nellie Cournoyea was born in Aklavik, NWT, in 1940. Her mother was Inuvialuit, or Inuit of the western Arctic. Her father, Nels Hvatum, was an adventurer turned trapper. He'd migrated from Norway and had worked his way across Canada before settling in the north. Nellie was the second of eleven children. During her childhood, her whole family worked a trap line some forty kilometres outside Aklavik, travelling entirely by dogsled. To this day, she can still skin a muskrat — or kill a muskox [14] — with the best of them.

There appears to have been little separation in roles between the male and female children. Nellie didn't inherit her mother's ability not to take life too seriously and to laugh off troubles, but her warmth of personality and her openness to people were obvious in the young woman from an early age. Her strength and stubbornness would appear to have come from her father. Two of Nellie siblings were killed in a fire when their home was destroyed. She was badly burned and scarred, but her hospitalization only seems to have added to her toughness of spirit.

She attributes her success to the sense of belonging and community she received from her family, where everyone was expected to do their part. She believes these attributes to be absent from many young people in the NWT today, which leads to their sense of isolation and dissatisfaction with their lives. Alcoholism and suicide are the result, she believes, of the breakdown of community.

Her education was mostly by correspondence from the Department of Education in Alberta. Soon after she passed Grade 10, at the age of seventeen, she met and married a Canadian Forces Officer who was based in Inuvik. For three years, she followed him to postings in Halifax and Ottawa. Shortly after their return to the North, they were divorced. She has a daughter, Maureen, and a son John, now both in their forties. She has never remarried.

She supported herself and the children by working for the CBC. She'd become interested in broadcasting through volunteering for the community radio station. Her first job was as a radio announcer. She was willing to do all the shifts no one else wanted. The resulting late nights and early mornings suited her life as

---

[14] Once, when attending a Western Premier's conference in Alberta, she startled her colleagues at a dinner held at a guest ranch, by showing up with the trophy head of a large muskox. She had shot the animal herself earlier in the week.

a working mother. She later became the station manager.

In more than ten years working for the CBC, Cournoyea fought a constant battle to get funding for Aboriginal programming produced in the north. She believed that programming had to be relevant to the audience and in order to achieve that, it had to be Aboriginal. Her battles with the CBC establishment prepared her for her lifelong battle to achieve better treatment for her people.

She left the stability of CBC North in order to work directly with and for her people. She founded the Committee for Original People's Entitlement (COPE), an organization dedicated to the self-determination of the Inuvialuit of the Western Arctic. In the 1970s, she worked as a negotiator for the Inuvialut, who were then working towards a comprehensive land claims settlement with the federal government.

These were difficult years in the north, as First Nations people were pitted against the oil companies that wanted to build the Mackenzie Valley Pipeline. Cournoyea was determined that land claims would be settled first. It was during these years that she earned her reputation as a workaholic. Though the oil industry was much better financed and their negotiators formally trained, they met their match in Nellie Cournoyea.

She even ran for and won the Mackenzie Delta seat in the NWT Legislature, as a way of furthering the settlement of those claims. She believed that, as a member of the legislature, she would have more prestige and credibility. The claims were finalized in 1984.

Until this time, she had opposed any pipeline in the NWT. Now that land claims had been settled, and any profits would be shared among First Nations people, she no longer opposed the pipeline, provided appropriate environmental controls were in place.

In addition to her already heavy workload, Cournoyea worked with others to establish the first Arctic Winter Games in 1970. The Delta Drummers, now an internationally recognized traditional dance, drum and song group, received her active encouragement. She was present in every aspect of her community.

Cournoyea has a well-deserved reputation for warmth and hospitality. Her house was, and remains, open to all, particularly those in trouble. If you were a student waiting for a plane back to your settlement, a patient awaiting transfer to a medical station, a visiting politician or an artist, you could always go to Nellie's for tea, talk, television and hot food at meal time. It's no wonder she's been a success in politics. Her roots in her community are deep and many of her constituents have had direct contact with her.

In 1989, she was a vigorous opponent of the Meech Lake Accord, as were many northerners. One of the less well-known provisions of Meech would have given provincial veto over the entrance of the territories as provinces. Prior to the Meech proposals, discussions on admission to provincial status were solely between the federal government and the territory. Québec particularly wanted the new provision, and it also had strong support from provinces like Alberta and Saskatchewan that border on the Territories and have direct road and air links with them. The people of the north believed it was unjust — none of the other provinces had been expected to abide by such criteria upon their entry to Confederation.

In addition, the Meech Lake Accord made it almost impossible for residents of the Territories to be appointed judges. Under Meech, provinces would make these appointments, and northerners didn't believe provincial governments would choose any but their own. Provinces would also appoint senators, while in the territories, the Prime Minister would still have that power. Cournoyea's opposition was firm and to the point. The people of the North were being treated as second-class citizens and that was unacceptable.

Cournoyea was elected for the first time in 1979, and re-elected in 1983, 1987 and 1991. Following her election in 1983, she became a cabinet minister. All members of the Northwest Territories Legislature are elected as Independents — there are no political parties. As a result, once the twenty-four members have been chosen, they must select from among themselves the Government Leader, now called the Premier, as well as the members of the cabinet.

During her years in cabinet, Cournoyea held four portfolios, including Health and Energy, Mines and Petroleum. It was while she was Minister of Health that she oversaw the transfer of services from the federal government to the territory. This was in keeping with her belief that the local community does it best when it comes to the delivery of any service. While Energy Minister, she began the negotiations for a Northern Energy Accord, the purpose of which was, once again, to devolve federal power to the Territory.

In the fall of 1991, the newly elected twenty-four members of the NWT legislature chose Nellie Cournoyea as Government Leader. In so doing, they made her the first female Aboriginal political leader elected in Canada.

Cournoyea is blunt, autocratic, hardworking and above all, a voice for her people. As Premier, she was faced with the same problems of most governments in the 1990s. A rising deficit forced a streamlining of services in all departments, including pay cuts for herself and her ministers. In addition to a drop in transfer payments, the oil and gas industry had pulled much of its investment from the territories. The result was a sharp rise in unemployment.

During the same period, she had to preside over the difficult breakup of the NWT. The eastern Arctic, Nunavut, was established as a separate territory in 1996. Prior to the devolution, she constantly reminded the federal government that it would be impossible to run the two territories with the money formerly given to one. She worked hard to achieve greater devolution of services from the federal government to the territory, and from the territory to the community. Her larger aim was to end the paternalistic governance of the NWT by the federal Department of Indian and Northern Affairs. In part, this was achieved in the land claims settlements on which she'd worked for more than a quarter-century, but progress was (and is) necessarily slow, given the time and resources required to reach final agreements.

To the surprise of most observers, Cournoyea announced on August 28, 1995 that she would not be running for re-election. She chose instead to return to development work on behalf of her people, where she could devote all of her time and energy to their future economic success. Today, she chairs the Inuvialuit Regional Corporation, and, as her recent *Life and Times* biography pointed out, is arguably one of the most powerful women in Canada.

On her retirement from politics, Cournoyea was asked about her contribution to the advancement of women in Canada. She answered by saying that, in her view, women have always been the backbone of northern communities. In the North, whenever you wanted something done, particularly with respect to the communities or families, you turned to women. As to whether being a woman had been a plus or a minus in politics, she stated, in her usual direct style, that she had never been a man, so she wouldn't know.

◆◆ ❖ ◆◆

Freedom requires individuals to be free to use their own resources in their own way, and modern society requires cooperation among a large number of people. The question is, how can you have cooperation without coercion? If you have a central direction you inevitably have coercion. The only way that has ever been discovered to have a lot of people cooperate together voluntarily is through the free market. And that's why it's so essential to preserving individual freedom.

Milton Friedman

The market has its own truth, on which reality does not intrude.

John Kenneth Galbraith

The 1980s was the decade when Communism was finally defeated. The Wall came down and the world cheered. But one of the effects of winning the Cold War was the transformation of capitalism from an economic system to a kind of triumphalist state religion, with Hayek, Friedman and Gilder as its high priests, Wall Street, The City and Bay Street as its new cathedrals and "We Are the Champions" as its anthem.

The commandments of this faith were already well known, though they'd been out of favour since the Gilded Age ended with the stock market crash of 1929 — the invisible hand, trickle-down economics, a rising tide raises all ships, and a host of other clichés. What it really boils down to is the belief that lower taxes and less regulation will allow business to create more wealth, which will inevitably ripple through the entire economy, making everyone better off.

The first part almost always works. As taxes drop, business does create more wealth and the owners and shareholders of those businesses do become richer. As for the second part, it depends what the owners and shareholders do with the wealth. Reinvest it in expansion and creating new jobs, and the ripple hypothesis might have some sustaining energy. Move the wealth, and the company, to a tax haven because of the still-onerous tax load (any level of taxation seems to meet this criterion in some circles), or use free-trade agreements to move the new jobs offshore to a lower-wage, zero-benefit environment and, like the Colorado River, the ripples die in the mud flats before ever reaching the sea.

Among the contented majority, much of whose net worth was controlled by pension funds and other large institutional investors that held major positions in the latter sort of company, there was a certain amount of guilt about the appeal of these ideas. After all, these were largely middle-class people — Catholic, Anglican, United Church — who, even if they did make their semi-annual pilgrimage in a Cadillac or Mercedes and preferred to send cheques instead of children, still shared a value system that was informed by those long-ago Sunday School mornings.

The guilt was not so much about their own circumstances, which were clearly earned and deserved. No, the problem was how to pay for the tax cuts that helped make it possible. As anyone who's balanced a cheque book knows, a drop in income means either a drop in spending, or borrowing to make up the difference.

So on a national scale, tax cuts either meant less money for social programs — benefits for those people out on the mud flats whom the ripples never reach — or rising budget deficits, debt that would be left for our children and grandchildren to deal with. Not an appetizing choice from a strictly moral point of view.

Happily, there was a new American philosophy — one that combined the very latest in postmodern moral relativism with an almost evangelical belief in the individual and his sacred right to control his own destiny … and money.

Neo-conservatism explained that poverty was actually the fault of the poor, exacerbated by the very programs designed to help them. This was because the real reason for social programs was not to help the poor, whose only salvation in a knowledge economy seemed to lie in a return to servitude. Oh no. Social programs were really designed to increase the power of the bureaucrats who created them — those minions of big government, the so-called New Class.

Expiation. Absolution. Amen.

> Canadian neoconservatives … reject the Canadian welfare state and the Keynesian consensus that undergirded it. They prefer a small federal state that interferes less with business, does not attempt state-sponsored social engineering, and they share the belief of their American counterparts that a liberal New Class of intellectuals and bureaucrats needs to be neutralized. Like their American colleagues, they call for restrictions on immigration, and support a heavy-handed approach to law and order. Given their affinity for American ideology, it is no surprise that they call for close relations between Canada and the United States. In their one purely Canadian manifestation, neoconservatives call for a hard line on the national unity question, opposing political and constitutional 'concessions' to Quebec and rejecting the dualist interpretation of Canadian history favored by Quebec intellectuals. There is more than a passing similarity between the Canadian neoconservative attitude toward Quebec and the American neoconservative attitude toward affirmative action for African-Americans.
>
> D. Rovinsky & Z. Madjd-Sadjadi
> *In Search of Canadian*
> *Neoconservatism,* 1998

So in the end, all of society's ills — poverty, permissiveness, the decline of the family, were actually the fault of, not any particular government, but of government itself. The problem with Canada, then, was that there was entirely too much public space, and not nearly enough private.

> It seems to us that the way to restore Canadian pride is to begin to serve our true interests. In the first place, the second place and the nth place, this means dismantling the welfare state. The welfare state has created a welfare state of mind. It must go. More to the point, we must destroy it with gusto! We ought to think of it as the burden … a shackle on our opportunity … an insult to our dignity and self respect.
>
> David Bercuson & Barry Cooper
> *Derailed: The Betrayal of the*
> *National Dream,* 1994

This, of course, brings us to Reform (or Reforrrrrrrrrm, as Don Ferguson memorably put it during Royal Canadian Air Farce broadcasts). Founded in 1987 by disgruntled Tories and led by Preston Manning, son of former Alberta Premier Ernest Manning, Reform was not, like so many new political parties before it, just a typical Western protest movement. Part populist, part neocon, Reformers regarded their erstwhile Conservative colleagues as not really so different from the Liberals — unrepresentative, too centrist, too focused on Québec and, despite Mulroney's free trade agreement, and the cancellations of FIRA [15] and the NEP [16], far too wedded to the state.

Given that Manning's father had continued to host the radio program, *Canada's National Bible Hour,* for the entire time he was Premier, and that Preston appeared regularly thereon, it's not surprising that in addition to neoconservatives, Reform also attracted people who were socially conservative on matters like abortion, homosexuality, education and the role of women.

Before Reform, this was a constituency that had very little presence on the national political scene in Canada. This had also been the case in the United States until the Republicans began actively recruiting in evangelical and fundamentalist Christian communities in the 1970s. Ronald Reagan's subsequent success showed likeminded people in Canada that the same thing could be done here.

Only in existence for one year when Mulroney called the Free Trade election of 1988, Reform failed to win a seat and only garnered 2.1 per cent of the popular vote nationwide. However, with more than fifteen per cent in Alberta, the signs of future potential were clearly present.

Potential began to turn to reality when the Mulroney government decided to return to the national unity question. The Prime Minister fancied himself the consummate deal maker. He became convinced that he could succeed where Trudeau had failed and bring Québec into the constitution.

The problem, as it turned out, was that the rest of the country, particularly the West, wasn't interested. In addition to the personal concerns we examined earlier, there was a real sense that the big, "future of the country" questions had been answered, at least for the present. The referendum had been won, the Constitution repatriated and the Charter put in place. Why were we being asked to consider this again? Was the Prime Minister bowing to pressure from his Québec caucus? Or was this the Brian Mulroney Memorial Legacy Project?

Neither answer was terribly satisfying to Canadians outside Québec, and it handed Manning an obvious hot button issue as he worked to convert western

---

[15] Foreign Investment Review Agency
[16] National Energy Policy

Conservatives. Seemingly oblivious, Mr. Mulroney invited the premiers to Meech Lake outside Ottawa and proposed a deal to amend the Constitution.

As drafted, the Meech Lake Accord would have recognized Québec as a distinct society, devolved more power to the provinces and put parts of the Charter at risk. The process's larger significance — the initiation of the series of events that would result in the destruction of the PC party and pose a direct threat to Canadian unity -— still lay in the future.

Any amendment to the Constitution has to be ratified by all ten provincial legislatures within three years of its initial acceptance. So, when the National Assembly in Québec voted in favour on June 23, 1987, the timetable was set — complete approval by June 23, 1990, or the whole thing failed.

By the spring of 1990, it was clear that Meech was in serious trouble. Newfoundland had rescinded its approval after a change in government, and New Brunswick and Manitoba were looking for improvements and had not brought it to a vote. Lucien Bouchard, hand-picked by Mulroney to be his Québec lieutenant, was adamantly opposed to any changes. He resigned from cabinet and then quit the party to sit as an Independent, a move that had a powerful effect on the party's Québec caucus.

With twenty days left to the deadline, Mulroney called the provincial leaders to Ottawa for a last-ditch effort to arrive at a compromise; a roll of the dice, as he later called it. As a labour lawyer, Mulroney was well versed in the various techniques of contract negotiation and he used them all to create a pressure cooker environment that would force an agreement. [17]

It appeared to work. The bleary-eyed premiers emerged from their lock up on June 9th to announce that they had a deal. All that was left was for the remaining provincial legislatures to give their approval. With the support of the various leaders, this was surely a mere formality … only it wasn't. In his effort to apply maximum pressure, the Prime Minister had cut it too fine.

In a very blunt demonstration of identity politics, native leaders made Mulroney pay for not consulting First Nations on the proposed constitutional amendments. Elijah Harper, Manitoba's first Aboriginal MLA, simply refused unanimous consent to any streamlining of parliamentary procedure, and then watched the clock tick down until time expired. When it became obvious that Manitoba would not meet the deadline, Newfoundland declined to hold its vote. Meech Lake was officially dead.

As an expression of his humiliation at the outcome, Lucien Bouchard formed the Bloc Québecois the following year. Mulroney, meanwhile, after

---

[17] For an insider's account of these negotiations, see Senator Carstairs' book *Not One of the Boys*, Macmillan, 1999.

thoroughly annoying Québec by failing to deliver Meech, infuriated the rest of Canada by introducing the GST, which came into effect January 1, 1991.

Segué to the fall of 1992. On dining room tables and coffee shop counters across the country, people are unfolding an infopak from the government. In the two years since the failure of Meech, we have been bombarded with consultations and reports until, finally, the federal government has our attention. Here we are, attempting to figure out what this new agreement will really mean for Canada.

Brian Mulroney may have had many perceived faults, but a lack of persistence wasn't one of them. By October 26th, Charlottetown Referendum day, the full-court press had been on for nearly a year: Senate reform, the Supreme Court, Aboriginal rights, an amending formula — everything addressed, all approved by every possible leader. All that was left was for the little people to give the OK, and it was forward to a New, Improved Canada.

Maybe it was the weakening of the central government. Maybe it was distinct society. Maybe Canadians were just so damn tired of the "jaw that walks like a man". Whatever the case, when the votes had been counted, it turned out even Québec and First Nations people had voted to send the Brian Mulroney Memorial Legacy Project to the constitutional dust bin.

NATIONAL REFERENDUM ON THE CHARLOTTETOWN ACCORD

Province	Voted Yes	% of Yes Votes	Voted No	% of No Votes
Newfoundland	133 193	62.9	77 881	36.5
P.E.I.	48 687	73.6	17 124	25.9
Nova Scotia	218 618	48.5	230 182	51.1
New Brunswick	234 010	61.3	145 096	38.0
Québec	1 710 117	42.4	2 232 280	55.4
Ontario	2 410 119	49.8	2 397 665	49.6
Manitoba	198 230	37.8	322 971	61.6
Saskatchewan	203 361	44.5	252 459	55.2
Alberta	483 275	39.7	731 975	60.1
British Columbia	525 188	31.7	1 126 761	68.0
Yukon	5 354	43.4	6 922	56.1
N. W. T.	14 750	60.6	9 416	38.7
Total Canada	6 185 902	44.6	7 550 732	54.4

Source: *Canadian Annual Review*, 1992, p. 27

It's no surprise that Manning and the Reform Party were firmly committed to the No side (Reform was the only "national" party to take this stand) and, as the table above shows, it was very effective in its home base in Western Canada.

> The Referendum held on October 26th, 1992, to determine the fate of the Charlottetown Accord was a double triumph for the Reform Party. Not only did the referendum result block the adoption of a constitutional package that most of the party's membership intensely disliked, but also the very fact that the referendum was held established an important precedent for the future. Most observers of Canadian politics think it unlikely that major packages of constitutional amendments will ever be adopted without referendum approval, which in itself was a Reform demand.
>
> Tom Flanagan
> *Waiting For the Wave,* 1995

Charlottetown was the final straw. Even to a man of Brian Mulroney's generous ego, it was clear that the Tories were sinking fast. With an election call less than a year away, the party's base in the West had been lost to Manning and his Reformers, and in Québec, to Bouchard and the Bloc. Since his personal popularity was plumbing depths never before explored by a Canadian leader, it was inconceivable that he could lead the party into another campaign. The Prime Minister announced his resignation on February 24, 1993, to be effective in June.

All of this would put the new leader, who would become Prime Minister before an election, in a truly unenviable position. The similarity to the situation that faced John Turner after he took over from Trudeau in 1984 was surely not lost on the Conservative leadership, but what could it do?

The only option was to select someone as different from Mulroney as possible, and then pray that during the campaign the new PM would, Jesus-like, transfigure from sacrificial lamb to Saviour. Coming from a party that was under attack from the right, the left and the centre, it was asking a lot. But, for a while, it looked as though she might actually pull it off.

◆◆ ❖ ◆◆

> In 1984, there was a large campaign to try to have me run for leadership of the Liberal Party of Canada … I knew that our party was going to lose in the next election — I knew that better that anyone, as the [party's] President. I did not want the party to be defeated if it were

KIM CAMPBELL

headed, even for a short time, by a woman, because the defeat would be laid at the foot of the woman, to some degree.

Iona Campagnola,
July 1999

Speaking to a conference on Women and the Media sponsored by the Canadian Association of Journalists in November 1992, the MP said she was often unspeakably lonely. She told them she was far from home and friends and was at the same time accused of being crushingly ambitious, a term she said would never be applied to a male politician. This was a woman who was already lining up her campaign team for a run at the leadership of the Progressive Conservative party and yet, soul searching about what this would mean to her life. The MP was Avril Phaedra "Kim" Campbell and seven months later, she would become Canada's first female Prime Minister.

Kim Campbell was born in Port Alberni, British Columbia on March 10, 1947, the second child of George Campbell and Phyllis Cook, better known as Lissa. George and Lissa had met and married during the war and Kim's older sister, Alix, had been born in 1945.

Shortly after her birth, the family moved to Vancouver so George could continue his studies. He attended law school at the University of British Columbia and was admitted to the bar in 1953. Meanwhile, Lissa worked to support the family. In 1954, they moved into a home in Kerrisdale, where Kim attended school.

The marriage had been deteriorating for a number of years. When Kim was twelve, Lissa sent her and her sister to St. Anne's, a Catholic boarding school in Victoria. Six months later their mother wrote to them, informing her daughters that she had left their father. Kim did not see her mother for the next ten years, though they continued to correspond by mail.

Neither the nuns, nor her friends in Vancouver (she returned to public school the next year), noted in Kim any display of sadness or angst about her mother's behaviour. Her one overt act was to change her name from Avril Phaedra, her mother's choice, to Kim. According to those who knew her, she was bouncy and bubbly and displayed not a care in the world. She later admitted, however, to being very lonely and unhappy and it's difficult to believe that losing a mother with whom you have been very close would not have been devastating. While her sister clearly showed her pain by dropping out of school, Kim internalized her sadness and, with a stiff upper lip, got on with living.

She was a very good student, later identified by the nuns as the brightest girl they had, with an IQ score so high it was unmeasurable. She was elected president of the student council in Grade 12 and was her class valedictorian. She dated, played the guitar and sang, and was clearly a popular member of her class.

Her yearbook said she wanted to study political science or medicine and with these ambitions in mind, she went to the University of British Columbia, graduating five years later with an honours degree in political science. In 1967, she met Nathan "Tuzie" Divinsky, twenty-two years her senior. He was a mathematics professor at the university and both were active in a group that performed operettas by Gilbert and Sullivan.

Within two years they were living together and in September of 1972, they married. Divinsky held very conservative and elitist views, often praising the British class system and extolling the virtues of educating the elite for leadership roles. There seems little doubt he had a significant influence on Campbell's personal philosophy.

During her years at university, Campbell was the frosh president and in her senior year, vice-president of the student council. While her grades were not brilliant, classes had been combined with an active extracurricular life. The summer following her graduation from UBC, she took a fourth-year course at the University of Oregon where Tuzie was teaching a summer course, and on their return to Vancouver began work on her M.A. in International Relations at UBC.

Instead of completing this degree, she applied for, and was given, a Canada Council doctoral fellowship to study at the London School of Economics. Tuzie joined her two years later when he received a year's sabbatical.

While she was at the LSE, she studied with Leonard Shapiro. During the '60s and early '70s, the LSE had become a hotbed of left-wing thinkers. One of the exceptions was Leonard Shapiro. He was adamantly opposed to centralization of government and Campbell was a willing and respected pupil. She toured the Soviet Union with him for three months and became strongly opposed to both communism and socialism. Her favourite political thinker, and one she would quote frequently during her political career, was Edmund Burke, an eighteenth-century philosopher and politician who strongly favoured government by the elites.

Returning to Vancouver before she'd completed her Ph.D., Divinsky decided to run for school board and with Campbell's help and her knowledge of running campaigns for student office, he was elected in 1974. For several years, she seemed content to be a housewife and hoped to be a mother. Unfortunately, according to her mother, she was told by doctors she could not conceive.

She then threw herself into work. A potential teaching career at UBC came to an end because she didn't have the appropriate letters after her name and appeared to have no interest in completing either her M.A. or her Ph.D. She then accepted a teaching position at the Langara campus of Vancouver Community College. When the instructor she replaced returned to teaching duties, Campbell was relegated to teaching evening courses. She had serious decisions to make and her work ethic kicked in with full force. In one year, she entered law school and replaced Divinsky on the Vancouver School Board, while continuing to teach at the community college. Obviously, she could handle a number of irons in the fire at one time and do it with verve.

Her career on the Vancouver School Board, two years as a trustee and two years as chair, was indicative of the style and philosophy she would bring to politics. She fought hard for what she believed and was unwilling to back down. She was clearly a leader, not a follower.

> I ran for the school board and was elected and found that I liked it very much. I found that I had what it took to do public policy. I loved the issues. But, more particularly, in terms of the temperament, I wasn't dismayed by criticism. It's not that you develop a thick skin … and you certainly are never immune to the meanness that comes to anybody who's a public figure. But you also come to understand that you can't be involved in making real decisions without making some people unhappy — that a certain amount of hostility and venting is part of the process, and that you should, in fact, welcome it, because it's a sign of the vitality of the democracy.[18]
>
> Rt. Hon. Kim Campbell

She fiercely defended the imposition of fiscal restraint imposed by the Social Credit government, even though other board members thought she should be leading the fight against the erosion of school board power. At the same time, she worked hard to establish special programs for gifted students. She also displayed her distaste for unions and their activities.

Meanwhile, she graduated from law school and accepted an articling position with Ladner Downs, a large establishment law firm. When the senior partners expressed concern that she would not devote the time necessary to her legal practice, she agreed to resign from the school board. They must have been shocked when, less than three months later, she accepted a Social Credit nomination to run in Vancouver Point Grey. She seemed to think this was acceptable because she knew she was going to lose. She did.

However, based on her effort in this election campaign, and the profile she'd gained on the Vancouver School Board, Premier Bill Bennett invited her to join his staff as a policy advisor. She went to work for Bud Smith and Norman

---

[18] All quotes by the Rt. Hon. Kim Campbell are from an interview conducted in Winnipeg by Tim Higgins on July 21, 1999.

Spector, who were to play significant roles in her political career, both in British Columbia and on the national stage.

She'd been on the Premier's staff for less than two years when Bennett decided to step down. In a bizarre political move, Campbell decided to run for the leadership. It was bizarre because she clearly had no base in the party, had never sat in the legislature and had no prominent backers. The result was predictable — she came twelfth out of twelve candidates with only fourteen votes cast for her on the first ballot. She immediately pledged her support to Bud Smith.

Why did she do it? Though she claims it was because no one was speaking to the serious policy issues of the day, she also became a figure of interest to the media, particularly when she said of the eventual winner, Bill Vander Zalm, that "charisma without substance is a dangerous thing". He was furious, but British Columbians would remember these comments when Vander Zalm's government began to fall apart. The media would also remind them that it had been Kim Campbell who'd warned them.

Despite her previous losses, she decided to run for election in the 1986 campaign and this time she was successful. However, with Vander Zalm now Premier, her chances of a cabinet seat were nil.

In response to the decision of the Supreme Court of Canada to strike down Canada's abortion law, Premier Vander Zalm announced that the government of British Columbia wouldn't pay for abortions. Campbell denounced the policy of her own government, and when the courts failed to support Vander Zalm's position, she was once again proven right in a highly public way. Kim Campbell was clearly becoming someone of substance in British Columbia politics.

Norman Spector had moved to Ottawa as a staff member to Brian Mulroney. He persuaded the Progressive Conservative Party in British Columbia that they should get Campbell to run for them in the 1988 election. The original proposal had her running against Liberal Leader John Turner in his home riding, thereby forcing him to spend a disproportionate amount of his time in Vancouver. She declined, believing it would be impossible to win. If she were going to leave the provincial scene and her political party, it would only be to win a federal seat.

She also had a more personal reason. Her marriage to Nathan Divinsky had ended in 1983 and in 1986 she had married Howard Eddy, a lawyer with the provincial government. They led an idyllic life, moving between his boat docked in Victoria Harbour, where he worked and she had duties as an MLA, and her house in her Vancouver constituency. She was loath to jeopardize their relationship.

However, Eddy's three children by an earlier marriage lived in Ontario and he thought that he could re-establish contact with them if he and Campbell were to live at least part time in Ottawa. With his agreement and support, she decided to accept the Conservative nomination in Vancouver Centre, the riding recently vacated by Pat Carney, who was stepping down due to poor health.

Campbell knew this too would be an uphill climb to victory, but at least she wouldn't be running against a national leader. In addition, though the polls showed the NDP ahead in the riding, Carney had been a strong constituency person. There was deep support for her in the riding and she did everything in her power to move that support to Campbell.

Both women were staunch defenders of the 1987 free trade agreement, which helped bring financial support on side. In addition, Campbell benefited enormously from the fact that, although the positions of the NDP and the Liberals were virtually the same on trade (against), John Turner had taken the leadership on this issue away from Ed Broadbent.

The NDP candidate was Johanna den Hertog, the national president of the NDP, who had been working the constituency for six months. She was clearly ahead at the beginning of the campaign, but as Turner began to make an impact on the trade issue, the Liberal candidate, Tex Enemark, picked up enough support to become the spoiler. In the end, Campbell polled only 38.7 per cent, but it was enough to defeat den Hertog by 269 votes.

She was off to Ottawa and, once there, her rise was meteoric. She was appointed to the cabinet on January 30, 1989 as Minister of State for Indian and Northern Affairs. This was an interesting choice; she had long opposed any settlement of Aboriginal land claims in the province of British Columbia, while the federal government was in favour of movement in this area.

Indian and Northern Affairs may have been a junior ministry, but it came with all the perks of power and she set out to learn as much as she could. Two of her staff members, Harry Swain and Fred Drummie, had been in the civil service for a long time and knew the ropes. She put herself in their hands, urging them to give her all the information they had about the operations of government. She worked long hours, from early morning to late at night and went to cabinet meetings not only well-briefed on issues, but also on process.

On February 23, 1990, Campbell became the first female Minister of Justice in Canadian history. In addition, she was made the senior minister in B.C. and thus a member of the prestigious and powerful Expenditures and Review Committee of Cabinet. She was clearly being examined for her leadership potential.

One of her immediately pressing issues was Bill C-43, the abortion bill introduced by the previous Justice Minister, Doug Lewis. The bill restored abortion to the criminal code, stating that abortions could be performed only if a woman's physical, mental or psychological health were at risk. The bill also included fines and imprisonment for doctors and other health care professionals who performed abortions where those criteria were not met.

The Conservatives were very divided about this legislation. Some, like Barbara McDougall, the Minister of External Affairs, were opposed to any law at all. She indicated she would support it only because she was a member of Cabinet and therefore required to do so. Others believed Doug Lewis' bill to be far too lenient and that the provisions for physical, mental and psychological health would open the doors to abortion on demand.

Prior to becoming Minister of Justice, Campbell had defended C-43 as better than no law at all and she continued this defence through to its passage in the House of Commons. The bill was subsequently defeated in the Senate on a tied vote and Campbell announced she would not attempt to pass another bill because C-43 had been the best compromise that could be forged.

While she lost the support of many women's groups over her stand on C-43, she gained tremendous respect by her initiation and staunch defence of the rape shield law. As with the abortion law, the Supreme Court of Canada had struck down a previous bill that denied the use of a woman's sexual history in a rape trial. The justices had argued that while it was not necessary in most cases, there might be some occasions where it was relevant. A self-avowed, though clearly non-doctrinaire feminist, Campbell consulted extensively with women's groups before introducing a new law, which, while upholding an accused's right to a full and fair defence, unequivocally stated that when the matter before the court is rape, no means no.

> I've always described myself as a feminist because I don't know a better word to describe someone for whom the advancement of women and the equality of women is a very high priority. It's not just an abstract value for me. … There are different forms of feminism. I don't run around ranting about the patriarchy and I don't see male chauvinist pigs under the bed everywhere I go … But, I don't shy away from using the word because I think creating some kind of negative connotation about the word feminism undermines women. I don't know of a better word to describe the deep commitment to equality for women, and I know men who are comfortable describing themselves as feminists, too. It's not gender apartheid. It's a commitment to enfranchising and creating a different relationship between men and women — one of greater equality and mutual support.
>
> Rt. Hon. Kim Campbell

During her time in Justice, she introduced legislation that toughened sentences for young offenders and tried, unsuccessfully, to draft legislation that would reduce discrimination toward homosexuals (too many of her colleagues had no desire to take a position). She was also required to deal with the even more controversial issue of gun control, a matter on which her caucus was hopelessly divided.

Greater gun control was demanded by the Canadian public in response to the shooting of fourteen women by Marc Lepine at Montréal's Ecole Polytechnique on December 6, 1990. Supporters of gun control legislation were dismayed at the weakness of the resulting legislation. However, it should be remembered that members of the rural caucus, many of whom would eventually switch to Reform, more largely opposed to any measures at all. Campbell may have been forced to make many more changes than she wanted to, but the bill passed. She'd shown herself capable of making the necessary compromises and building consensus. Within a party that was showing increasing signs of disarray, this was recognized as a significant quality for leadership.

Campbell lost personally as a result of her hard work through this period. In 1991, Howard Eddy left her. In his view, she had not found enough time for him in her busy life and, dissatisfied with his work with the Immigration and Refugee Board, he returned to the West Coast. Hurt and upset by his actions, she also went West to visit her sister, but in her usual pattern soon put on her "I don't have a care in the world face" and quickly returned to work.

She was given a significant role in the selling of the Charlottetown Accord. Because she was a woman and was perceived through her work in Justice as concerned with women's issues, it was her job to allay fears that the accord jeopardized Section 15 of the Charter, which guaranteed equality rights for women. As we've seen, the accord failed, but she had done her part and was once again perceived as a team player in the Conservative caucus.

It had been hoped that the Charlottetown Accord would be Brian Mulroney's final triumph, allowing him to retire wreathed in the glory of his constitutional achievement. Denied the place in history a successful accord could have given him, the Prime Minister was at a loss. What to do?

The party's standing in opinion polls was declining as rapidly as his personal popularity. Should he accept the future campaign loss himself or was he the only one who could still carry the Tories to victory?

Mulroney decided he might be a liability and asked his friend and cabinet colleague Marcel Masse to introduce Campbell to the power brokers in Québec. He wanted to know if she was saleable in his native province — was she the catalyst that could cement the coalition he'd forged during the 1984 election? It was clear after her trip to Québec that the answer was yes.

On January 3, 1993, Campbell was appointed Minister of Defence. As with Justice, she was the first Canadian woman to be given this portfolio. While some in the media saw it as a demotion and interpreted the demotion to be the result of her seemingly overly ambitious leadership plans (along with Michael Wilson and Perrin Beatty, she'd had a loose organization since the spring of 1992), many more saw it as an opportunity for her to show her stuff in what had always been considered male turf. It also removed her from further defence of the sexual orientation bill, which was again causing her problems within caucus.

The Defence portfolio allowed her to cement her relationship with Marcel Masse, who had resigned from cabinet, but not before he had orchestrated the most expensive purchase in the history of the federal government — the five-billion-dollar contract for the purchase of EH 101 helicopters.

She defended the purchase of these aircraft throughout the campaign, despite public opinion polls showing that sixty-nine per cent of Canadians were opposed to it — polls that included seventy-seven per cent of people in Québec, where most of the contracts would be awarded. The Prime Minister was pleased with her performance; on February 24, 1993, he tendered his resignation as leader of the Progressive Conservative Party, to take effect upon the election of a new leader. The leadership race was on.

Almost immediately public opinion polls were released showing a clear victory for the Tories if Kim Campbell became the leader. The *Globe and Mail* published a Com Quest poll showing the PCs, with Campbell as leader, with forty-five per cent of the vote, the Liberals with thirty-two per cent and the NDP with nine per cent. Angus Reid released a poll showing forty-three per cent support for the Tories if Campbell were their standard bearer and Gallup showed the Tories with fifty per cent. The other leadership campaign hopefuls were thrown for a loop. Wilson, Beatty and others were not going to run for the leadership with a guarantee of failure.

I find, in Canada, a lot of young women come and talk to me and say, 'I'm going to be PM.' Not, I want to be PM, I'm *going* to be PM. Their sense of what is possible has been changed by having a woman there. [So] though the timing couldn't have been worse, and there were a lot of difficulties, I've never had the sense that people say, well, you shouldn't have been there; you were incompetent to be there. What they say is, boy, it was the wrong place at the wrong time and it was an impossible situation. And, that was something I thought a lot about before entering the leadership, because I knew how difficult it would be to win that election. But then I thought, will having a woman who loses the election discredit women as leaders? I gambled that it would not, and I don't think it did. It created a sense that this was something that was possible for young women. Elsewhere in the world, it had a very powerful effect. First of all, aside from the fact that it gave me genuine experience that I can share with people, it was a great source of encouragement for women in other countries as well. What American women say to me is, if Canada can do it, why can't we do it? And they redouble their efforts to get a woman into the White House.

Rt. Hon. Kim Campbell

Within weeks, all the serious contenders had bowed out, giving excuses of family or simply admitting as Beatty did after he joined the Campbell team, that it was clear there was a universal choice. It appeared there was going to be a Campbell coronation. From a strictly political point of view, this caused problems for the party, which ran the risk of a public loss of interest since there didn't appear to be a fight for the job. Also, there was a feeling that a coronation would expose Campbell to too much scrutiny — not an advantage when there was also an election campaign to be fought later in the year.

The only candidates to announce were backbenchers with little or no profile. Patrick Boyer and Garth Turner from Ontario were not household names and Jim Edwards, from Alberta, somewhat better known because he had been the Tory caucus chair, were the only announced candidates. Campbell flew to Vancouver and on March 25, 1993 made the announcement that she was in the race. The announcement photo-op went very well: lots of people, lots of enthusiasm. But her interview on CBC's *Prime Time* the following night with Pamela Wallin and Peter Mansbridge didn't go quite so well, facing Campbell with one of the verities of the late twentieth century — politically, one news cycle can be an eternity. She recalled the events of the campaign this way:

> The challenge, I think, for the media, is to have some humility, to understand, first, how important is the role that they play. Because we know that campaigns are much more mediated than they used to be. If you look at the length of a sound byte on radio or television, or the length of a direct quote in the print press, it's about a tenth of what it used to be twenty years ago. So, the frustration that politicians face is trying to get through all that, and communicate directly.
>
> Rt. Hon. Kim Campbell

It was on the basis of this and a few other campaign stumbles that Jean Charest was persuaded to enter the race. He had considered a bid earlier as the first step in a climb to leadership in the tradition of Mulroney and Turner before him. Both had run for the leadership while quite young and had reached the top on their second run. However, the game plan demanded a respectable showing and since the earlier polls showed such massive support for Campbell, Charest believed he would be decimated. With the Campbell campaign showing a few flaws, he accepted the entreaties of the Prime Minister to make it a horse race and entered the campaign. No one anticipated that he would come as close as he did to ending the Campbell sweep.

The contrasts in the campaigns were clear. Campbell had gender on her side. However, she also had two failed marriages and members of the right-wing family caucus were dismayed by what they saw as her lack of stability. Even the fact that she had no children was held against her. Charest was considered by some to be, at thirty-four, too young. But he was fluently bilingual, had a wife and two children and was seen as the ideal family man.

Campbell didn't shine in the leadership debates held within the party, but broadcast nationally. The spark expected of her wasn't there and, some potential delegates began to have second thoughts. Her continued defence of the helicopter purchase hurt, but even more problematic was her lack of acceptable response to the Somalia affair.

This involved two incidents that had brought shame to members of Canada's Airborne Regiment. The first involved the killing of two Somalis, one of whom, according to medical evidence, had been shot in the back. The other, more serious offence, was the beating death of a sixteen-year-old Somali boy. The reality of the utter chaos in Somalia notwithstanding, pictures of a Canadian soldier grinning as he posed over the bloodied body of a Somali child had a powerful effect on a Canadian public raised to believe in the near sainthood of our peace-keepers. That their Defence Minister was portrayed as being too busy campaigning to treat these incidents with the seriousness they deserved was not helpful.

Then, in a speech in May, Campbell referred to citizens who couldn't understand the seriousness of the country's deficit and the wisdom of the govern-ment's decision to cut it as "enemies of Canadians". The media interpreted this to mean that if you don't agree with Kim Campbell, then you are not only wrong, you are unCanadian. She later admitted her use of the words was inappropriate, but it was an example of the kind of scrutiny to which she was subjected and her need to control what she said. Charest, meanwhile, was not subjected to anywhere near the same level of criticism and was sailing through the leadership campaign.

Also in May, an interview she gave to Peter Newman received a dispro-portionate amount of publicity. Things she said were pulled out of context, making it appear that she was anti-Catholic and had been critical of Joe Clark.

I think the media is one of the most conservative elements in
Canadian public policy. When I talk to people who work closely with
the press, including producers in television, they agree with me. I think
the public is much more willing to be experimental, to be welcoming of
new kinds of people. There, is, particularly among the national political
press, or the press gallery around any capital city a sense of ownership
of the process. And, if you're new and different, their reaction is, well,
who is this person? We didn't make that person! How dare they come
in! They often have their own ideas about who should be in positions
of leadership. And they can really be a problem. The other thing is,
they're often totally oblivious to the stereotypes that they carry around
with them.

Rt. Hon. Kim Campbell

But perhaps her most devastating comment was about Canadians who
don't participate in their nation's activities. She referred to them as "condescend-
ing SOBs". One interpretation might have been that she was tired of uninvolved
people always complaining about government and politics. Many politicians have
made similar complaints. What actually emerged, however, was that if you're not
willing to become a politician, you have no right to complain.

Canadians were furious at being called SOBs and Charest's popularity
increased, but it was far too late. By this time most of the delegates had been
chosen, and they were committed to Campbell.

Though she didn't win the first ballot victory that had been forecast,
she did take 1,664 votes, or forty-eight per cent. It was an unbeatable number.
On the second ballot, she went over the top with 1,817 votes or 52.7 per cent.
Charest came second with 1,630 votes — 47.3 per cent of the convention delegates
had chosen the underdog.

In her acceptance speech, she referred to Charest as "one hell of a tor-
toise", but this was the only mention she made of him. This omission would come
back to haunt her in the weeks that followed. Though her first choice for Deputy
PM had been Perrin Beatty, she was forced to appoint Charest when it became
clear she would lose Québec if she didn't bring him on side.

Kim Campbell became Canada's first female Prime Minister on June 25,
1993. She immediately announced a restructuring of government with a leaner
cabinet than Mulroney's, then travelled for most of the summer. Her first foreign
trip, representing her country at the G7 conference in Japan, was portrayed as a
success, and she returned to visit most provinces in the country in a get-to-know-
you tour. Her public appearances were long on handshakes, if short on speeches,

but the gaffes of the leadership campaign, while noted by many, were set aside in a willingness to give the new Prime Minister a chance. Public opinion polls showed the Conservatives running neck and neck with the Liberals, and it looked as if the campaign would be a two-way battle between Canada's traditional parties.

This changed almost immediately with the dropping of the writ. In the scrum immediately following the formal campaign launch on September 8th, she was asked how long it would take to get Canada's economic house in order. The Prime Minister said that she couldn't envisage any significant improvement for ten years. She was correct in that it would take a number of years for Canada's deficit, and therefore debt, to be brought under control. However, the Liberals pounced on her words and made it appear that working people would continue to be jobless for the next ten years. It was not an auspicious beginning and things went downhill from there.

When asked about social policy review, the Prime Minister stated that an election campaign was not the time for serious policy discussions. Again she was factually correct — the length of an election campaign is not sufficient to under- take a serious analysis of social policy. But her statement was interpreted as meaning she was unwilling to discuss the matter with ordinary Canadians, the implication being that we were not quite capable of understanding the issues. To the Canadian public, this new-style Tory leader was beginning to sound a lot like the former leader, whom many regarded as elitist.

Perhaps the greatest blunder of the campaign was the Tory ads showing Liberal leader Jean Chrétien's face in a number of poses with the phrase, "Can you trust this man to be Prime Minister?" superimposed over it.

Most Canadians never saw the ads but they heard about them on radio and television and were dismayed at what they believed to be an attack on Chrétien's facial deformity, the result of a birth defect.

This kind of negative advertising might have been popular in the United States, but it was definitely not acceptable in Canada. Though Campbell ordered the ads pulled after less than a day on air, her grudging apology further hurt the campaign. She didn't fire her campaign manager, which could have communicated her personal outrage, and she didn't announce to Canadians how despicable she thought the ads were. Instead, she said if Mr. Chrétien was personally hurt by the ads, then he could have her apology if he wanted it.

She performed relatively well in the two debates. If a knock-out punch was delivered, it was landed by Lucien Bouchard rather than Chrétien, but the Prime Minister wasn't going to be forgiven for her gaffes.

On the other hand, the Liberal campaign had been flawless from opening to closing. Chrétien's popularity grew continuously, starting with the publication of the Red Book, and his tour hummed along, in sharp contrast to the growing Tory fiasco.

On election night, the Progressive Conservative Party, one of the major Canadian political parties since Confederation, was reduced to two seats, one of which was won by Jean Charest. The irony couldn't have been lost on Campbell, who lost her seat in Vancouver Centre. The party's popular vote was sixteen per cent — the same result the party had been getting during the final days of Brian Mulroney's leadership. The party's decision to put a fresh new female face on Conservatism had failed utterly.

Campbell was still the leader of her party, though no longer Prime Minister. However, it was quickly clear that the party wanted to rid itself of her immediately. She was informed that she would no longer be paid. She had only been an MP for five years so her eligibility for a pension was questionable. She had no other source of income because, though she was eligible for a Prime Minister's pension, she wouldn't qualify to collect until she turned sixty-five. She tendered her resignation as party leader and, after serving as Canada's Consul General in Los Angeles, accepted a teaching appointment at the Kennedy School of Government at Harvard University.

Campbell's career has been labelled a failure at home, but to the rest of the world, a female leader in North America, under whatever circumstances, has been regarded as a wonder.

> You have to face the fact that women have half the world's talent and energy and courage and commitment, and I don't think the world can survive without all [its] resources brought to bear. I think it's a matter of enfranchisement ... The question, "Why should we have women in politics?" is a tautology in a democracy. The real question is, "How have we gone so long putting up with the exclusion of women?"
>
> Rt. Hon. Kim Campbell

On the Brink of the Twenty-first Century

(1993 –)

◆

Nellie

Scene: 1998

We're in a provincial legislature during debate on bill M-49, legislation that would mandate the provincial government to provide universal daycare. The opposition health critic is speaking.

Opposition critic: This is bad legislation, Mr. Speaker, a direct threat to the traditional values that have served us well for so long ...

(Deborah Halingford, Minister of Health, leans over to a colleague on the front bench and mutters loudly enough to be heard across the aisle)

Halingford: Here we go again. Back to the kitchen, girls.

(The opposition critic hesitates for a moment. Then looking straight at the Minister)

Opposition critic: As I said, Mr. Speaker, traditional values. Ones with which the Minister is sadly unfamiliar. Perhaps if the Honourable Member had embraced those values, perhaps if she'd stayed home and been a real mother to her children when they were young, instead of placing them in one of these daycares she's so insistent on ramming down our throats, perhaps then her daughter wouldn't be living in sin with another woman today.

(There's a split second of disbelieving silence. Then the House erupts with shouts of 'Shame' from the government side, and somewhat tepid applause from the opposition benches.)

(Halingford rises and is recognized by the Speaker.)

Halingford: Mr. Speaker. My office also receives letters from people who are convinced that daycares are part of a communist plot. So we have childcare outside the home undermining traditional values, corrupting our youth, maybe even a treasonous activity. What's next? Daycares as a fifth column for alien invasion?

Mr. Speaker, that the Honourable Member undoubtedly knows people who hold these views should perhaps be of some concern to her party. And if the Honourable Member chooses to be a mouthpiece for such people instead of representing her constituents as she was sent here to do, I'm sure that's something those constituents will address at the next election.

Even if the other side of the House is afraid to admit it, Mr. Speaker, they know that Bill M-49 is intended to correct a terrible wrong being done to the women and children of this province.

Despite the Honourable Member's despicable attack on every Canadian working mother, the fact is that most of us have little choice in the matter. We have to work to feed and clothe our children, to provide them with shelter and nutrition so that they have the chance to become productive members of society.

Given the rising gap between the rich and the rest in this country — a gap, I might add, that those on the other side of the House did so little to address when they were in government — given this gap, Mr. Speaker, the need to work exists for a large percentage of mothers, regardless of their marital status.

What are we to say to these women? That it's all right for your children to face malnutrition as long as you're there to watch them? Are we to say, well, if you weren't woman enough to keep your man, or your husband wasn't man enough to land a decent job, then it's welfare for you and good riddance?

Mr. Speaker, I'm proud to be part of a government that says, that's not good enough. These people, these citizens, are an important resource for this province, and every one of their children is precious.

As a society, we have a collective responsibility to see that all citizens have at least the opportunity to reach their full potential. Mr. Speaker, it does this province no good to force many of our best and brightest to stay home because they are unable to find adequate care for their children while they work. It does this province no good if, during the early years of their lives, when so much of their development depends on variety of experience and social interaction, these children are denied the safest, highest quality environment we can provide.

So, Mr. Speaker, this government will provide the parents of this province with the best daycare system it is possible to construct. Failure to do so would be dereliction of our duty to the people who elected us, and a direct threat to future generations, upon which the wellbeing of this province so vitally depends.

Halingford sits, while her colleagues rise in a standing ovation.

	POLITICAL	SOCIAL / TECHNOLOGY
	T I M E L I N E	
1994	• O.J. Simpson tried for murder • ANC wins first multi-racial election in South Africa • North American Free Trade Agreement in effect • Genocide in Rwanda begins	• Extrasolar planets discovered • IRA declares cease-fire • Netscape Navigator first released • Kurt Cobain (Nirvana) found dead • Films: *Forrest Gump, Pulp Fiction*
1995	• Isreali PM Yitzhak Rabin assassinated • NATO begins peacekeeping in Bosnia • Quebec referendum on separation • Oklahoma City bombing	• Sarin gas attack on Tokyo subway • *Toy Story* is first movie completely created with computer graphics • Carol Shields wins the Pulitzer prize for Literature for *The Stone Diaries*
1996	• Yasser Arafat: President of the Palestinian Authority • Dunblane massacre (Scotland) • Mad-cow disease hits Britain • U.S. President Bill Clinton's Whitewater scandal	• Prince Charles and Diana, Princess of Wales, divorce • Child beauty pagent star Jon-Benet Ramsay murdered • Summer Olympics in Atlanta
1997	• **Madeline Albright: first female Secretary of State (U.S.)** • Confederation Bridge opens (PEI to mainland) • Jean Chrétien re-elected Canadian PM • Scotland votes to re-establish own Parliament	• Dolly the sheep successfully cloned • Tiger Woods is youngest golfer to win Masters • NASA's Pathfinder lands on Mars • Diana, Princess of Wales, dies in car crash
1998	• War in Kosovo • Pakistan tests missles that can reach India • Iraq will not cooperate with UN weapons inspectors • Microsoft antitrust case begins	• European nations forbid human cloning • President Bill Clinton's scandal with Monica Lewinsky • U.S. abortion doctor killed by sniper • **Carol Shields wins Orange Prize for *Larry's Party*** • Winter Olympics in Nagano, Japan
1999	• Euro currency introduced • Prince Abdullah becomes ruler of Jordan • Nunavut established as a Canadian territory	• Y2K paranoia mounts with countdown to year 2000 • JFK Jr., wife Carolyn Bessette, sister Lauren killed in plane crash • Anti-globalization protests in Seattle
2000	• Vladimir Putin elected Russian President • UN Millennium Summit • George Bush Jr. becomes US President • **Hillary Clinton elected to the U.S. Senate (N.Y. State)**	• Beginning of the end of the dot-com boom • Scientists discover ocean beneath the surface of Jupiter's moon, Europa • First *Lord of the Rings* film • **Margaret Atwood wins Booker Prize for *The Blind Assassin*** • Summer Olympics in Sydney, Australia

POLITICAL	SOCIAL / TECHNOLOGY	
	T I M E L I N E	
• September 11th attacks in U.S. • Jean Chrétien re-elected Canadian PM • U.S. invasion of Afghanistan: "War on Terrorism" • Slobodan Milosevic charged with war crimes	• First legal same-sex marriage in Canada • Enron files for bankruptcy • Harry Potter craze: books and films	**2001**
• Bali nightclub bombing • UN weapons inspectors arrive in Iraq	• Netherlands: first country to legalize euthanasia • Ice-water deposits found on Mars • Winter Olympics in Salt Lake City, U.S. • Yann Martel wins the Booker Prize for *The Life of Pi*	**2002**
• U.S. invades Iraq; large global protests follow • International Criminal Court founded in the Hague • SARS virus erupts, kills hundreds	• Widescale power outage in U.S. and Canada • Final flight of the *Concorde* supersonic airliner	**2003**
• U.S. lifts travel ban on Libya • Haitian President Jean Paul Aristide resigns • Paul Martin elected Canadian PM • Madrid train bombings	• NASA Mars rovers land on Mars • Cassini orbits Saturn • Summer Olympics held in Athens, Greece; second time in modern era • TV: *Survivor* and reality TV craze continues	**2004**

On the Brink
of the Twenty-first Century

In 1992, Francis Fukuyama wrote in *The End of History and the Last Man* that the end of the Cold War also marked the end of History. By this he meant that "liberal democracy may constitute the endpoint of mankind's ideological evolution and [be] the final form of human government." The important point for Canadians is that liberal democracy is not necessarily synonymous with the nation-state as we now experience it. Philip Bobbit has argued in *The Shield of Achilles* that the innovations required to win the ideological wars of the twentieth century — primarily innovations in weaponry, computers and communications technology — have so changed the environment in which nation states operate, that they may lose their legitimacy.

In their place, Bobbit sees what he calls the market state coming into being. He points out that, "whereas the nation state justifies itself as an instrument to serve the welfare of the people (the nation), the market state exists to maximize the opportunities enjoyed by all members of society."

Like the nation state, the market state assesses its economic success or failure by its society's ability to produce more and better goods and services, but, in contrast to the nation state, it does not see the State as more than a minimal provider or redistributor … For the nation state, a national currency is a medium of exchange; for the market state, it is only one more commodity. Much the same may be said of jobs: for the nation state, full employment is an important and often paramount goal, whereas for the market state, the actual number of persons employed is one more variable in the production of economic opportunity and has no overriding intrinsic significance ...

If the nation state was characterized by the rule of law ... the market state is largely indifferent to the norms of justice, or for that matter to any particular set of moral values so long as law does not act as an impediment to economic competition ... The sense of a single polity held together by adherence to fundamental values, is not a sense that is cultivated by the market state. This cultural difference does, however, make the market state an ideal environment for multiculturalism.

Philip Bobbit
The Shield of Achilles, 2002

To serve the people, the nation-state has two broad responsibilities: 1) to devise a constitutional order inside the country (laws, system of government, etc.), and 2) to defend that order in the international arena. In a Western democracy, as long as there's a consensus among citizens that the state is fulfilling these responsibilities to their general benefit, the state is recognized as legitimate. Thus, while governments come and go, the entity that is Canada endures.

In the Canadian nation-state, in addition to a parliamentary system of government, the constitutional order includes such things as universal health care, the redistribution of wealth from richer regions to poorer, support programs for the poor and disadvantaged, a commitment to cultural independence and a somewhat higher tax level (at least by North American standards) to pay for them.

By writing that the world's developed countries are becoming market states, Bobbit is suggesting that the consensus among the citizenry of those countries, including Canada, is beginning to erode. In fact, Canada may be more vulnerable to this process than most liberal democracies.

Our history of "two solitudes" obviously plays a role. So does our commitment to multiculturalism, simply because we have so many new citizens who are in the throes of adjusting to their new home. As birth rates continue to fall and population growth comes primarily from immigration[1], this kind of "loyalty in transition" will be an ongoing reality.

But the greatest internal threat to the Canadian nation-state may in fact come from identity politics and the culture of Me. When too many citizens start to value their own interests (or their group's interests) above all else, they call into question the very idea of a national consensus and the kind of compromises (the

---

[1] The prairies are an exception to this trend. With lower immigration and comparatively high birth rates among First Nation peoples, there is another transition taking place. Native Canadians will form a larger and larger proportion of the prairies' population, creating an increasingly powerful group with its own reasons for ambivalence toward Canada.

political process) that sustain it. This is true whether the citizen is an United Empire Loyalist from Southern Ontario who's tired of supporting welfare bums, a farmer from Alberta who thinks the Wheat Board is a government rip-off, or a recent arrival from a more traditional culture who is here for the economic opportunity and has no intention of being corrupted by what he or she deems to be a godless society.

So, we're faced with a situation today where fewer people in Canada are interested in supporting the traditional constitutional order. Hence the rising support for Reform, the Alliance and now the new Conservative party, whose neocon, "it's your money" approach to governance has such clear appeal for the contented majority. The only reason Stephen Harper didn't become Prime Minister in 2004 was his inability to stifle the social conservatives in his party long enough to get elected.

There is no better evidence of the way self-interest and middle-class angst is transforming our society than the changing role of money in our lives. In a capitalist economy, money is an obvious fundamental and as the consumer society we created in the twentieth century has multiplied our needs, our demand for personal income to meet those needs has grown in lockstep. On the other hand, our nation-state consensus has always dictated the availability of public funds (taxes) for services that don't necessarily benefit individuals directly, but are clearly good for Canadians as a whole.

Implicit in our consensus is the idea that where a good or service is deemed essential because of its impact on the health and welfare of Canadians, the state has a responsibility to ensure delivery to the greatest number possible. Crown corporations, public utilities, Medicare and subsidized transport to northern communities are examples. While there are legitimate (and vigorous) discussions about the definition of essential, the majority of Canadians have traditionally agreed that there exists a class of goods and services that should be public and thus not for sale.

In the market state, on the other hand, everything is a commodity. Money becomes the sole arbiter, and anything that impedes the business of setting a price is needless, even dangerous, interference with market forces. The state, left with no role in any activity that could be undertaken by the private sector, therefore can (and should) be much smaller. Individuals can then use the resulting tax savings to "invest" in goods and services that were previously provided communally, thereby accelerating their journey from citizens to customers.

In Canada, the trend has been demonstrated by the sell-off of phone companies and other public utilities and the contracting out of municipal services like garbage pick up. But to get a real idea of where this may be going, one only has to look south of the border, where welfare is being transferred to private companies, [2] the private penitentiary system is growing, and American administrators in Iraq are guarded by "contractors" (read "mercenaries") instead of U.S. soldiers. [3]

The self-interest generated by Me-ism has had another unfortunate consequence. People who have money are increasingly convinced that their wealth and success have been earned almost exclusively by the sweat of their own brows, and owe little, if anything, to the stable business environment provided by the state or the accumulated social capital of Canadian society (which they take for granted). It follows that no one — particularly some bureaucrat — should have any say on how that wealth is spent.

So if a foreign company wants to buy your local highway or water system and run it at a profit (a Margaret Thatcher specialty), there should be nothing to stop it from doing so. If you need an MRI and don't feel like waiting, you should be able to buy your way to the head of the line.

And, to take an example from the 2004 election, if the media and political parties are not giving your opinion the weight it deserves during an election campaign, you should be able to buy as much advertising as you can afford and say pretty much anything you want to within the confines of the slander laws. After all, free speech is protected by the Charter, and in the market state, money is speech.

Not surprisingly, this last concept has also gained far more acceptance in the U.S., where candidates, their supporters and various interest groups spent $2.4 billion during the 2000 election and are projected to go over $3 billion in 2004. The problem for Canadian proponents — and their ranks are growing, as the Conservative's ninety-nine seats in the 2004 election attest — lies in convincing citizens here that rewarding their self-interest is worth the growing inequality this shift will bring — i.e. no money, no vote.

They're not quite there yet. Despite relentless lobbying from both identity groups and neoconservative organizations like the National Citizen's Coalition — until recently headed by Mr. Harper — which are seeking to use the Charter as a vehicle to transform Canada into a nation more in line with their particular viewpoints, the Supreme Court remains unwilling to bestow constitutional blessing on the supremacy of money.

... the right of meaningful participation in the electoral process is not

---

2 Florida, where the Governor in 2004 was President Bush's brother Jeb, is a leader in this field.

3 The overwhelming majority of these contractors are former U.S. (and British) military personnel, who are earning many times what they did while saluting the Stars and Stripes or taking the Queen's shilling. Their cheques still come from the taxpayer. Its just more ideologically acceptable to funnel the money through private security companies first.

limited to the selection of elected representatives and includes a citizen's right to exercise his or her vote in an informed manner. In the absence of spending limits, it is possible for the affluent or a number of persons pooling their resources and acting in concert to dominate the political discourse, depriving their opponents of a reasonable opportunity to speak and be heard, and undermining the voter's ability to be adequately informed of all views. Equality in the political discourse is thus necessary for meaningful participation in the electoral process and ultimately enhances the right to vote. This right, therefore, does not guarantee unimpeded and unlimited electoral debate or expression.

Supreme Court Ruling, 2004
Harper vs. *Canada*

This obstinacy on the part of the Court elicits anguished cries of judicial activism from the unsuccessful petitioners and certain quarters of the media. Any reasonably objective observer would have to conclude that attempting to identify the moneyed as an oppressed minority is laughable at best, but it's clear the pressure will continue.

That's because rulings like this are affirmations of the nation-state, as is the continued existence in Canada of programs like universal health care. In our view, the importance of Medicare goes beyond its obvious and far-reaching benefits for Canadian citizens. Medicare is a symbol — perhaps *the* symbol — that our nation-state consensus has not completely disappeared in this era of "sink or swim", as Angus Reid has termed it.

Through our continuing support for Medicare, Canadians demonstrate our continued belief that health, at least, is not a good like a car, or a restaurant meal (if you can't afford it, you don't get it). That's why it remains illegal to refuse aid to an injured person (lawsuits notwithstanding), cut off the gas for non-payment during a Canadian winter, or sell a kidney or a womb for cash.

And yet, the pressure to privatize and commoditize continues, not only from the true believers and the rich, but also from much of the middle class, erstwhile charter members of the contented majority. Why? With economic pressure exacerbated by another huge round of layoffs after the collapse of the tech bubble at the end of the '90s, it's fair to say that for many people in Canada, contentment has not continued into the new millennium.

The rich are sick of sharing. The middle class is desperately trying to cling to the middle of the ladder, despite all the broken rungs. Its members (and many of its former members) are trying to determine who is responsible for doing them in — corporations, governments, governments in concert with immigrants, government in concert with the poor, and so on. This is a new mentality in a country where frontiers were opened up by government and which has been nourished by government for much of its 129 years. It reflects the viewpoint that much of what Canada has always been about, at least in economic and social terms, has been wrong. This allegation captured widespread support in English-speaking Canada just as a majority of French-speaking Canadians were voting to support the contention that much of what Canada had been about, in cultural and political terms, had also been wrong. Needless to say, it's difficult to keep a country's spirits up when two of its three most muscular political movements (Reform and the Bloc) keep hammering home that the essence of Canada's political, social, economic and cultural heritage is fundamentally flawed. Is it any wonder that the spirits of Canadians, already battered by the vicissitudes of massive economic change, are flagging a bit?

Angus Reid
*Shakedown: How the New Economy
is Changing Our Lives,* 1996

This odd combination of dyspepsia, fear and boomer self-indulgence is being expressed in a number of ways. Automobiles, always isolating, have morphed into giant SUVs, mobile fortresses that continue the assault on social capital by making neighbourhoods places we move through rather than live in. Home theatres recreate the movie going experience without exposure to sticky floors and potentially dangerous strangers. Exclusive nurseries, play dates and private schools extend the same protection to our children.

But as an expression of the sheer cynicism and lack of trust that permeates society, nothing beats reality TV, or "non-fiction improvised drama" as the god-father of the genre, Mark Burnett, has termed it.

Professor Alison Hearn of the University of Western Ontario points out that the success of reality TV "[depends] on the dominant cultural impetus to laugh at the misfortune of others. The whole dynamic of humiliation is central to reality TV. There's certain car wreck mentality."[4] For that reason, she suggests that *schadenfreude* TV might be a better description. How else to explain the popularity of Donald Trump (again!) and his "You're fired!" shtick?

---

[4]   Quoted in the *National Post*, May 8, 2004.

In addition to being extremely profitable, reality TV captures the true *zeitgeist* of the times — the market as a model for our lives. We're all in this together becomes Outwit. Outplay. Outlast™. In a world where money and celebrity are more highly valued than reputation and accomplishment, and entitlement has become the basis of public discourse, what better entertainment could we have devised?

•• ❖ ••

In a BBC interview at the World Aids Conference in Bangkok, on July 10, 2004, Dr. Peter Piot, UN Under-Secretary General, said:

> Let's not forget that in Africa there have been decades of policies by governments, by the donors, by the IMF, by the World Bank, to destroy public services. The mantra was that what's private is good and what's public is bad. Inflation has to be controlled, government spending [reduced]. And, of course, there was some good grounds for that. But, it went too far. Without a well-functioning state, you cannot deliver goods to the poor. And that's what we're paying a price now for.

The movement toward the market state has a name. It's called globalization and globalization has meant, among other things, that individual states have less power to control their own economic lifeblood — the flow of money across their own borders. While international investment can be hugely beneficial, governments also find that they've become vulnerable to the calculations of people who have no interest in the welfare of their citizens. Argentina, Malaysia, Indonesia and Korea — far from a complete list — experienced the downside of globalization in the 1990s. International investors decided that these countries were no longer good investments and pulled out billions, leaving the national economies on the verge of collapse.

> We have the currency going down and down and down, and we have the stock market doing the same. The index kept on going down, no matter what we [did]. And we felt totally helpless. We felt that there was no way we could recover. So, I mean, the feeling was very bad, very frightening. [5]
>
> > Mahathir Bin Mohamad
> > Prime Minister of Malaysia, 1981-2003

---

[5] As quoted in the television series, 'The Commanding Heights', 2002.

In 1997, the economy and then the government of Indonesia did collapse, while South Korea, the world's eleventh-largest economy, was only saved by the biggest international bailout in history — $55 billion worth of loans and guarantees arranged by the International Monetary Fund.

What these countries experienced first-hand was the loss of sovereignty that will inevitably accompany globalization. This loss of sovereignty undermines a nation-state's legitimacy on the basis of its second fundamental responsibility — defending its constitutional order in the international arena.

As with the rightward drift within Canada, the culture of Me plays its role in globalization. Part of the money we don't want to give to our governments in the form of taxes is the money that went into (and out of) places like the Southeast Asian countries, Korea and Argentina, invested by our banks, mutual funds and pension managers. If we're honest with ourselves, the small (and temporary) drop in net worth we may have experienced from these episodes was far more significant to us than the plight of, say, the Argentinean middle class, many of whom were reduced to selling their belongings at flea markets because their life savings evaporated in the collapse.

In short, if a reduction of governmental ability to interfere in business means more money in my pocket, where's the downside? After all, Canada, the world's twelfth-largest economy, isn't Indonesia or even Korea. Is it?

Perhaps not. However, when one considers the continuing blackmail-bribe cycle over private-sector job creation, the unrelenting pressure on the Wheat Board and softwood lumber industry and the enormous (and apparently successful) pressure put on Health Canada by drug companies over internet pharmacies, it does give one pause.

The most powerful example of this external influence was our so-called debt crisis of the early 1990s. Despite the *Wall Street Journal*'s harumphings about our being "the Mexico of the North", there was never any chance that Canada would default on its external debt. The drop in our credit rating can therefore be regarded more as international disapproval of the way we were doing things — a reminder that we weren't moving quickly enough toward the market state. Our vulnerability to this kind of pressure, both as a trading nation and as a smallish economy [6] in the emerging global economic system, was made obvious in subsequent Paul Martin budgets.

The point here is not whether the spending cuts in 1995 and subsequent years were right or wrong, though we think that, on balance, they were beneficial

---

[6] There is a huge gap between first and twelfth in terms of Gross Domestic Product. In 2002, the American defence budget alone equalled a third of Canada's entire economy.

for the country. The point is, given the circumstances, how little real choice the Chrétien government had in making them.

Enthusing in the *Financial Times* about the export of North American jobs to low wage economies (job "mobility" being another feature of globalization), William Dudley, Peter Hooper and David Resler succinctly sum up the preferred role of government in the market state and provide another subtext for the conversion process — resistance is futile.

> … while the costs are huge for those who lose their jobs, the beneficiaries are either unaware that their jobs are linked to liberalized foreign trade or do not appreciate that outsourcing is holding down the prices of the goods and services they buy … Trying to slow the process of outsourcing is no solution. Instead, the United States (and presumably all developed countries) must make the adjustment process less painful and ensure that it has full access to markets.
>
> First, the government should assist displaced workers. The benefits of free trade can only be realized if those people find alternative employment. More could be done to set up job-finding services … and to provide financial assistance for severely hit local communities to attract replacement jobs.
>
> Reprinted in the *National Post*
> March 27, 2004

One is left with the impression that market state enthusiasts see only one real role for governments — that of insurance provider, where the premiums (our tax dollars) are used to bail out overeager investors, while easing the transition to exciting new careers in burger-flipping for the rest of us. It's hard to imagine Canada having much of a place in such a future.

In the end, we have to conclude that Fukuyama may have been somewhat premature, and not necessarily because the world is entering a time of Samuel Huntington's clash of civilizations (though the forces of tribalism and mediaeval morality are certainly abroad, and not just in the Muslim world). Even if the left-right divide of the Cold War ended with the fall of the Berlin Wall and demise of the Soviet Union, the centre-right fight over the fate of the nation-state is still far from over.

Ideological endpoint? Not yet. But how it turns out will have a profound effect on social progress in Canada, including the eventual role of women in public life.

‥ ❖ ‥

When I was running for president of the Liberal Party — this was in 1982 — there had never been a woman president. So there was a great deal of the old clichés. You see, every time a woman walks through one of those doors that has been closed — every time you breach that barrier — the process takes you right back to the beginning of women's breakthrough. So, it's like 100 years ago ... Can a woman do it? Is a woman able? Is it possible for a woman do this thing? As a result, there were high emotions and I received some notes under my door, full of misogynistic hate. You know, how dare you do this, etc ... But, I won.

Hon. Iona Campagnolo
Lieutenant Governor of B.C.
July 1999

The 1990s and first part of the new millennium have not been particularly kind to women. Partly, this has been because the economy has put so many people into survival mode. Partly, it's been the radical right's success at labelling most female activists as extremists or "feminazis", in Rush Limbaugh's odious phrase. Partly it's been the rightward political shift we've been examining — a shift that's been particularly sharp in the United States, inescapable source of so much of our cultural iconography.

But the main problem, and one that's been with us throughout the twentieth century, is that despite the consciousness-raising of two waves of feminism, the fundamentals of how we live and work still haven't changed. Working or not, in 2004 women still bear primary responsibility for home and children, and society still depends on that unpaid labour. This is the true patriarchy — not a plot, but another excruciatingly persistent period of social inertia. Women have gained access to the world of men ... but so far, mostly by moonlighting.

Which brings us to the final female politician in this study, a woman whose career was directly affected by the trends examined in this chapter. If there was ever a woman who was willing and able to enter the male arena and take on all comers, it had to be Sheila Copps. Many felt she had the potential to take the final step and become the first woman elected to be Prime Minister. But in politics, as in life, timing is everything.

"Shush Sheila, Shush!" "Send her back to kindergarten." "Can you imagine being married to that." "A big mouth never gets anything, baby." "God damn ignorant bitch." These are just a few of the epithets that have been hurled at Sheila Copps. Why has she caused such invective?

❖ SHEILA COPPS ❖

Was it because she was one of the youngest women to ever mix it up with the boys in what they considered to be their game and they didn't much like the competition? Was it because she was physically attractive and while they were willing to tolerate older women, they were not willing to accept parliamentary give and take from someone they'd like to date? Was it because she was unwilling to be treated as anything other than their equal and unlike many women would not grin and bear the insults? Whatever the reason, she rose above it all and proved she was, as her own book proclaims, *Nobody's Baby.*

Sheila Copps was born in Hamilton on November 27, 1952. Her father, Victor Kennedy Copps, was a former Mayor of Hamilton and her mother, Geraldine Florence Guthro Copps, had served as an alderwoman in the same city. From a family of four, Sheila was the second eldest of three girls and one boy. Her father ran for the Board of Controllers in Hamilton when Sheila was eight and she immediately wrote and performed his theme song along with her sisters. It was clear from the beginning that she had good political instincts.

It will surprise no one who has observed the Canadian political scene that Sheila was an effervescent young woman. She was the leader of the pack. Her mother has commented that if it hadn't been for her tough hand, Sheila might have become a juvenile delinquent. That appears somewhat harsh, as Sheila was never engaged in any dangerous or illegal activities. She was simply … high spirited.

She also felt the burden of being a politician's daughter. She was hurt and angry when informed by the boy whom she had just beaten in an oratorical contest that she had only won because she was the Mayor's daughter. She also recalls arriving at school with a new leather coat shortly after the city council had voted itself a raise, and being confronted by: "Did you get that out of your father's raise?" In fact, her father had given his raise to charity and the charity wasn't Sheila.

She also experienced the hard side of politics. Her father had given years of dedicated service to the people of Hamilton. Yet, when he was left brain damaged as a result of oxygen deprivation caused by a heart attack, he had no pension to support either himself or his family. She also saw first hand the generosity of the people of Hamilton, who promptly raised $170,000 for a trust fund dedicated to the former Mayor's support.

Why did she choose a political career? Certainly her education didn't point in that direction. She attended the University of Western Ontario and graduated with Honours in English and French. She then attended the Université de Rouen in France and spent some time at McMaster University. Her ability to speak both of Canada's official languages fluently, as well as her ease in Italian, certainly helped her in her political career, but they were not the kind of courses that educate in the art of politics. Indeed, upon her return to Canada from France she chose a job as reporter for the *Ottawa Citizen* in its Hull branch, not to learn more about politics, but primarily to work on her language skills.

She left this work when her father had his heart attack, returning to Hamilton to help her mother in what was a stressful time for the whole family. Copps had the further burden of a broken marriage. She speaks very little of her first partner, Bill Miller, an American who also worked for the *Ottawa Citizen* and *Reuters* news agency, other than to say they were incompatible. He was apparently as right wing as she was left wing in ideology. There was no meeting of the minds and the marriage ended in an annulment.

She decided to stay in Hamilton and took a job with the *Hamilton Spectator*. Her very first night at the paper, she received a phone call from the Liberal Party of Ontario asking her to run as its provincial candidate in Hamilton Centre. There were only twenty-three days left in the provincial election campaign, but she was told not to worry; there would be plenty of money and workers. It was clear the party members wanted to run on the Copps name — they'd asked her uncle the night before.

He perhaps knew better than Sheila not to trust desperate organizers who promise the moon, but she decided to take the gamble. She knew she was a long shot but, with youth on her side — she was only twenty-four — her attitude was essentially one of nothing ventured, nothing gained.

She soon learned there was no money and most of the Liberal workers had moved to other constituencies, believing there was a better chance of their work counting for something where campaigns were up and rolling. That Hamilton Centre had not voted Liberal since 1934 only added to their lack of enthusiasm, but it didn't deter Copps.

As she was to do in every campaign that followed, she campaigned flat out. She has always claimed that any politician must run scared. Not panic scared, but scared enough to make the candidate, workers and voters believe that this is truly the campaign of their lives. She didn't win in 1977, but since she only lost by fifteen votes, she immediately set her sights on winning in the next campaign. She was hooked.

In the process, her provincial leader, Stuart Smith, was so impressed with her savvy and hard work that he immediately hired her to be his constituency assistant in Hamilton West. She was able to use the next four years to learn everything she could about running a constituency.

On nights and weekends, she furthered her own cause in Hamilton Centre, working on community projects, school initiatives and hospital boards. She was determined to win and when the next election was called, she did — her fifteen-vote loss of 1977 became a 3,000-vote victory in 1981. Sheila Copps was off to Queen's Park.

When she arrived, she was the only woman in a caucus of thirty members. She quickly learned that if she appeared to be unambitious, the rest were delighted to have their token woman. What they didn't want, however, was someone who would compete with them for high office, or cut into their media coverage.

Copps has a sparkling personality. She also has a sense of righteous indignation. When the two are combined, she can out debate, out talk and sometimes out outrage anyone within listening distance. She also has a woman's voice. This means it has a higher register. It also means, when at full strength, it can be heard above the rest — not because she is louder necessarily, but because her voice carries better.

For some, this was considered a negative. For her own growth as a politician, it was a positive. Everyone knew when Copps had something to say and she was never shy about voicing an opinion. She was a quick study, not afraid to make mistakes and swift to apologize when she was wrong, all of which made her hot copy in the media. Her stands on issues were clear. She led the fight for inclusion of sexual orientation in the Human Rights Amendment and worked tirelessly in her caucus for pay equity.

Less than two years after her election, at the age of twenty-nine, Copps ran for the leadership of the Liberal Party in Ontario. The media wrote her off as a dark-horse candidate, but ended with considerable egg on its collective face when she came second to David Peterson, and finished handily ahead of three other male candidates. In addition, she had been able to increase support between the first and second ballots, thereby dispelling any belief that voters had simply parked their vote with Sheila until they saw the lay of the land. The final results were 1,138 for Peterson and 774 for Copps. She had shown Ontarians that women could be credible leadership candidates in competitive races.

Once back in Queen's Park, Copps had to deal with a change in attitude on the part of other caucus members. She had crossed the line from token female MPP to a strong, high-profile politician who was their equal or superior. Some egos had been damaged, and she needed to do some repair work.

A quality for which she is now famous began to be recognized. Copps is loyal, both to her party and to her leader. She can fight in caucus with the best of them. But once a decision has been taken, she will be its staunchest defender, even though she may in her heart be opposed. The same can be said of the loyalty and support she gives to her leader

David Peterson, whom she had opposed for leadership, has said that Sheila is loyal to a fault. He had proof of it in her unflinching support for his leadership in the Ontario Legislature. She supported John Turner and then Jean

Chrétien with the same fervour. She clearly believes that if you cannot support the leader, you leave the party. You do not undermine from within.

Under Peterson's leadership, Copps was given the responsibility of health critic. She fought for an end to premiums for health care and a ban on extra billing, both of which were put into effect by the Peterson government when it came to office. In addition, she supported more community-based programming in health, compulsory family life education in the schools and the availability of birth control information at all community health units. That all these issues were considered to be political minefields did nothing to deter her.

In 1984, after three years in opposition, her concern that Conservative Premier Bill Davis would decide not to resign and probably be reelected led her to leave provincial politics and to enter the federal arena. Unfortunately, Davis did resign and Peterson formed the next government in Ontario, one in which Copps undoubtedly would have had a cabinet position. However, she had no regrets about her decision to run federally, even though it ended up meaning another nine years in opposition.

Copps decided to run in the federal seat vacated by John Munro. Munro was a political veteran who had been extremely disappointed by his poor showing in the Liberal Party of Canada leadership convention of June 1984, and the ensuing failure of the new leader, John Turner, to appoint him to cabinet.

Copps' relationship with Munro went back a long way. He had helped her in the 1977 provincial election and in subsequent campaigns. Munro was one of the few politicians to visit her ailing father and it was John Munro who had spear-headed the raising of the former mayor's trust fund. Because of his generosity to her and her family and because he was the "local son" candidate in the 1984 leadership campaign, she supported him in his bid for the leadership. She also encouraged him to take his vote to Jean Chrétien on the second ballot, when it was clear he could not win.

However, Munro and his supporters did not encourage Copps to run in his Hamilton East seat. It was true they were tired and discouraged, but it also seems they felt that because of her age, Sheila would want the seat for a long time. They would have been happier with an older candidate prepared to keep the seat warm in case Munro wanted to make a comeback. While it would have been helpful to have their support, Copps was now well enough known, and her value as an elected representative sufficiently high, that their help was not essential.

As in previous campaigns, Copps went flat out. The national campaign was a disaster and this began to have an impact on the Hamilton riding. The campaign team watched their ten percentage point lead dissipate. They clearly had nothing to lose, so they gambled.

The campaign team spread the message that it was clear that Canadians were tired of the Liberals and were going to get rid of them. However, it would still be necessary to have a fighter in opposition and Sheila Copps was the best fighter they could send. It worked. When count was finished, Copps was moving to Ottawa with a plurality of 2,700 votes.

In Ottawa, her reputation as a tough fighter quickly grew. The front benches of the governing Conservative Party disliked her intensely and, their comments reflected their disdain. She became part of the so-called "Rat Pack", a group of Liberals who constantly harassed the Tories in the house — a challenging task since there were only forty Liberals and 211 Tories.

Among the permanent members of the "Rat Pack" were Don Boudria, Brian Tobin, John Nunziata and, of course, Copps. Jean Claude Malepart and Bob Kaplan joined on occasion. When asked today who the "Rat Pack" were, most Canadians will immediately identify Copps. They have forgotten most, if not all, of the men. In fact, she was not the most active member of the group, but it was a new role for a woman. While some didn't like it, many, both men and women, applauded the feistiness of her attacks.

In 1985, Copps married for the second time. She met her husband, Ric Marrero, while on vacation in Florida. He agreed to move to Canada and eventually opened a sound studio in Ottawa. The marriage lasted less than five years. However, on March 22, 1987, Copps gave birth to Danelle, an eight-pound baby girl.

She had been in the House of Commons the day before, as usual giving John Crosbie, the Conservative Minister of Trade, a difficult time. Like any good politician, her timing was perfect. She gave birth just before Question Period and her leader, John Turner, announced minutes later that, for the first time in Canadian history, a child had been delivered of a sitting member of the House of Commons.

Copps was back at work full time six weeks later, though she was actually present on Parliament Hill ten days after Danelle's birth for the visit of U.S. President Ronald Reagan. It was clear from the start she was to be a thoroughly modern parent, combining motherhood and career. During the first few months, Danelle accompanied her mother to the office in her bassinet so that she would be available for her mother to both cuddle and breast feed. The baby went to tactics meetings and when necessary, for lack of a sitter, to committee meetings.

Everyone loved the baby and some even saw Copps in a new light — something she found more than a little amusing. She was the same old Sheila, but where before the birth certain media portrayed her as a harpy, now she became the caring mother. It was a short-lived interlude as Danelle, like all babies, grew.

A child-care centre was found and Sheila and her husband worked out a schedule that allowed Danelle to have at least one parent present when she was at home.

For most analysts, the outcome of the 1984 election was a foregone conclusion. After twenty-one years of Liberal government, Canadians had wanted change and they had seen that change in the person of Brian Mulroney. On the other hand, Liberal Party members believed the 1988 election was theirs to win and they went all out.

However, both the Liberals and the NDP were campaigning in opposition to the Free Trade Agreement and they split the vote. The Liberals increased their seats in the House of Commons from forty to eighty-four, but Brian Mulroney remained Canada's Prime Minister, and although she increased her personal plurality to 8,138 votes, Sheila Copps remained an opposition member.

In 1989, John Turner announced his decision to step down as leader. The Liberal Party of Canada decided to delay the convention until June 1990 and in an utterly bizarre decision, called the convention for the exact weekend that the Meech Lake Accord had to be ratified by all the provinces. It should have been abundantly clear to the executive even in 1989 that Meech was in serious trouble in the Manitoba, Newfoundland and, to a lesser degree, New Brunswick. So, it's difficult to explain why they would have deliberately chosen that particular time.

It was apparent from the beginning of the leadership campaign that Jean Chrétien, narrowly defeated in 1984, would be the man to beat. However, there was also an ABC movement, Anyone But Chrétien. There were Liberals who believed he had not been adequately supportive of John Turner and others who believed he was past his prime. The theme of "Yesterday's Man" became a constant refrain of his opponents.

Paul Martin, the son of the late Honourable Paul Martin, had been elected to the House of Commons in the 1988 election and was seen as a contender. Martin was a wealthy businessman turned politician who spoke well, was fluently bilingual and had a well-developed policy package.

Copps was perceived to be running a strong third, the idea of choosing a woman as leader being less revolutionary as it might have seemed even a year before. The New Democratic Party had elected Audrey McLaughlin as the leader of their party in December 1989, and it was clear that Copps was far more qualified than McLaughlin in terms of political experience. If the Liberal Party chose to buck tradition, Copps was the odds-on favourite. She was bilingual, from urban Canada, and a politician with substantial front-bench experience at two levels of government. The biggest problem she faced was overcoming the belief, held by many Liberals, that it was Jean Chrétien's time.

As usual, from the very beginning of the campaign it was obvious that the Copps' candidacy was going to be treated differently from the rest. The media was interested in her clothes, her hair-style, her child-care arrangements and her recent separation from her husband. She had already experienced this invasive coverage during the leadership race in Ontario, so she was prepared for it.

She was also ready to go on the attack. In her opening press conference in January of 1990 — she was the second to announce, after Tom Wappel — she laid out a campaign based on youth and loyalty. These were clearly attacks on Chrétien and Martin. Both men were in their fifties compared to her thirty-seven, and there was a perception among some Liberals that Chrétien had been less than loyal to Turner.

She also reminded delegates that she represented small-town Canada and the middle class, as opposed to the wealth and privilege of the two front-runners, particularly Martin. However, she saved her strongest attacks for Brian Mulroney. He was the one whose job she was after and she left no doubt that she relished the prospect both of his defeat and her own leadership.

Copps had been unswerving in her support for the Meech Lake Accord. This, combined with her fluency in French and the support of Yvon-Marc Coté, a leading member of the Québec Liberal Party, made her a favourite in that province. Paul Martin, because he was from Québec, had hoped to get Robert Bourassa's support. But with Coté, a Bourassa insider, supporting Copps, Martin's chances of taking the entire Québec delegation with him were diminished.

Strongly positive media coverage and the support of other influential Liberals did not, however, translate into delegate support. In one constituency after another, Chrétien and to a lesser degree Martin slates were being elected. The problem was simple. The delegate selection meetings were run on the basis of winner takes all. Each constituency chose seven delegates but even if forty-nine per cent of those attending the meeting supported Copps, as long as Jean Chrétien had the support of the other fifty-one per cent, he received all seven delegates. In reality much lower percentages were required because of the number of candidates.

Copps also had problems raising money. The party had set a limit of $2 million per candidate. Even with their deep connections to the corporate community, this sum was going to be difficult for Chrétien and Martin to raise. It would be impossible for Copps. Her campaign committee only budgeted for $500,000 and had great difficulty raising even this. When it comes to fundraising, as Kim Campbell has said, they quickly learned there is no advantage to being a woman in Canadian politics.

I think that women themselves are often much cheaper
than men when it comes to making political donations. I don't know

the reason for that. It may be that women think of their money as family money and don't feel so free to give it as donations. Most party fundraisers will tell you that if the wife answers the phone at a home where they're used to getting a donation, they'll get about a tenth of what they'd get if the husband answers. That often has an impact on women and their ability to raise money for campaigns. If they're not that well-connected in the corporate world, or in the worlds where people have money and are used to giving money to political campaigns, that can be a problem.

Rt. Hon. Kim Campbell

July 1999

Less money meant a lower travel budget, fewer staff members, less computer help, a reduced communications budget and less hoopla at the convention. Her campaign knew that with the overwhelming support for Jean Chrétien, her only hope for success rested with her ability to grow on the convention floor. In other words, they had to convince the delegates to make Copps their second choice in an ABC (Anyone But Chrétien) movement.

By the time the convention began, opinion polls showed that Copps was second only to Chrétien in public popularity — she actually led the polls in Québec. Unfortunately, most delegates had been selected prior to the release of the poll numbers.

Chrétien was unbeatable on the convention floor. He won on the first ballot with 2,662 votes, fifty-seven per cent of the ballots cast. Paul Martin came second with twenty-five per cent of the vote and Copps placed a third with eleven per cent. However, the new leader understood her growing popularity across the country, and respected both her talent and her loyalty. He also recognized the need to have women in prominent roles in the Liberal Party of Canada. So in January 1991, Copps was made the Deputy Leader of the Liberal Party.

She worked tirelessly during the 1993 election campaign. She was in demand across the country and was a willing campaigner. She won her own riding handily with a plurality of over 17,000 votes. Then, like all newly elected members of the government, she had to wait to hear the plans of the new Prime Minister. When the new cabinet was announced, in addition to being named Environment Minister, Copps again made history by becoming Canada's first female Deputy Prime Minister. It was to be (to date, at least) the high point of her career.

It's true the Liberals won 177 seats in 1993 — a landslide. Remember, however, that ninety-eight of those seats came from Ontario. Since these were the same voters who gave Mike Harris an overwhelming majority for his neo-conservative Common Sense Revolution just two years later, it's fair to say that if these voters perceived the Liberals as the party of the centre, the centre in Canada had moved rather smartly to the right.

Copps, on the other hand, was the standard bearer for the Liberal left. So after 1995, as the government's focus changed to deficit reduction and response to the Québec referendum, she began to drift out of Chrétien's inner circle.

Her GST stance didn't help. The Liberal platform for the 1993 election had promised to do away with the GST, and replace it with another revenue generator, but it quickly became obvious the new government could not keep this particular pledge. Copps, in a move many of her colleagues considered grandstanding, promised to resign if her government didn't keep its word.

When Paul Martin's 1995 budget made it clear that the government had decided it needed the money the GST generated, she astonished almost everyone by announcing her resignation. She easily won the resulting by-election and returned to cabinet, but the gesture did nothing to endear her to party insiders.

The Liberals won again in 1997. Herb Grey was named the new Deputy PM, while Copps was demoted, receiving the lesser portfolio of Culture and Heritage. It was now that divisions in the Liberal party began to become obvious, as Martin and his clique manoeuvered to unseat Chrétien as Prime Minister. Still loyal to her leader, Copps would clearly be in trouble if the coup attempt succeeded.

Succeed it did. Chrétien gave the Liberals a third majority in 2000 and then was persuaded (some would say forced) to retire, which he officially did on December 12, 2003. There was clearly no place for Sheila Copps in a Martin government, especially since, in typical Sheila fashion, she'd been the only one with the temerity to run against him in the November leadership convention.

She refused to accept a patronage post, choosing instead to stay on as an MP. The thought of having rat pack tactics used against them from their own backbench was more than the Martin team could stomach. So, redistribution was used as an excuse to deny this stalwart of the party the nomination in her own riding, forcing her to return to private life. As a long-time Liberal Senator recently remarked, "I've never seen such a bunch of sore winners in my life."

The Liberals won their fourth consecutive election in 2004, but with only 135 seats, the Martin government is in a minority position. Historically, that's meant another election within two years, by which time Martin will be sixty-eight and Copps, only fifty-four. Will she make another comeback? It seems long odds, but the former member for Hamilton East has never been a quitter.

Whatever the future holds in store for Sheila Copps, she has already made an outstanding contribution to Canadian politics. She has shown women, particularly young women, what can be accomplished. And she's done it her way.

◆◆ ❖ ◆◆

As we write in the summer of 2004, the "War on Terror", the American-led response to the 9/11 attacks on Washington and New York, is drifting toward the end of its third year. Governments have been replaced in Afghanistan and Iraq, but the new regimes are clearly not in control of their own territories, and will not be for years to come. The semi-permanent presence of foreign troops in these and many other countries around the world, many of them ex-colonies, is an eerie reminder of the nineteenth-century world we outlined at the beginning of this volume.

But, of course, this is not the nineteenth century. In 2004, the forty-odd independent states of 1902 have become 191, as defined by membership in the United Nations. This is up from 166 at the beginning of the 1990s, the increase driven by the breakup of the Soviet Union and rising nationalism in Southeastern Europe. Militarily and economically, there is one Great Power — the United States — with a second tier that includes China and Japan, the old colonizing countries, and a few successful ex-colonies like India and Canada.

With a population of more than 32,000,000, Canada has become one of the most multicultural countries in the world — more than a third of us have a background other than European. Urbanization is almost complete, with nearly eighty per cent of us living in towns and cities. Our birthrate of 1.61 children per woman is one of the lowest on the planet, following a trend that's been repeated throughout the developed world (the exception being the United States). Even with immigration, our population is growing slowly and aging quickly, a combination that that will soon have serious implications for our social safety net.

Television,[7] whether delivered by cable, telephone line or satellite, has long since eclipsed any other form of popular entertainment or public communication, at least for people over twenty-five. Canadians now spend an average of three hours every day having their attention spans lowered and hearing damaged by ever larger and louder home entertainment systems.

The fact that television is, above all else, a visual medium, and therefore singularly bad at the presentation of complex ideas, has had a profound effect on the practice of politics, where the trading of thirty-second sound bites has almost completely replaced reasoned discourse.

---

[7] We include the movie industry in this general category as much of its output is aimed directly at the home market.

The effect has been to blur the boundaries between politics and a peculiar television hybrid called infotainment, a category that today includes newsmagazines, celebrity trials and, increasingly, news programs themselves — presentations that seem to have little purpose beyond selling anti-flatulence pills, feminine hygiene products and impotence aids. So, Question Period or reports by the Auditor General seem no different than reality game shows, and more and more public business is done outside the House of Commons, timed to take advantage of the ever-shortening news cycle.

The result, along with the other trends we've examined in the latter part of this book, has been a growing political disengagement. In the 2004 election, the most interesting and significant contest in a quarter-century, only 60.5% of the electorate bothered to vote — the lowest turnout in Canadian history.

All of this — Meism, the rise of the market state, the decline of the middle class — is, in our view, bad news for the cause of equality. That's because it's not only the voters who are disengaging. The women who should be taking leadership roles in government and business — the women who are now the majority of our university graduates — are opting out, either disgusted by the choices they're forced to make, or exhausted by the attempt to smash the glass ceiling.

> For two generations, we have been advised that life was a footrace and that the best and fastest would win. Ambitious girls planned for the main event by taking math and acquiring job skills. Earnest mothers read self-help books and enrolled their daughters in sports so they would acquire team and leadership skills.
>
> But millions of females aced algebra and high-fived their way through adolescence only to discover that business is not so much a sport as a blood sport. The metaphor that applies is war, not baseball, and success belongs to those in full metal jackets rather than track suits.
>
> Diane Francis
> *National Post*, November 1, 2003

Even the women who have donned their designer armour and fought their way to the top will admit they're still the exception. As Francis goes on to note, there are still very few female CEOs in Canada, and women make up less than ten per cent of boards of directors.

The situation in politics is not much different. Susan Thompson, Winnipeg's first female Mayor, has also used the term "blood sport" to describe

CATHERINE CALLBECK

Canada's First Elected Female Premier

CATHERINE CALLBECK was born on July 25, 1939 in Central Bedeque, Prince Edward Island. Her parents, Ralph and Ruth Callbeck, were long-time Islanders in a province that counts the generations. Her father, as had his father before him, operated Callbeck's, a general store that drew people from all over the island to buy stoves, groceries and hardware.

Catherine left P.E.I. to take a Bachelor of Commerce degree at Mount Allison University in Sackville, New Brunswick. She graduated in 1960, the only woman in her class. She earned her Bachelor of Education at Dalhousie in Halifax, and did post-graduate work in Business Administration at Syracuse University in New York State. This led to a teaching position in the business faculty at the St. John Institute of Technology, where she was the only female on staff.

In 1973, she successfully ran the Prince Edward Island centennial celebrations in Bedeque. The following year, she was approached by the provincial Liberals to run in the Fourth District of Prince constituency. Callbeck was a "small c" conservative, but party affiliations run deep on the island and her family had been Liberal for generations. She accepted the nomination and became the second woman in P.E.I. history to be elected to the Legislative Assembly. After one term as Minister of Health and Social Services and Minister for the Disabled, she returned briefly to private life to wind up the family business, before being returned as the MP for Malpeque in the 1988 federal election.

After serving on the front bench in opposition, she fully expected to be included in a future Liberal cabinet, but others had different ideas. The popular Liberal Premier, Joe Ghiz, had decided to retire, and soon, the phones in Callbeck's offices were ringing off the hook, urging her to run for Premier.

The leadership convention, held on January 22 and 23, 1993, was quick and decisive. Callbeck received 1,228 of the 1,556 first ballot votes, a whopping seventy-nine per cent. She was the new leader of the Liberal Party of Prince Edward Island and, two days later, on January 25, 1993, she was sworn in as Premier.

Interestingly, gender never became a media issue, either during the leadership race or in the election that followed. The reason was that Tory leader Pat Mella was also a woman, so there was no doubt the new Premier was going to be female. It is somewhat ironic that, in the only province where there is no access to abortion and only a single shelter for battered women, the citizens were presented this particular electoral choice. As it turned out, the election was more a coronation. On March 29, 1993, the Liberals under Callbeck won thirty-one of thirty-two seats with fifty-five per cent of the popular vote, and Canada had its first elected female Premier.

Callbeck made it clear from the beginning that she didn't believe that women's issues needed special attention from a female leader. She denied being a feminist, stating that women's issues were the same as all other issues and they would get on the legislative agenda in the same manner. Her focus throughout her time as Premier, as her background might suggest, remained firmly on economic matters — balancing the budget, increasing exports and building the fixed link that would connect Prince Edward Island to the mainland.

Catherine Callbeck retired as Premier of P.E.I. in 1996, and was called to the Senate in 1997, where she is an active member of the Social Affairs committee that works on health-care policy. In addition, she contributed to the recent report on *Women As Entrepreneurs*.

her two terms at the municipal level. And, more than eighty years after women received the vote, only Pat Duncan of the Yukon, has managed to join Nellie Cournoyea and Catherine Callbeck as an elected provincial leader.

Federally, there will be sixty-five female MPs in the 38th Parliament out of a total of 308 members. This representation rate of twenty-one per cent is actually a slight drop from the final Chrétien government, and continues a trend that's been ongoing since 1993. In addition, the new Martin cabinet will have two fewer women than the one he named in December 2003, and though Anne McLellan is Deputy Prime Minister, none has been given a senior portfolio.

This slide in representation is at least partially the result of an even larger drop in participation. In 1993, 476 women ran in the federal election, an all-time high. By 2004, the number of female candidates had dropped to only 265.

Why? Part of the drop can be explained by the growing popularity of the political right, which tends to attract fewer women — in 2004, only eleven per cent of Conservative candidates were female. The continuing difficulty of achieving positions of real power obviously lessens the attraction to competent, ambitious women. And then there's the job itself, which is pretty much the same as when Agnes Macphail started doing it in 1921.

> [You need] enormous physical good health and stamina, off the top. It takes a measure of calm, emotional security, and a good healthy intellect doesn't hurt either, you know, because you're constantly learning. But the physical demands, particularly on western members of Parliament — and I, as a British Columbian, can tell you first hand about that — [it's] the sheer weight of travel. That long flight to Vancouver, the flight north (Campagnolo was the member for Prince Rupert), then taking the midnight flight back, over and over and over, every weekend. Night sittings. Flying off in the middle of the week to be a fundraiser for the party. There was no rest and the fatigue was beyond belief. So, physical endurance was [needed] as much as intellectual endurance.
>
> Iona Campagnolo,
> July 1999

Now imagine that this hard-working elected representative has a second full-time job, as every woman with children does. Even when she finally makes it home, it's catchup rather than respite. Allison Pearson captures the poignancy of the experience in her recent novel, *I Don't Know How She Does It*.

Before I was really old enough to understand what being a woman meant, I already understood that the world of women was divided in two: there were proper mothers, self-sacrificing bakers of apple pies and well scrubbed invigilators of the washtub, and there were the other sort. At the age of thirty-five, I know precisely what sort I am, and I suppose that's what I'm doing here in the small hours of the morning of the thirteenth of December, hitting mince pies with a rolling pin till they look something like mother made. Women used to have time to make mince pies and had to fake orgasms. Now we can manage the orgasms, but we have to fake the mince pies. And they call this progress …

… There have been times over the last year when I have tried to explain to my daughter — I felt she was old enough to hear this — why Mummy has to go to work. Because Mum and Dad both need to earn money for our house and all the things she enjoys doing like ballet lessons and going on holiday. Because Mummy has a job she is good at and it's really important for women to work as well as men. Each time, the speech builds to a stirring climax — trumpets, choirs, the tearful sisterhood waving flags — in which I assure Emily that she will under-stand all this when she is a big girl and wants to do interesting things herself.

Unfortunately, the case for equal opportunities, long estab-lished in liberal Western society, cuts no ice in the fundamentalist regime of a five-year old.

Given all this, it's fair to ask at the dawn of the third millennium, why would any woman want to become a politician? Our answer is, just look around you. There's so much work to be done.

In 2003, sixty-three per cent of Canadian women with children under three were working. Given the static income levels for most of the middle class through the nineties, one has to presume that most were working because they have to. So opting out of the rat race or hiring a nanny is not a readily available option (although becoming one may be).

For the vast majority of working women — the women who care for our aged parents, who serve us our lattes and microbrewery beer, who make sure that our paycheques are deposited into the correct account — for these women, maternity leave is inadequate or non-existent, and that much-promised daycare spot has yet to materialize. In a final indignity, according to Statistics Canada, the women who do all these jobs are still being paid thirty per cent less than men.

JOYCE FAIRBAIRN

Canada's First Female Government Leader of the Senate

FRUSTRATED BY THE BANALITIES of Question Period, the Prime Minister stormed out of the House of Commons and up the stairs. He was greeted by his legislative assistant, who reportedly said, "Well, aren't we a sweetheart today?" It was a telling moment between Pierre Elliot Trudeau and the newly-hired Joyce Fairbairn. Had he resented her comment, her career in the Prime Minister's office would have been very short. Instead, he saw the truth in her aside and Trudeau and Fairbairn developed a close working relationship for the next fourteen years, culminating in his resignation and her appointment to the Senate, where she continues to work for literacy and Aboriginal rights in Canada.

Joyce Fairbairn was born in 1939 in Lethbridge, Alberta, where her grandfather, the town sheriff, had fought in the Riel Rebellion. Her father, Judge Lynden Eldon Fairbairn, died young. So the greatest influence in her life was her mother, Mary Elizabeth Young, though Joyce soon ended her mother's penchant for dressing her in pastels. Instead, Joyce opted for red, a fitting symbol of her independence, rebellious heritage and Liberal affiliation.

Following high school, she studied English at the University of Alberta, where she met Jim Coutts, who would become Pierre Trudeau's principal secretary. During the summers, Fairbairn worked for the *Lethbridge Herald*, and following her B.A., she went to Ottawa to study at Carleton, then the only university in Canada to offer a journalism degree. In 1961, she became a reporter for the *Ottawa Journal* and a year later, parliamentary press gallery reporter for *United Press International*, one of the first women to work in the field. It was the start of a life-long love affair with politics. In 1964, she moved to *FP Publications,* where her reports were carried across the West, in the *Winnipeg Free Press, Calgary Herald, Vancouver Sun* and *Victoria Times*, among others.

Her first contact with Trudeau was when he was Minister of Justice. Both liked boiled eggs for breakfast and a cautious friendship developed as they cracked eggs together in the parliamentary cafeteria. In 1970, then Prime Minister Trudeau asked Fairbairn to leave journalism and to come to work for him. It was an offer that promised new horizons. Election campaigns in 1962, 1963, 1965 and 1968 had meant long hours and short holidays. Though Fairbairn had found time in 1967 to marry Michael Gillan, she was ready for a change.

Her primary job was to ensure that the Prime Minister was thoroughly briefed on the day's issues, including preparing him for Question Period. Trudeau was supplied with a black book with a summary of the issues, answers to possible questions and hints as to how to stay out of political hot water. Her work also took her across the country, which kept her in touch with the issues on the ground inside and outside the party. During the campaigns of 1972, 1974, 1979 and 1980, she was an integral part of Trudeau's campaign team. She assisted John Turner in the 1984 and '88 campaigns, and worked for Jean Chrétien in 1993.

Her Senate appointment was a surprise to Albertans, for most believed that her home base was now Ottawa. To assure them that she could ably represent them in the upper chamber, she began a travel schedule equalling that of any elected MP, returning to Alberta most weekends. She also dedicated herself to the cause of literacy. Dropping in on learning centres, speaking to business groups, addressing educators, volunteer groups and the Senate, she worked to effect change.

In the Senate, she opposed the Goods and Services Tax, which she believed was a tax on reading, and the Abortion Bill of 1993, but she had another agenda — to encourage female candidates to run federally, in winning constituencies. As campaign co-chair for the Chrétien Liberals, she was at least partly responsible for the fact that there were thirty-seven women among the 177 Liberals elected in 1993. When Prime Minister Chrétien announced his cabinet two weeks later, Joyce Fairbairn became the first female Senate Government Leader. With Anne McLellan named as Minister of Energy in the same cabinet, Alberta became the first province to be represented by only women in cabinet.

These are clearly not issues of interest to business in a society where women are encouraged to inject their faces with poison in order to appear younger and have toes surgically removed so they can wear the latest anatomically incorrect shoe; where internet pornography makes billions by objectifying women and game shows that allow psychiatrists and plastic surgeons to engage in human experimentation pass for entertainment. And they will not be of concern to the neo-conservative right, many of whom believe that all the world's a market, and all the men and women, mere consumers.

External lobbying is no longer enough, as NAC has found to its sorrow. Equality will only be achieved when women are fully represented on the public stage.

Governance is a ongoing dialogue, where competing priorities and ideas are in constant flux. Without strong advocates at every level of government, issues important to women fail to gain attention and support, because the arguments are less likely to be made with the understanding, passion and commitment required to take them from proposal to policy.

> Democracy is based on the notion of the rule of the people, and there are many ways in which women experience the world differently from men. And I don't think their reality will be fully articulated unless they are part of the public policymaking process. This isn't to say that men can't support the concerns of women, or that women can't support the concerns of men. But I think, certainly, to create gender literacy, to create a political system in which the reality of life as women live it is one of the premises on which public policy is made, you need the involvement of women.
>
> Rt. Hon. Kim Campbell
> Prime Minister of Canada, 1993

♦♦ ❖ ♦♦

First-wave feminists are recognized as great Canadians today, and justly so. But their fight was always more about improving the status quo than seeking true equality. The struggle for equality initially defined second-wave feminism, and great progress was made before the movement became lost in the ideological minefields of the late twentieth century.

It's time for a third wave of feminists — women who are willing to step through the doors that have been opened by the women we've met in this book. The uncertain world of the twenty-first century desperately needs their enthusiasm,

BEVERLEY MCLACHLIN
First Female Chief Justice of the Supreme Court of Canada

"We all possess a certain image of a judge. He is old, male and wears pinstriped trousers. He decides only what is necessary, says only what is necessary and on no account ever talks to the press." So said The Right Honourable Beverley McLachlin, PC, on May 5, 2004, when speaking on The Role of Judges in Modern Society. Beverley McLachlin is the antithesis of all this. She is sparkling, vibrant, extremely attractive and totally female. And she will change, for all time, the image of what a Canadian judge should be.

With her appointment on January 7, 2000, as Chief Justice of Canada's Supreme Court, one could now say that all of the top positions in all branches of government – legislative, executive and judicial – have, at one time, been occupied by a woman. Yet her appointment by Prime Minister Jean Chrétien was not the first example of her leading the way. In 1981, she was the first woman to be appointed to be appointed to the Supreme Court of British Columbia and in 1985 she became the first woman to be appointed to the Court of Appeal in her province. Three years later, she was the first female Chief Justice of the B.C. Supreme Court and in 1989, she was appointed to the Supreme Court of Canada, only the third woman in Canadian history to be so honoured.

Beverley McLachlin was born on September 7, 1943 in Pincher Creek, Alberta, a small town in the southwestern corner of the province. Like most kids growing up on a ranch, she did chores, helped feed the hired hands and looked after her four younger brothers. But above all, she read books.

After finishing high school, she moved on to Edmonton and to the University of Alberta, where she earned a B.A., an M.A. in philosophy and a law degree, all by the time she was twenty-five. Called to the bar in 1969, she practised in Edmonton for two years before moving to British Columbia. She practised for a year in Fort St. John and another three in Vancouver before joining the law faculty at the University of British Columbia in 1974. She also married Rory McLachlin, whose death from cancer in 1988 left her as sole parent of their son, Angus. She readily admits that he had put her career ahead of his and she was devastated by his death, which occurred just three days after her appointment as Chief Justice in B.C. She later married Frank McArdle, with whom she lives in Ottawa.

As Chief Justice of Canada, she not only serves as both the chair and a member of the Supreme Court, but is now one of four female members on a nine-member court. She is also the administrative head of the court. Among her responsibilities are deciding on the panels of judges which hear all cases before the court, heading a public service staff of 150 and chairing the Canadian Judicial Council, which is made up of the chief and associates of all federally appointed courts. In addition, she is the chair of the advisory council of the Order of Canada and, if all this were not enough, she replaces the Governor General, should she become incapacitated or when she is out of the country. Combined with her talents on the piano, in the garden and the kitchen, and as a seamstress, she certainly has the attributes of a superwoman.

She has been an active writer of judgements while on the bench and many believe that she will bring greater stability to the court in ensuring that decisions will be more unanimous. To date, it appears that this is the case, but only time will tell. She is only sixty-one; given that the court's compulsory retirement age is seventy-five, she could continue to put her stamp on the interpretation of our laws and particularly on the Charter of Rights and Freedoms for another fourteen years.

their energy and their insight. There's no doubt the task is a daunting one, but then, that's true of anything worth doing.

The critical mass of education and talent is in place, the groundwork has been laid and the goal is in plain sight. All that's needed now, is the will.

> You just have to keep reminding women that a tremendous battle has been fought, and to respect that battle and to protect it. We lose what we don't respect and we lose what we don't pay attention to. I think the message has to be that, if you don't get in there, it can easily go backwards … [so] it's essential for women to become involved, to become part of the law-making and decision-making of a country … If you want to make a difference, I think you absolutely have to do this.
>
> Susan Thompson
> Mayor of Winnipeg (1993–99)

Scene: 2016

Thursday, January 28th, 2016

Rt. Hon. Deborah Halingford-Cho
Prime Minister of Canada
speaking in Winnipeg
on the occasion of the 100th anniversary
of women's suffrage in Canada.
(Manitoba, January 28th, 1916).

Your Honour, Mr. Speaker, Premier, Honourable Members, ladies and gentlemen. First, let me thank the Government of Manitoba for its gracious invitation. I understand that I am the first Prime Minister to have the opportunity to address this assembly, and to be here on such an occasion is truly an honour.

Exactly one hundred years ago, perhaps two hundred metres from where I now stand, one of our great reformers rose in this Legislature to change the course of Canadian history. Premier T.C. Norris declared that, henceforth, the women of Manitoba would have the same right to vote and stand for office as was enjoyed by the men of this great province.

With that announcement began the series of events that ultimately led to my being here with you today. It wasn't an easy road. As remarkable as it may seem now, a quarter-century after Manitoba led the way, there were still Canadian women who couldn't vote in a provincial election. And nearly a half-century later, in 1960, we still barred some women from standing for public office.

By the 1990s, a woman had held virtually every major portfolio at all three levels of government, including, briefly, Prime Minister of Canada. There were women in board rooms and executive suites. But, inevitably, these cases were still the exception. Female representation in Parliament, Legislative Assemblies and City Councils remained far below percentage of population. The same was true in business. Canadians eventually realized that mainstream feminists had been right all along — our political system, the way business was run, our society itself — all of it was designed for a world that had long since disappeared.

The single-income nuclear family had already ceased to be the norm in this country by the 1970s, but we continued to behave as though nostalgia were fact. It was perplexing. By the turn of the present century, we'd extended what are now perceived as basic human rights to gays and lesbians, visible minorities, people with disabilities, prisoners, even those addicted to drugs.

But suggest that families might need society's help in raising their children, or businesses should recognize that their employees' familial obligations are just as important as their contractual ones, and suddenly, there was a marked change in tone. 'Well, we certainly want to do everything possible, but when you look at the cost... and really, aren't children better off with a mother who's there for them?' Honestly, you knew they were looking at a research scientist or a financial analyst or an engineer, but you couldn't help thinking that what they were seeing was a frilly blouse, an apron and a steaming tray of cookies.

Drawing attention to those inequities and working to change them has been a major goal of my government, and I'm proud to say we've had some real successes. But, I'll be the first to admit that we can't take all the credit.

There is no doubt that, in the effort to build a society where there's true equality between men and women, the corporate sector has been an enthusiastic partner over the last decade. Their reasons are perhaps more pragmatic and bottom-line oriented than ours, but, isn't it interesting how often doing what's right converges with enlightened self-interest?

There comes a time when a solution that's always been considered too controversial or expensive or dangerous becomes the preferred choice because the parameters or magnitude of the problem have changed so radically. Who could have predicted at the turn of the century that Western countries would be invited to recolonize parts of sub-Saharan Africa and the South Pacific?

In North America, the same sort of shift in thinking has finally occurred with regard to the family. Traditionally, family responsibilities were regarded as an impediment to commerce by both public and private employers. This attitude only intensified when married women began entering the workforce in large numbers.

The problem, of course, was that the corporate structure that emerged in the '70s — some have said re-emerged, because of its startling similarities to the working world before the Second World War — this structure functioned best when workers were regarded as skill sets, rather than people. Efficiency was what was wanted, and manipulating job descriptions was so much more efficient than having to deal with the messy realities of real human beings.

So, by the turn of the century, a majority of workers — even those in white-collar or high-tech positions — were regarded as little more than expenses. If a worker had family responsibilities, the expenses went up — more days off, less overtime, more benefits, lower productivity.

This scenario meant that women with children, single or married, were at a severe disadvantage in the workplace, a disadvantage only made worse by another reality of the late twentieth century. Individualism, mobility and urbanization had broken down the old community support structures — extended families, neighbourhoods, marriage itself — on which working women often depended.

This lack of social support was as effective a glass ceiling as any old boy's network. After all, who could complain if the good old, unadulterated competition that defined liberal democracy and capitalism tended to keep women out of positions of power in government, business and the professions? Our system was the greatest generator of wealth and freedom in the history of the world. It had defeated all comers. It was the culmination of economic and political development. It was Right.

Except ...

By 2005, OECD countries were beginning to recognize that we were facing an imminent labour shortage. Birthrates were continuing to fall, and with no end in sight to what was then called the "War on Terror", immigration was increasingly restricted. That situation, of course, only got worse after the nerve gas attacks on the Washington and Paris subways in 2007.

Aided by free trade agreements, the corporate response to skilled labour shortages and rising costs during the '90s had been to offshore manufacturing and, increasingly, the service sector, to low wage countries — a practice that had the happy side effect of pleasing both shareholders and consumers. That response became less viable when the radical Jihadis proved you don't need weapons of mass destruction when you have a seemingly endless supply of suicide truck bombers.

At the same time, we baby boomers kept retiring, continually removing vital skills and experience from the workforce at a time when both were needed more than ever. In short, we had to find more qualified workers, and soon.

Of course, the workers were right there all along, just as they've always been — competent, educated women who weren't working, or were underemployed because they wanted the best for their children. Partner quality lawyers who couldn't generate the billing hours without neglecting their families. Academics passed over for tenure because they chose to have children during their assessment years. Women in administration, women on the factory floor, all constrained by the same problem — a system that refused to take children and family seriously.

Canadians decided to put their trust in my party in part because we promised to remedy this situation once and for all. Frankly, given the economic crisis we faced, we had little choice. We needed those minds, those abilities. Business had come to the same conclusion, and between us, we've accomplished some amazing things.

To take just one example, when I became Prime Minister, to imagine that I would be able stand before an audience such as this one just six years later and say that there is now affordable, flexible, high-quality childcare available for virtually any Canadian parent who needs it, would have seemed the height of hubris. And yet, here I am.

Availability is not the only challenge. As important as it was to give every Canadian the opportunity to be both parent and fully participating citizen, any viable civilization is ultimately about the future. We've all heard the old greeting card saw, every child is precious. As a society, we are finally coming to realize just how important those four words are to the survival of our nation.

The first three years of a child's life are critical. During this time, the brain is literally rewiring itself as genetic heritage interacts with environment. If that environment is made safe and stimulating by caring adults, then children gain the trust needed to explore, to interact with other children, and to develop to their full potential.

This is the time that doctors and teachers, entrepreneurs and Prime Ministers can be lost to us forever. It's a loss we can no longer afford. So, with our partners, we are committed to seeing that every Canadian child has the chance to succeed.

Using arguments that Premier Norris would have recognized, critics have claimed that this is radical feminism triumphant. It is not. It is, and has been from the beginning, about serving the real and vital interests of this country. And it's working. To come back to my first example, in this Parliament, forty-two per cent of MPs are women, a figure double that at the turn of the century. The same sort of increase is occurring at every level of government.

As our economic expansion continues, more and more women are moving out of the so-called Pink Ghetto into the positions for which their education and abilities so clearly qualify them. The result? Productivity, job satisfaction, earnings — all rising.

I think we've accomplished still more. The disastrous history of the past century is largely a story of elites — political or intellectual — trying to force people to conform to some ideal political construct — elites who said, given these absolute truths, society must be thus — adapt or die.

Whatever form this ideal took, whoever the Prophet — Hitler or Stalin, Adam Smith or Karl Marx, Mohammed or Jesus Christ — forcing people to conform was, in the end, fundamentalism, no different than the sort we've so recently defeated.

Blind defence of traditional roles and, in particular, the elevation of woman as Wife and Mother to quasi-sacred status, fell into this same category. A woman is not a role. A man is not a role. What we have to do; what we are doing, finally, is building a society that reflects our very real needs as human beings, while letting go of those things that no longer serve us. Is the task difficult, exhausting, frustrating? Of course. Is it inspiring, fulfilling, exhilarating? Every. Single. Day.

Much of the credit for the speed of this transformation must go to Canadian men, whose attitudes have undergone such a radical shift over the past two decades. But, there is no doubt in my mind that we could never have arrived at this moment without the women whose efforts culminated here, 100 years ago today.

As you might imagine, the visitor's gallery was packed that day. History was being made, and people wanted to be able to tell their children, "I was there." Among the throng that afternoon, was a woman named Amelia Hardesty Crawford, a suffragist from Ontario. Amelia Crawford was what they used to call a force of nature, a powerful speaker who seemed to fill a room simply by entering it. She was a friend of Nellie McClung, corresponded regularly with Emily Murphy and, I'm proud to say, my great-grandmother.

My mother tells me that Amelia's favourite question, right to the end of her life, was "Why? Why does such and such have to be so?" And, heaven help you if you answered with a cliché. To her mind, if a subject was worthy of serious attention, then sloppiness, or "good enough" simply wasn't acceptable. I've thought of Amelia often over the past six years — her intelligence, her directness and her unswerving devotion to a cause she knew to be right.

My friends, as we struggle together to build a truly equal society, these are the qualities that have been unfailingly demonstrated by the government and people of this great province. Given the nature of the event we celebrate here today, your support comes as no surprise. Being Manitobans, you're doing what you've always done — leading the country. As your Prime Minister, as a woman, as a Canadian, I thank you.

GENERAL BIBLIOGRAPHY

Allen, Frederick Lewis. *Only Yesterday: An Informal History of the 1920s.* Harper Collins, 1931.

Artibise, Alan. *Winnipeg: A Social History of Urban Growth, 1874–1914.* McGill-Queen's University Press, 1975.

Bacchi, Carol Lee. *Liberation Deferred? The Ideas of English Canadian Suffragists, 1877–1918.* University of Toronto Press. 1983.

Barber, Benjamin R. *Jihad vs. McWorld: How Globalism and Tribalism are Shaping the World.* Random House, 1996.

Bell, Daniel. *The Cultural Contradictions of Capitalism.* BasicBooks. 1976.

Bercuson, David J. and Cooper, Barry. *Derailed: The Betrayal of the National Dream.* Key Porter Books, 1994.

Berton, Pierre. *The Great Depression 1929–1939.* McClelland & Stewart, 1990.

Birkerts, Sven. *The Gutenberg Elegies: The Fate of Reading in an Electronic Age.* Ballantine Books, 1994.

Blaker, Kimberly, ed. *The Fundamentals of Extremism: The Christian Right in America.* New Boston Books, 2003.

Bobbitt, Philip. *Shield of Achilles: War, Peace and the Course of History.* Knopf, 2002.

Boorstin, Daniel J. *The Image: A Guide to Pseudo-events in America.* Vintage Books, 1992.

Brendon, Piers. *The Dark Valley: A Panorama of the 1930s.* Ramdom House (Vintage), 2000.

Broadfoot, Barry. *Six War Years 1939–1945: Memories of Canadians at Home and Abroad.* Doubleday Canada Ltd., 1974.

Broadfoot, Barry. *Ten Lost Years, 1929–1939.* Doubleday Canada Ltd, 1973.

Brown, Robert Craig and Cook, Ramsay. *Canada 1896-1921: A Nation Transformed.* McClelland and Stewart, 1974.

Bumstead, J. M., *A History of the Canadian Peoples.* Oxford University Press, 1998.

Bumstead, J. M., ed. *Interpreting Canada's Past. Volume Two: Post Confederation.* Oxford University Press, 1993.

Canadian Panel on Violence Against Women. *Changing the Landscape: Ending Violence—Achieving Equality.* Minister of Supply and Services, 1993.

Crawley, Tilly ed. *Canadian Women: A History.* Harcourt, Brace, Jovanovich Canada, Inc., 1988.

Campbell, Kim. *Time and Chance: The Political Memoirs of Canada's First Woman Prime Minister.* Doubleday Canada, 1996.

Canada in the 50s: Canada's Golden Decade. Penguin Books Canada Ltd. (Viking), 1999.

Creighton, Donald. *The Forked Road: Canada 1939–1957.* McClelland and Stewart, 1976.

Davey, Frank. *Reading "Kim" Right.* Talon Books, 1993.

Ehrenreich, Barbara, *Fear of Falling: The Inner Life of the Middle Class.* Random House of Canada, Ltd., 1989.

Ehrenreich, Barbara and English, Deirdre. *Complaints and Disorders: The Sexual Politics of Sickness.* The Feminist Press, 1973.

Eksteins, Modris. *Rites of Spring: The Great War and the Birth of the Modern Age.* Lester & Orpen Denys, 1989.

Ferguson, Niall. *The Pity of War.* Basic Books, 1999.

Fekete, John, *Moral Panic: Biopolitics Rising.* Robert Davies Publishing, 1994.

Flanagan, Caitlin. How Serfdom Saved the Woman's Movement. *The Atlantic Monthly,* March, 2004.

Flanagan, Tom. *Waiting for the Wave*. Stoddart Books, 1995.

Firestone, Shulamith. *The Dialectic of Sex: The Case for Feminist Revolution*. William Morrow and Company, 1970.

Foot. David, K. *Boom, Bust & Echo 2000*. Macfarlane, Walter and Ross, 1996, 1998.

Forty Medical Specialists. *Pictorial Medical Guide*. American Life Inc., 1953.

Fraser, Sylvia, ed. *A Woman's Place: Seventy Years in the Lives of Canadian Women*. Key Porter Books, 1997.

Frederick, Christine. *Selling Mrs. Consumer*. The Business Bourse, New York, 1929.

Friedan, Betty. *The Feminine Mystique*. W. W. Norton & Co., 1963.

Fukuyama, Francis. *The End of History and the Last Man*. MacMillan, 1992.

Fukayama, Francis. *The Great Disruption: Human Nature and the Reconstitution of Social Order*. Simon & Schuster, Inc., 1999.

Fussell, Paul. *The Great War and Modern Memory*. Oxford University Press, 1975.

Galbraith, J. K. *The Affluent Society*. Houghton, Mifflin Co., 1958.

Galbraith, John Kenneth. *The Contented Majority*. Houghton Mifflin Company, 1992.

Granatstein, Jack. *Canada 1957–1967: The Years of Uncertainty and Innovation*. McClelland and Stewart, 1986.

Gwyn, Richard. *Nationalism Without Walls: The Unbearable Lightness of Being Canadian*. McClelland and Stewart, 1996.

Harding, Sandra. *The Science Question in Feminism*. Cornell University Press, 1986.

Heath, Joseph. *The Efficient Society*. Viking, 2001.

Hobsbawm, Eric. *The Age of Empire: 1875–1914*. Random House (Vintage), 1989.

Hobsbawm, Eric. *Age of Extremes*. Little, Brown & Co. (Abacus), 1994.

Hoff Summers, Christina. *Who Stole Feminism: How Women Have Betrayed Women*. Simon & Schuster. 1994.

Homer-Dixon, Thomas. *The Ingenuity Gap*. Alfred A. Knopf Canada, 2000.

Kaus, Mickey. *The End of Equality*. Basic Books, 1992.

Kealey, Linda, ed. *Not An Unreasonable Claim: Women and Reform in Canada, 1880s–1920s*. University of Toronto Press, 1979.

Kennedy, Paul. *The Rise and Fall of the Great Powers*. Random House, 1987.

Lasch, Christopher. *The Revolt of the Elites*. W. W. Norton & Company, Inc., 1995.

Lasch, Christopher. *The Culture of Narcissism*. W. W. Norton & Company, Inc., 1979.

Lewis, Michael. *The Money Culture*. W. W. Norton & Company, Inc. 1991.

Light, Beth and Roach Pierson, Ruth ed. *No Easy Road: Women in Canada, 1920s to 1960s*. New Hogtown Press, 1990.

Matthews, Glenna. *Just A Housewife*. Oxford University Press, 1987.

May, Elaine Tyler. *Homeward Bound: American Families in the Cold War Era*. Basic Books Inc., 1988.

Megyervy, Kathy, ed. *Women in Canadian Politics*. Dundurn Press, The Royal Commission on Electoral Reform and Party Financing, 1991.

Morton, Desmond and Granatstein, Jack L. *Marching to Armageddon: Canadians and the Great War, 1914–1919*. Lester & Orpen Dennys, 1989.

National Council of Women of Canada. *Women of Canada: Their Life and Work.* Ministry of Agriculture, 1900.

Owram, Doug. *Born At the Right Time: A History of the Baby Boom Generation.* University of Toronto Press, 1996.

Pankhurst, Emmeline. *My Own Story.* Hearst's International Library Company, 1914.

Pearson, Allison. *I Don't Know How She Does It.* Anchor Books, 2003.

Pevere, Geoff and Dymond, Greig. *Mondo Canuck: A Canadian Pop Culture Odyssey.* Prentice Hall Canada, Inc., 1996.

Postman, Neil. *Building a Bridge to the Eighteenth Century.* Alfred A. Knopf, Inc., 1999.

Public Works and Government Services Canada. *A History of the Vote in Canada,* 1997.

Putnam, Robert D. *Bowling Alone: The Collapse and Revival of American Community.* Simon and Schuster, 2000.

Ralston Saul, John. *Reflections of a Siamese Twin.* Penguin Books, 1997.

Ralston Saul, John. *On Equilibrium.* Viking, 2001

Ralston Saul, John. "The Collapse of Globalism and the Rebirth of Nationalism". *Harper's,* March, 2004.

Reid, Angus. *Shakedown: How the New Economy is Changing Our Lives.* Doubleday Canada, 1996.

Rieff, Philip. *The Triumph of the Therapeutic.* University of Chicago Press, 1966, 1987.

Roszak, Theodore. *The Making of a Counter Culture.* University of California Press, 1968, 1969.

Royal Commission on the Status of Women. *Report of the Royal Commission on the Status of Women.* Information Canada, 1970.

Sayers, Dorothy L. *A Matter of Eternity.* William B. Eerdmans Publishing Co., 1973.

Sharpe, Sydney and Braid, Don. *Storming Babylon: Preston Manning and the Rise of the Reform Party.* Key Porter Books, 1992.

Sharpe, Sydney. *The Gilded Ghetto: Women and Political Power in Canada.* HarperCollins, 1994.

Shirer, William L. *The Rise and Fall of the Third Reich.* Simon and Shuster, 1960.

Strasser, Susan. *Never Done.* Random House (Pantheon), 1982.

Strong-Boag, Veronica. *The New Day Recalled.* Copp Clark Pittman, Ltd., 1988.

Taylor, Graham D. and Baskerville, Peter. A. *A Concise History of Business in Canada.* Oxford University Press, 1994.

Tuchman, Barbara. *The Proud Tower.* The MacMillan Company, 1962.

Underhill, Paco. *Why We Buy: The Science of Shopping.* Simon and Schuster, 1999.

Watson, Peter. *A Terrible Beauty: The People and Ideas that Shaped the Modern Mind.* Phoenix Press, 2000.

Whyte, William H. *The Organization Man.* Doubleday, 1954.

Wolfe, Tom. *The Purple Decades: A Reader.* Farrar, Strauss and Giroux, Inc., 1976.

Vance, Jonathan F. *Death So Noble. Memory Meaning and the First World War.* UBC Press, 1997.

Wolff, Edward N. *Top Heavy: A Study of the Increasing Inequality of Wealth in America.* The Twentieth Century Fund, Inc., 1995.

SELECTED BIBLIOGRAPHY

Louise McKinney

Bannerman, Jean. *Leading Ladies Canada.* Mika Publishing Co., 1977.

MacEwan, Grant … *And Mighty Women Too: Stories of Notable Western Women.* Western Producer Prairie Books, 1975.

Qualyle Innis, Mary. *The Clear Spirit.* University of Toronto Press. 1966.

The Married Woman's Home Protection Act (Alberta): April 1915.

Nellie McClung

Hallet, Mary and Marilyn Davis, *Firing the Heather: The Life and Times of Nellie McClung,* Fifth House, 1994.

Savage, Candace. *Our Nell.* Western Producer Prairie Books, 1979.

Emily F. Murphy, "What Janey Thinks of Nellie." *Maclean's Magazine,* September 1921, pp. 15; 34-35.

May L. Armitage, "Mrs. Nellie McClung." *Maclean's Magazine,* July 1915, pp. 37-38.

Nellie McClung. "What Will They Do With It." *Maclean's Magazine.* July 1916, pp. 36-38.

Nellie McClung, "All We Like Sheep". *Maclean's Magazine,* March 20, 1920, pp. 14-16; 63-64.

Nellie McClung, "A Woman on the Warpath." *Maclean's Magazine,* January 1920.

Nellie McClung, "I'll Never Tell My Age Again!" *Maclean's Magazine,* March 15, 1926.

Nellie McClung, "Can a Woman Raise a Family and Have a Career?" *Maclean's Magazine,* February 15, 1928.

Agnes Macphail

Crowell, Terry. *Agnes Macphail and the Politics of Equality.* James Lorimer & Co. 1990.

"Canada's First Woman M.P. is Honoured." *The Canadian Unionist,* March 1955.

Agnes Macphail, "If I Were Prime Minister." *Chatelaine,* January 1933, pp. 13, 46.

Agnes Macphail, "A Report on Penal Reform." *The Canadian Forum,* December 1946, pp. 206-208.

Genevieve Lipsett-Skinner, "The Little Farmer's Daughter Who Became World Famous." *The Canadian Magazine,* September 1926, pp. 8-9.

Gertrude E.S. Pringle, "The only M.P. who can bake, churn, cook, milk, sew, hitch, teach, talk…" *Maclean's Magazine,* January 15, 1922.

"What Politics Needs Most–More Laughter." *Maclean's Magazine,* March 28, 1959.

Emily Murphy

Qualyle Innis, Mary. *The Clear Spirit.* University of Toronto Press, 1966

Kome, Penny. *Women of Influence.* Doubleday Canada Ltd., 1985

MacEwan, Grant … *And Mighty Women Too: Stories of Notable Western Women.* Western Producer Prairie Books, 1975.

Thérèse Forget Casgrain

Ann Charney, "Thérèse Casgrain: enfant terrible at 78. " *Maclean's Magazine,* September 1974, pp. 37; 52-55.

Ed Bantey, "The Practical Idealist." *Saturday Night,* Vol. 66, No. 30, 1951.

"Quebec CAC President Appointed a Senator" *Canadian Consumer,* January/February 1971.

Senate Debates: Tribute to the late Honourable Thérèse F. Casgrain, November 3, 1981.

Thérèse F. Casgrain, "Can Women Unite for Peace?" *Independent Woman,* November 1942.

Susan Mann Trofimenkoff, "Therese Casgrain and the CCF in Quebec." *Canadian Historical Review,* LXVI, 2, 1985.

Wayling, Thomas. "Therese Casgrain." *Saturday Night,* May 6, 1933.

Cairine Wilson

Franca Iacovetta, "The Political Career of Senator Cairine Wilson, 1921–1962." *Atlantis,* Vol. 11, No.1, Fall 1985, pp. 108–121.

Valerie Knowles, "Senator Cairine Wilson: First Lady of the Red Chamber." *The Beaver,* Vol. 72, No. 5, October/November 1992, pp. 16–19.

Charlotte Whitton

Fellman, Anita. *Rethinking Canada: The Promise of Women's History.* Copp Clark Pitman Ltd., 1986.

Rooke, P.T. and R.L. Schnell, "An Idiot's Flowerbed: A Study of Charlotte Whitton's Feminist Thought, 1941–50", in *Rethinking,* First Edition, pp. 208-225

Rooke, P.T. and R.L. Schnell, *No Bleeding Heart: Charlotte Whitton, A Feminist on the Right.* UBC Press, 1987.

James Struthers, "Charlotte's Web", *Horizon Canada,* Vol. 7, No. 7, pp. 1844–1848.

Lawrence Elliot and James Finan, "The Mayor is no Angel." *The Reader's Digest,* July 1963.

P.T. Rooke and R.L. Schnell, "Chastity and Power: Charlotte Whitton and the Ascetic Ideal." *American Review of Canadian Studies.* XV, 4, 1985, pp. 389-403.

"Quebec Liberals Win Sweeping Victory…" *Globe and Mail,* November 15, 1962, p. 8.

"The Door of My Lips" *Newsweek,* November 16, 1961.

"The Incomparable Charlotte Whitton Can't be Beaten", *Canada Month,* Vol. 3, No. 6, June 1963, pp. 15–17.

"The Unsinkable Charlotte Whitton", *Maclean's Magazine,* April 22, 1961.

Ellen Fairclough

Fairclough, Ellen Louks. *Saturday's Child: Memoirs of Canada's First Female Cabinet Minister.* University of Toronto Press, 1995.

"A Lady's Day in the Commonwealth." *Newsweek,* July 1, 1957.

Austin F. Cross, "Parliamentary Personalities." *Canadian Business,* September 1950.

"Boston Conference on Distribution Honors Minister of Citizenship and Immigration." *Canadian Business,* November 1958.

"Canadian Women as Citizens", an address by the Honourable Ellen L. Fairclough, Thursday December 12, 1957.

Doyle Klya, "Ellen Fairclough is always in a hurry." *Weekend Magazine,* Vol. 8, No. 9, 1958.

Edwin Copps, "Ottawa: No One-Man Government." *Saturday Night,* February 14, 1959.

Edwin Copps, "The Tories Need a Tonic." *Saturday Night,* August 5, 1959.

Ellen Fairclough, "1958 Immigration Into Canada Returns to More Normal Level." *The Monetary Times Annual,* 1959.

Ellen Fairclough, "Indian Affairs in 1959." *The Monetary Times Annual,* 1960.

Ellen Fairclough, "Indian Affairs in 1960." *The Monetary Times Annual,* 1961.

Eva-Lis Wuorio, "Ellen goes to Ottawa." *Maclean's Magazine,* August 1, 1950.

Frank Flaherty, "Diefenbaker government faces big problems and commitments." *Canadian Business,* October 1957.

Mary Lowrey Ross, "Ellen Fairclough: First Woman in the Cabinet." *Saturday Night,* August 1957.

"Make Way, Men." *Saturday Night,* May 30, 1950.

"New Zonta Treasurer Elected." *The Canadian Chartered Accountant,* November 1972.

Peter C. Newman, "Ellen Fairclough." *Maclean's Magazine,* August 30, 1958.

Peter C. Newman, "Women are Equal-Especially Ellen Fairclough." *Maclean's Magazine,* August 30, 1958.

"Women as Chartered Accountants." *The Canadian Chartered Accountant,* June 1966.

Bertha Wilson

"A Judge Beyond Judging." *Western Report,* April 16, 1990.

"A Tribute to Bertha Wilson." *Canadian Labour Law Journal,*Vol. 1, No. 1 & 2, Spring/Summer 1992.

Bertha Wilson, "Will Women Judges Really Make a Difference?" *Law Society Gazette,* 1990.

Bertha Wilson, "Constitutional Advocacy." *Ottawa Law Review/Revue de droit d'Ottawa,* Vol. 24, No.1, 1992.

Bertha Wilson, "Family Violence." *RFD/CJWL,* Vol. 5, 1992.

Bertha Wilson, "The Scottish Enlightenment." *The Law Society Gazette,* pp. 185-212.

Bertha Wilson, "Women, The Family, And the Constitutional Protection of Privacy." *Queen's Law Journal.*

David Beatty, "A matter of finding the right Justice." *Globe and Mail,* Monday November 26, 1990.

David Vienneau, "Speaking her Mind" *Toronto Star,* September 13, 1990.

"Justice and Gender." *Western Report,* February 26, 1990.

Kirk Makin, "Top court's first woman judge retires to seek more normal life" *Globe and Mail,* November 21, 1990.

Rudy Platiel, "Years in manse and in courtroom aid commissioner" *Globe and Mail,* December 1992.

Sandra Gwyn, "Sense and Sensibility." *Saturday Night,* July 1985, pp. 13–19.

"Wilson, Hon. Bertha." *Guide parlementaire canadien,*1986.

"Wilson, Hon. Bertha." *Canadian Who's Who,* 1994.

Papers presented at a symposium to honour the contribution of Madame Justice Bertha Wilson, Dalhousie Law School, October 5, 1991. Delivered by Brian Dickson.

Remarks given at the call to the Bar Ceremony and on being awarded the degree of Doctor of Laws.

Retirement Ceremony of the Honourable Bertha Wilson, Supreme Court of Canada.

Introduction from the chair: "Touchstone for Change: Equality, Diversity, and Accountability."

Rosemary Brown

Brown, Rosemary. *Being Brown: A Very Public Life.* Random House, 1989.
"A Canadian Woman Prime Minister?" *Chatelaine,* July 1980.

"Brown, Rosemary" *Canada's Who's Who,* 1994.

Jusy Steed, "Outside Chances." *Canadian Forum,* January 1990.

Lisa Hobbs, "Why is Rosemary Running?" *Chatelaine,* July 1975, p. 30; 73–78.

Sharon Batt, "The Radical Tradition of Rosemary Brown." *Branching Out,* July/August, 1975.

Rosemary Brown, "Running a Feminist Campaign." *Branching Out,* November/December, 1977.

Nellie Cournoyea

Guide parlementaire canadien, 1994, p.1024

Charlotte Gray, "Waiting in the Wings", *Chatelaine,* October 1991

Cooper Langford, "Native woman government leader in N.W.T.", *Winspeaker,* November 22, 1991

"Cournoyea becomes premier of territory." *Whitehorse Star,* March 3, 1994.

"Guarding her territory", *Maclean's Magazine,* August 10, 1992

Hugh Winsor, "Liberals face anger of North over accord", *Globe and Mail,* August 16, 1989

James Hrynyshyn, "Inuit displeased by constitutional plan." *Whitehorse Star,* July 21, 1992.

Kathleen Kenna, "An Amazon of the North: She has critics but no foes", *Toronto Star,* May 7, 1989

Larry Johnsrude, "N.W.T. premier vacates government seat." *The Ottawa Citizen,* September 3, 1995.

Larry Johnsrude, "N.W.T. leader ponders future." *Toronto Star,* September 5, 1995.

Laurie Sarkadi, "Meet Canada's Newest Premier." *Edmonton Journal,* December 14, 1991.

Laurie Sarkadi, "New leader gives herself wage cut to aid cash-strapped government", *Vancouver Sun,* December 11, 1991, A6

Miro Cernetig, "New N.W.T. head a scrapper", *The Globe and Mail,* November 14, 1991

Rick Halliechuk, "N.W.T. leader wants more power over mines", *Montreal Gazette,* March 7, 1995,

Kim Campbell

Davey, Frank. *Reading "Kim Right."* Talonbooks, Vancouver, 1993.

Dobbin, Murray. *The Politics of Kim Campbell: From School Trustee to Prime Minister,* James Lorimer & Co., Toronto, 1993.

Fife, Robert. *Kim Campbell: The Making of a Politician.* Harper Collins, Toronto, 1993.

Allan Chambers, "There's life after politics for Campbell." *Edmonton Journal,* May 4, 1996.

Brenda Bouw, "Kim Campbell lands consul postion in L.A." *Vancouver Sun,* August 9, 1996.

"Campbell, RT. HON. A. Kim." *Guide Parlementaire canadien,* Globe and Mail Publishing. 1994.

"Campbell, The Right Honourable Kim." *Who's Who in Canada.*

"Campbell suited to post." *Regina Leader Post.* August 13, 1996.

Charlotte Gray, "Politicking: Singing in the Rain." *Saturday Night,* October 1991.

"Chretien defends plum L.A. post for Kim Campbell." *Toronto Star*, September 17, 1996.

Cockman, Judith. "Former PM's play premiers." *Toronto Star*, July 9, 1997.

Dalton Camp, "Kim Campbell's catharsis can be painful reading." *Toronto Star*, May 15, 1996.

E. Kaye Fulton and Mary Janigan "The Real Kim Campbell" *Maclean's Magazine*, May 17, 1993.

E. Kaye Fulton and Mary Janigan, "A Separate Identity" *Maclean's Magazine*, Vol. 106, No. 14, April 5, 1993.

Ed Feuer, Ed. "Kim Campbell hardly a 'human sacrifice'" *The Winnipeg Sun*, July 16, 1997.

Edison Stewart, "Campbell posting 'token': Reform MP" *Toronto Star*, August 10, 1996.

"Empowered by People." *Winnipeg Free Press*, March 21, 1993.

Ezra Levant, "Campbell choice puzzling." *Calgary Sun*, August 12, 1996.

"Former PMs play premiers" *Toronto Star*, July 9, 1997.

Heath Macquarrie, "A political tragedy of a bright star." *The Hill Times*, Monday May 20, 1996.

Hunt, Stephen. "Partying with a drag queen and an ex-PM." *Globe and Mail*, August 9, 1997.

Jean Sonmor, "Kim Cambell: Lessons for a teacher" *Toronto Star*, April 21, 1996.

Jean Sonmor, "Kim Campbell: Reborn in L.A." *The Ottawa Sun*, July 19, 1997.

Jeff Sallot and Edward Greenspon, Edward. "Chretien gives Campbell L.A. job." *Globe and Mail*, August 9, 1996.

Jim Bronskill, "Prime Minister names cronies, foe to plum jobs." *Ottawa Citizen*, August 9, 1996.

Joe Woodward, "On the fast-track to PM." *Alberta Report*, Vol. 20, No. 2, December 28, 1992.

Kathleen Kenna, "Former PM shakes up Tinseltown." *Toronto Star*, March 13, 1997.

Lana Payne, "Chretien singing Campbell's tune." *The Evening Telegram*, June 2, 1996.

Lorri Goldstein, "Poor Kim was right…and we kissed her off." *Toronto Star*, February 23, 1997.

"Ms. Prime Minister." *Maclean's Magazine*, Vol. 106, No.25, June 21, 1993.

Murray Dobbin, "The Crowning of Kim" *Canadian Forum*, May 1993, p.10–15.

"Passing Out Political Plums." *Daily Gleaner*, August 29, 1996.

Peter C. Newman, Peter C. "Citizen Kim." *Vancouver Sun*, May 1993.

Richard Gwyn, "Campbell shows she wasn't fit to be PM." *Toronto Star*, April 21, 1996.

Sharon Doyle Driegdger, "Playing Gender Politics" *Maclean's Magazine*, October 4, 1993.

Shawn McCarthy, "Chretien names Campbell to plum Los Angeles job." *Toronto Star*, August 9, 1996.

Timothy Appleby, "Kim goes to Hollywood." *Globe and Mail*, September 28, 1996.

Audrey McLaughlin

McLaughlin, Audrey (with Archbold, Rick), *A Woman's Place: My Life and Politics*, Macfarlane Walter & Ross, Toronto, 1992.

"A fork in the NDP's road." *Globe and Mail*, April 15, 1994.

Alan Toulin, "Politics would be all the poorer without NDP." *Financial Post*, June 26, 1993.

"Audrey McLaughlin: Mastering the Art of the Impossible." *Chatelaine Magazine*, Vol. 63, No.3, March 1990, p.60–62, 111–113.

Audrey McLaughlin in *Who's Who in Canada.*

Audrey McLaughlin, "I work for all Yukoners." *Whitehorse Star,* 1993.

Audrey McLaughlin, "How NAFTA affects the environment." *Whitehorse Star,* January 29, 1993.

Audrey McLaughlin, "Swimming upstream: equality in backlash times." *Whitehorse Star,* March 11, 1994.

Audrey McLaughlin, "Reviewing this week's events in Parliament." *Whitehorse Star,* September 23, 1994.

Audrey McLaughlin, "Canadian programs standards are vanishing." *Whitehorse Star,* January 13, 1995.

Audrey McLaughlin, "35th Parliament faces extremely troubling times", *Whitehorse Star,* February 9, 1996.

Audrey Mclaughlin, "In the end, it's us who make it work", *Whitehorse Star,* March 1, 1996.

Audrey McLaughlin, "What do those women want anyway?", *Whitehorse Star,* March 13, 1996.

Audrey McLaughlin, "The 'right' approach is the wrong approach" *Whitehorse Star,* May 24, 1996.

Audrey McLaughlin, "Rounding up the parliamentary session" *Whitehorse Star,* June 21, 1996.

"Audrey McLaughlin tire sa reverence." *La Presse,* Le 11 janvier, 1997.

"Audrey's adieu marks NDP decline." *Toronto Star,* April 19, 1994.

Audrey McLaughlin's speaking notes: "Women, Politics, Education, and Quality of Life." November 26, 1992, St. John's.

Bud Robertson, "Canada's Jurassic Park is Senate." *Winnipeg Free Press,* June 25, 1993.

Carol Goar, "McLaughlin's 'Decency Problem." *Toronto Star,* February 6, 1993, B4.

Carol Goar, "Non-Conformity costs McLaughlin dear." *Toronto Star,* Saturday September 14, 1991, D5.

Dale Eisler, "Leader among reasons for NDP slide." *Regina Leader-Post,* June 26, 1993.

Dale Eisler, "Axworthy vs. McLaughlin-style NDP." *Regina Leader-Post,* December 6, 1994.

Dalton Camp, "It's hard to remember such a forgettable politician." *Toronto Star,* April 20, 1994, A19.

Daniel Drolet, "Living by her own rules." *Ottawa Citizen,* December 23, 1992.

Daniel Drolet, "Analysts find flaws in NDP blueprint." *Ottawa Citizen,* February 19, 1993.

Dave Traynor, "NDP leader speaks out." *Regina Leader-Post,* September 9, 1994.

Douglas Fisher, "Lauding Audrey", *Ottawa Sun,* April 22, 1994.

Duncan Cameron, "The Way Back for the NDP." *Canadian Forum,* September 1993, p.14–18.

Edison Stewart, "Party bickering leaves unity talks down to the wire", *Toronto Star,* February 28, 1992.

E. Kaye Fulton and Bruce Wallace, "The New Face of the NDP." *Maclean's Magazine,* December 11, 1989.

E. Kaye Fulton, "McLaughlin's Mission." *Maclean's Magazine,* August 13, 1990.

"Embattled McLaughlin says difficult '92 made her tougher." *Toronto Star,* Sunday January 3, 1993.

"Empowered by People." *Winnipeg Free Press,* March 21, 1993.

"Farewell to Audrey McLaughlin" *Montreal Gazette,* April 20, 1994.

"Former NDP leader says goodbye to politics", *Ottawa Citizen,* January 11, 1997

"From teacher to first woman to lead a national political party in Canada" *Winnipeg Free Press,* April 19, 1994.

Geoffrey York, "Federal NDP seeks silver lining." *Globe and Mail,* June 17, 1993

Geoffrey York, "Langdon slapped down." *Globe and Mail,* April 30, 1993.

Geoffrey York, "Anti-woman bias worries NDP leader." *Globe and Mail*, October 18, 1993.

Geoffrey York, "McLaughlin lends dignity to much-heralded defeat." *Globe and Mail,* October 23, 1993.

Geoffrey York, "McLaughlin attacks lucrative MP pensions." *Globe and Mail*, February 25, 1992.

Geoffrey York, "A Voice in the Wilderness." *Globe and Mail,* October 23, 1992.

Gerald Flood, "McLaughlin's embattled chief of staff quits" *Winnipeg Free Press,* December 8, 1992.

"High Anxiety in the NDP." *Toronto Star,* June 6, 1992.

Hugh Winsor, "McLaughlin a puzzle for historians." *Globe and Mail*, April 19, 1994

Ian Austen, "Why McLaughlin missed." *Montreal Gazette,* April 16, 1994.

Ian Austen, "Robinson might be a contender." *Montreal Gazette*, April 16, 1994.

Irshad Manji, "Audrey's Legacy." *Montreal Gazette,* April 25, 1994.

IrwinBlock, "BQ ruining government system: NDP chief." *Montreal Gazette,* March 6, 1994.

James Laxer, "McLaughlin's selfless move allows time for renewal." *Toronto Star,* April 24, 1994.

Jane Taber, "McLaughlin writes off Parliamentary Press Gallery banquet." *Ottawa Citizen.* April 25, 1992.

Janet Wilson, "NDP cancels August convention." *Hill Times,* April 21, 1994

Jim Butler, "God help those who would succeed her." *Whitehorse Star,* January 15, 1997

John Douglas, "Help Wanted for the NDP." *Winnipeg Free Press,* April 19, 1994.

John Lownsbrough, "Sister Audrey." *Saturday Night Magazine,* May 1992.

James Rusk, "McLaughlin attacks Candu deal." *Globe and Mail,* November 21, 1994.

Judy Steed, "Can You Imagine Her as PM?" *Toronto Star,* Sunday February 3, 1991.

Judy Steed, "The Real Audrey." *Toronto Star,* December 6, 1992.

Karan Smith, "McLaughlin gives retiring address, but promises not to fade away." *Whitehorse Star,* April 28, 1997.

Larry Welsh, "McLaughlin is taking a chance with church-basement strategy.", *Telegraph Journal,* May 28, 1993.

"Leaders departure allows NDP renewal." *Times Colonist* (Victoria), April 19, 1994.

Lisa Blackburn, "McLaughlin leadership era concludes." *Whitehorse Star,* April 19, 1994.

Lisa Murray, "NDP leader urges consensus on environmental issues." *The Northern Miner.* September 20, 1993.

"McLaughlin asks labour to rebuild NDP." *Globe and Mail,* August 24, 1994.

"McLaughlin going on vacation to 'rest her soul', ponder future." *Montreal Gazette,* December 15, 1993.

McLaughlin cruise into sunset called off because of bad press." *Vancouver Sun,* December 29, 1994.

"McLaughlin to remain as MP." *Vancouver Sun*, December 30, 1994.

"McLaughlin's popularity unstoppable." *Whitehorse Star,* October 26, 1993.

Mark Kennedy, "You just have to move on." *Ottawa Citizen,* September 19, 1993.

Mary-Jane Egan, "McLaughlin's penthouse interview." *London Free Press,* September 30, 1993.

Michael Smyth, "Socialism not dead, McLaughlin tells party." *Times Colonist* (Victoria), March 28, 1994.

Michel Gratton, "Well, so much for all the good intentions." *Ottawa Sun,* April 20, 1994.

MP going to Democrats' meet" *Whitehorse Star*, August 22, 1996

Neal Hall, "Audrey McLaughlin's campaign from hell." *Vancouver Sun,* October 9, 1993.

"NDP leader slams NAFTA." *Leader Post.* August 17, 1992.

"Neither a legend nor a footnote." *Whitehorse Star.* April 20, 1994.

Paul Gessel, "Federal NDP leader regrets Ontario decision to bring in casino gambling." *Ottawa Citizen,* May 3, 1992.

Peter O'Neil, "McLaughlin never tried to be more than she was–very ordinary." *Vancouver Sun,* April 19, 1994.

Randy Burton, "Abolish Senate, McLaughlin says." *Regina Leader-Post,* September 21, 1993.

Shawn McCarthy, "NDP chief to quit but not till '96." *Toronto Star,* April 19, 1994.

Shawn McCarthy, "NDP leader to weigh future during 4-week trip to Asia." *Toronto Star*, December 19, 1993.

Stewart MacLoad, "Audrey McLaughlin breaks unwritten rule of Commons." *St. John's Evening Telegram*, March 3, 1992.

Stewart MacLoad, "McLaughlin stoically awaits a successor to NDP leadership." *St. John's Evening Telegram*, April 2, 1994.

Stewart MacLoad, "Few politicians envy Audrey McLaughlin." *Guardian*, April 28, 1994.

Susan Delacourt, "Trailblazing politician's legacy crucial to women." *Globe and Mail*, April 15, 1994.

Tim Harper, "Two years later, McLaughlin still won't play Ottawa's game." *Toronto Star*, December 2, 1991, A5.

Tim Harper, "Last Chance for McLaughlin?" *Toronto Star*, August 29, 1992, A19.

Tim Harper, "McLaughlin, plummeting in polls, distances herself from Rae." *Toronto Star*, July 17, 1993.

Tim Harper, "Federal NDP at odds over Rae." *Toronto Star,* August 11, 1993.

Tim Harper, "NDP chief goes on attack over drug-price legislation." *Toronto Star,* September 15, 1993.

Tim Harper, "McLaughlin's next decision: When to quit." *Toronto Star,* October 25, 1993.

"The missed blessing of the federal role." *Whitehorse Star.* August 18, 1993.

"Time for Change: Will A.M. be our next P.M.?" *Herizons.* Spring 1993, pp. 28–32.

"Will it be a race or a coronation?" *Whitehorse Star.* November 20, 1996

Virginia Galt, "McLaughlin stands firm over demotion of Langdon." *Globe and Mail*, May 7, 1993.

Beverley McLachlin

1999 Globe Information Services

Department of Justice website

Julian Beltrame, "Judging Beverley: The Chief Justice is putting her stamp on the Supreme Court." *Maclean's*, May 20, 2002.

Margaret Wente, "The Making of Beverley McLachlin", *Globe and Mail*, November 9, 1999.

Supreme Court of Canada website

INDEX

Pankhurst, Emmeline, 45
Paris World's Fair, 18
Parkinson, Ray, 207–208
Parlby, Irene, 82, 83
Parti Québecois, 214–215, 223
Paul VI, Pope, 186
pay equity, 127, 154, 168, 317
peace organizations, 124
Pearson, Alison, 316–317
Pearson government, 184
Pelletier, Gérard, 214, 217
Penikett, Tony, 248
Pépin, Lucie, 258
Person's Case: background, 77, 78, 81; group of five, 82; in Privy Council, London, 84–85; in Supreme Court, 83–84
Peterson, David, 306
Peterson government, 307
Pettkus v. Becker, 194
Phillips, Carol, 251
Piot, Peter, 299
Pipeline Debate, 167
Pius XI, Pope, 63, 66, 111
political advertising laws, 296–297
political disengagement, 314
political life: for R. Brown, 208; for I. Campagnola, 316; for E. Fairclough, 166; for A. Macphail, 74
Polykoff, Shirley, 201
Ponzi, Charles, 68
postmodernism, 255–257, 258–260
Pratt, A.M., 120
Price Spreads Committee, 99
Prince Edward Island, 315
Princip, Gavrilo, 41
private sector. see business sector; capitalism
progress, idea of: death of, 62; in 1902, 16–17; and WWI, 43, 44, 52; in 1950s, 140, 143
Progressives, 75–76
prohibition: blocked by WWI, 41; federal law, 51–52; in the provinces, 46, 50; and WCTU, 34–35, 46
property rights: Dower Act of 1917, 50–51; in Québec, 115; in 1902, 16; in 1920s, 70, 85
Protestant church, 33–34, 38, 44. see United Church
Putnam, Robert, 239

Q
Québec: and Catholic church, 110–112, 116; FLQ crisis, 214; and K. Campbell, 279, 283; Meech Lake Accord, 268–269; and neo-conservatism, 267; 1980 referendum, 215, 223; and Parti Québecois, 214, 215; and Person's Case, 83; prohibition in, 35, 52; Quiet Revolution, 186, 212–214; T. Casgrain and fight for rights, 114–119, 128–129; and WWII, 127–129
Quiet Revolution, 186, 212–213
Quinn, Herbert F., 111
quotas, 185–186

R
racism: in 1920s, 85–86; in 1930s, 100; in 1950s, 204, 206; in 1980s, 192–193
radio: in 1902, 12; in 1920s, 66, 68; in 1930s, 99–100, 125
Rae, Bob, 199, 251, 253
rape shield law, 278
"Rat Pack", 308
RCMP (Royal Canadian Mounted Police), 109, 214
Reagan, Ronald, 216, 268
REAL Women, 197–198
reality TV, 298–299
rebellion of 1960s, 161–162. see also student movement of the 1960s
recession, 200
referendum, Québec (1980), 215, 223
referendum on prohibition (1898), 35
reform movements. see social reform movements
Reform Party, 268, 271
refugee law, 195–196
refugee relief, 124–125, 130, 157
Regina Manifesto, 110
Regina v. Morgentaler, 196–197
Reid, Angus, 297–298
Reid, Horace, 188, 192
relief camps, 98
relief programs, 98
religion (see also Catholic church; Protestant church): in Québec, 110–112, 116; and social reform, 17–18
Resler, David, 301
Riche, Nancy, 251
Riefenstahl, Leni, 100, 125
Riesman, David, 146
Riis, Nelson, 249
Road to Wigan Pier, The (Orwell), 102
Robinson, Svend, 249, 250
Roblin, Rodmond, 46–48
Roblin government, 48
rock and roll, 182
Rolston, Tilly Jean, 148
Rowell, Newton Wesley, 83
Royal, Joseph, 39
Royal Commission on the Status of Women, 184–186, 207
Rubens, Paul Alfred, 44
Russia: and Cold War, 131, 144–145; and communism, 103–104; in WWI, 42

S
Sabia, Laura, 184, 188
Sanger, Margaret, 18
Sankey, Lord John, 84
Saturday Night, 155
Saul, John Ralston, 257
Sauvé, Jean-François, 219, 221
Sauvé, Jeanne: early years, 216–217, 219; as Governor General, 215–216, 226–227; marriage

THE RT. HONOURABLE SHARON CARSTAIRS, PC

It might truthfully be said that politics was in Senator Carstairs' blood, for her father, Harold Connolly, was a provincial cabinet minister at the time of her birth in Halifax, Nova Scotia. Her degrees in political science, history and teaching led to a twenty-year career in education, followed by her own entry into politics in 1984. She has been Leader of the Liberal Party in Manitoba, Leader of the Official Opposition, Leader of the Government in the Senate, where she still serves, and Minister with Special Responsibility for Palliative Care.

Her first book, *Not One of the Boys*, was published in 1993. She was also a contributing author to *Dropped Threads*.

TIM HIGGINS

Born into a Canadian Forces family during a posting to Washington, D.C., Tim Higgins has lived in Winnipeg since 1952. His B.Sc. in zoology and graduate work in human genetics naturally led him to a twenty-year career in acting, directing and writing for television.

He has received two Manitoba Motion Picture Industry "Blizzard" nominations for screenwriting; one for an historical documentary, the other for drama. He has written and directed two plays adapted from previous Heartland publications: Shipwreck!, based on Frances Russell's *The Great Lake* and BROADWAY, based on Marjorie Gillies' *Street of Dreams*.

Dancing Backwards is his second book.